Studio
Affairs

Studio Affairs

My Life as a Film Director

Vincent Sherman

THE UNIVERSITY PRESS OF KENTUCKY

Copyright © 1996 by Vincent Sherman

Published by The University Press of Kentucky
Scholarly publisher for the Commonwealth,
serving Bellarmine College, Berea College, Centre
College of Kentucky, Eastern Kentucky University,
The Filson Club, Georgetown College, Kentucky
Historical Society, Kentucky State University,
Morehead State University, Murray State University,
Northern Kentucky University, Transylvania University,
University of Kentucky, University of Louisville,
and Western Kentucky University.

Editorial and Sales Offices: The University Press of Kentucky
663 South Limestone Street, Lexington, Kentucky 40508-4008

96 97 98 99 00   5 4 3 2 1

Library of Congress Cataloging-in-Publication Data

Sherman, Vincent.
   Studio affairs : my life as a film director / Vincent Sherman.
      p.   cm.
   Includes index.
   ISBN 0-8131-1975-8 (cloth : alk. paper)
   1. Sherman, Vincent. 2. Motion picture producers and directors—
United States—Biography.   I. Title.
PN1998.3.S453A3   1996
791.43'0233'092—dc20   96-14263
[B]

This book is printed on acid-free recycled paper meeting
the requirements of the American National Standard
for Permanence of Paper for Printed Library Materials.

Manufactured in the United States of America

To Hedda,

whose loyalty, devotion, and wisdom
were far greater than I deserved

Contents

Foreword by Eric Sherman   ix

Acknowledgments   xi

Raison d'Etre   xiii

1   Moment of Decision   1

2   Unknown Territory   9

3   Meeting Hedda   22

4   Hollywood—First Time   37

5   Moving Left   47

6   Hollywood—Second Time   67

7   Moving Up   85

8   *The Hard Way*   106

9   Bette Davis   119

10   *In Our Time*   134

11   Midway   151

12   Errol Flynn   163

13   London   176

14   Joan Crawford   195

15   Freelancing   219

16   Red Scare   243

17   Back to Warner's   267

18   Twilight Years   289

Postscript   298

Filmography   306

Index   315

Illustrations follow pages 114 and 210

Foreword

I grew up in Hollywood, the son of a well-known and well-respected movie director. I spent Saturdays "on the lot," watching my father direct the likes of Clark Gable, Ava Gardner, Paul Newman, and Richard Burton. I had no concept that this was a special or privileged life. "Dad makes movies for a living." That was all. Much later, when I was in college in the late 60s, I came to understand that the business and professional environment in which I grew up was indeed special—that it was the subject of much admiration, devotion, and study by others. I suddenly became envious of my own childhood and wished that I had paid more attention! But something *did* rub off on me during those early years, something that I came to appreciate much later when I started making my own films. It was a kind of ease on the set—the sense that it was an acceptable and appropriate activity for men and women to be creating universes of light and color and motion for others to watch and live through and, hopefully, to learn from.

When I knew that I, too, wished to spend my life associated with this industry and art form, I had a series of discussions with my father, and I rapidly came to consider that there was only so much one could learn about film directing *technique* from others. However, I became fascinated with the job of living, and I decided that other than the natural learning that occurs during the rigors of experience in any field, it was *viewpoints* that were interesting. Exposure to more and more people and their unique attitudes about existence were my primary source for developing my own take on things.

This was further confirmed when I was writing my second book, *Directing the Film* (American Film Institute/Little, Brown, 1976; Acrobat, 1988). Of the more than eighty directors we interviewed, I discovered that no two of them agreed on anything, whether it was the choice of story material, the directing of actors, the selection of camera position, the creation of editing rhythms, or even methods for dealing with critics. However, virtually all the directors agreed on what their *problems* were, what situations had to be resolved if one wished to make a movie. It was the *solutions* that were unique.

Thus, when my father told me a few years ago of his plan to write a book, I recommended that he be sure to include not only his view of filmmaking, but also his experiences of life. I felt that memoirs could be even more interesting and useful than a manual on directing, because, after all, it is a life and its accumulated impressions, rather than some abstract dogma, that shapes one's work. As I started reading chapters of this book, I was enthralled to learn of my father's early days in the South, of his move to Hollywood, of his interactions with the major stars of his time. Most of the information in this book was revelatory to me. I had heard my father talk about film directing, but I had never really learned of the *livingness* that went into creating those attitudes. I now understand much better.

Perhaps the single value that most strikes me in this book and, in fact, in my father's life, is his tendency to survive. At eighty-nine years old he is healthier, more energetic, and more full of life than many people half his age. Not only have nearly all his friends and colleagues from his own generation died, but many from the subsequent generation are gone, too. Recently, after burying a writer with whom he had often worked, Vincent looked at me and said, "I thought it was supposed to be a *good* thing to live a long life—but everyone's gone." I reminded him that in his book he was leaving a valuable message, and that at this stage of his life one of the best services he could provide would be to record his own problems and solutions so that others could learn from them . . . and be entertained by them. He agreed, and shortly thereafter he announced that he planned to start another book and to rewrite a screenplay he had started in the 1950s. He would be headed to Europe for a tribute in Lyon, would be interviewed for a special week of his films on the Turner Classics network, and would be judging at a film festival in the United States.

So, in this presentation of a life, there is much to be learned—about survival, about strengths and weaknesses, about hopes and regrets, and about how a person's desire to communicate can lead to a body of work to be viewed around the world, now and for generations to come.

—Eric Sherman

Acknowledgments

Several persons helped me with this book. To them I wish to express my thanks.

First, Joanne Yeck: One day she phoned to ask for an interview. She was preparing an article about me for Magill's Cinema Annual of 1985. She sounded intelligent and businesslike, and I invited her to my home so that she could look through some of the still pictures of my films and other memorabilia. After an hour or so of questions and answers, which she recorded, I discovered that she had a Ph.D. from a midwestern university and had taught film history at a southern college.

Later, she brought me a copy of the interview for my approval. It was simple and well written. Again we talked for hours about films, actors, directors, and producers, and after I told her some of my experiences, she suggested that I write an autobiography. I hesitated, but she encouraged me and helped me get started. I was about to ask her to collaborate with me, when she met a man she fell in love with and got married; they now have a delightful little daughter. We are friends, and she still writes for various publications.

A year later, I received a letter addressed to me and my wife Hedda. It was an invitation to see a one-woman show written and performed by Donna Cameron, who, for a short while in 1953, worked for me as a secretary at Columbia Pictures. I was surprised because I had no idea that she had any ambition as an actress. But I remembered that she was gracious, wide-eyed, and innocent. I phoned her. She was sorry to hear about my wife's death. I promised to see her show, *Cut on the Bias,* which was playing weekends at a dismal little theater on Santa Monica Boulevard. What I saw was a well-written and beautifully acted series of sketches about some ladies who were slightly offbeat—both comedic and dramatic.

When I told her that I was working on an autobiography, she volunteered to help me in any way possible if, in exchange, I would consider taking a little time off to help her improve her show. I said it was a deal. Thus began a relationship that lasted for eight years until her untimely death from cancer on February 25, 1994. She was of enormous help to me, not only as a delightful companion, but with suggestions for rewriting and editing this manuscript. She had a great sense of humor and a keen awareness of what would appeal to audiences and readers.

I also must pay tribute to my son, Eric, and my daughter, Hedwin, for their suggestions, corrections, and editing assistance. They have written various works of their own that have been published, and their advice and knowledge about the contents and presentation of their father's experiences have been invaluable and deeply appreciated.

I want to offer a special thanks to Daveda Lamont, who typed and prepared this manuscript. She also made important recommendations regarding its content.

Finally, I cannot end these acknowledgments without a thank you to the staff of the University Press of Kentucky for their detailed and insightful suggestions for revisions. Without their help I might never have completed the work.

Raison d'Etre

The distance from Vienna (pronounced Vy-anna), Georgia, a small town in the Deep South, where I was born July 16, 1906, and spent the first fifteen years of my life, to Hollywood, California, where I have lived and worked since 1937, is more than the actual two thousand miles. And the transition from Abe Orovitz, whose ambition was to become a great criminal lawyer, to Vincent Sherman, who became an actor in New York and eventually a director of motion pictures, was more than a change of name and career. They were moves from one world to another—from the relaxed, unhurried, gentle atmosphere of bucolic life, ordinary folks, and mundane thinking to the feverish pursuit of both art and commerce by sophisticated intellectuals and astute individuals in New York and Hollywood. How I made that transition and found a place for myself in the maelstrom, I hope to make clear. I will address questions I am frequently asked: How did a Jewish boy happen to be born in south Georgia, and how did I fare? What does a director do? What films did I make? What was it like working with the big stars in the golden age of the Hollywood studio system?

To begin with, never did I expect to work as an actor with such great talents as John Barrymore, Alfred Lunt, Lynn Fontanne, Alla Nazimova, Claude Rains, and Sydney Greenstreet. Nor did I ever dream that someday I would be directing such stars as Humphrey Bogart, Richard Burton, Joan Crawford, Bette Davis, Errol Flynn, Glenn Ford, Clark Gable, Ava Gardner, John Garfield, Rita Hayworth, Miriam Hopkins, Ida Lupino, Dennis Morgan, Patricia Neal, Paul Newman, Debbie Reynolds, Ann Sheridan, Robert Young, and many other well-known personalities, including former president Ronald Reagan. Nor did I, in my wildest fantasies, ever anticipate that three of the ladies—each a glamorous, talented, and exciting star—would one day profess their love and affection for me. To write honestly about those individuals will necessitate revealing intimacies, and inevitably, there will be readers who believe that private matters should be kept private. To them I can only say that to exclude these episodes would be to draw a veil over some of my most vivid experiences. Moreover, this is a record of all the events that shaped my life. I hope that readers, especially young people who are struggling to get a foothold in the theater or in films, will find it interesting and that my children and grandchildren will acquire a sense of their roots.

So, in the jargon of film, permit me to flash back.

1
Moment of Decision

In July 1927 I made a decision that was to determine the course of the rest of my life. I had written a play with James Larwood, a former classmate at Oglethorpe University in Atlanta, from which I had graduated two years before. Confident that we had created the potential of a success, I decided to give up the study of law, go to New York, and seek fame and fortune in the theater. I even talked Jimmie into it, though he needed little persuasion; he had spent a year at the Columbia School of Journalism and was anxious to get back to the big city.

The play was about a college student we had both known. After indulging in a profligate lifestyle, he suddenly gets religion and sets about trying to convert everyone else to his way of thinking. Living in a fraternity house, he comes into conflict with a realistic medical student, a physicist, a psychologist, an engineer, an economist, a journalist, and a business major, who decide to test his beliefs by introducing him to an attractive but amoral young lady. He tries to convert her, but the plot ends in tragedy, much as the plot of the film *Rain*, based on the Somerset Maugham story "Miss Sadie Thompson." In that story a devout minister, Reverend Davidson, trying to convert Sadie, a whore, instead seduces her. He is found dead the next morning, a suicide.

Jimmie and I wrote *The Steeple* in twelve weeks. It gave us a chance to speak the truth about many of the false concepts of our time. Meanwhile, my parents and friends were shocked to hear that I was abandoning what promised to be a successful career as a lawyer. I had won a prize for public speaking and had been president of the Debating Society at Oglethorpe, and now I planned to embark on a profession that was remote, hazardous, and, to many, even disreputable—fit for bums and fly-by-night adventurers. A few companions secretly expressed their admiration and said that I had a lot of guts to leave the small city of

Atlanta, with three hundred thousand souls, where I had friends and knew my way around, for the giant metropolis of over two million Yankees, alien and wily.

But it was not guts that prompted me to brave whatever lay ahead—only naïveté, the overconfidence of youth, and an accumulation of repressed desires finally asserting themselves. I also wanted to help my family—Papa, Mama, a brother, and four sisters—regain economic security and respectability, which had sadly deteriorated during the few years prior.

My family name is *Orovitz*. Some relatives spell it *Horovitz*, some *Horowitz*, some *Hurwitz*. Family members are scattered in Miami, Philadelphia, New York, and California. My cousin, the late Michael Landon, who was born in Philadelphia, began his illustrious career as Eugene Orowitz. When I asked my father why he removed the *H* from our name, he replied, "To Americanize it." My mother once told me that the family name was originally Gurewitch, but that officials at Ellis Island had changed the *G* to *H* and simplified the rest of it. The immigrants were so thrilled to set foot on these shores that they gratefully accepted the names they were given.

Papa had once been a prosperous merchant in Vienna, Georgia. He had left Russia as a young man around 1900 with the help of relatives, including an older brother, Ben, who preceded him and began operating a small dry goods store in the town of Vienna. Papa made his way to that distant little town and became a peddler, traveling through the countryside in a horse and wagon selling various items of merchandise to the farmers of Dooly County, even before he was able to speak English. But he did know how to make change, and he ingratiated himself with customers. In less than a year, he taught himself not only how to speak, but also to read and write the language. He earned enough to send for his young wife from the old country. When I was born in 1906, he gave up peddling and went to work in Ben's store. I was five or six when Uncle Ben, a handsome, adventurous bachelor, decided to go to California and sold the store to Papa. I was sad to see him leave—I loved him almost as much as I did Papa. I would not see him again for twenty-one years.

Cotton was king, and black labor was plentiful and cheap. Vienna became a thriving agricultural center. As the town's population grew from a thousand to over twenty-five hundred, Papa's business grew. So did our family. I was the oldest child and began working in the store when I was five. Papa was a great salesman, and I started out by imitating him.

I remember a night in September 1918 when Mama, who had tended the cash register on Saturdays, the big shopping day, had gone home with my brother and sisters. Papa counted the day's receipts and, in a euphoric mood, told me he expected to gross sixty thousand dollars for the year—equivalent to over a million dollars today. We hoped we were on the way to becoming rich.

Two months later our hopes diminished. November 11, 1918, World War I ended, and so did inflation. Papa's stock of merchandise, worth one hundred thousand dollars, dropped in value 40 percent. In 1919 the boll weevil, which had been slowly making its way from Texas to Georgia, destroyed almost the entire cotton crop. Farmers and merchants were devastated, especially Papa, who sold on credit during winter, spring, and summer but was paid in the fall when the cotton crop came in. Hopes for a remedy led the farmers to plant cotton again in 1920 and 1921, but the results were equally disastrous. They finally gave up cotton and tried desperately to plant other crops, but it was a struggle to keep body and soul together. Papa and Mama saw everything they had worked for begin to disintegrate. More heartbreaking was the gradual loss of Papa's spirit. He never fully recovered.

Nevertheless, Mama insisted that I go to college, get an education, and acquire a profession—either doctor, lawyer, or dentist—the obsessive goal of most Jewish mothers. It was a hardship, but in 1921 I began my prelaw studies at Oglethorpe. Several times during the next two years I was on the verge of giving up college, but somehow Mama found a way to keep me going.

In my senior year Papa and Mama could no longer help me. Dr. Thornwell Jacobs, the president of Oglethorpe, arranged for my tuition, and my fraternity, Tau Epsilon Phi, gave me my room and board in exchange for managing the kitchen (hiring the help, preparing menus, paying bills, and so forth). I covered my other expenses (books, pipe tobacco, and clothing) by selling cigars from office to office three afternoons a week and by working at Edison Brothers shoe store on Decatur Street every Saturday. Thus, I was able to graduate.

An event that year threw me off course and contributed to my eventual "downfall." I was asked to play an old man in the Oglethorpe Players' yearly theatrical production. The day after the performance, my favorite professor, Dr. James (Babe) Routh, head of the English department, called me into his office. "Orovitz," he said, "I don't know what you plan to do when you graduate, but if you can afford it, I suggest that you go to New York and give yourself a chance as an actor. I think you have a talent for the theater." I thanked him but explained that I had to go to work because my family was having a rough time. He had planted a seed, however.

A few weeks later, the college received a request from the Forsyth Players, a professional stock company in Atlanta. They needed someone to play the small part of an old uncle in *Seventh Heaven.* I read for them and got the job. It was an exciting and happy experience, especially when I received forty dollars for the week. The director liked me well enough to use me in two more plays; the seed was watered and grew, even though I tried to suppress it.

By the time I graduated, Papa, after struggling in vain to get back his former status, finally took my advice and scraped together enough money to move the family to Atlanta, where I took a job with Enterprise Distributing Corporation selling silent moving pictures throughout the Southeast. The pay was better than most jobs, twenty-five dollars per week plus expenses, with chances for promotion. And the job kept my hand in the field of entertainment. The company product consisted of eight Buddy Roosevelt and eight Buffalo Bill Jr. westerns and six Reed Howes action pictures. I had never heard of any of them, but I sold them, based on still pictures, for a rental fee of $7.50 per night. I also had six "society" pictures. Any film in which the men were dressed in suits and the women wore dresses and everyone just stood around and talked (by titles—sound had not yet been invented) was a society film. You couldn't give them away.

After the first two weeks out, although I did well, I was wasting most of my time waiting for trains. When I got back to Atlanta and explained the situation, Bill Jenkins, the head of the company, suggested I buy an automobile. They loaned me enough for a down payment, and I bought a used Model T Ford coupe for three hundred dollars. Instead of one town a day, I was able to cover three. They soon gave me a raise to thirty-five dollars a week and six cents a mile on my car, plus 10 percent on any cash transaction I was able to negotiate. I averaged over seventy-five dollars a week, which was fantastic at the time and was often the only money coming into our house, because Papa was having trouble finding work.

One night in Birmingham, Alabama, the company was launching a biblical film made in Italy and had engaged a fine theater. (DeMille's first version of *The Ten Commandments* had been a huge success.) They wanted me to attend the opening night and check the receipts. What I saw left me aghast! There was no story, no one with whom you could identify, only vast crowds moving about, battle scenes in which you did not know or care who won or lost, nothing but endless pageantry with subtitles to tell you what was going on. I was so mortified that I sneaked out of the theater before it was over.

When I returned to my hotel, depressed and ashamed to be associated with such a dreadful picture, a bellboy suggested that a pretty young lady was willing to come to my room for three dollars. I was still a virgin, and although I had often yearned for sex, I rejected the idea of sleeping with a prostitute. I was saving my clean, healthy body for the woman I'd love and eventually marry. Moreover, I had no great sexual urge at the moment, only an overwhelming desire to escape thinking about the movie I represented. As it turned out, the sex was as disappointing as the picture, and I vowed never again to have anything to do with ladies of the evening.

Before going to sleep most nights, I spent time reading plays I took out of the Atlanta library. I must have read five or six a week, American and famous foreign plays. I was preparing myself for the future without realizing it.

After six successful months on the road, the company wanted to transfer me to the New Orleans territory, but Mama objected. Our situation had improved; Papa had found a job in a store, and Mama wanted me to find work in the city, stay at home, and start going to law school at night.

Through John Ottley Jr., who was working on the *Atlanta Journal* ("Covers Dixie Like the Dew") and who had been a friend at Oglethorpe, I got a job with the paper as a police reporter and enrolled at the Atlanta Law School. The pay was only $20 a week, but they gave me a $2.50 raise when I helped get out an extra edition late one afternoon. After five months, however, I was fired over a misunderstanding about a story I had written. Even so, it was a valuable experience. Covering the police station, the Fulton County Tower (for felons) and the Grady Hospital (the county emergency facility), I became acutely aware of the violence, the harsh reality, and the unpredictability of life. I saw men, women, and children arrive with gaping wounds, some fatal, others causing painful suffering. I met and talked with petty criminals and murderers, prostitutes, lawyers, and judges. I saw corruption and chicanery in high places and low. Every day was a raw emotional shock that kept me awake most of the night until I became hardened and cynical.

As a child and a youth growing up in a small southern town, I was idealistic, hypersensitive, and overemotional. I was, however, reluctant to reveal these qualities. I was afraid they were unmanly and would set me apart from my Christian playmates. Horatio Alger's novels provided me with guidelines: hard work and honesty led to success; living a good clean life and believing in God resulted in happiness. I was a forerunner of Forrest Gump!

My first experience with death had been when I was five years old. One morning, my friend "Hash" Jolly and I went swimming at the County Campground about two miles from town. As we cut through a plum orchard, Hash ate a lot of green plums. Later, I was having a sandwich at home when my mother rushed in from town, highly agitated, and started asking questions. How many green plums did I eat? Did my stomach hurt? When I replied in the negative, she was relieved but urged me to tell her if I felt any pain. I wanted to know why she seemed so upset, but she said it was nothing. I became suspicious, however, and stole away into town. On the way I passed Hash's house. Several men stood on the porch speaking quietly, and two cars were parked out front, one Doctor Daves's. Something grim and ominous hung in the air.

When I got to the store and asked Papa what was wrong, he said, "Didn't Mama tell you?" I shook my head, fearful of what I was about to hear. Hash had died of "acute indigestion." In those days the term covered a multitude of ailments. Years later a doctor friend surmised that Hash might have had a ruptured appendix. At any rate, that night I became hysterical with fear, and Mama took me into her bed and assured me that God was looking out for me and that as long as I believed in him I should not worry.

A few years later, the summer I was eight or nine, another incident shook my faith. After basketball practice at the school grounds, my friends and I decided to stop long enough to go home for lunch. On my way I had to pass through town where I saw, on an empty lot, a parked mule and wagon. Standing nearby was one of the saddest, sweetest looking hound dogs I'd ever seen. I could not resist going over to pet him. He wagged his tail joyously, but I was concerned because he was not tied to the wagon or on a leash. The town, fearful of rabies during the summer, had passed a law that such dogs would be shot. I wanted to warn the owner, but no one seemed to know who that was, so I went home hoping that our town marshal, Chief Morgan, would not see the dog.

After lunch, as I went back to join my friends, I passed the empty lot and stopped, horrified. On the ground near the wagon lay this sad sweet animal, dead in a pool of his own blood, his tan coat smeared with dirt and already drawing flies. I surmised what had happened, gave up to the grief and pain that overwhelmed me, and ran back home just ahead of my tears. Once inside the house, I began to sob uncontrollably, and Mama tried to comfort me. I never told anyone else about it, but my belief and faith in God was shaken.

Religion was always gently poured down my throat. After my Bar Mitzvah in Macon, Georgia, I prayed every morning until I was nineteen years old. But as the years passed, I felt the disillusionment after World War I ("the war to end all wars") and heard the comments: it was a rich man's war and a poor man's fight. I read about the failure of the League of Nations, heard about the Chicago Black Sox, saw *What Price Glory?* and began reading H.L. Mencken's *American Mercury* magazine. I was slowly discarding my illusions.

Then, with the help of a course that Dr. Jacobs taught for seniors only, modestly called Cosmic History, I learned about evolution and revolution, the constant changes in nature, man, and society. I also realized that my religious belief was shallow and my concept of God was narrow and limited; I came to believe that he had not created the earth in six days but that it had evolved over billions of years, as had man himself; that our planet was only a small part of our universe; that life was a struggle for survival and a mixture of good and evil. As it must to every young man, my time for rebellion had come. When I told my mother of my feelings, she was disturbed, but she did not retreat from her blind faith, nor did I ever go back to my old ways. My father was too concerned with his economic situation to care either way.

So by the end of my newspaper experience I had concluded that life was like a child's undergarment, to quote an old German saying—short and full of shit. I decided that one should do whatever was necessary to live—without hurting others—and should indulge in every pleasure available. I gave vent to my sexual desires by seducing a beautiful young nurse at the hospital whose thinking was the same. More important, I realized that young criminal lawyers, unless their families were wealthy, had to depend upon ambulance chasing to make a living. Achieving a reputation while hoping and waiting for a wealthy client to call could take years. And although I refused to admit it, my intuition also told me that what appealed to me was not the law itself, but the *theater* in law. I saw myself fighting for justice, defending the poor, and pleading for those whom life had deprived of a fair chance. So I went to Mama and explained my hopes for success in New York. She reluctantly agreed that I had to follow my heart.

My only hesitation was that, besides Papa, I was the only one in the family who was working, and my contribution was vital. Fortunately, I was able to arrange for my brother Nathan, who was four years younger than me and just finishing high school, to take over my temporary job of selling hats at Kaufman's Hat Store on Peachtree Street. I promised that I'd send for him and the family as soon as I made it on Broadway.

My friend Jimmie's parents were no problem. He was an only child, and they did not need his help. He left before I did to find us a place to live, and in a few days he wrote that we had a room in an apartment at Ninety-eighth and Broadway for ten dollars a month.

Tears rolled down Mama's cheeks, doubts and disapproval showed in Papa's face, and fear for the future swam in the eyes of my brother and sisters as we said good-bye. They wished me luck as I left for the Great White Way with dreams in my head, the play that Jimmie and I had written in my suitcase, and sixty-five dollars in my pocket.

2

Unknown Territory

If Atlanta was a step up from Vienna, New York was a quantum leap. The moment I arrived, I knew that the tempo of my body and mind were destined to change; it would have to if I wanted to survive in the midst of this incredible mass of aggressive humanity. Its drive and energy were awesome. And the noise was deafening. How could people think, work, and sleep? Despite these negative aspects, I was tingling with excitement. I was also a little apprehensive. Would I be able to compete and make a place for myself in the city? These thoughts crowded my mind as Jimmie met me at Penn Station. We took a subway uptown to Broadway and Ninety-sixth Street, then walked to Ninety-eighth, where he had rented the room for us.

I met our landlady, unpacked my bags, and went downtown with Jimmie. He had made an appointment with Alice Kauser, an elderly playbroker who had been recommended to us. She had a small, cramped office. Manuscripts were piled high on her desk, the floor, and in cabinets. We asked if she'd read our play and handle it for us. She said that she would read it, but it would be two weeks before she could give us an answer. We left it with her, our optimism subdued as we realized that we were not the only aspiring playwrights around.

Jimmie spent the next few days showing me New York: the Bronx Park Zoo, the aquarium at Battery Park, various museums and ethnic areas. Every moment was stimulating and enlightening . . . and free! We ate mainly at Apthorpe's Cafeteria at Ninety-sixth and Broadway or at the Automat Midtown. Breakfast was ten cents, lunch and dinner and blue plate specials, forty cents. Our pleasure was reading the *Morning World* newspaper with Alexander Woollcott, Heywood Broun, Franklin P. Adams, and Harry Hansen on its editorial page—all for two cents.

I had relatives in New York I had not seen since I was twelve and

9

they lived in Savannah, Georgia: my cousin Nat Orovitz, his wife, Anna, and Nat's stepmother, whom we all called Aunt Ida, a kind-hearted, generous soul who had three children of her own, including Louis, who was my age. Nat was advertising manager of Bloomingdale's basement, and Louis was his assistant. During several difficult periods Aunt Ida and Louis helped me with dinners, an occasional loan, and moral support. Nat and Anna helped as well, and I used to babysit now and then for their two children, Buddy and Naomi, who were then ages six and four. (Later, during World War II, a handsome young captain in the Air Force knocked at our door in Hollywood. It was Buddy!) Knowing that I had relatives in the city gave me a bit of security.

Jimmie and I began seeing plays to get a feel for what was successful in New York. Each night we went to the basement of the Longacre Theater at Forty-second Street and Broadway. Joe LeBlang's ticket agency was located there. A few minutes before showtime, most of the theaters would send over half-price tickets for some of their unsold seats. By waiting patiently, we saw almost every hit play from the second balcony for fifty-five cents a seat. The first we saw was *The Squall,* with Blanche Yurka; she was a fine actress, but we thought the play was poor. In his review of the play, Robert Benchley described the gypsy seductress who enters an old Spanish home and says, "Me Nubi, me stay." In response, the critic offered his famous line, "Me Benchley, me go!" As we left the theater, we congratulated ourselves. If *The Squall* was a success, our future was assured. We could write better. The next night we saw Molnar's *The Play's the Thing,* with Holbrook Blinn and Reginald Owen, and we came out depressed. It was a masterpiece of humor and sophistication. We knew we were not as good as Molnar—not yet, anyway.

The most exciting show we saw was *Broadway,* produced by Jed Harris and directed by George Abbott. It was not a play of any great depth, but it was superb entertainment, and its pace was breathtaking. I became aware that I was drawn to the theater like iron filings to a magnet. If only we could sell our play, all would be well. But until we did, I'd have to be careful. In two weeks, I'd already spent half of my sixty-five dollars.

When we went back to the Kauser office, we received what can only be described as a rude awakening. She thought our play showed promise but was not yet good enough to submit to producers. We decided she didn't really understand the story, and we began to look for another playbroker. We heard about Frieda Fishbein and met with her. She read our play and thought it had possibilities. But a dozen producers that she submitted it to turned it down. Gradually, we had to accept defeat. It was, as they say, a bitter pill to swallow. We had counted on someone paying us five hundred dollars for an option, which we thought would give us enough to live on until the play opened. But it was not to be. Looking back, I am amazed that we could have been so immature as to expect to sell our first play so quickly and easily. We realized we'd better find work and earn some money.

Because of his past experience working on the *Atlanta Georgian,* a Hearst newspaper in Atlanta, Jimmie was able, through my cousin Nat, to get a job as a copy reader on the *New York Evening Journal.* I decided to look for a job as an actor. I began by going to offices of agents and producers who were listed in theater news columns and in the yellow pages of the phone book, and I listened as other actors inquired about work. I followed their routine, which was mainly to exaggerate experience. After a week or two with no results, I heard that the only busy agent in New York was Chamberlin Brown. I went to his office and spoke to a young man at the reception desk.

"Excuse me," I said, "but yawl doin' any castin' today?"

He smiled and replied, "What part of the South you from?"

"How'd yawl know I wuz from the South?" I inquired innocently.

He laughed, thinking I was making a joke. "What's your name?"

"Abe Orovitz." He frowned (at that time, ethnic names were avoided) and asked me to repeat it. I did. "That'll never do," he said. "Nobody could pronounce it, let alone spell it. Let's get something simpler. What was your mother's maiden name?"

"Schurman or Scheerman, I'm not sure," I replied.

He thought for a second, then said, "Sherman. That's not bad. What was your father's first name?"

"Harry," I told him.

"That's ordinary. What is your mother's first name?"

"Vinnie."

"Vinnie . . . hm . . ." He repeated the name several times. "Vinnie, Vinnie, Vincent." He turned to another young man who had come out of the inner office to get something from a file. "Hey, Larry, what do you think of Vincent Sherman for a name?"

Larry thought for a second. "Sounds good to me."

"Okay, kid," the receptionist said. "That's your name from now on—Vincent Sherman. Come back tomorrow, and I'll try to get you in to see Mr. Brown."

I thanked him and walked out, repeated the name to myself several times and found it pleasing. Suddenly, it dawned on me that Vincent was Italian or Irish, and Catholic, and Sherman was anathema in the South, especially in Georgia. So what was a nice Jewish boy with a southern accent doing with an Italian or Irish Catholic first name and a second name of Sherman? After thinking it over, I decided that it had a nice sound to it, and maybe the incongruity was intriguing.

The next day, on my way to the Brown office, I ran into an actor I had met before, and I told him what had happened.

"Good luck," he said, smiling. "But watch your step. Brown's a fairy." Stunned, I became wary and decided I had better keep away from the Brown office. I never went back. Over the years I have become enlightened by working with many gay men and women, and I have come to accept them as fellow human beings who simply have different sexual desires than I.

When I wrote to my mother that I had taken the name of Sherman, she was pleased—she thought it was a good omen. But my father implored me to forget the theater and return to Atlanta, where he was sure I'd find a job in a law office. By now, however, the theater had thoroughly hooked me. I wanted to remain close to it, become a part of it. Where else was that possible, except in New York? I was also ashamed to return home in defeat. So I resumed looking for work as an actor, walking downtown every day from Ninety-eighth Street to Times Square in order to save the nickel subway fare. Fortunately, I went to an office that booked actors for a stock company in Whalom Park, Massachusetts. They had just received a request for a juvenile who would be willing to work for forty dollars a week and had two suits. I volunteered, was given the job, and left the next day.

The company consisted of the leading man and his wife, several young actors, and a few old-time character actors. I think they were very disappointed with my southern accent but found me adequate. It was the end of their summer program. I played the juvenile in three productions and returned to New York with fifty dollars I had managed to save.

I began again to look for work. Going from office to office, "pounding the pavements," and being told there was nothing for me, I began to wonder whether I had made a mistake; maybe I should admit my defeat and crawl back to Atlanta. But then I was told at one office to come back in a few days when there might be something for me.

It was the only office that promised even the possibility of a job. It was, ironically, that of Jones and Green, the producers of *The Squall*, the play I considered so awful. They were planning to send out a road company, and because the play had a Spanish background and I was a "Latin type," they would consider me. I was so desperate for a job and so short of money that I would have taken any part in any kind of play. I returned a few days later and was told by the secretary that the producers were still trying to make up their minds and that I should come back again in a day or two. For weeks I went back and forth, hoping with each visit that they would at least let me read for them, but they kept delaying. Finally, I was told I could expect a definite answer the next day. I slept fitfully that night, awoke early the next morning and, after coffee and a roll, walked briskly downtown, hoping that the answer would be positive.

The same secretary informed me, while she filed her nails, that because business had fallen off with the New York company, the producers were not going to send out a separate company but instead would use the New York company for the road tour. My heart seemed to hesitate for a moment. I had pinned all my hopes on it. I tried to cover my disappointment and asked a few questions while I regained my composure. As I went down in the elevator to the street below, I was confronted with the question of what to do next. I had no other office to go to, even to look for a job. I walked zombielike from the Longacre Building, where Jones and Green had their offices, up Broadway to Forty-fourth Street, pushed along by the crowd. At Forty-fourth I started to cross the street toward the Astor Hotel, again carried forward by the crowd. In the middle of the street I stopped and asked myself why I was crossing, since there was nothing on the other side for me. I started to turn back, when it occurred to me that there was no reason to turn back, either. I had no place to go, no one to turn to, nothing to look forward to. How long I stood there I don't recall, but the traffic light changed, and I became aware of cars starting to move, horns blowing, and voices yelling at me to get out of the way. I wanted to move, but I couldn't. Someone mercifully dragged me to a place of safety, and gradually I realized what had happened. Hopeless and down to my last few dollars, I considered walking west to the Hudson River and ending my troubles. It was the lowest point of my life, and I have never forgotten it. But the will to live and the determination to fight failure rescued me. I walked back to Ninety-eighth Street. In my room, I sat staring out the window, when our landlady began playing the Brahms waltz Opus 39 on her piano. I do not know what motivated Brahms to compose it, but for me it expressed the sadness that I felt and the hope I clung to underneath it. (Fifteen years later, as the director of *Old Acquaintance*, I had Miriam Hopkins play the same number when she was sad about having lost her husband but was hopeful of getting him back.) The next day, I remembered that there was one place I had not yet tried for a job: the Theater Guild on West Fifty-second Street. They had achieved high marks as producers of artistic works, not just commercial plays. Because of my lack of experience, I felt inferior to their standards and thought it was useless to contact them. But, desperate and with nothing to lose, I decided to try them.

Cheryl Crawford was the assistant casting director. After listening to my story, she offered me a job as an extra in Eugene O'Neill's *Marco Millions* for sixteen dollars a week. The production was to begin rehearsals soon with Rouben Mamoulian, a young Armenian, directing. Although the sixteen dollars was just enough to live on, and being reduced to playing an extra did nothing for my ego, I consoled myself that I would be with a fine company and perhaps would learn something.

My thinking, for a change, was correct. Mamoulian was gifted, and I was privileged to watch rehearsals with Alfred Lunt as Marco Polo and a superlative cast of supporting players. Lunt, I thought, was a great talent, and O'Neill was America's foremost playwright. He came to rehearsal several times, sat quietly at the rear, and rarely commented. I had read most of his plays and admired him. In *Marco Millions* he was contrasting the commercialism of the West with the beauty and philosophy of the East. The play reads better than it acts.

Among the extras were Clifford Odets, Johnny Mercer, and Eric Linden, all of whom later achieved recognition. Playing a small role in one scene was Sanford Meisner, who became a good actor and a master teacher of acting. Another small role was played by Albert Van Dekker, who later became a well-known film actor.

I had eight changes of costume to make, which kept me running up and down five flights of stairs at every performance. Mamoulian also assigned me to carry a small pillow for Marco to kneel on whenever he arrived in the presence of the Great Khan. One time, I got it underneath Lunt at the last moment just as he was kneeling, and it got a laugh. He liked the idea and later told me to repeat it. For the first time, Lunt seemed to take note of me.

After the opening, understudies were assigned, and I was given several small roles to cover. I did not tell my family that I was merely an extra but wrote that I was with one of the best theater groups in the country. I told them they didn't have to send me any more money.

At every performance I would watch Lunt from the wings. It was from him that I learned how to create an effect by a dramatic pause, how to build a line for a laugh, and especially how to concentrate and listen to other actors. Another benefit I derived from working at the Guild was an association with people who talked glibly about theater, music, dance, painting, and sculpture. They tossed about names I'd never heard of: Stanislavsky, Eleanora Duse, Grasso, Chaliapin, Mierhold, Vachtangov, Stravinsky, Mahler, Schoenberg, young Aaron Copland, Gide, Stendhal, Picasso, Van Gogh, Gertrude Stein, Gordon Craig, Stieglitz and others. Nor had I known anything before about cubism, dadaism, surrealism, impressionism, or stream of consciousness writing. I hesitated to ask questions for fear of revealing my ignorance. But I was determined to find out what they were talking about. My quest for knowledge about the arts began. I became an omnivorous reader. Three or four times a week I'd spend the day in the New York Public Library or visit the Bloomingdale branch on Fifty-eighth Street, where they had an excellent drama section.

One aspect of my learning, which at first I did not appreciate and found upsetting, came from listening to snide remarks by some of my colleagues about southerners' ignorance and prejudices. These people were certain that most southern Whites went about with a rope ready to lynch black people on the slightest whim. I told them that in all the years I had lived in Vienna, I had never seen any overt antiblack activity. On the contrary, there was a warm, friendly relationship between the races. Black and white children often played together until they were ten or twelve years old, and many black women ran the white households they served. Of course, segregation was a way of life: Blacks had separate schools, churches, and eating places, and they lived in a separate area. They rarely voted and never, to my knowledge, held public office. In terms of civil rights, they were second class citizens, but there were no public expressions of unhappiness about it that I knew of. Unless you lived in the South, and especially in a small town, you would find it difficult to understand the relationship that existed there between Whites and Blacks.

I also pointed out that although my mother and father were Orthodox Jews and we observed Jewish holidays such as Rosh Hashonah, Yom Kippur, and Passover, I was never subjected to nor witnessed any anti-Semitism. The only time I can recall a period of anti-Semitism was during the Leo M. Frank case in 1913 in Atlanta. Frank, a Jew who had moved from New York to Georgia to manage his uncle's pencil factory, was charged with the rape and murder of Mary Phagan, a fourteen-year-old girl who worked in the factory. He was convicted on circumstantial evidence and sentenced to die. Jim Conley, a young black janitor, was also arrested as an accessory and sentenced to one year on the chain gang. Governor Slaton had doubts about Frank's guilt and commuted his sentence to life imprisonment, but Tom Watson, a racist politician, added Jews to his hate list of blacks and Catholics, and an angry mob lynched Frank. In 1982, Alonzo Mann, who was a fourteen-year-old office boy at the factory in 1913, confessed that he saw Conley carrying the limp body of the girl to the basement but said nothing because Conley threatened to kill him if he did. Conley died in 1962. Mann said he was glad to get it off his chest. But in Vienna, my father actually took up a collection to help Frank.

I was well aware that our religion was different: that we didn't believe in Jesus Christ as our savior, didn't eat hog meat, were circumcised. But there were so many other activities I shared with my Christian friends—playing baseball, going swimming, fishing and hunting, shooting marbles, competing for girls, and having fun at parties—that I ignored the differences. In fact, during my last year in high school, I was captain of the baseball team and represented Vienna in the declamation contest of the Third Congressional District. Coached by Ruth Lewis, my beautiful elocution teacher, and Senator Walter F. George, I won first place. The town later took up a collection to send me to the state meet at Athens, but there I lost. I understood eventually that because there was only one other Jewish family in Vienna (the Feldsers), we represented no threat; our neighbors came to know us as human beings rather than as members of a stereotyped minority.

A few years ago I was invited to my hometown by the Kiwanis Club to help celebrate the ninetieth birthday of my beloved Ruth Lewis. Over a hundred citizens attended, and I was given a warm welcome. The mayor who introduced me as the principal speaker was a black man. Despite the tragedy of racial violence over the years, there has been progress with respect to equal rights and the improvement of economic conditions for African Americans. Although we have a long way to go to eradicate racial prejudice, I still have hopes that the good people of the South will lead the way to granting all Americans equal rights.

Midway in the run of *Marco Millions*, the Guild decided to do a production of *Volpone*, the Stefan Zweig version of Ben Jonson's play of the same name. This alternated with *Marco* and used as many as possible of the same cast. It was a bawdy, satiric comedy and was to be directed by Philip Moeller, a member of the board of the Theater Guild. Dudley Digges played Volpone, and Lunt played Mosca, his toady. Again I had the privilege of watching a talented cast and director as they extracted every laugh from a brilliant play.

On a particular day of rehearsal for *Volpone,* Sanford Meisner, who was playing a court attendant, was late, and Moeller pointed at me. "You, young man," he said, "walk across the room and yell out, 'Clear the Court!'" I had seen Sandy do the scene, knew what was required, and belted it out. Moeller told me to keep the line, and he gave Sandy another bit to do. I was also assigned to understudy Voltore, an important role. The result was that for *Volpone* I received forty dollars a week. I no longer walked from Ninety-eighth to Fifty-second Street to save a nickel. The show opened to good reviews, and again I watched the actors from the wings at every performance. Lunt's creative ability was a joy to behold as he'd embellish every scene with his inventiveness.

During the run in New York, we were invited to see a special matinee of another Guild production, *Porgy,* brilliantly directed by Mamoulian. I also watched a dress rehearsal of *Strange Interlude,* a five-hour show written by O'Neill and directed by Moeller. It starred Lynn Fontanne, Lunt's wife. She was tremendous. The play seems dated now, and its asides tend to hold up the action, but it was one of the most powerful experiences I have ever had in the theater. It was a huge success. In fact, with *Porgy, Strange Interlude, Marco Millions* and *Volpone,* the Guild had its greatest season ever.

Before *Marco* and *Volpone* ended their runs, we were told that both shows would go on the road the following September, but with a different cast: Earl Larimore would replace Lunt as Marco Polo and would play Mosca in Volpone; Claude Rains would replace Digges in both plays. As an understudy I was required to rehearse with them, and it was the beginning of my friendship with Claude Rains. He was from the London theater and was fascinating to watch. At first I thought he was very slow to grasp the essence of the roles, but gradually I began to see that he wanted to motivate every move he made and every line he spoke. Claude had an unusually fine speaking voice and brought something original to his performance. Only recently did I learn that he once taught acting in London and that John Gielgud was one of his students.

Cheryl Crawford advised me to study with a voice teacher in order to get rid of my southern accent. I did and was told that when the road tour began I would play the small roles in *Marco* that I had understudied and that I would continue to cover Voltore in *Volpone.*

My confidence, which had been so badly bruised, was beginning to be restored. I became so preoccupied with learning about the world of theater, art, and culture that I spent little time thinking about women or sex. It was a period of sublimation. When summer arrived, I was offered a job in a boy's camp as a dramatic counselor. It would give me a chance to get away from the city during the hot, humid, stifling summer months, and I'd receive a small salary plus a nice vacation. Having nothing better at hand, I accepted it. Thus ended my first season in New York.

Camp Mohican, at the edge of a lake in Massachusetts, was surrounded by a large wooded area. A kitchen and a huge dining room overlooked the lake. Nearby were a recreation hall and a row of log cabins, which housed the boys and staff. In front was an open field for various athletic events. I bunked with several young men about my age who were counselors. They were all pleasant, and I looked forward to an enjoyable summer.

The recreation hall had a small stage. After things got organized at the camp, I cast one of the plays I had brought with me and began rehearsals. It was my first attempt at directing, and I enjoyed it. The boys, most of them not yet in their teens, were fun to work with, and it was a rewarding experience for me. I learned how to direct children and observe the audience response to various effects I had strived for. During the final weeks, I planned to do a night outdoor production of Eugene O'Neill's *Emperor Jones*. I would play Jones myself, since I had a good southern Negro accent and we had an ideal setting for an audience, a section of white birch trees. I had never heard of its being done outdoors but thought it would be a good entertainment for the boys and their parents, who came often for weekends.

A few days before rehearsals, a friend of one of the owners came for a visit. He was Milton Stiefel, formerly a stage manager for Max Reinhardt. With him was Joseph Pevney, a young actor. We met, and when I told Stiefel my plan, he thought it was a good idea and suggested that I use Pevney to play Smithers, the white trader. Joe was only seventeen, but I soon discovered that he was a good actor and that we worked well together. We built a huge chair for the emperor's throne, decorated it with colorful cloth, and placed it in the center of the setting that represented the emperor's palace. The day scenes were lit by two white spotlights, one at each side. After the opening scenes, when Jones begins his escape, we removed the chair and other decorations and put blue gels in the spotlights for the night scenes. The birch trees became a ghostlike jungle, and we used the same setup for different areas in the jungle simply by changing a few pieces in the foreground. Deep in the woods, unseen, one of the counselors was beating the tom-tom (an old drum).

Because we had no curtain on the exterior, Stiefel suggested how we could simulate one: we dug a trough where the curtain would normally be, and we sprinkled red flash powder in it. As each scene ended, we'd have the stage manager put a lighted match to the powder; the flash would give us an exciting finish, and the rising colored smoke would make a good curtain. We added fresh powder for every scene. All this, plus the aura of the outdoors at night with the entire camp sitting on benches and chairs or on the ground, gave the show the eerie quality it needed. It was a great success.

It was also the start of my friendship with Joseph Pevney. We worked together in subsequent years at other camps, and later he came to Hollywood, where he had a long and successful career acting in and directing films and television. Our friendship has continued to this day.

The production opened up for me new areas of creativity: staging a play, visualizing the background, using light effects and sound. And since I was directing, I had no reason to try to impress or please anyone but myself during the rehearsals, so I simply worked quietly until I began to sense the true feeling of the Jones character—his guilt and his fears. It was a revelation to me. I began to get a sense of what the art of acting could be. At the end of the summer I returned to New York full of energy and happy that I had chosen the theater for a career.

In September of 1928 we began our tour of the major cities of the East and the Midwest with *Marco Millions* and *Volpone.* My salary was increased to ninety dollars per week. In less than a year I had gone from sixteen dollars to ninety dollars. I bought a portable typewriter and planned to write a play based on Lafcadio Hearn's *Youma,* the story of a noble black woman during a revolt on the island of Santo Domingo.

Jimmie and I had to split up, but he had a new job and was ready to take an apartment alone. We remained close friends and saw each other frequently until I moved to Hollywood in 1937.

On tour, I enjoyed seeing all the cities and the art museums; I went to afternoon concerts, except on matinee days. In Cleveland I heard a young Vladimir Horowitz play a Rachmaninoff concerto with the local symphony. It was one of the most exhilarating experiences of my life. I also had the pleasure of seeing Ruth Draper, Victor Chenkin, Mei Lan Fang, Mary Wigman, Cornelia Otis Skinner, and Harold Kreutzberg with Yvonne Georgi. My taste for artistic work was slowly being honed.

We completed the tour in the spring of 1929. It was a success. The Guild decided that for the following season they would send out *Marco* and *Volpone* again, but to smaller cities, and they would add a revival of

R.U.R., a futuristic play by Karel Capek, to be directed by Mamoulian. Cheryl Crawford informed me that I could repeat my roles in *Marco* and understudy in *Volpone* and *R.U.R.* I asked if there was a chance to get my brother Nat a job as an extra in the company, and she agreed.

I finished writing *Youma* during the 1928-29 tour and gave the play to Miss Fishbein. I also left a copy with Harold Clurman, who was in charge of reading plays for the Theater Guild. Then I went home to Atlanta to spend a few weeks with my family. They were happy to see me and overjoyed to hear that I had a job for Nat. He seemed pleased that we'd be working together and to know that he'd be paid forty dollars a week as an extra. It was my attempt to repay him for going to work at Kaufman's Hat Store and helping the family while I was trying to break into the New York theater.

Rehearsals began in August. Sydney Greenstreet replaced Rains, who was going into a new play at the Guild. I introduced Nat around, and he was well liked. I also called Harold Clurman. He was extremely kind to me and suggested that, although my play *Youma* was not for the Guild, I should send it to David Belasco, who might be interested in doing it as an operetta. Miss Fishbein sent a copy to Belasco, but he didn't buy it.

In September we started on the tour. Whenever possible Nat and I took a furnished apartment so that we could cook our own meals, do our own laundry, and save money. We sent some of our savings home every week and even put aside a few dollars for ourselves. While we were playing in Richmond, Virginia, in 1929, the stock market crashed. On the train between towns I was working on another dramatization of a short novel, *Class Reunion*, by Franz Werfel. Meanwhile, Nat played poker with the crew and almost always won. Our property man approached me one day and told me that he considered Nat the best born gambler he had ever met. He suggested that I should finance Nat once the tour was ended. Nat was barely nineteen. This knack, which I tried to discourage, plus alcohol, proved to be his downfall years later.

After twenty weeks on the road, we returned to New York, found a small apartment, and through a friend met Burt Kelly, who worked for Paramount Publix Theaters. While talking with Nat, Burt offered him a job in the New York office. Nat had no intention of pursuing a career in the theater, so he took the job. It paid only twenty-five dollars a week to start, but in no time he was given a raise and Paramount began grooming him for an important job in the booking department.

Although the effect of the stock market crash was more pronounced on Wall Street than elsewhere, the Great Depression soon began to set in over the rest of the country. By late spring of 1930, the American people were becoming disillusioned with Herbert Hoover, then president, who had promised "a chicken in every pot and two cars in every garage." Fortunes had been lost in the stock market, men were jumping out of buildings, thousands were losing their jobs, and bread and soup lines began to form in cities. Solid, middle-class, respectable citizens began selling apples on the street for five cents each. Fear was slowly but surely mounting everywhere.

Along with many others, I began to ask questions and take an interest in politics. What was wrong? Why was it that in a country as rich in resources as ours, there had to be poverty, hardship, and starvation? Why was there such a breakdown of the machinery of finance, industry, and government? I started reading magazines like *The Nation* and *The New Republic* and books by sociologists and economists. I even read some Lenin. I was looking for answers. It was the beginning of my social consciousness and the second stage of my rebellion against the establishment.

3

Meeting Hedda

I completed my dramatization of *Class Reunion* and took it to Frieda Fishbein, who now had an office on Broadway and had a young lady named Hedda Comoro working for her. Hedda seemed bright and efficient. She was also attractive, had a trim figure, dressed smartly, and was pleasant. She said that Frieda was busy at the moment, but as Frieda's new secretary and reader, she took the play and promised to read it and let me know her own thoughts. At a desk in the far corner was a man in his thirties, introduced as Lester Sweyd, who had recently brought Frieda a new client, his friend Moss Hart. Hart had written the play *Once in a Lifetime*, which Frieda had promptly sold to Sam Harris, a well-known producer.

When I returned to the office several days later, anxious to know whether Hedda had read my play, she introduced me to Moss Hart, a tall, dark-haired young man about my age. Soon he was ushered in to see Frieda, and I had an opportunity to talk with Hedda. She and Frieda had read *Class Reunion,* liked it, and planned to submit it to producers. As we chatted, I told her a little of my history, and she volunteered a few facts about herself: she had once worked on the *Evening World* newspaper as assistant to the editor of a children's column and had conducted a radio program for children when she was only eighteen years old. Just before taking the job with Frieda, she had been doing publicity work. When I told her my age, she unhesitatingly revealed she was nine months older. I realized that she was bluntly honest and without feminine guile. Also, years older in worldly sophistication. She had a great sense of humor. That day she had done her hair differently, with a braid around her head that gave her the look of a Scandinavian bride, and was very pretty. Until then, I had not asked about her background and was surprised to learn that she was Jewish, although not religious. I was drawn to her.

Moss emerged, and I said a quick hello to Frieda, who was, as always, gracious but had some business to discuss with Hedda. I promised to come back later and left with Moss. We walked to Walgreen's at Forty-fourth and Broadway, where we had a cold drink and talked for half an hour. He asked what I did during the summer, and when I told him I'd done a few plays with kids over previous summers, including staging *Emperor Jones* outdoors, he was interested. He had once acted Smithers (the white trader) with Charles Gilpin, a fine black actor, in a New York production of *Jones.*

He asked if I thought I could direct well enough for adults. For several summers, he explained, he had been a social director on what was called the "borscht circuit"—large summer camps where middle-class young Jewish men and women went for their vacations and to look for potential husbands and wives. He earned enough in those three months to keep him going the rest of the year and also to help his family. His assistant was Dore Schary. The previous year he had worked at Flagler, and this summer he was scheduled to go to Camp Copake, where he was to receive two thousand dollars and all expenses. Because he now had to stay in New York to work with George Kaufman, a well known director and playwright, on the rewrite of his play, he couldn't take the job. He advised me to see the owner of the camp, Sam Suzuli.

When I called on Mr. Suzuli, he was courteous but explained that he could not use me. "Sherman," he said, "you seem like a bright guy, and since Moss recommended you, I'd like to give you the job. But I have two thousand tough, sophisticated New Yorkers who come up for weekends. They're theater wise, and unless you can give them something good, they sit on their hands. I need someone with experience. But I have two friends who have a small camp not far from Poughkeepsie. They need a good social director, and their crowd is not as tough as mine. You go see them."

He wrote out their names, and the following day I had a job at Camp Beekman on Sylvan Lake. They agreed to pay me six hundred dollars for the summer, plus all expenses. I thanked Moss, and a few days later his brother Bernie kindly spent time with me going over the kinds of shows Moss had presented during the past few summers.

One day Hedda phoned to tell me that Guthrie McClintic, the husband of Katherine Cornell and a director, was interested in *Class Reunion.* Nothing came of it, though. She also invited me to a violin concert to which she had complimentary tickets. I accepted, and afterward we went to her apartment for a drink. We talked for hours and revealed much more about ourselves to each other. She was an independent, liberated young woman and a former Greenwich Village rebel. Later I learned she had attended the Rand School of Social Science, where Will Durant was one of her professors. She was the winner of several prizes for shorthand and speed typing. I enjoyed being with her and realized that she was an unusual person, superior to most of the girls I had known in the past. We ended up going to bed.

Before I left for Camp Beekman, Moss invited me to a new apartment he had just taken for himself and his family—mother, father and Bernie—at the Ansonia Hotel on upper Broadway. I had dinner with them and enjoyed Moss's stories of his experiences. They became part of his *Act One,* a delightful and exquisitely written autobiography of his early years.

I took Joe Pevney with me to Beekman to play juvenile leads, and I assembled a good all-around cast and staff to help with the variety of shows that I was planning. In addition I had a dance orchestra whose members I could use when necessary, and a host of waiters, usually talented college boys, who were not averse to acting roles when called upon. One was Irving Fein, who was George Burns's manager and was formerly with Jack Benny.

That summer, in addition to vaudeville nights, cabarets, indoor games, and campfires, I staged and acted the leads in *The Play's the Thing, White Cargo, The Racket, Volpone,* several one-act plays, and another outdoor production of *Emperor Jones,* which surpassed the one I had done at the boys' camp.

In the middle of the summer a guest introduced himself as Lou Bandler. He said he sold wholesale groceries to most of the large summer camps, including Camp Tamiment in the Pocono Mountains of Pennsylvania. They were building a new recreation hall for next summer and needed a social director. He said he had seen several of my shows, liked them, and had recommended me to Tamiment. I thanked him and promised to get in touch with Tamiment when the summer was over.

On my return to New York, I came upon Moss Hart again in Frieda's office. He wanted to know how the summer went and was happy to hear it was good. He kindly invited me to a dress rehearsal of *Once in a Lifetime.* It was obvious that the play had the makings of a success, but it needed to be pulled together, which was Kaufman's specialty. In addition, Cheryl Crawford told me that there was a part for me in the upcoming Theater Guild production of Maxwell Anderson's *Elizabeth the*

Queen. With the assurance of work for the fall, I sent half of the summer earnings to my family in Atlanta and suggested that they sell everything, buy a used car, and drive to New York, where Nat and I would find an apartment for all of us. They were quite ready to leave Atlanta.

Before they arrived, I saw Hedda several more times. She told me more about herself. In her teens she'd gone through an unhappy love affair with a writer. After he deserted her, she fell apart, lived a crazy, promiscuous life for a short while, and finally came to her senses. I, too had had a disappointing affair with a girl whose parents had stopped her from seeing me when they found out I was an actor. So Hedda and I had come together at a time when we were both unattached and in need of a warm, friendly relationship.

Rehearsals of *Elizabeth the Queen* began, with Alfred Lunt playing Lord Essex and his wife Lynn Fontanne playing the queen. The director was again Philip Moeller. To watch them rehearse and develop their roles was a lesson in acting and directing, and I was happy to be in the same production with them. I was given a small but difficult role: I had to break through a group of the queen's ministers as she was holding court, throw myself at her feet, and warn her that Lord Essex, a popular hero with whom she was in love, was returning in rebellion from Spain to London. She had ordered him to give up his mission there before it had started, and he was angry. She refused to believe the news, and I had to convince her it was true. She and Lunt were most complimentary. For this small scene the Guild paid me $110 a week, a generous salary at the time.

The play opened to good reviews, and I felt sure of a good season's work. With a little help from my brother, I was able to rent and furnish an apartment large enough for the entire family in Astoria. They arrived safely and we were all together once again. My father and my oldest sister, Tillie, got jobs with my cousin Nat, who had left Bloomingdale's and opened a small department store called Carson's at Sixth Avenue and Fourteenth Street.

In November of 1930 I made an appointment with Bertha Mailley and Ben Josephson, the supervisors of Camp Tamiment, to discuss the job of social director for the summer of 1931. After two meetings I signed a contract with them to begin on Decoration Day and continue through Labor Day. I was to get one thousand dollars and all expenses. They would also allow me to hire an adequate staff to assist me.

The future was promising. I was seeing Hedda once or twice a week, and we were getting to know each other more with each visit. She was easy to be with, down to earth, practical, made no demands on me, and accepted the fact that my first obligation was to my family.

From experience I knew that life was unpredictable, but a few blows now fell that startled me nonetheless. The Guild decided to do a production of Shakespeare's *Much Ado about Nothing,* to be directed by Robert Edmond Jones, utilizing as many of the cast from *Elizabeth* as possible, and to stage the two alternately. I was interviewed by Jones, who was a great scenic designer but not a good director. He wanted me to play a foppish character, wear a blonde wig, and sing songs. I did not feel I was right for the part, nor did he, so, along with a dozen other members of the cast, I was dropped from *Elizabeth* a week before Christmas and left without a job. I was not only hurt but surprised that they would let me go, since Lunt and Fontanne had been so complimentary.

At the same time my mother, who was going through the change of life, began giving us a difficult time. Then, confirming that it never rains but pours, my brother developed a cold and an earache. One night when I came home, I saw that his face had a deathly pallor. The next day, through a friend, I got him to an ear doctor. Nat had mastoiditis and needed to be operated on at once. The doctor got him into Saint Vincent's Hospital, and the operation was successful.

A few days later Hedda accompanied me to the hospital to pick up Nat and take him home. She had not yet met my family. Nat was waiting, head bandaged, but in good spirits. I told him how close we had been to losing him, and he was grateful that things had turned out well. We took a taxi to Astoria. As we entered the apartment, my mother rushed forward to embrace Nat, held on to him for a moment, then told him how worried and ill she had been. When she saw Hedda, she released him. I introduced Hedda to everyone, and we had a delicious dinner that my sisters had prepared. Afterward, I walked Hedda to the subway and asked her how she felt about my family.

"I love your father and all the rest of your family, but your mother shocked me. She said very little to comfort your brother but began telling him how sick *she* had been." It was true, but I became very defensive. I had always thought my mother was the most loving and unselfish parent who ever lived. But I could not deny what had happened.

When I asked my family what they thought of Hedda, they all said they liked her, but my mother said that I should stop seeing her. She declared that until my sisters were married, it was my duty not to get involved with any girl. I was stunned, never having thought she could be so unreasonable. From that moment on, living at home became a strain.

I told Hedda my feelings, and she invited me to use her place to work. I was grateful because I was trying to write another play, and it was impossible at home. I spent two or three days a week at Hedda's and often remained overnight. My mother objected, but I refused to discuss it. I was twenty-five years old and felt she had no right to interfere in my life.

Hedda's family lived in Brighton Beach, and she thought it was time we met. One Sunday we took the long ride on the subway and spent the day with them. Her father was a kind, gentle, intelligent man who in his younger days had leaned toward anarchism, read Kropotkin, and believed that power led to corruption and tyranny. He considered Stalin monstrous, and although he held no brief for capitalism, he thought it was the least objectionable form of government. He had come to America from Russia about the same time my father had, with the great wave of immigrants. He became a streetcar conductor, then ran a delicatessen, and eventually tried farming. He failed at each. His wife, a Jewish intellectual, ran away with another man and left him with their two small daughters when Hedda was six and her sister, Claire, was four years old. Despondent and penniless, her father was rescued by an unmarried Jewish woman who was sympathetic to his plight and especially to that of the children. She moved in with him and became a mother to the girls. They referred to her as Auntie. She was energetic and a go-getter who badgered politicians at City Hall until she obtained a license to operate a newsstand in the Wall Street district. That's how they made their living. Through Auntie's efforts they eventually bought a house at Brighton Beach, and she paid for it by renting out rooms. She and Hedda's father had a son, Leo, who was in high school. He and I became friends and are still close.

Early one evening, after Hedda and I had been seeing each other for several months, I planned to go home for a night. She said she had been thinking things over and that, if I wished to continue our relationship, we'd have to get married. I was dumbfounded. It was the first time the subject of marriage had ever arisen. Until then she had led me to believe that she considered marriage a bourgeois convention and that the certificate meant nothing to her. That suited me perfectly, for I was in no position to even think about marriage. I was curious about this sudden change.

"Well," she explained, "it's true the legal document itself means little to me, but you happen to be very bourgeois minded, and I think it means a great deal to you. I am ready to commit to you, but unless we're married, I doubt you'd feel the same toward me. So, if you don't want to marry me, we'll have to reconsider things."

I argued with her, pointing out that her proposal was so sudden that I needed time to think. Marriage was the last thing on my mind. I was trying to write a play and looking for a job as an actor, and the only work I could look forward to, at the moment, was for the coming summer. True, I was fond of Hedda and respected her, her honesty, and her strength of character, but I was not romantically in love with her, nor could I have fallen in love with anyone since I was concerned solely with my future and that of my family. As I rode home on the subway, I weighed my choices: to refuse to marry her and lose a good and sensible companion, a desirable sex partner, and a place to work; or to marry her, become obligated, and lose my freedom. I had almost decided to terminate our relationship, but when I arrived home, I went through a terrible time with my mother. She accused me of abandoning the family and said I did not love her anymore. She had heard from friends that Hedda's parents were anarchists, immoral, did not believe in marriage, and that I was living in sin. I wanted no more of this turmoil. It was my last night at home.

The next morning I packed a bag, slipped away, and went to Hedda's place. That night I told her I was ready to marry her as long as she realized I was broke and could not contribute anything toward our expenses. She understood and accepted the situation. The next day we took a subway downtown to City Hall, filled out the necessary papers and, at the height of the Depression, March 9, 1931, with Frieda Fishbein as a witness, we married.

That evening we discussed the future. I was concerned about leaving her alone in New York for the summer while I went off to Tamiment. She suggested that I talk to the managers and ask if there was an office job available. When I learned that they were looking for a registrar, I told them about Hedda but did not tell them we were married, because married social directors were not considered desirable. They interviewed her and were so impressed that they immediately hired her for the summer. Hedda was sorry to leave Frieda Fishbein but was relieved that we'd be together.

Several days later I paid a short visit to my family and told them I was married. My mother became hysterical and threatened to kill herself. My father calmed her down and wished me luck. He had always liked Hedda. My brother and sisters kept out of the argument.

While I was preparing for the summer at Tamiment, still bitter at having lost my job at the Guild (especially since I learned that the Guild board, after seeing a dress rehearsal of *Much Ado about Nothing,* had decided to cancel it), the phone rang early one evening and Hedda answered it. After a moment she turned to me.

"It's a woman—she says she's Lynn Fontanne and wants to speak to you."

"Somebody's being funny," I replied. I took the phone.

"Okay, who is it?" I said.

"Vincent, this is Lynn." I recognized her voice and became flustered.

"Oh yes, Miss Fontanne. I'm sorry. I just didn't think it could be you."

"Let me tell you why I'm calling," she began. "Both Alfred and I are very angry that they let you go, and we've tried to get you back. So far, we've had no luck but we'll keep trying."

"I'm very grateful," I replied.

"Meanwhile, I wonder if you'd do me a favor. Tomorrow a dear friend of mine, Noel Coward, is coming to see the show, and I do want him to see a good performance, but I simply cannot play the scene with this boy the way I used to with you. If I can arrange it, would you be willing to go on for one performance?"

I was overcome with emotion and could hardly speak. My ego, which had been so depressed for months, suddenly soared.

"Miss Fontanne," I replied, "I would be more than happy to do it, and I can't tell you how much I appreciate your thinking of me."

"Very well, I'll speak to Terry Helburn [the president of the Guild] and call you in the morning."

When I hung up and told Hedda, she was happy for me and was impressed. The next day, Miss Fontanne called to say that, after checking with Equity, Helburn was told that they could not permit it, that the actor had been engaged for both plays. The fact that *Much Ado* was called off did not give the Guild the right to dismiss him from *Elizabeth,* nor could they allow him to be humiliated by replacing him for one performance. I understood and told her that just to know she and Lunt had been thinking about me made up for everything.

The summer at Tamiment was hard work—often sixteen hours a day—but rewarding. During the week they had hundreds of guests, and on weekends over a thousand. I had most of my former staff plus a few added performers. I was also fortunate in having a string quartet led by Irving Kolodin, who later became music critic for the *New York Sun,* an afternoon paper. After the *Sun* folded, Irving was the music editor of the *Saturday Review of Literature.*

Near the social hall was a special bungalow for me and the male members of my staff. But during the week Hedda, as registrar, would know which bungalows were occupied and which were not; she would whisper to me at dinner, and we'd meet and spend the night together in one of them. I'd slip out early the next morning and go back to my group, and Hedda would go to the bungalow she shared with another female employee. Several times, early in the morning, a maid would pop into the bungalow we were in, and Hedda would quickly cover me with the sheet. I was sure, after different maids had seen her in various bungalows, that they must have thought she was with a different man each time and was the biggest tramp in the camp.

The guests were pleased with the shows, and the management was happy. After the final show on Labor Day, I took a week's rest while Hedda helped clear up details in the office. We also told Mrs. Mailley and Josephson that we were married. They had guessed it. We returned to New York with my one-thousand-dollar salary intact and with most of Hedda's earnings.

What pleased me most about the summer was that it was the first time Hedda was able to observe my work as a director and as an actor playing the leads in dramatic and musical shows. She liked what she saw and assured me that it was only a matter of time before my big chance would come. I valued her opinion because she was not given to empty flattery.

We found a small apartment in Manhattan, and Hedda took a temporary job as a secretary. Soon after, I was given a role in the Chicago company of Elmer Rice's new play, *Counsellor at Law,* which was already a hit in New York. It starred Paul Muni as a successful Jewish attorney who had worked his way up from the ghetto and was married to a gentile socialite. Otto Kruger was to play the Muni role in Chicago. My part was small but effective, that of a poor young Jewish boy who is beaten up by the police and arrested for making communist speeches. After his mother pleads with the lawyer to help, he bails the boy out but berates him in his office and scorns his speechmaking. The two have a powerful confrontation about wealth and betrayal of class. Despite the communist jargon, I was sympathetic with the sentiments expressed. The part paid seventy-five dollars per week, which was good for the peak of the Depression. Hedda and I agreed that until we were certain the play was a hit in Chicago, she should remain in New York and hold on to her job. We had become more concerned than ever about money and the necessity of saving it.

The opening in Chicago was well received. My scene with Kruger came at the end of the second act, and the applause was gratifying. Hedda gave up her job and took a bus to Chicago; I found a furnished apartment for us in a new building in Lincoln Park. Our stay in Chicago became our honeymoon. On days when I was not doing a matinee and on Sundays when we had the day off, we took walks along the lakefront, visited the museums, attended the symphony orchestra concerts, went to the Adler Planetarium, and made love often. On several occasions after the show, we were invited to the College Inn at the Sherman Hotel to hear Ben Bernie, the old maestro, and his orchestra. Twice he introduced me to the crowd. At Sportsman Park, they once named a horse race in my honor. It was my first taste of a little glory and public recognition since entering the theater, and I confess that I relished it. So did Hedda.

In the cast, playing an office boy, was Jules Garfield. We became friends immediately and shared the dressing room for twenty weeks. Julie was eighteen years old and one of the most eager young men I'd ever known. His education had been limited, but he was yearning to know about everything: theater, art, music, literature, and politics. I started him reading *The Nation* and *The New Republic,* which he devoured.

As usual, I was sending money home, but I became worried about my father, who had suffered a bout with emphysema and had to stop working. My two oldest sisters had jobs, were living at home, and were contributing to the family, but sadly, my brother was sending little from Scranton, Pennsylvania, where he was earning over a hundred dollars a week as a booker for the Comerford chain of movie houses.

After a run of twenty weeks we returned to New York in May 1932 and decided that until we knew what lay ahead, we'd take a room with Hedda's family at their home in Brighton Beach. My family had moved to Brooklyn to be near one of my mother's relatives. My father's health, which had deteriorated, seemed to be improved, although he was not yet able to go back to work.

It was too late for a job on the borscht circuit. The good positions were filled. Max Liebman had been engaged, months before, as the new social director at Tamiment. He was to achieve recognition later as producer of the TV series *Your Show of Shows* with Sid Caesar, Imogene Coca, Carl Reiner, and Howard Morris.

Through a friend, Hedda was soon offered a job with the Democratic Campaign Committee to Elect Roosevelt President, and she began work in June. She, along with several other skilled secretaries, was to answer the mail that was pouring in from people all over the country who were in economic straits, telling Roosevelt that they were going to vote for him and asking him, if he was elected, to please help them. Most of the letters, she said, were heartbreaking.

I began gathering material for another play, but in August I received a phone call from Joe Pevney. He was at Green Mansions, a popular summer camp, where he had been working with Harold Hecht, the social director. The program there had not turned out too well, and the owner, who knew that Joe had worked with me in the past, asked him to find out if I would do the last few shows of the summer. The pay was fair, and since it was only for a few weeks, Hedda thought I should take the offer. I left for Green Mansions with a promise from Hedda that she would come up after the Labor Day weekend.

I directed and acted in three shows there, and the season ended successfully. Confidence in my ability to create entertainment continued to build. Hedda came to the camp, and we relaxed for several days before returning to New York. Soon after, I was called by the Theater Guild for a role in *The Good Earth,* a play based on Pearl Buck's novel about China. It was written by Owen Davis and his son Donald and was to star Alla Nazimova, with Claude Rains playing her husband. My role was that of a young revolutionary (this time Chinese) who appears on a city street and tries to incite the poor to rebel against the terrible conditions they face. It was only a short scene, but it was flashy, and they paid me well. I was pleased to be working again with Claude and to be directed by Philip Moeller, who had sent for me.

I had heard about Nazimova, her great performances years before in New York, and her femme fatale roles in silent movies in the early twenties. I was curious about her. She was now in her fifties but looked much younger, had a slim figure, and was obviously a highly talented actress. At the end of the first reading of the play, Moeller gave us a short break before starting the second reading. As I was getting a drink of water, Nazimova approached me.

"What is your name, young man?" she asked. I told her. She stared at me for several seconds then took a step back, looking me up and down until I became slightly self-conscious. I didn't know if she was going to offer me some advice or criticism. Then she leaned close and whispered, "You are very good." I was flattered, naturally, and ended up a devoted admirer. I never thought it possible that one day I'd direct her.

The Good Earth notices were only fair, but we had a nice run because of the Guild subscription list, theater parties, and so forth. Before it closed Claude was summoned to Hollywood to play the lead in the Universal film *The Invisible Man,* based on H.G. Wells's thriller. I said goodbye to him, wished him good luck, and was sorry to see him go, not knowing whether I would ever see him again. He was replaced by Earl Larimore.

In November Roosevelt was elected by a landslide, and the country was waiting desperately for him to take over. In March Hedda was invited to attend the White House reception after the inauguration. *The Good Earth* had closed, and I went with her. We took an inexpensive midnight excursion train to Washington and arrived early the next morning. As we entered the terminal station, I recalled the first time I had been in it, when my father took me with him on a buying trip to Baltimore in 1915 and we stopped off in Washington for a day. It was a thrilling experience then, but this morning's newspaper headlines announced that the nation's banks were closed and a bank holiday was declared. Hedda and I were worried about what we'd do when we got back to New York because what little money we had was in a bank.

We didn't go to a hotel but carried a bag that Hedda took into the ladies' room to change into her outfit for the affair. After breakfast we checked the bag and walked to the lawn of the Capitol grounds for the inaugural ceremony. I was sure the huge crowd was anxiously waiting to hear what the new president would have to say, not only about the banks closing but about the condition of the country. I was mistaken. There was a long wait as Ted Husing described over the radio and loudspeaker the progress of the march to the rotunda of the Capitol, where the oath of office would be administered. Finally, Roosevelt appeared, dressed in frock coat and striped trousers, walking upright on the arm of his son Jimmy, his steel braces unseen under his trousers. The oath of office was administered by Charles Evans Hughes. The moment the ceremony ended and Roosevelt began to speak, I was astounded to see many of the people in the crowd begin to drift away. They weren't interested in what the new president had to say but were there merely out of curiosity to see the man who had been struck down by infantile paralysis. They wondered if he would arrive in a wheelchair or attempt to walk in and stand for the oath. It was a sad comment on the public's interest in political and economic matters. This was the speech in which Roosevelt said we had nothing to fear but fear itself and in which he spoke about the four freedoms. It was inspiring and for years much quoted.

Afterward, I walked Hedda over to a side entrance of the White

House, where I waited as she went in to shake hands with the president and Mrs. Roosevelt and to greet some of her fellow campaign workers. It was almost an hour before she came out, but I was enjoying myself as I watched and recognized some of the important people who went inside.

We returned to New York that night with high hopes for the future. Within a few days the banks reopened, and people felt that something would at last be done to bring relief to the country. It was a time of many and great changes. Some felt that Roosevelt was saving the country from a revolution, as Kerensky had done in Russia, while others were convinced that he was leading us down the road to socialism. Roosevelt was both loved and hated.

Summer 1933 was not far off. Hedda and I decided that we would forgo any jobs that might be available on the borscht circuit. Aside from the hard work, the long hours, and the nervous strain, such a job meant that I was not able to get back to New York until after Labor Day, when many of the fall shows were already cast, and I might miss out on a good role in a new play. With both of us working during the few months before and living for five dollars a month rent in the basement room with Hedda's family at Brighton Beach, we had saved up over nine hundred dollars even though I was still contributing to my family.

I had been reading about the life of Samuel Insull, the utility tycoon of Chicago, and what went on in that dynamic city during his rise and fall; the time of Big Bill Thompson, the anti-British mayor; and Al Capone's gangsterism. I thought there was a play in it that could have a vigorous style like that of Hecht and MacArthur's *The Front Page*. Hedda encouraged me to write it, and in May we packed our few belongings and took off for Provincetown, Massachusetts—famous as a writer's and artist's resort. In no time we found a small furnished house belonging to a gracious Portuguese couple who owned a grocery store in the town. It was a few yards behind their own home. We had a tiny kitchen with a kerosene stove and an ice box, but no bathroom or toilet—only an outhouse. However, the kitchen did have a large sink where we washed our dishes, clothes, and bodies. Now and then we'd go to the beach for a swim.

We enjoyed every moment in Provincetown—the atmosphere of the town, the fishermen, the ocean breezes, and the tangy salt air, garnished now and then with the odor of fish. I wrote steadily every day from early morning until late afternoon. Then we'd take a walk. There was a Provincetown Players Theater, but I didn't get involved. I was too busy writing *Light and Power*.

Not far from our place there was an old cemetery we used to wander through, reading the names on the tombstones. Many of them went back to the year 1600. Some of the men and women had died at sea, some on land. On the road to the cemetery were blueberry and blackberry bushes that were loaded with fruit, which we picked free of charge. Fishermen would sell us, for a pittance, the plentiful fresh mackerel or whitefish. Once or twice a week we'd dig for clams or go with our landlord at dawn to check his lobster pots. We almost always came back with one or two lobsters for ourselves. That summer, we lived almost entirely on seafood, which cost us very little.

After dinner I'd indulge in a five-cent cigar, followed by a short walk into town to see the tourists; then I would come back home to make love and sleep. Often, during the day, Hedda would slip up behind me, put her arms around me, and I'd stop for an hour of love. As I recall that summer, I have a warm, sweet feeling. We were optimistic about the future. Although we had married primarily out of a need for each other, we began to know what love was about: a complete envelopment with each other. Hedda was dedicated to helping me with my career, reading and discussing my work, and making my life pleasant, and I was determined to justify her belief in me and achieve success for both of us. In eight weeks I completed a first draft of *Light and Power,* which I thought captured the conflict between Insull and the people of Chicago (led by Donald Richberg, later an important figure in the Roosevelt administration) in their struggle for low utility rates.

We returned to New York in the middle of August healthy, happy, and tanned from a wonderful summer that cost us the grand total of $175. I was prepared to begin polishing my play when a phone call came from Jane Broder, the agent who had gotten me my job in the Chicago company of *Counsellor at Law.*

"How would you like to go to Hollywood?" she asked.

"Hollywood? For what?" I replied.

"To test for the part of the young communist? They won't promise that you'll get the job, but they'll guarantee you four weeks at $250 a week whether they use you or not."

I had heard that the play was to be done as a film by Universal Pictures with John Barrymore playing the role Muni had created on Broadway. The rest of the cast would be made up from the New York company.

"I thought Marty Wolfson was going to play the part," I questioned, since he had created the role.

"He made a test," Jane said, "but the director wants a different type, and Mr. Rice recommended you. But you'll have to fly out tomorrow."

In 1933 flying was not as commonplace as today. Hollywood was three thousand miles miles away. I hesitated, wondering whether Providence was giving me a break with one hand but intended, through an accident, to take it away with the other.

"Well . . . would you like to go?" Jane said. I conferred briefly with Hedda, and we decided I should take the chance. My family lived in Brooklyn, not far away, and I rushed to tell them the news and say goodbye. They were delighted and pointed out that I would be able to see my Uncle Ben, who now lived in Los Angeles and worked for the May Company department store. I could also see another relative, Dora, a first cousin, who was married to Morris Horovitz, a dentist. I looked forward to seeing them, especially Uncle Ben, whom I only vaguely remembered.

Because it was uncertain whether I'd get the role, Hedda felt she should remain in New York until we knew more. Even if they used me, it would require only a short stay, and if they didn't, I'd soon be on my way back with the one thousand dollars.

The next afternoon Jane was at the airport with my ticket and introduced me to John Qualen. He had played the Swedish janitor in Rice's *Street Scene,* in both the play and the film, and then the role of Breitstein in *Counsellor at Law;* he later became well known as Papa Dionne, the father of the quintuplets, in the film about them. He was all set for the movie version of *Counsellor,* and we were flying together. Our plane, a TWA tri-motor, took thirteen hours to get to Los Angeles. We arrived at the airport early the next morning and were met by Bill Woolfenden of the Edward Small Agency, Broder's western tie-in. He drove us to the old Hollywood Hotel at the corner of Highland Avenue and Hollywood Boulevard.

On the way he said, "Too bad you boys won't have a top director looking out for you." We asked who the director was, and he replied, "Oh, one of the Laemmle relatives [Carl Laemmle was the head of Universal Pictures], a fellow named Wyler, never made anything important." Neither Qualen nor I had ever heard of Wyler, but we were ready to do our best for him.

4
Hollywood—First Time

The lazy sunshine of southern California, its palm trees, and the odor of orange and lemon blossoms drifting through the clean, dry air were immediately seductive. The tension of New York seemed to dissolve and melt away. A languid relaxation such as I had not felt since leaving the South came over me. In short, Hollywood was a pleasant surprise. I called my cousin Dora. She lived with her husband and her son, Leon, in a house at the corner of Wilton and Franklin. She invited me for dinner that evening and promised to have my uncle Ben there.

That afternoon Qualen and I took a walk down Hollywood Boulevard, from Highland to Vine Street. There were few people on the street, practically no traffic, and the only noise was from a red streetcar that passed up and down the boulevard every hour. It was quite warm, but the heat was dry and not uncomfortable. The atmosphere was that of a sleepy village, peaceful and restful.

Dinner with my relatives was a pleasure. We talked until midnight, as I filled them in with all the news from back East. My uncle was in his fifties, still dapper, still unmarried, and my cousins were intelligent and warm human beings. We became good friends.

For a day or two, Qualen and I stuck close to the hotel in case there was a summons from the studio. Later we were told not to worry about it; they'd let us know in plenty of time when they wanted us. It occurred to me that Claude Rains might still be in Hollywood, where he had gone months before to make *The Invisible Man* for Universal. I called the studio and learned that he was at the Chateau Elysée on Franklin. When I phoned, he was most cordial and invited me for dinner. We met at Musso and Frank's and had an appetizing meal. Driving his new black Ford Roadster with red wire wheels, he took me to the beach at Santa Monica to show me the Pacific Ocean. After a few days he finished his film and went back to New York to do a play. He later returned to Hollywood, where he worked for many years and gave many fine performances. I never dreamed that I would one day be directing him.

A week passed before a call came from the studio telling me that Mr. Wyler was ready to see me. I am ashamed to say that I was one of those snobbish young New York actors who looked down on movies and had no great respect for most of the movie directors and their imaginations. I thought I'd best look as much like the conventional concept of a communist as possible if I wanted to get the part. I didn't shave, left my hair uncombed, and wore my oldest clothes. I took the streetcar over the Cahuenga Pass, got off at Lankershim, and walked to Universal studios. I was directed to the stage, where Mr. Wyler and John Barrymore were waiting. Normally, I would have been nervous to meet the great Barrymore, but because he had deserted the theater—sold his soul for the "filthy lucre" of Hollywood—I regarded him with a touch of scorn, which matched the feelings of the young communist. He didn't faze me one bit.

Wyler introduced himself and Barrymore. I was polite but sullen. After looking me over, Wyler said, "Would you do the scene with Mr. Barrymore the way you did it on the stage?"

"Okay," I replied and took a moment to get ready. I had not played it since we closed in Chicago over a year before, but it was in my gut, having performed it every night for twenty weeks. I had also refreshed my memory of it while I was coming out on the plane. Barrymore read from the script as I played the scene with full emotion. When we finished, he put his arm around my shoulder and said warmly, "Makes me feel like I'm back in New York."

I did not expect such a generous reaction, and I was flustered. My attitude toward him changed; I was immediately won over. Wyler seemed pleased and said he'd like to make a test. He ordered a camera to be sent to the set. We repeated the scene on film, and the next day I was told to come to the studio to see the result. As I started into the projection room with Wyler and Barrymore, the latter said, "I want to warn you, if you've never seen yourself on the screen, it'll be a shock to you, the way you look and sound. The first time I saw myself I went outside and puked." I didn't puke, but it *was* a shock. My voice sounded much higher pitched than I expected, and I looked much more rugged and menacing than I had imagined. The next day I was told I had the part and that they would call me when it was time for the actual shooting. I didn't ask when that would be or how long it would take. But I wrote to Hedda to tell her the good news and promised to let her know as soon as possible if she should come out.

Qualen and I decided to take an apartment so that we could have a kitchen and prepare a snack whenever we wanted and not have to run out for it. We found a place at the Shelton Arms on Wilcox just off Hollywood Boulevard. It had a living room with twin pull-down beds, a kitchen, and a bath.

After two or three weeks I was called to the studio to do my first scene, a simple matter of sitting in the outer office of Barrymore's character and glaring at his two spoiled stepchildren. One of them was played by Richard Quine, who later became a good director. In between the lighting and the rehearsals, I had an opportunity to talk with Barrymore about theater, films, actors, and kindred subjects. Perhaps he was finding excuses for having deserted the theater, but he said, "You know, in the theater, some nights you feel well and give a good performance, and some nights you feel bad and give a lousy performance. But in movies, they pick the best take of every scene you've done, and all over the world audiences see you only at your best." When I mentioned that I had heard his performance of Hamlet was great, he told me that he had bought the scenery from the Arthur Hopkins production and was paying storage on it, hoping some day to return and repeat his performance. He never did.

One day, discussing actors, he said, "I'm always amused by those actors who, when offered a role, want to know how many scenes they have, how many big speeches? . . . That never interests me. . . . I only want to know *who does the suffering.*" I laughed but later realized how shrewd he was: With whom does the audience identify? With whom do they sympathize?

Barrymore was in his early fifties at the time but looked older. His jowls hung loosely, and the makeup man had to tape them up every morning. He was married to the beautiful Dolores Costello, whose father was Maurice Costello, a famous actor and a matinee idol. She had starred with John in several films at Warner Brothers. There was talk that their marriage was foundering, which later, with their divorce, proved correct.

At last the day came when we were to do our big scene. I was sure that it would not require more than a few hours. It took almost four days. Barrymore was having trouble remembering his lines, and the studio was concerned how he would handle his scene with me. It was highly emotional for both of us. (In the play, it was the second act curtain.) The scene began, as in the play, with him lacing into me for making communist speeches, getting arrested and beaten up by the police, and causing my mother grief. I resent his remarks, turn on him angrily, and point out that since he has become a wealthy lawyer, he has forgotten his roots, the poor of the east side. Barrymore had only a few short speeches at the climax, whereas I had long, emotional ones. For some reason he'd dry up and go blank. He was apologetic to Wyler, who was patient, and especially to me, as we had to repeat take after take. They finally put up a blackboard for him at the side of the set with key lines on it in large letters, which he was skillful at using. A sidelong glance or turnaway that seemed natural would allow him to focus on his next line.

In spite of the trouble we were having getting the scene, I found it fascinating to see how he worked. At that time the word *improvisation* was not used in Hollywood, but he literally improvised his scenes: he knew his intent and attitude but couldn't remember the author's exact words. So he'd play the action in his own words. After each take, when Freda Rosenblatt, who was Wyler's longtime script clerk and secretary, would correct him, he'd ask, "What did I say?" She'd tell him, then give him the correct words, and little by little he made the author's words his own. It was, and always will be, the method every good performer uses to create a role: Know the character, his or her attitude, feelings, intent, basic desire, and need in every scene.

By the time we had done twenty takes and still had not completed the scene, I was physically exhausted. I asked Wyler if I could rest for a few minutes. He said quietly, "I don't blame you." He ordered the stage doors opened and told me to go into a dressing room and lie down until I felt better. I detected that he was becoming annoyed with Barrymore but was holding back his anger. After a short rest I recovered my energy, and we began again. Seven more takes, twenty-seven in all, and Wyler thought he had what he needed. Subsequently, he became well known for his many takes, but in this case I think he was justified.

Before Barrymore became an actor, I was told, he had been a cartoonist for one of the San Francisco newspapers, and I was curious to see what he was constantly doodling on the large pad at his desk. When he wasn't looking, I stole a glance at it. He had drawn several faces of himself in the attitude he had toward me in the scene. I was also interested in Barrymore's hands: they were small and gnarled, but strong. At the end of each day as I left the studio, I felt genuinely sorry for him. He had been warm and friendly to me all through the shooting, and I could sense that he was deeply troubled. Everyone was afraid that he might start drinking, which often had happened in the past, but so far he remained sober. In fact, I was told that his contract with Universal was for five thousand dollars per day for twenty days, and if he didn't work he wasn't paid.

One night, as I waited for Qualen to come from the studio where they had been shooting his scene with Barrymore, he didn't arrive until 10:00 P.M. I wondered what was wrong, and he explained: They had started his scene after lunch, worked straight through dinner, and made fifty-four takes before Wyler finally gave up, saying they would try to get the scene right tomorrow. Qualen felt something was decidedly wrong with Barrymore. The next morning Barrymore came in bleary-eyed, face swollen, wearing one red sock and one blue. They sent him home and shot other scenes. When Gene Fowler was preparing to write his novel *Goodnight Sweet Prince*, about Barrymore, he called Qualen to ask him about the day of fifty-four takes. Then Fowler informed Qualen that that night, when Barrymore went home, he was so upset that he called his neighbor, John Gilbert, and went to his house, where he spent most of the night drinking. Barrymore told Gilbert that he was afraid he was losing his mind. I heard later that Barrymore was haunted by the fear of insanity; his father had died in an institution.

A few times he invited me to his dressing room, where he had corned beef or pastrami sandwiches and dill pickles brought in for lunch. Afterward he reeked of garlic, and I could see the disgusted faces of some of the ladies he worked with, especially Doris Kenyon, who played his snooty wife. But he seemed to enjoy her discomfort.

He was, I discovered, in addition to being a great actor, a truly cultured man, well read, with a knowledge of music and painting. Yet there was something simple and down to earth about him. Years later, after his career was in disarray and his drinking was out of control, his sense of humor and cynicism took over, and he mocked himself as the Great Profile. But I cannot forget his performances in *Topaze, Grand Hotel, Bill of Divorcement*, and other films. Occasionally, I listen to some of his great recordings made for Columbia Records with scenes from Shakespeare. I treasure my memory of him.

It was also my good fortune to become friendly with William Wyler, for whom I developed a genuine admiration and who proved his great talent in the years ahead. Recently, I saw a print of *Counsellor at Law,* and it still holds up! It was Wyler's first important production, and he was already a keen judge of film. The story was confined to a suite of offices and consisted mostly of talk, but he kept things moving, and the result paid off.

When my scenes were completed, the Small agency informed me

that Universal was interested in having me do a test. Wyler and Barrymore had suggested that they sign me to a long-term contract. Naturally, I was elated. An appointment was made for me to meet Mr. Laemmle, the head of the studio. He was a man in his sixties, short and balding, with a ready smile and thick-lensed glasses that seemed to enhance his wise eyes. He was most cordial, complimented me on my work, and suggested that I get dressed up and pick a nice scene with a girl for the test. I knew I would not be comfortable playing a romantic love scene on a balcony under the moonlight, nor had I ever thought of myself as a typical juvenile, so I selected something with a rough texture. Unfortunately, the studio was looking for romantic types, such as Robert Taylor, which I was not, so they decided to function without me.

However, I was not discouraged. I felt that something would turn up—a role in a film or a play—and that I should remain in Hollywood for a while and give myself a chance. I wrote Hedda to come out. She arrived, and we rented a house for a month. I bought an old 1922 Buick for twenty-five dollars from one of the actors in *Counsellor at Law* who was returning to New York and no longer needed it. He had paid fifty dollars for it.

Within a short time, the Small office called to tell me that a man named Seymour Robinson was going to produce and direct a play at the Pasadena Playhouse titled *The Terrible Turk*. It was about Jed Harris, the mercurial but talented producer and director of many successful plays in New York. He said Robinson would like to talk to me about playing the lead. They said it didn't pay anything, but the Playhouse was a great showcase. I read the play and liked it. It caught the volatile quality of Harris, who was a legend in New York. Robinson liked my interpretation, and I was given the role.

I received a call from Wyler. He was seeing a young actress, Sheila Bromley, who was trying out for the female lead in *The Terrible Turk*, and asked if I would help her because she was inexperienced. I told him it would be my pleasure to repay his many kindnesses to me. When Sheila appeared for a reading, she was shy and slightly nervous but as pretty and delicate as a Dresden doll. She had exactly the quality called for in the play and was given the role. We became good friends and remain so to this day. She also became a fine actress; she later married Arthur Applebaum, a successful attorney who recently died.

The reviews were gratifying. Katherine T. Von Blon of the *Los Angeles Times* was especially kind to me. She wrote, "Vincent Sherman, who is practically the play, performed with gusto and power. He has a genuine liking for the theater and managed terrific intensity without over-stressing. He was pathetic, humorous and dominating." I felt and hoped that I had finally become a good actor.

In December 1933 the film *Counsellor at Law* opened at Radio City Music Hall in New York. Some of the reviewers wrote that, although Barrymore did not have the Jewish characteristics that Muni had in the play, he gave an excellent performance. Wyler was praised for the terrific pace of the film. No one ever said again that Willy was "just one of the Laemmle relatives." The New York reviews for me were all that I could have hoped for. Regina Crewe of the *New York American* summed it up when she wrote, "Perhaps there is a sign of the times audible in the applause that echoed through the marble halls of the Radio City Music Hall at the conclusion of the communistic denunciation of the hero as a 'class traitor,' during the film's first showing. Or perhaps it was just a well-won tribute to the histrionics of Vincent Sherman, who makes a moment all his own, face to face and eye to eye with John Barrymore in a convincing, thrilling scene." Ed Sullivan selected it as the best "bit" performance of the week.

A few days after the opening, I received a letter from my father, who wrote that he had taken my mother and my two youngest sisters to the first showing at the Music Hall. When my scene was over, the audience burst into applause. But he added apologetically, "Maybe I started it, Sonny." So he insisted that the family stay for the second showing and made them promise *not* to applaud unless others did first. He finished by writing, "Sonny, the audience still applauded."

Soon after, my agent called to say that Columbia Pictures wanted me for a film. I was anxious to work, in order to earn as much money as possible, and was not too critical of what I was offered. The role was that of a gangster, something I had never before played, but I thought I could use the experience. It was produced by Irving Briskin, head of the department for B-budget films and was to be made in twelve or fourteen days. I had time to run through the lines once, then shoot. I had a good third-degree interrogation scene that was effective, and because I always knew my lines, they dubbed me "one-take Sherman." I did six pictures in a row for Irving, several with "third-degree" scenes, in which the dialog was almost always the same. Some were with Ralph Bellamy, who was not only a good actor but also a nice man.

During this period the country was still suffering from the effects of the Wall Street crash; the economy had not yet recovered. Europe was even in worse shape. In Germany an Austrian house painter had become chancellor, was drawing large crowds, and was telling them that international Jewish bankers were the cause of their troubles. In Spain a battle between democratic forces and right-wing reactionaries was looming on the horizon. It was difficult to know what was really happening because the Los Angeles papers were singularly free of bad news, and the relaxed atmosphere of southern California added to the torpor.

A call came from Warner Brothers for me to play another gangster, this time in a picture with Richard Barthelmess titled *Midnight Alibi.* I was one of his henchmen, along with three other actors, but we never appeared in scenes with him. In fact, I had little to do until a courtroom sequence where I was a witness and had five or six speeches. Alan Crosland Sr. was the director, and that morning he was having trouble with several actors who had only a couple of lines each to deliver and with a girl who was said to be the friend of one of the producers at the studio. After several maddening hours, he turned wearily to his assistant, Russ Saunders, and said, "Okay, who's next?" Russ pointed to me and introduced me. Crosland said, "Know your lines?" I nodded. "All right," he replied, "Run over 'em and we'll try a take." I ran through the lines with Robert Warwick, a good actor, who was playing the district attorney. Then Russ yelled "Quiet!" and afterward "Roll 'em." Warwick and I were letter perfect, and Crosland printed the first take, then moved in for a closer shot and again printed the first take. When I stepped down from the witness stand, Robert McQuade, a fine character actor, came to me. "You should have seen the look on the director's face when you finished," he said. "He turned to me wide-eyed with surprise and, with a big smile, winked." That night, Woolfenden called to say that he was told I did a sensational job. I explained that I only did five speeches without a fluff. Even so, he replied, they were talking about a possible contract for me. It did not happen then, but the payoff would come later. Had anyone told me that in five years I would be directing Richard Barthelmess, I would not have believed it.

While we were in Hollywood, we met several actors, including Lee J. Cobb. He had appeared in plays at the Pasadena Playhouse, one of which we saw, and I thought he was excellent. I was told he wanted to meet me. We invited him to lunch at our rented house in Burbank. He was about my height but heavyset, slow moving, with a large head that was almost bald, and as a result he appeared to be much older than he really was. We enjoyed a lunch that Hedda had prepared and began immediately to talk about theater, acting problems, films, and the ominous rise of Hitler and Nazism. We soon discovered that our tastes and feelings were similar in so many areas, it was as though we had each found a long lost brother. We spent the entire afternoon talking and finished off a bottle of wine. We even had a few laughs, despite the fact that Lee was deeply depressed about his career. He felt he was going nowhere; he had played one small role of a villain in a B western that he disliked and was convinced he had no future in films, nor in the theater. He had played half a dozen roles of old men at Pasadena and had received praise, but no agent had approached him. I tried to console him by telling him about my own struggle in New York and those of many of my friends.

Afterward, he was at our house two or three times a week. We listened to his complaints, did our best to cheer him up, and fed him many meals. Hedda was becoming a good cook, and he enjoyed eating with us. We became close friends. Finally, one day when I realized that he was in a hopeless rut and unlikely to get out of it unless he was helped, I suggested that he go to New York and look for a part in a good play. In fact, I was myself considering going back. I was tired of playing one gangster after another, even though the money was welcome and we loved the sunshine. The more I urged him, the more he seemed to reject the idea. I thought it best to drop the subject.

About this time a telegram arrived from Jane Broder, telling me that Elmer Rice wanted me to play a young American lawyer in his new play, *Judgement Day,* a courtroom drama that paralleled the Reichstag fire trial in Germany. Rehearsals were to begin late in August. Would I like to do it? I wired Jane that I was happy to accept the offer and that Hedda and I would soon be leaving for New York. We had no regrets. We thought Hollywood was a place to vegetate and remain isolated from the mainstream of life. We said goodbye to our friends and relatives and had Lee to the house for a farewell dinner. We suggested one last time that he come to New York. I promised to send him our address the moment we got located. He was sorry to see us go.

It was July 1934 and hot, so I suggested to Hedda that we take a leisurely drive back east but travel mostly at night. I had traded in our 1922 Buick for a later-model used Deluxe Roadster that cost us three hundred dollars. Hedda thought it was a good idea, so we left late one afternoon and arrived at dawn in Las Vegas. It was an ugly, dirty, windswept little town, with (we soon learned) two whorehouses for the workmen who were building Boulder Dam, and a couple of coffee shops and gas stations. We got out of Las Vegas as soon as possible. In 1950, when we visited the more modern Las Vegas, Hedda refused to believe it was the same place we passed through in 1934.

We stopped for a day in Chicago to see an old friend, Meyer Levin, who was the movie critic for *Esquire* magazine and who had given me a great review for *Counsellor at Law.* We also visited the World's Fair.

Back in New York, we found a simple apartment on Fifty-fifth Street. Our families were happy to see us, and rehearsals for *Judgement Day* soon began. Everyone in the cast had hopes for a successful show and a long run. But the critics were not impressed. Although we took salary cuts to keep the play open, Mr. Rice finally had to close it down.

5

Moving Left

Not only was the closing of *Judgement Day* disappointing, because we thought it was an important play, but furthermore, finding another job was not easy. The theater was at an all-time low, and acting jobs were scarce.

During the six months Hedda and I were in Hollywood, there seemed to be little concern for what was going on elsewhere: strikes, unemployment, and bread lines in the United States and the growth of fascism abroad. Hollywood was apolitical, but in New York the newspapers were full of the problems. We became increasingly aware of the conflicts and felt that we should do whatever we could to help worthwhile causes.

I agreed to direct a one-act play for a left-wing organization, The Theater Collective. It was about the breakdown of a typical middle-class family in the depression and the effort of the father to hang on to his old beliefs. The play was called *God's in His Heaven,* and it was written by Philip Stevenson. I was beginning to look for someone to play the father, when I received a call one evening from Lee Cobb. He had taken my advice and come to New York. I was happy to hear from him. He was trying to get an agent but having no luck. Could I help him? It suddenly struck me that he would be ideal for the father in *God's in His Heaven.* I invited him to our apartment for lunch the next day and explained that although no one was being paid to do *God's in His Heaven,* it was a chance for him to be seen by a producer or an agent. He thought I was right, read the play, liked it, and agreed to do it. I looked forward to a happy experience, based on our relationship in Hollywood. But because I had limited time to get the play ready for a performance, I might have been asking for results sooner than he felt like giving them. I tried to reason with him, but he was stubborn and insisted on doing things the way he

47

wanted. The result was a conflict that got nastier each day. We finally compromised, but our friendship was damaged. However, because of his performance, one night at the Fourteenth Street Theater he was invited to join the Group Theater. I envied him. Later, although I played a few small roles in several Group Theater productions, and many of its members were old friends from my Theater Guild days, I was never asked to join them.

Then came a call from Clifford Odets, formerly a close friend. He was playing Dr. Benjamin (the role created by Luther Adler) in his own dynamic *Waiting for Lefty*. It was a highly charged role, requiring a kind of emotional burst that was comparable to my role in *Counsellor at Law*. Cliff wanted to know if I'd like to replace him, because he wanted to give full time to his play *Awake and Sing*. It was in rehearsal, with Harold Clurman directing and Luther Adler playing Moe Axelrod. I was happy to do it, if only for a few weeks' run and a minimal salary. That night Hedda and I were invited to a party, where we saw Lee Cobb. He was playing a small role in *Lefty*. I said, "We'll soon be working together."

"Oh?" he replied. "How do you mean?"

"Cliff called me. I'm replacing him as Dr. Benjamin."

I thought he'd be happy for me and gracious enough to say "Welcome." Instead, his face clouded over as he said, disappointedly, "Cliff promised to let *me* do that part."

I could not believe that after all the lunches we had served him in our home in Hollywood, all the talks we had had to cheer him up, and my having been responsible for his coming to New York and appearing in the play that got him into the Group, he could be so uncharitable. Hedda was standing at my side with a shocked expression on her face. She pulled me away and said, "If you ever speak to that selfish, ungrateful bastard again, I'll leave you." Many years passed before Lee and I spoke again.

Months later, when the Group did the Odets play *Paradise Lost*, I was given a small role in it. I also acted in two productions of the Theater Union, *Black Pit*, by Albert Maltz, and *Bitter Stream*, based on Silone's novel, by Victor Wolfson, both directed by Mike Gordon. They too paid only small salaries, but they were trying to dramatize important social issues, and I was pleased to participate.

About this time I learned that Papa was not well. Hedda and I took the subway to Brooklyn to see him and the family. His emphysema was troubling him, but he did not seem to be in pain or worried, so we hoped it was not too serious. My brother Nat was back at home, having lost his job in Scranton. When we tried to find out what happened, he was reluctant to discuss it, saying only that he'd had a run-in with one of his bosses. We were concerned, especially my father, who wondered why Nat was not looking for another job, because arguments with management were commonplace. Nat evaded the issue.

Within a few days my father's condition worsened, and his doctor ordered him to go to the hospital for treatment. But when an ambulance arrived, he refused to be carried out on a stretcher. He got dressed and walked downstairs. The next day Hedda and I went to see him at the Kings County Hospital and found him in an oxygen tent. He smiled and seemed cheerful, however, and we felt sure that after a few days he'd be coming home. Early the next morning, October 2, 1935, my brother phoned to tell me that Papa had died just before dawn. I was distraught and refused to believe it; I thought a mistake had been made and called the hospital frantically to get the truth. They told me simply that his heart had given out. He was only fifty-two years old. My shock was so profound, my grief so overwhelming, I was unable to utter more than a few words during the next several days. I truly loved Papa.

My mother, when she was told, fell apart and was unable to attend the funeral on Staten Island. We were strapped for cash at the time and barely making ends meet, but we were helped by my mother's cousin, who belonged to a burial society. On Yom Kippur, when I went to synagogue with my brother to say the Prayer for the Dead, he broke down outside and confessed that he felt partly responsible for Papa's death. While in Scranton he had been leading a crazy life—drinking, whoring, and gambling—which led to the loss of his job and reputation. Papa had surmised the truth. I tried to console Nat, but it was not easy for either of us. Not long after, he left New York and went to Miami, where he got a job with our cousin Max Orovitz, an attorney who was building houses. My oldest sister, Tillie, had gone there a few months earlier with her husband, Harry Carr, a nice young man she'd met while they were both working in New York at Carson's Department Store.

Nat was bright and sharp in business matters and was soon serving as foreman for Max and his company. A few months after he went to Miami, my mother and my two youngest sisters, Evelyn and Barbara, followed. They all took a house together. My sister Minnie remained in New York, having married Morris Weiss, whose father owned one of the biggest laundries in the city.

Conditions in New York and in the theater were discouraging. Actors were required to rehearse free for four weeks. If the play was a flop and ran only two weeks, the actors were guaranteed only two weeks' pay for six weeks' work. If it was a success, there was no extra compensation. Along with many other actors, I felt this was unfair, and I spoke about it several times at group meetings. After many bitter words "pay for rehearsals" was finally approved by the majority of the members of Actors Equity. Today, young actors find it hard to understand why it was ever called a communist cause and its advocates reds.

Shortly thereafter, Elmer Rice called together a group of thirty or forty actors. Some had worked for him in the past, and others had not, but he admired the talents of all. He wanted to form a theater company in New York. I was flattered that he had included me. As he outlined the project for the Theater Alliance, we were all enthusiastic. He was also going to Washington to see whether he could get funding from the federal government. I was chosen as one of the members of the board, along with Sam Jaffe, Philip Loeb, and George Heller. We spent several days discussing with Rice the plays we would do, how salaries would be handled, profits, and so forth. The Belasco Theater was to be our home base. Rice had bought the building several months before, presumably with his profits from *Street Scene* and *Counsellor at Law,* and until we were established he would not expect any rental fee.

After several days in Washington, he returned with a surprising report. The president and Mrs. Roosevelt were not interested in funding a small group of thirty or forty actors, but they wanted to put five thousand theater people to work—those walking the streets, some literally starving, not only in New York but in every major city in the country. Hallie Flanagan, a friend of Mrs. Roosevelt, was already making plans for a Federal Theater project. It was welcome news. At last the government was paying some attention to the arts, although it meant that, for the moment, we would have to give up the Theater Alliance. Mr. Rice later became head of the New York branch of the Federal Theater. Knowing of my past experience and my desire to write and direct, he suggested that I join the Experimental Theater, which was to be headed by a friend of Hallie Flanagan's, Virgil Geddes, who had written a few minor but interesting plays.

I filled out an application, along with Charles Friedman and James Light. But because those who were setting up the Federal Theater were not aware of the requirements of a theater, there was no provision made for directors, so we went in as accountants for $150 per month. In the meantime Actors Equity established guidelines for salaries and rehearsal time for those involved in the Federal Theater. Actors were to receive

$25 per week and were permitted to rehearse only four hours a day instead of the normal eight hours.

I soon discovered that although Geddes was a pleasant man and talented, he had no idea of what was necessary to organize a theater. Friedman knew, but he was preoccupied with some other work and could not give us full time; James Light was a talented director and a favorite of Eugene O'Neill's but was said to be often on the bottle; so much of the work fell to me. After we assembled sixty or seventy actors for our company, I organized a play department, requisitioned several readers, and notified play agents that we were looking for material. Soon plays began to pour in. The first one recommended was *Chalk Dust*. I read it at once and suggested that we do it. Geddes, Friedman, and Light agreed, and Light was assigned to direct it. He did a good job, and the play was well received. We had made a start.

The next play that I thought we should consider, although it needed work, was *Battle Hymn*, written by Michael Gold and Michael Blankfort. Gold was a recognized author, having done a successful novel, *Jews without Money*. He was also a well-known communist. Blankfort was a promising writer. *Battle Hymn* was about John Brown of Harper's Ferry fame, and it seemed a worthwhile subject. What was wrong with the Gold and Blankfort play, in my opinion, was a failure to dramatize the political situation in the country at the time, one of the most vital and violent periods in our history. Another weakness was the stilted quality of the dialog, with Brown uttering pompous declarations as though he was already aware of his place in history. (Lincoln had said Brown hastened the Civil War by ten years.)

I told Geddes I'd like to direct *Battle Hymn*, and he approved. I read Oswald Garrison Villard's biography about Brown and, luckily, came across *God's Angry Man*, an excellent novel about Brown by Leonard Ehrlich. From the two books I began to get an insight into Brown's character. I had also learned a lesson about presenting a hero to an audience by watching a Russian film, *Lenin in October*, with the great Boris Schukin playing Lenin: Never let the character become aware of the importance of his role in history or how great his work is; play it down; keep reducing him to a normal human being with a few failings—but one who has the courage to fight for what he thinks is right.

To create the background of the times, Blankfort proposed doing stylized interludes before each act. I thought the idea excellent, and he came back in a few days with substantially what is in the published version. The credit for staging them should have gone to Aaron Foxman, my assistant. After weeks of rehearsals, the play opened to good reviews and had a long run.

At the same time the Living Newspaper branch of the Federal Theater did an exciting dramatization of the housing problem, directed by Joe Losey. It offended some members of Congress, and when they tried to interfere, Elmer Rice resigned in protest. We were sorry to see him go. Phil Barber, his capable assistant, was put in charge.

Before *Battle Hymn* ended its run, word was spread about that Sinclair Lewis, the Nobel and Pulitzer prize winner, had turned over his novel *It Can't Happen Here* to the Federal Theater for production. It would be done simultaneously all over the country at the various Federal Theaters. This was a real coup. We took it for granted that the job of directing it would go to Joe Losey, who had directed *Jayhawker*, an earlier play of Lewis's, for the Broadway theater. I was surprised, therefore, when I was called to Eighth Avenue, where the main office of the New York Federal Theater was located. Barber introduced me to Hallie Flanagan, a plain but nice-looking, pleasant, intelligent woman, who was the head of the Federal Theater. She informed me that they had decided, because of my work on *Battle Hymn,* that I was the one to direct the Lewis novel. I was lifted skyward. This was a prize assignment, one that every director in the Federal Theater coveted. Lewis was well known, and the production would command worldwide attention. When I asked why it was not given to Losey, who had done such a good job on the Living Newspaper, the reply was that Mr. Lewis wanted someone else.

Barber gave me a copy of the novel, which I had not read, and the play. He asked me to read both and report to them the next day. I rushed home and with great anticipation began reading the novel. By midnight I had also read the play. The novel was about the rise of fascism in the United States and was effective, but the play, I thought, was bad. There were two names on it, John C. Moffitt and Sinclair Lewis. I told Hedda that I would have nothing to do with it, that because Lewis was so well known and the material so popular, it would be doubly subject to criticism. Anyone who attempted to direct it was in for big trouble.

The next morning, as I entered Barber's office, Flanagan was waiting. I thanked them both for their confidence in me and for offering me the job, but I told them how disappointed I was. It was not that the play needed a little work; it had to be thrown out completely and a fresh start made. They agreed that it was not good but explained that they were caught in a bind. Lewis and Moffitt were no longer speaking. They had begun working at Bronxville, where Lewis and his wife, Dorothy

Thompson, had a home. Moffitt was given a room in the house so that he and Lewis could work closely together. Lewis found Moffitt pompous, and they disagreed about everything. Now they were split, and the Federal Theater was stuck not knowing what to do. Although I was sympathetic, I could see no way to solve their problem and begged to be relieved of directing the play. At that moment a man entered the office, whom I recognized as Harry Hopkins, a close friend and associate of the president. After being introduced, he was told how I felt about the play. He responded quietly but firmly. There were, he said, certain congressmen in Washington who were determined to shut down the Federal Theater, claiming that it was a boondoggling project and a haven for communists. Unless something important was done soon, something that would gain national attention and, hopefully, some praise, it was likely that we would soon see the end of the Federal Theater. I sensed that he was giving us the bald truth.

After a moment he rose, apologized for the short visit, wished us luck, and left. I was impressed by his simple but direct and businesslike manner. What he said changed the complexion of the meeting. I felt that no matter how difficult it would be, or how badly I might get clobbered by the critics, it was my duty to get the production done. But I had to know whether Lewis would permit rewriting and would be willing to help us.

"You'll have to talk to him," Barber replied.

"Unfortunately," Flanagan added, "he's not in a very good mood, so you'll have to be careful of what you say, or he might just call the whole thing off."

"I'll do my best," I said. Barber called the Essex House, where Lewis had a suite, and told him that I would direct and wanted to discuss some changes. Lewis said he would be waiting for us. As we made our way uptown, Hallie Flanagan and Barber cautioned me once again to be tactful. With trepidation we entered Lewis's suite. He was tall, knock-kneed, had a pockmarked face and thinning red hair, and spoke with a high-pitched nasal twang. After being introduced and exchanging a few words of small talk, he turned to me.

"I understand you have some changes in mind."

I nodded, but began by telling him what a great pleasure it was to meet him, how much I admired his work and what an honor it was to direct *It Can't Happen Here.* He thanked me curtly, as if to say, "Cut the bullshit," and got to the point of our meeting: "Let's hear your changes."

A pause, and I started. "Mr. Lewis, I read the novel before the play, and some scenes are so much better in the novel that I wonder if we couldn't use them, even if cut down?"

"It's possible. Which scenes?"

I could see that he did not want to waste time and wanted to hear what I had in mind. I went over the work scene by scene and explained how I thought we could improve the dramatic impact. After listening patiently to my suggestions for nearly a half hour, during which he said only, "I see," or "Maybe," he suddenly rose from his chair, crossed to the mantle and turned to me. "Just a minute, young man," he said with an edge. "You began by saying how honored you were to be working with me and how happy you were to be doing my play, but you've just been telling me that you want to change every damn scene in it!" The silence was thunderous. I looked at Barber and Flanagan. They were pale with fear. I knew I had scuttled the project. I was trying to think of how to apologize and save the situation when Lewis added, "It's all right with me. I think it stinks, too."

I have never seen or heard such a sigh of relief as that from Hallie and Phil. I told Mr. Lewis how happy he had made us and added, "If you are willing to help with the rewrite, I can't promise you a big hit—we don't have the time to do that kind of a job, but I feel we can get the dignity of a serious review; at least merit a column of criticism from Brooks Atkinson [the *New York Times* critic], whereas if we do it as is, we might be dismissed with a one-line review."

I told them a story: "When I first came to New York, a play opened called *One Shot Fired*. The next morning, one of the critics wrote: '*One Shot Fired* opened last night. We doubt the second shot will ever be heard.' That was all. That was the review. I don't want the critics to say '*It Can't Happen Here* and didn't!' Period." Lewis agreed, and we relaxed.

We began work the next morning in his hotel suite. Now and then he'd digress to ask about my mother and father, the South, how I got into the theater, and so forth. I did not ask him many personal questions, thinking it would be rude of me, but I did explore his thinking about current issues. He was not a student of politics or economics; he steered away from them since he considered them ephemeral and constantly changing; but he did have an extraordinary feeling for people, especially Americans—their values and aspirations, their weaknesses and prejudices. In speaking of his novel *Babbitt,* he surprised me.

"You know, people think I was poking fun at *Babbitt,* that it was a satirical portrait of a certain type of American. The truth is that in some ways I admired him; if it wasn't for the George Babbitts, this country might not be what it is." As I worked with him, I realized that he saw all sides of a human being.

We had barely gotten started rewriting when I had to begin casting at the Adelphi Theater. I asked him if he'd like to be present at these sessions, and I soon realized he was infatuated with the theater and wanted to participate in every phase of the production. I would have preferred that he use the time for writing, but he promised to do that in the afternoons and evenings.

I knew that the play was mild compared to its dynamic subject matter, but to do it right, give it the kind of excitement and suspense it called for, would require a different concept and structure and take weeks or months we didn't have. Time was the villain. I made up my mind not to worry but to forge ahead and do the best I could under the circumstances. The privilege of working with Sinclair Lewis was worth the harsh reviews I knew I would later receive.

He was a fascinating man with a great sense of humor. He told me about his divorce from his first wife, Grace Hegger, and how it cost him most of his royalties from *Babbitt, Main Street, Elmer Gantry* and *Arrowsmith* ($1 million). I asked him what the problem had been between them. He thought for a second, then said ruefully, "I guess I just never lived up to what the husband of Mrs. Sinclair Lewis should have been."

Slowly the play began to take shape. But as opening night approached, we still had no sets. Props and furniture had not yet been selected, and Lewis was growing impatient. At one point he was so incensed by the delays that he threatened to stop the whole show. I convinced him that it was no one's fault, just the bureaucracy of a government organization that was plowing new ground. At last opening night came. We had barely gotten the sets up for one dress rehearsal when it was curtain time. The performance was ragged, some of the actors not knowing whether to open a door by pulling it or pushing it, but the audience was sympathetic. There was a big hand for Lewis after the curtain came down, and the audience called for a speech. He took out his watch and said, "I have been making a speech for the last two hours and a half."

Later, there was a party at one of the large hotels. Hedda and I were invited, and for the first time we met Lewis's wife, Dorothy Thompson, the well-known columnist. She was tall, buxom, dynamic, and attractive. Hedda and I met many of the Lewises' friends. From the short talk we had with Dorothy, we gathered that she was not too happy with Lewis's desire to write plays. She felt he should stick to his novel writing.

Although the reviews were not good, we did accomplish what I set out to do, namely, merit the dignity of a column of criticism by Brooks Atkinson and not be dismissed. Also, I was happy to note that despite the poor reviews, audiences seemed to enjoy the show. It began to do fair business and settled in for a nice run. The play opened simultaneously at various theaters around the country. They were sent as many changes as possible and made some of their own. Finally, the objective of winning attention for the Federal Theater was achieved, and for the time being its enemies in Congress were subdued. I was happy to have contributed a small part to it.

A few days after the opening, Lewis asked me to come to his hotel to talk. "I want you to leave the Federal Theater and collaborate with me on a play," he began. "I've got an idea for Walter Huston. He's a professor of biochemistry at a small college, and although he is not Jewish, he is confronted with anti-Semitism as it relates to a colleague. I want to contrast one of the most advanced sciences with one of the most backward prejudices. Huston's fight to protect a young Jewish professor of economics is what the play will be about."

I was overwhelmed. I did not know how to reply except to say that it would be a privilege to work with him and a great honor to have my name on a play with his.

"How much do you make at the Federal Theater?" he asked. I told him, and he continued, "All right, I'm making out a check to you for $2,500 against future royalties. But from now on you work with me." I rushed home to tell Hedda about it and showed her the check. She was happy for me. That night we splurged—we had dinner out and spent almost five dollars. The next day I informed Virgil Geddes and Phil Barber of my good luck, and they wished me well.

Lewis called to say we had an appointment for tomorrow with Ben Harrow, a professor at City College of New York, to learn about the work of a biochemist. Harrow was serious but had a great sense of humor and had written several books on biochemistry. He told us about his work, and after an hour with him in his combined laboratory and office, Lewis proposed we go to lunch. He asked first, "Which way to the bathroom?"

"Number one or two?" Harrow asked.

"One," Lewis replied with a smile.

"In that case," Harrow said, "would you mind putting it in this?" and handed Lewis a chemical vial.

"Don't tell me you're saving the stuff?" Lewis asked.

"Oh yes," Harrow replied. "You see, we collect it in this," he said, pointing to a five-gallon glass water bottle, half-filled with urine, "and eventually extract the male hormone."

"Ben," Lewis observed, "you've got five thousand students up here. Why don't you just hook up the pissoirs, and you can extract all the male hormones you need?"

"You're right," Ben replied. "I spoke to the dean about the possibility of doing just that, and he said that he was sure it would be all right with the science department, but he didn't know how arts and humanities would react." Lewis roared with laughter. It was a stimulating day, and we got an idea of the kind of work that was being done by biochemists and the importance of their research.

The next appointment Lewis made for us was to talk to an assistant rabbi of the Steven Wise Temple about the problems of anti-Semitism. He made a luncheon date for the upcoming Friday, and I was to come to the hotel before noon to greet the rabbi and make him feel comfortable. Friday arrived, and I went to the Essex House. The maid was cleaning the living room. I asked where Mr. Lewis was. She smiled and pointed to the bedroom. As I opened the door, a sour odor of stale whisky greeted me. Lewis was in bed, dead drunk. I tried to wake him. He was half-conscious. I reminded him of our appointment with the rabbi. He muttered, "You apologize, tell him I'm not well but ask him all the questions, and order lunch." He closed his eyes and went back to sleep. I had heard about his drinking, but this was the first time I was confronted with it.

Half an hour later, the rabbi arrived. He smiled tolerantly when I told him Mr. Lewis was indisposed. He, too, had heard stories about Lewis's drinking. I ordered lunch and plied him with questions. He was most helpful and recommended certain books that we should read. Once or twice I looked in on Lewis, and he seemed to be sleeping. But just before the rabbi was ready to leave, we heard from the bedroom a terrible crash and the sound of breaking glass. I rushed inside and saw Lewis on the bathroom floor clinging to the toilet, his head drooped over, almost into the bowl itself, and broken glass all about him. He apparently had gone in to urinate, began to sway, lost his balance, grabbed for the glass stand just under the medicine cabinet, and pulled it down together with two drinking glasses, which hit the marble floor and broke. I quickly asked the rabbi if he would excuse me, explaining that there had been an accident. He understood and left. I went back into the bathroom, where I struggled to get Lewis up on his feet, which was not easy because he was so tall and gangly. His pajamas were wet with urine, and he began to retch. As I helped him up, he cut his hand on a piece of glass, and blood began to drip on the floor and into the toilet. At last I dragged him back into bed, pulled off his pajamas, wet a large bath towel, did my best to clean him up, and finally got him into fresh pajamas. I put a piece of plaster tape on his bleeding hand. It took a half hour, and I was physically and emotionally exhausted. I called his secretary, a man named Lou, who said he would come in to help and would speak to Dorothy. The next day they moved Lewis up to Bronxville, where he and Dorothy and their son, Michael, five or six years old, lived with two servants.

A few days later I received a call from Lewis saying he was much better and wanted me to join him and drive us up to Connecticut to see the Hartford Federal Theater presentation of *It Can't Happen Here,* which had been delayed until now. He sounded sober on the phone, and I was happy to accommodate him. My old Buick was still functioning, so I drove up to Bronxville. But the moment I entered the house and he greeted me, I realized that he had been drinking again. I was not happy. Nonetheless, we started out for Hartford in his auto, which I drove. I was hopeful that by the time we got there he would be all right and everything would turn out well. But on the drive up he said he needed a drink, and we stopped at a bar in one of the small towns we passed through. I had already been told by Lou that once he started to drink, it was unwise to try to stop him—he would drink even more. So I said nothing.

Inside, a half dozen working men were at the bar, some on their way home. Lewis started a conversation with one of them and introduced me as a salesman for the Singer Sewing Machine Company and himself as a supervisor who was breaking me in. He asked whether the man's wife had a machine and if not, why not, and carried on a conversation that soon included other men at the bar and other subjects: baseball, politics, Roosevelt, and the New Deal. When he insisted, I joined in but did not enjoy the pretense as much as he seemed to.

I was intrigued, however, with his ability to joke with the men on their level, elicit information from them, then shake hands and say goodbye. None of them suspected that they were talking to a noted writer and Nobel prize winner—such was his simple, down-to-earth language and behavior. When we continued our journey, he described what he thought their lives were like—their homes, their wives, and their children. He even improvised dialog for them. His imagination ran rampant, and the few drinks seemed to have given him a kind of high. We made one more stop at a bar in a country inn before reaching Hartford.

There he had another drink and once again engaged the customers in conversation. This time I was a shoe salesman, and he was the northeastern representative of Endicott-Johnson Shoes. Because I had sold shoes on Saturdays while going to college, I was better able to participate in this pretense.

We arrived in Hartford just before dark, checked into a hotel, had a light meal in the restaurant, where he ordered another drink (always scotch and soda), then proceeded to the theater. We went backstage, where we were met by the director, who did not at first realize that Lewis was drunk (he could disguise it up to a point). Lewis asked to have the cast brought on stage—he'd like to say a few words to them. In no time the actors, their makeup half finished, were assembled, and the director introduced Lewis. They were thrilled to meet the famous man and anxious to hear what he had to say. I was on tenterhooks for fear that he would say or do something that would embarrass everyone. Sitting in a chair center stage, he began by telling them he was sorry that the play was not better, introduced me as the director of the New York production, and told them how hard we had worked, but that time had defeated us. He wished them luck, rose, and started away. The actors seemed a little confused by his slurring of words and frequent mumbling. They had no idea he was inebriated.

I was holding him up as we walked offstage when a man pulled Lewis away from me, saying that the governor of Connecticut, Wilbur Cross, had just arrived, and newspaper reporters wanted to get pictures of the two together. I was afraid the governor would be embarrassed to appear in pictures with Lewis, who was now bleary-eyed and beginning to wobble about, but as it turned out, the governor was a former schoolmate of Lewis's at Yale, knew about his drinking, and insisted on having the pictures taken, even as he held Lewis up. I suppose it was still good politics and good publicity to get your picture in the paper with the famous author.

I wanted to take Lewis back to the hotel and put him to bed, but he insisted on seeing the performance. We were ushered to two seats midway in the orchestra section just behind Dr. and Mrs. Hepburn, the parents of Katherine Hepburn. Lewis seemed to know them well; he tapped them on the shoulder to say hello and introduce me. I felt miserable for fear they'd think it my fault that he was drunk. But I was wrong. They were friendly and gracious and well aware of his problem. The curtain went up, and he was talking to them so loudly that I begged him to give the actors a chance. He became quiet and began to nod. By the end of the first act he was fast asleep and beginning to snore. The moment the lights came up for intermission, I got him to his feet and managed to get him back to the hotel and into his bed. It had been a strange day.

The next morning he slept late but was willing, after toast and coffee, to start back to Bronxville. Unfortunately, he insisted on stopping for a drink or two even on the way back. When we arrived at Bronxville, Lou was at the house and helped me get him inside and to bed. I went back to New York and awaited word from him.

Two or three days later, he called and said he was better and ready to go to work and that I should come up prepared to stay for a few days in one of the guest rooms. He sounded sober, but I was not sure. Over the phone it was not easy to detect that he had been drinking. I packed a bag and told Hedda I might be gone for a few days. She was still doing secretarial work; she had met Lewis on several occasions and liked him. She encouraged me to stick with him even though I was becoming discouraged and disillusioned by his behavior. This time, when I arrived, he was ready to work. We began by making notes about the characters and events of the play, which he chose to call *For Us the Living*. It was a slow process because he would start inventing dialog for a character and reel off pages of material, often irrelevant. The extent of his imagination was unbelievable, and I became aware of the fountain of creativity inside him that had made him the best-selling novelist in America.

One morning, when I came down to breakfast, he was already awake and searching through a thick notebook for names of our characters. This was one in which, for many years, he had been gathering unusual names, along with those that simply appealed to him. When I thought about it, I realized that many of his novels were noted for the names of his protagonists: George Babbitt, Elmer Gantry, Martin Arrowsmith, Dodsworth, Ann Vickers, and others.

The second or third day of work, during which he was cold sober, I was shocked to see him eat piece after piece of chocolate candy until, by the end of the day, he had consumed almost two one-pound boxes. I could only assume this was his body's need following the aftermath of his drinking. It was this day, as I recall, that he asked me to stop calling him Mr. Lewis and to call him Red. I told him I could not comfortably do that, but if he insisted, I'd call him what Dorothy and her sister called him, which was Hal for Harry. His full name was Harry Sinclair Lewis.

In the evening, whenever I stayed overnight, I used to tell stories to the Lewises' son Michael, a lonely, winning little boy, before he went to bed. I was sorry for him. Dorothy was always busy and often stayed overnight in New York, and Lewis had no patience with children. He once confessed that he was not cut out to be a father, and he went so far as to excuse his lack of paternal affection by saying that perhaps it was not a bad idea for fathers to keep away from their sons; that way they could grow up without any pressure from fathers and just be themselves. I did not think I was old enough or wise enough to argue with him.

I always admired Dorothy and found her stimulating to be around. She was well informed and often made keen and amusing observations: "Jews are like everyone else," she once said, "only more so."

Lewis and I had completed notes for the first act of the play when he suddenly informed me that he was leaving Bronxville and moving into the Algonquin Hotel in New York, where we would continue working. There was a rumor that he and Dorothy had separated, but I did not ask him if it was true. I figured he would tell me if he wanted me to know. I went to his room at the hotel the next morning and found him in bed, drunk again. All work stopped, and for the next six weeks he lived on pinch bottle Haig and Haig scotch, with an occasional glass of milk. During this period I went every day to see him, took turns with Lou to sit with him, help him to the bathroom, and take care of other personal needs he couldn't manage on his own. Several friends came to see him. Two I remember well: Louis Untermeyer, the poet, and Sam Behrman, the playwright. When Behrman called from downstairs, I wanted to stop him from coming up, but before I could say anything, he was on his way. I opened the door for him and began to apologize, saying Mr. Lewis was not well, but he jumped in quickly and, with a smile, said, "Drunk again?" I nodded, and he went right into the bedroom and spoke to Lewis for several minutes. He was warm and friendly, an unpretentious, delightful, and talented playwright whom I greatly admired and was happy to be able to meet.

As the days dragged on, I became worried about Lewis's health. How long could he go without nourishment? One morning, when he was semiconscious, he told me that he had to get away from New York and that we were going to Bermuda to write the play. He instructed Lou to get tickets for the three of us and make hotel arrangements. (Lou told me that he thought Lewis was disturbed by a rumor that Dorothy was having an affair with David Sarnoff, the head of RCA. I remembered that Lewis was once asked how Dorothy was and replied, "I don't really know. She disappeared somewhere in the RCA building.") Lou got the tickets, and we were preparing to leave, when I decided to call Dorothy to let her know what was going on. She had not, to my knowledge, seen

Lewis in several weeks. She said she would come by the hotel that afternoon. We had a drink in the lobby and talked. She told me that what was troubling Lewis was the fear that he didn't have another novel in him. I wanted to tell her what I thought was really causing him to drink so heavily: jealousy, shame, and humiliation. But I said only that I was concerned about him and hoped something could be done for him. She called a doctor who had taken care of Lewis in the past. He came to the hotel, went upstairs, and soon came down to tell us that Lewis had to be hospitalized at once, that he would have to be dried out and fed intravenously for a few days. That night an ambulance took him to Doctors' Hospital. The trip to Bermuda was canceled.

I visited him a few days later. He was thin and emaciated. Again he apologized for the way things had gone, and I tried to let him know that I understood and was sympathetic. When he was released from the hospital, Dorothy drove him up to Bronxville. He was told that he had to rest for the next few months. I knew it would be a long time before we could expect to resume work on the play. I felt that until his situation with Dorothy was resolved, it would be hopeless. I drove up once to Bronxville to see him. He was warm and solicitous but depressed. I offered to return the check he had given me. He refused to consider it, because he had asked me to resign my job at the Federal Theater. I thanked him for his kindness and told him I would feel more comfortable if he would at least allow me to return half of it. He agreed, and I gave him back $1,250. I said good-bye, begged him to take care of himself, and promised I would see him again when he was fully recovered.

I had spent almost a year with him. It had been a stimulating and enlightening period. I had gotten to know an important literary figure and, through him, had met many other prominent persons. My hope that I would be able to write a play with Sinclair Lewis faded, but I considered it a good year nevertheless.

Once again I began to look around for an acting job or a play to direct. I did not have long to wait. Martin Gabel, an actor who had played the pal of the gangster Baby Face Martin in Sidney Kingsley's successful play, *Dead End,* called to tell me that he was going to direct a road company of *Dead End* for Jules Leventhal. I had worked for Jules one summer, and he had recommended me for Baby Face Martin. Would I care to read for the part? I liked Jules, even though he was well known for paying low salaries and many actors scorned working for him. I also liked Gabel. I read for him and was offered the role. It only paid seventy-five dollars per week, the highest salary in the company, but what interested me was that the tour was to be cross country, ending up in Los Angeles.

The past two and a half years had been disheartening and hectic: I had lost my father, most of the rest of my family had moved to Miami, I had acted in four plays and directed two for the Federal Theater, and I had done the one-act play with Lee Cobb. None of the plays were smash hits or completely satisfying. I felt in need of a rest, a change of scene, maybe the California sunshine. Perhaps I was also hoping that some part in a film might turn up. I discussed it with Hedda, and she felt I should take the job. She was always ready to do whatever she thought was good for me and go wherever I asked. In addition, she herself had a desire to see California once again and enjoy the sunshine. But she asked to be excused from the first few weeks of the tour, which covered many small cities in the East for two- and three-night stands. I understood, and we decided that she would join me in Denver, where we were to play for a week before moving on to San Francisco for four weeks, then to Los Angeles for four weeks. If nothing happened in Hollywood, we'd return to New York. But in the meantime we'd have a vacation.

The tour of *Dead End,* as we made our way across the country, was only mildly successful for the producer, but it was a great boost to my morale. The critics' reviews of my performance of the gangster were unusually good, much better than I had expected. I began to hope that when we opened in Los Angeles, an offer of an acting job would turn up from one of the studios.

As we had planned, Hedda joined me in Denver, and we enjoyed being together again. San Francisco was an especial treat, with its cable cars, fine restaurants, Fisherman's Wharf, aquarium, and Chinatown. My ego was further enhanced when one of the critics who had interviewed me prior to the opening devoted most of her review to my performance.

But our opening in Los Angeles at the Biltmore Theater was less than spectacular, and my performance was only mildly praised. However, a few nights later, Sheila Bromley, with whom I had worked at the Pasadena Playhouse, came to see the play with a friend and afterward paid a visit backstage. Her friend was Bryan Foy of the Seven Foys family, well known in theater and film circles. In his forties, tall, thin, and nice looking, he was a producer at Warner Brothers Studios in charge of the smaller-budget or B films. Many referred to him as the "Keeper of the Bs." Hedda and I joined them at the Biltmore Hotel next door, where we talked about films, the theater, and Hollywood. It was easy to see that

Brynie, as everyone called him, was showbiz wise. He asked what my plans were when the play closed. I told him that I intended to concentrate for a while on my writing rather than acting.

"How would you like to try writing for films?" he asked. The question took me by surprise. It had never occurred to me that I might qualify for such a career, much less pursue it. Motion pictures were interesting, and now and then a good one would impress me, but I still felt, as did most serious young actors in New York, that they were a shallow form of entertainment, mostly for the masses. Hollywood was just a place to earn money, whereas the theater was the only place where serious and lasting drama could be created. So the prospect of writing for films, and especially B pictures, did not necessarily excite me. However, I did not want to appear haughty or ungrateful, so I replied that, although I had not considered it, I would like to think about it. He suggested that I come out to the studio for a talk, and if I had anything with me that I had recently written, I should bring it along. We made a date for the following week.

We were staying with my cousins Dr. and Mrs. Horovitz, who lived in Hollywood with their son Leon, so I took a streetcar over Cahuenga Pass, got off at Barham Boulevard and thumbed a ride to Warner Brothers. I brought with me two one-act plays that I had written while on the road tour. As I was ushered into Brynie's office, he asked to see the plays and glanced through them quickly.

"Sheila has told me all about you," he said. "If you'd like to go to work for me as a writer, I'll get you a hundred dollars a week for ten weeks. Then we'll see how it goes." I thanked him and told him that I could not tie myself up for such a small sum. He hesitated and suggested that I go down to the commissary for lunch, where I might run into an old New York friend, while he had a talk about me with Jack Warner in the executive dining room.

There were four separate eating places at Warner Brothers. A huge commissary was where most of the people who worked on the lot ate: cameramen, grips, electricians, carpenters, painters, office employees, small part actors, and extras. In a smaller but quieter area of the same building was the Green Room, for the stars, directors, and writers. In the same building in an even smaller area was the room for unit managers. The executive dining room, where only producers, top executives, and special invited guests ate, was in a different area.

I went into the commissary and looked about for someone I might know, but seeing no one, I sat at one of the counters and had a sandwich and coffee. Afterward I took a walk around the lot. It was a busy, thriving studio with dozens of actors and extras in various costumes moving about. In transit from one stage to another were cameras, lights, and scenery, while trucks and cars moved through the narrow streets. There were ten or more large sound stages and several buildings with offices for writers, directors, producers, and other employees.

On the backlot were streets and facades representing New York brownstones, western buildings, and structures of Fifth Avenue, the tenement district, Broadway theater, and the small town, both business and residential buildings. There were also a church, a school, a courthouse, a small park area, and several foreign-looking exteriors. The possibility that I might become a part of this bustling enterprise was enticing, but any thought that I'd spend the next fifteen years here and become one of its directors was remote.

When I returned to Brynie's office, he pulled out a slip of paper from his coat pocket, the wrapper from a package of spearmint gum, with some figures written on the back.

"I talked to Mr. Warner," he said. "If you're willing to sign a three-way contract as actor, writer, and/or director for seven years, he'll start you off at (reading from the paper) $200 per week for the first year and $250 for the second year, with six-month options, until, if you make good, by the seventh year, you'll be earning $750 a week."

Not until years later did I learn, from Max Arnow, the casting director at Warner Brothers, what had happened that day at the executive dining room. When Brynie told Warner that he'd like to hire me as a writer, Warner asked, "What has he had published or produced?"

Since Brynie could not cite anything specifically, Warner asked again, "Then why should we hire him?"

At that point, Arnow, sitting not too far away, spoke up. "Did I hear you say Vincent Sherman?"

Brynie nodded, and Max turned to Warner. "Jack," he said, "he's the boy I suggested that we sign up two years ago after he did *Counsellor at Law* at Universal and *Midnight Alibi* for us."

"Oh, he's an actor, too? That's different."

"He's also done some directing," Brynie added.

"Good," Warner said, as he opened a package of Spearmint chewing gum. "We'll sign him, and if he doesn't work out as a writer, we can always get our money's worth out of him as an actor or dialog director." He then wrote out the figures that Foy had read to me.

I thanked Brynie and explained that I would have to talk to Hedda before I could give him an answer. He ushered me into a small room adjoining his office, pointed to a telephone, told me to dial 9, then my number, and discuss it. He added, "I'd like to wrap it up before Warner changes his mind."

Hedda was not elated about the offer. She thought I should go back to New York and wait for a better offer. She was sure one would soon appear because I was becoming better known as an actor. I might also get my play, *Light and Power,* produced. "Besides," she argued, "we don't need the money. We have almost twelve hundred dollars in the bank." When I pointed out that it would give me a chance to write while earning a living, plus the security of knowing that for the next six months we had nothing to worry about except the blow to my ego (working on B pictures), she reluctantly agreed.

After *Dead End* closed, I reported to the studio, and Brynie submitted a contract to me. When I began to look over its many pages he said, "Don't bother reading it. They've got you by the balls. Just sign it and get started." I did.

6
Hollywood—Second Time

Although I knew we were to be residents for at least the next six months, I felt no greater sense of permanence than the first time we were in Hollywood. Hedda soon found us a nicely furnished house on one of the hills off Beachwood Drive for forty dollars a month. It had a small balcony where we could sit outside at night and see the city lights below. We also bought a new Plymouth car for nine hundred dollars.

For my first two weeks at Warner's all I did was to sit in my new office and read scripts, at Brynie's suggestion, to get the feel of screenplay writing. By the time I had read and studied the techniques of a dozen successful movies, I became aware of the difference between writing for the theater and writing for movies. Dialog was the basic ingredient of plays, whereas films relied more upon action and reaction, keeping dialog at a minimum. As Sidney Howard, the well-known playwright, once said, "Dialog for film should be written like a cablegram."

Warner's was undoubtedly the most vital studio in Hollywood. Their pictures were topical and realistic. They dealt with the nitty-gritty of life more often than did the films of MGM or Paramount. Hal Wallis was the executive producer of the A department, the larger-budget films, and made an average of twenty to thirty features a year, while Foy made thirty or forty smaller films. They had a roster of stars under contract: James Cagney, Edward G. Robinson, Paul Muni, Errol Flynn, and Pat O'Brien; the featured players were George Brent, Humphrey Bogart, Dick Powell, Claude Rains, Alan Hale, John Litel, Barton Maclane, Frank McHugh, Donald Crisp, Dick Foran, Allen Jenkins, Hugh Herbert, and Guy Kibbee. Kay Francis was the top leading lady, followed closely by Bette Davis and Olivia De Havilland, with Joan Blondell, Glenda Farrell, Ann Sheridan, and Jane Wyman moving up rapidly. A dozen or more other actors and actresses were under contract for smaller roles.

Brynie's right-hand man was Bill Jacobs, a producer and a kind, gentle human being, whom I soon got to know. He invited me to sit in with him as he talked to other writers about screenplays they were developing. Some of the writers had worked during the silent era and still referred to dialog as titles. I soon became aware of the jargon of the picture business: Who are we rooting for? Give it some heart; What's the climax? We need some laughs; Not enough suspense; What's at stake? Not enough conflict; We need a time bomb ticking away; and Let's get to the chase.

There were also the many different script terms I needed to learn: fade in; dissolve to; wipe, pan or whip to; long, medium, and close shots; tracking or dolly shots; process, matte, glass, stock, or crane shot; iris in, iris out; high and low angle, and fade out. I found out later that most directors ignored the labels and used their own judgment about shots.

Brynie invited me to look at rushes (now called dailies, film shot the day before and developed overnight for the next day's viewing) with him. I tried to understand the instructions he'd give the editor: Use the master until they sit, keep away from her close-up, play it all in the two-shot, cut the next line, pick up a wild line, use the over-the-shoulder. He talked all through the running, and I wondered how he could pass judgment so easily, but as I learned later, those quick evaluations were usually right. Many people in the business, I soon discovered, looked down on Brynie and the kind of films he made, but I confess I learned much from him. He was shrewd and sharp and also an expert at switching, that is, taking stories from movies that have been made before, changing the background and a few details, and presenting them as new. He knew how to build suspense, get a laugh, set up a character, steal a plot or a situation from another story, and use stock footage to make a film look more expensive, and he rarely paid for a new story or script. In fact, he eventually switched almost every well-known Warner A film that was made, and he so disguised the plot that few people caught on. I soon learned that it was a common Hollywood practice, and I used it myself later on. In addition, Brynie had been a gag writer, had appeared in vaudeville, had written the Gallagher and Shean song, and had produced the first all-talking picture, *Lights of New York,* plus a variety of independent films.

During story conferences, which quickly bored him, he would hastily summarize what had to be done to make a story work and then regale us with tales of his past experiences, which kept everyone in the room howling with laughter. Once he made a film called *Elysia* about a nudist colony. He gained the consent of the members of the colony by assuring them that he wanted to present their case with dignity. They agreed, provided the crew would also work nude. Eventually he assembled a crew, and all went well until one day the head grip complained that he had to waste a lot of time walking back and forth to get a hammer or a pair of pliers every time he needed them. Could he wear his work belt? Brynie had to stop shooting and have a conference to get this concession. Another time his director played a long scene with a man and woman seated on a log, but as they rose to walk away the imprint of the log was so deeply imbedded on their behinds that it got a bad laugh and had to be reshot. An awkward moment occurred when a male nudist was photographed as he was swinging on one of the park swings. Unfortunately, he was so well endowed that his penis could be seen hanging over the edge of the board, and the scene had to be redone with an actor of lesser proportions.

During one of Brynie's lean periods, he raised enough money to hire the great actor Richard Bennett, father of Constance and Joan, for a day's work as a doctor in a scene with a sick child. It was a heartrending scene in a bedroom, but in the rushes they saw small fish swimming back and forth in the upper part of the room. They had been using short ends of film in order to save money and were unaware that the film had been exposed before. (Short ends were the last parts of film rolls, sometimes as much as a hundred feet, that the major studios assumed had not been used. They were sold cheaply to "poverty row" independents.)

I soon realized that although producers, directors, and writers avoided using the word *art* in discussing picture problems, they were, nevertheless, definitely concerned with artistic problems: creating interesting characters and situations, conflict and suspense, laughter and tears. It never occurred to them that movies would one day be looked upon seriously or that the work of directors, writers, cameramen, editors, and others associated with the making of a film would be regarded as cinematic art. They were simply craftsmen creating entertainment.

Once when I complained to Brynie that we needed more character development in a story, he said, "Vince, you're not writing for the Theater Guild. Two guys are talking, one says to the other 'Here comes that shit-heel' except you can't say shit, but now you know he's a shit-heel. A guy kicks a little dog, you know he's a no good bastard. A boy looks at a girl, she looks at him in close-ups; he smiles, she smiles, you know they're in love. You don't need much exposition—let the audience find out about the character by what he or she does." His fundamentals were valid, even if he was only a B producer.

A short time after I began, he asked me to shoot a close-up of an actor who had also been recently signed by the studio. He was formerly a radio sports announcer from the Midwest and was to do a scene for one of Brynie's films. I went down to the stage at the scheduled time, found a desk with a microphone on it, a chair in place, and the camera already set up for a shot. The crew was standing by. Ronald Reagan soon appeared. We met, and he did the scene, a short broadcast of a sporting event. He was affable and anxious to work and to please. He knew his lines, and we did the scene in one take. It was my first experience as a director of a scene for a film and Ronnie's first experience in acting for film. During the Warner years we pronounced his name *Reegan*, not *Raygon*. We did not work together again for a long time—not until I was asked to do some retakes on a film called *Juke Girl,* in which he starred with Ann Sheridan. Years afterward I was sent to London, where I produced and directed *The Hasty Heart,* in which Ronnie played Yank and gave one of his best performances. More about him later.

My first official assignment as a writer came when Mark Hellinger, a columnist for one of the New York dailies, was signed by Jack Warner as a producer. He expected to work under Hal Wallis, who soon turned him over to Foy. Later, it was revealed that there was no love lost between Hellinger and Wallis. Foy recommended me to Hellinger. It was to be Mark's first picture as a producer, and I was to do a switch on a story that had been made years before about a girl and a boy in New York, recently married, and their trials and tribulations during the depression. Mark was a genuine New Yorker. He knew all the Broadway types Damon Runyon wrote about: big shot racketeers, politicians, prize fighters, agents, managers, show people, actors and actresses, chorus girls, and everyone who was anyone on the Great White Way.

The story was lightweight, but we thought we might be able to get a warm human comedy out of it. After several conferences I began writing the screenplay and a few weeks later turned in a script called *Spring in New York.* It was given to Lew Seiler, a director also recently signed by Warner's, and an old friend of Brynie's, as possibly his first film. Seiler reported that he liked the characters and dialog but thought that it needed two stars with a great deal of charm to make it work. Because this was a B film, he was not going to get the kind of actors required. So he turned it down. Brynie agreed that for him to rely upon charm to sell a picture would be a gamble, so he decided not to make it. Naturally, I was disappointed, but I could understand their reasoning. I was sure that this meant my option would not be picked up. And although I thought I was prepared for it, the truth was that I was beginning to find films fascinating and wanted to succeed. But I thought it was now too late: my first screenplay had been shelved. Hellinger was not too upset. He had his eye on more important projects. In fact, he was writing an original story that eventually became *The Roaring Twenties,* a hit film with James Cagney and Humphrey Bogart.

A few days later, as I sat in my office trying to come up with an idea that would salvage my waning prospects, I received a call from Brynie that was to change my future completely. As I entered his office, he said, "Pick up a script of *The Mayor of Hell,* made with Cagney a few years ago, and a copy of *San Quentin,* made with Pat O'Brien and Ann Sheridan. Use the first half of *Mayor* and the second half of *San Quentin.* We're going to make a picture with the Dead End Kids called *Crime School.* Seiler will direct, and Humphrey Bogart will play the lead. I'll need a first draft screenplay in a week, so call the story department and get to work." I was slightly bewildered. How could I write a script in a week? It would take me almost that long just to read the two, think about them, and figure out what to do. But I didn't let him know my feelings. I said "Okay," and left.

He must have sensed my fear, for by the time I reached my office, he phoned. "Listen Vince, you're new at this, so maybe it's unfair to saddle you with it. I'm going to give the job to an old hand, Crane Wilbur. But the minute he gives us a first draft, you can go to work and start polishing it. Seiler likes your dialog, and you know the type of work the Dead End Kids do." I was relieved.

The Dead End Kids, as they were called, those from the original New York stage show (not the road tour), were Billy Halop, Huntz Hall, Leo Gorcey, Bobby Jordan, Gabriel Dell, and Bernard Punsley. They had appeared in the film version of *Dead End* that was recently released, with Humphrey Bogart and directed by William Wyler. Afterward, Mervyn LeRoy persuaded Warner to sign them for a film at Warner's to be written by Bob Rossen, a contract writer, whom I had met briefly years before in New York. The project never came to life, and Warner, annoyed with having to pay the Kids' salaries for months when nothing was being done with them, voiced his feelings one day at the lunch table. Foy said he could put the boys to work quickly by doing a switch, remaking and combining two old studio A films. Warner said, "Go ahead. You've got 'em."

Sure enough, within a week Crane Wilbur delivered a first draft of *Crime School.* He had adroitly put the two scripts together and changed the names of the characters, but the second part did not always mesh properly with the first part. I pointed out some of the discrepancies in the script to Seiler. He agreed and said, "You start fixing them. I've got to look for sets and locations and see some actors." I worked for the next few days on revisions and gave them to Seiler, who was being pushed to get started. He approved the changes and gave them to Foy, who put them through as *blue pages* (script revisions on a different color of paper than the normal white).

The day before Seiler began shooting, Brynie called. "Vince, I've been thinking, maybe you should go down on the set with Seiler, be his dialog director." Dialog director, a job no longer active in the film industry, was a holdover from the transition between the silent and sound era.

"I'd like that," I replied. And so began an experience that was to lead to my achieving identity among two thousand employees. On the set I met the Dead End Kids and Bogart, and also the other actors and the crew. They were all friendly. *Crime School* was supposed to be made in eighteen days, so everyone went about his job in a businesslike manner. There was no time for discussion of motivations or relationships. They were supposed to be apparent from the script. My duty, I was told, was to rehearse the actors in their lines so that they knew their dialog, but not try to tell them how to play their scenes; that was the director's job. I did just that. I looked on as Seiler worked out the staging with the actors and then discussed the setup with the cameraman.

At the end of the third day's shooting, after we had seen the rushes of the first two days' work, I thought the scenes were workmanlike but lacked spontaneity and a sense of life: The Kids seemed to be constrained by the individual lines of dialog assigned to them. I felt they needed to be free to ad lib, as we called it then; now we say "improvise." I talked to Seiler about it, and he thought I had a point but wondered what could be done. I asked whether, when he had determined the layout of the scene and knew where he wanted to make his cuts, he'd let me take the boys offscene and rehearse them. He agreed, and the next day while the crew was lighting the set, I gathered the boys outside the stage.

"Now you know the situation in this upcoming scene and what the intent is," I began. "So let's rehearse it, but forget what's written. Feel free to express the action in your own words, and don't be afraid to talk over each other." I sat nearby with a pad and pencil, and as they ad libbed I jotted down as much as I could, especially those lines that were good, and there were plenty. I asked them to run over the scene again and preserve the lines I thought worth keeping. They did and added new ones. When I thought we had a good scene, I rushed back into a dressing room on the stage, typed up the new scene, and gave it to Seiler. He liked what I had done. The script girl (now called script supervisor, the person in charge of keeping track of visual and aural continuity) quickly made copies, and the scene was shot. When Bogart was in the scene, he participated in the improvisation, as did the other actors. The rushes became lively, and we all felt we were getting what could turn out to be a better-than-average B picture. As new scenes were written, they were sent to stenographic, where blue pages were put through. At the end of the film we had 120 blue pages, which meant the entire script had been rewritten.

Bogie, as he was called, and I got along well. He was from the New York theater and knew I had played Baby Face Martin on the road (the role he played in the film directed by William Wyler). We often talked about both. Bogie liked Wyler but thought he was somewhat inarticulate. However, we agreed that he had great dramatic instinct. His many awards later confirmed his talent. Most important for Bogie at the moment was the fact that he was playing the lead, a good guy, not another villain or *heavy*, which had been his fate in many Warner films. In a documentary about him made several years ago, he was shown being killed and dying an ignoble death in a series of twenty or thirty Warner films.

The Dead End Kids were not only fun to work with but also highly talented and disciplined. They quickly grasped what was needed in a scene and responded. Seiler, although an old-timer who had made mostly independent small-budget films, was a solid craftsman, and I learned much from him.

Prior to *Crime School* I became fully aware that being a writer for Brynie was low on the totem pole, so low that I did not have the courage to eat at the writers' table in the Green Room. Instead, I ate alone in the commissary at one of the counters. Now, the feeling that I was helping to create some good scenes and learning the craft of picture making gave my spirits a lift.

As we approached the last week of shooting, we were several days behind schedule, a serious breach for a B film. But there had been no flack, so far, from the front office. Then I had my first fight with the production department. One evening, after viewing the rushes, Seiler took me aside and said he was worried about the scene we had to shoot the next morning; it was not very good. He was right, but I had not had time to work on it, nor did I have any idea what to do with it. But I promised him that after dinner I'd think about it and try to come up with something. The truth was that I was tired. But I finally got an idea that I thought might work and called him. It was ten o'clock; he was already in bed.

When I told him the idea, he said, "Good, type it up and bring it to me first thing in the morning." I told him that I was exhausted, but I would come to the studio early and get it ready as quickly as possible.

The next morning I was working away in the dressing room when he arrived. A few little problems had arisen, and I was not quite finished. He told me to keep working, that he would vamp with the kids (fake rehearsing) until I was finished. At nine o'clock, when he was supposed to start shooting, I was on the last page. The door to the dressing room flew open, and Tenney Wright, the head of the production department, confronted me.

"What the hell are you doing?" he demanded.

"I'm fixing up the scene we're going to shoot and am just about finished," I replied.

"Goddammit!" he yelled, flying into a rage. "This picture is behind schedule and it's all your fault! You're nothing but a dialog director, and you've got no business rewriting the script! I'm going to tell Mr. Warner that you're responsible for the delay."

No one had ever yelled at me like that, and I deeply resented it. "Mr. Wright," I said quietly, but with all the inner fury I could muster, "I have been working until eleven and twelve o'clock every night since this picture started in an effort to make it better. If you and Mr. Warner don't like what I'm doing, you can take this job and stick it you know where!" He glared at me for a moment and started to speak, but held his temper, slammed the door in my face, and walked off the stage. I called Brynie. His advice was to forget it. But the next day I was told to report to Mr. Warner's office on the lunch break. I went alone, prepared to stand my ground. I had never met Mr. Warner but was not afraid to face him because my conscience was clear.

After waiting in his office for a half hour, I was told that he was delayed and would speak to me some other time, and that I should get back to the set. I did not actually meet him or talk with him until a year later. Maybe Brynie talked to him. But Tenney Wright did not forgive me for a long time. I had dared to talk back to him. Later, we became friends, and when he invited me one Sunday to visit him and see how he flew his pigeons (a hobby), I knew everything was okay between us.

Within a short time *Crime School* was ready to send to New York, where it opened at Warner's Strand Theater as an A release, and to fairly good reviews. Even better, it was doing A-picture business. The film had cost $186,000 and grossed over $2 million, one of the most successful Warner films for 1938, next to *Robin Hood,* but with an even greater profit percentage because it had cost so little. The irony was that because I had been blamed for the film being behind schedule, rewriting every day, and working with the Dead End Kids on the side, with its success I received the lion's share of the credit. In reality the Kids, Bogie, Seiler, and Brynie all contributed. On the screen I was not only given dialog director credit but shared screenplay credit along with Crane Wilbur. My option for another six months at two hundred dollars a week was picked up.

As a result I suddenly found myself the fair-haired boy. Other writers began to speak to me. Abem Finkle, Paul Muni's brother-in-law, whose wife had been friendly with Hedda in New York, suggested that I eat at the writer's table in the Green Room. I was also given an office in the Writers' Building, and Bob Rossen began to drop by each day to talk to me about a play he had been working on for a long time called *Corner Pocket,* which dealt with pool rooms and hustlers. Years later, he was to do *The Hustler.* At the lunch table in the Green Room, I met the other Warner writers, Casey Robinson, Julius Epstein, Seton Miller, Warren Duff, Milton Krims, Aeneas MacKenzie, Norman Reilly Raine, Jerry Wald, and Dick MacCauley. They were all friendly, and it was a delight to join them.

Brynie and I became good friends, and during the next few months he kept me busy writing and rewriting various scripts. One day he called to tell me that Warner, in an effort to get rid of Kay Francis, who had once been a big money maker for the studio but whose last few pictures had failed, had notified her that she would be assigned to making pictures for him (Brynie). Warner hoped that she would refuse and walk out on her contract. She was getting, I was told, five thousand dollars per week, making her one of the highest-paid leading ladies in Hollywood. However, she did not walk out. She said that as long as they paid her her salary, she would sweep the stage if they gave her a broom. I admired her.

Brynie, consequently, needed a script in a hurry and gave me an old play, *Courage,* done in New York years before with Janet Beecher. It was now to become the basis for a picture with Kay Francis. He had assigned another writer to work on the script but asked me to take over, and he informed me that the film had to start the next week. Thus, he needed a script by Monday morning. It was now Thursday afternoon. (Brynie thought it should take no longer to write than to type.) I called Hedda, explained the situation, and told her that I'd be working late. She always understood. After working until midnight Thursday and all day Friday, Saturday, and Sunday with my secretary, Helen Fahringer, who was one of the fastest typists on the lot, I turned over on Monday morning the script of *My Bill,* which Brynie handed to John Farrow to direct. The cast consisted of Kay Francis, Anita Louise, John Litel, Bonita Granville, and Bobby Jordan. The performances were good, and so was Farrow's direction, but the story was old hat and the film one I would like to forget.

A few days before starting, Farrow invited me to have lunch with him. As we entered the Green Room, he saw Orry Kelly, the designer, seated alone at a table and asked if we might join him. Orry was most cordial. Farrow introduced me and, after we shook hands, I decided to remind Orry of the first time we had met. "I don't suppose you remember me," I began, "but when my wife and I were first married in New York in 1931, a friend, Lester Sweyd, asked us if we needed any furnishings. We did, and he suggested that we contact you and Archie Leach [now Cary Grant] because you were both leaving soon for Hollywood. We bought your drapes and a daybed from you."

"Oh?" Orry replied, turned abruptly away from me as if he was offended, and began to talk to John. Throughout lunch he barely spoke to me. I was puzzled. Lester had said that Orry and Archie operated a kind of speakeasy in their apartment, somewhere in midtown Manhattan, and that Leach had recently signed a contract with Paramount. Not until two years later did I get an explanation for Orry's strange behavior. I was directing a film on which he was assigned to do the star's wardrobe.

"I owe you an apology," he said. "I was rude to you the day Farrow introduced us, but I had just had a falling out with Cary, and I didn't even want to hear his name mentioned."

Subsequently, Orry and I worked together on several films. He was not only a top designer but also a delightfully amusing fellow. He was gay and would often tell me, in his light-hearted manner, about his off-and-on friendship with Cary Grant, who was said to be bisexual.

Before *My Bill* was released, Brynie had put a writer to work on another project for Kay Francis, a remake of a Paul Muni film, *Dr. Socrates.* Again Brynie asked me to help. I could not imagine how he could make the switch. He explained that it was simple. In *Dr. Socrates* Muni had been a successful doctor in a big city, but because of the death of his beloved wife, he became disillusioned with life and moved to a small town. He shunned people, and the townsfolk did not like him. But one day some gangsters descended on the town after picking up Ann Dvorak, who was hitchhiking alone and out of work. They were led by Barton Maclane and terrorized the town while holding Dvorak captive. Muni, wanting to rescue the girl and help the town, tricked the gangsters into believing they had a fatal illness and unless he could give them certain injections they would die. They agreed, and the injections put them to sleep so that the authorities were able to capture them. Muni became a hero. His love for the girl and his admiration of the townspeople restored his desire to live.

Kay would play Muni's part. She is a doctor in a big city whose husband is also a doctor but innocently becomes involved with gangsters. In a police raid he is accidentally killed, and she retreats to a small town, as Muni did, keeps to herself, and is not well liked. The same bunch of gangsters, now led by Bogart instead of Maclane, appear in the small town, having picked up a hitchhiker, James Stephenson (in the Dvorak role), a writer out of work and alone. Bogart wants him to write the story of his (Bogart's) life, comparing him to Napoleon. When the gangsters rob a local bank, Stephenson gets away but is wounded and taken to Francis for treatment. They fall in love. Later, the gangsters forcibly take Stephenson to their hideout so that he can continue writing Bogart's story. Bogart becomes ill from a wound he also received during the bank holdup, and his men pick up Francis and bring her to the hideout to treat Bogie. When she sees Stephenson and realizes he is a captive and his life is in danger, she tells Bogie that he is suffering from an infection and he and his men might die unless she gives them shots. They accept her advice and the shots. I felt that we could not use the same device, putting them to sleep, so I had Kay give them shots to distort their vision. It was, I thought, more filmic and would allow for some gunplay at the finish to give us a better climax. The gangsters are finally captured.

Seiler directed this one, and I not only helped rewrite the dialog but also served as his dialog director. Brynie had made his second Kay Francis film. It was titled *King of the Underworld*. I was not proud of it, but I was working with professionals and learning more about the craft of writing for films.

Not long after, I wrote an original story and screenplay, based on a story in *Time* about a woman who had trained a blind horse to jump— an almost unheard-of feat. The film was called *Pride of the Bluegrass* and became a story of faith between a young boy and his horse. There were some good scenes in it.

At home Hedda and I were enjoying our lives when we had time to be together. We were meeting new people, seeing relatives, and taking walks at night down Hollywood Boulevard after dinner at Musso and Frank's restaurant. We attended all the Warner previews and saw the films of other studios. I was especially intrigued by the foreign films, French, German, and Russian, that played in a small theater on Fairfax Avenue. They seemed to have greater reality than ours. We saw *La bête humaine*, directed by Renoir; *Un carnet de bal*, by Duvivier; *La grande illusion*, by Renoir; *The Baker's Wife*, by Pagnol; *Poil de carotte*, by Duvivier; *La kermesse héroïque*, by Feyder; *M*, by Lang; *La maternelle*, by Jean Benoit Levy; and two Russian films, *Baltic Deputy* and *The Road to Life*. At the same time Hedda and I were becoming more concerned about the growing social, political, and economic problems confronting the United States: Hitler in Germany, Mussolini in Italy, and Franco in Spain.

When we left Hollywood in 1934, we felt we had been living in the proverbial ivory tower. The local newspapers were sparse when it came to world news, and few people seemed to be aware of or care about what was going on. Politics was rarely discussed. But now the town was seething with activity. The League against War and Fascism was building a strong organization, campaigns were being launched to raise money for Spanish loyalists, anti-Nazi films were being prepared, liberal democrats and leftists were cooperating, and there was a surge of social awareness. It was a tremendous change. We were happy to see it and participated, although we were a little concerned that it also seemed to have become the fashionable thing to do.

Feeling that the future was not all bleak, we turned our thoughts toward having a baby (we had tried before in New York). I was thirty-two and Hedda was nine months older. We felt the pressure of time and wondered why we were having no luck. Then, Hedda found a Dr. Holmes, a woman in whom she had confidence. Under her supervision we began taking pills of various kinds and doing special exercises. We also submitted to a series of tests she prescribed. Once I had to have intercourse with Hedda at home, withdraw just before the climax, ejaculate into a small glass jar, place it under my arm to keep it at body temperature, and drive as quickly as possible to the doctor's office so she could make a special type of sperm count. We now lived in a rented house on Laurel Canyon, but the doctor's office was in Beverly Hills. As I raced up Sunset Boulevard early one morning on my way there, I was stopped by a motorcycle officer for speeding.

"What's your hurry, young fellow?" he asked. I was afraid that if I told him I was rushing to the doctor's office with a jar of sperm under my arm, he'd take me to a mental hospital for observation. So I said nothing and later paid the fine.

Hedda did become pregnant, and on the night of September 23,

1938, our daughter, Hedwin, was born. We wept with joy as Hedda held the baby in her arms and nursed her. At the studio I handed around cigars. Life was looking up. My option for a second year at $250 a week was picked up. Hedda was enjoying motherhood, and I was learning the craft of picture making. We moved to a nicer house, not far from Schwab's Drug Store in Hollywood. We also hired a maid. As each day ended, I rushed home from the studio to play with my enchanting little daughter. Afterward I would hold her on my lap as I enjoyed dinner with Hedda. Except for world events, we felt secure and believed that President Roosevelt was a good man who was aware of the evils of fascism and anti-Semitism that were spreading through Europe. We also thought he knew they were growing in our country, and we felt he would resist them.

Before long Brynie called me to his office to tell me that Warner wanted to develop some new directors and that when he suggested me as a possibility, Warner heartily agreed. I was sure it was Tenney Wright's complaint about me during the making of *Crime School* that had brought me to Warner's attention. Brynie wanted to know how I felt about it. I thanked him and told him that I thought I knew how to tell a story and could handle the actors, but I was still uncertain about the camera, lenses, angles, and cutting. On the few films for which I had been a dialog director, I was so preoccupied with rewriting that I had little time to study the technical factors. He told me not to worry about them, that I would learn them in no time. Meanwhile, he'd put Syd Hickox on my first film to help me. He was the cameraman with whom I had become friendly on *My Bill* and *King of the Underworld*. Then Brynie offered me one of two stories to direct, a remake of *Kid Galahad* or *The Return of Dr. X*, a mystery horror yarn that was being developed into a screenplay by Lee Katz, a friend and former assistant director who had wanted to become a writer. I chose *Dr. X* immediately. It offered better visual opportunities and commercial prospects, and I did not want to have to compete with the original *Kid Galahad*, which had had a great cast: Edward G. Robinson, Bette Davis, Humphrey Bogart, and Wayne Morris. Lee and I made a few script changes, and I began to prepare for my first film as a director. The cast assigned to me was Wayne Morris, Dennis Morgan, Rosemary Lane, Lya Lyss (a stunning foreign import), and, to play a criminal who had died in the electric chair but was brought back to life, Humphrey Bogart. The doctor who revived him for his own purposes was played by John Litel.

Before shooting began, Brynie took me to Warner's office. We still had not met, although I had been on the lot a year and a half. After wishing me good luck and telling me to keep on schedule, he added a final request.

"I'm giving you this guy Bogart, and for God's sake see if you can get him to play something besides Duke Mantee." This was the gangster role Bogart had created on the stage in *The Petrified Forest,* with Leslie Howard, and had also played in the film version made at Warner's. He gave an extraordinary performance, but I soon found that most of the directors and producers felt the same as Warner about Bogart, that he was a good gangster or "heavy" but was unsuited for anything else and would never, in an A film, be accepted as a leading man who would "get the girl." If anyone had predicted at that time that Bogie would one day play a romantic lover opposite Ingrid Bergman, as in *Casablanca,* and become the idol of millions, surpassing Cagney and Flynn, he would have been considered daft. I was not concerned with how others felt. Bogie was a good actor, and I was happy to have him.

Bogie and I spent some time discussing his character. We decided that because he had been electrocuted in the past and brought back to life, we would have him made up with a white, pasty look and put a white streak in his hair (from the electric shock). In addition I gave him a white rabbit to carry around, which he was always stroking, a symbol of his desire for life and warmth. Obviously, it was a hokey story and a cornball role, but Bogie and I were both from the theater and were used to working seriously on whatever was handed us, so we did our best to make it as palatable as possible.

The first scene I had to shoot was with Wayne Morris, a reporter, and his young doctor friend, Dennis Morgan, in Dennis's office. After the rehearsal, during which Wayne comes to tell Dennis about having seen Bogart, the head grip offered me the viewfinder to look through (the customary procedure), so that I could determine where I wanted to put the camera. I took it, looked through it for a moment, then turned to Syd Hickox. "Listen Syd, what's the use of me looking through this damn thing. I don't know anything about lenses, angles, and cutting. You've seen the way I think the scene ought to be done, now you tell me how I can get what I want."

He smiled, took the finder, and said, "Just keep on staging the scenes the way you'd like, and we'll work it out." With his help I made a few adjustments, and we shot the scene. Later, I learned that the crew appreciated my honesty and became big boosters for me. We made more films together. The more familiar I became with the camera, the easier it was to know where it should be placed, the angles to choose, the size shot I'd need (close, medium, or long), and which lens to use.

Film savants and critics sometimes think, and often write condescendingly, that contract directors at the major studios in the "golden days" were forced to shoot according to a set of rules laid down by the moguls. I cannot speak for the other studios, but no one at Warner's ever told me how to shoot a scene. Yes, Jack Warner wanted to know where the scene took place, what the geography was, and that the characters and events appeared believable. But how you shot it was up to you. There was no hard and fast rule that you had to start with a long shot master scene and move closer as it progressed, nor was there a rule about the cutting. There was only one important rule: that you not cut with the camera, but cover yourself so that later, if you or the producer didn't like a certain angle or the reading of a line, or wished to add or drop a line, you could do so smoothly. The most important thing was that the performances seem truthful in relation to the story.

I am especially irritated when I read some so-called expert on films refer to Mike Curtiz as a "hack" contract director. He was, in my opinion, one of the most skillful directors we have ever had, and his use of the camera was superb. Recall *Captain Blood, Robin Hood, Charge of the Light Brigade, Four Daughters, Sea Hawk, Dodge City, Santa Fe Trail, Kid Galahad, Angels with Dirty Faces, Casablanca, Mildred Pierce, Yankee Doodle Dandy, This Is the Army,* or *White Christmas,* to name only a few of his films. How many other directors made such a variety of pictures and so successfully?

True, Jack Warner had many likes and dislikes, and I soon learned about them. He said never to let an actor yawn in a scene, because it becomes catching—the audience relaxes, you lose the dramatic tension of the story, and you'll have trouble getting them back again. We were never to allow an actor to wear a tie with too many dots or stripes or an actress a dress or outfit that was too busy with figures or flowers. It takes away from the face. All lines should lead to the face.

I also learned that each morning Warner would read the reports made out by the script supervisor the night before, which recorded the time everyone arrived on the set, when shooting began, how many takes each scene required, how many angles and pages were shot, and so forth. I was tipped off about how to please him. You were supposed to start shooting at 9:00 A.M. So, instead of a long rehearsal of a difficult scene that might result in a first shot at 10:00 A.M., you began the day by shooting an insert: a key being slipped into a lock, a hand opening a letter, or a gun being fired. The crew arrived at 8:30, and it took them only a few minutes to light it. You shot it quickly and easily, and the report would read that you made your first shot at 9:02 A.M., which proved that you were on the job. Then you could take time to rehearse the next scene, which was more important. Another way to avoid trouble when you had to make too many takes of a scene (more than five or six) was to move the camera a few inches and put a new number on it. Warner would only read the figures and not analyze the report, so he would be happy.

Because it was my first time directing film, I was concerned with keeping things moving. I used many dolly shots and hoped that Warner would think I was an expert with the camera. Syd was a great help; I learned much from him, as I did from every cameraman I ever worked with. Some of them had been making films for twenty years, and it would have been foolish of me not to take advantage of their knowledge and experience.

Syd once called for a human skull to be placed in Litel's office, and whenever we did a close shot of the doctor at his desk, the skull loomed large and menacingly in the foreground. Not only did it give depth to the shot, but it also enhanced the grim atmosphere I was trying to create. I learned a principle of photography: try to find and include in your shot those elements and objects that are associated with and symbolic of the mood you are trying to create.

I had to get used to some differences between the theater and films. Whereas in the theater the entire stage is almost always visible, with the camera you need only show what you want the audience to see. Furthermore, there is no need in film for what is called projection in the theater, that is, speaking loud enough to be heard in the second balcony. The sound can record a whisper, and the close-up can practically record what a character is thinking. Some of the most powerful moments in a film are those silent close-ups that show the actor going through a deep emotional experience before making a decision.

I have always felt that audiences should be unaware of the mechanics of filmmaking, such as cuts or camera moves. They should feel they're watching one long continuous strip of film. I formed a policy for myself to help accomplish this: go to where the audience wants to go, show the reactions it wants to see. Arbitrary and unmotivated cuts can make a film seem choppy, just as unmotivated camera moves can make an audience conscious of the mechanics and thus destroy the illusion of reality. A good film for me is one in which I become so absorbed in the story and the cutting is so organically related that I am never made aware of the mechanical skill involved.

The many technical and artistic problems encountered in directing are endlessly fascinating and stimulating, and each film is a challenge. Before I became knowledgeable about lenses, angles, cutting and when to move the camera and when not to, and began to be in full control of the various elements of filmmaking, having developed a sense of composition and photography, I had directed at least six films. I learned on each one of the six and continued to learn thereafter. Even when I had directed thirty features and started directing television, I was still learning. That has always been one of the most stimulating and exciting factors in directing—the challenge of determining how to bring a story to life and how best to stage and photograph each scene for maximum dramatic effect.

Above all, a director must be a good storyteller. He must know how to establish interest in his characters and their problems so that an audience will become anxious to know how the problems are finally solved. The skill with which he builds the conflict and keeps the suspense going until the final resolution is the test of his ability to entertain. This includes being able to work with actors, to give them a feeling of confidence and security, to stimulate their subconscious and dredge up their true feelings concerning the given circumstances. The director must become a mirror for the actor, so that he can know when he is doing too much or not doing enough to convey what is needed. One thing every director is concerned with is the laughs. Every legitimate laugh is valuable, and every bad or unintended laugh can hurt a film; indeed, too many bad laughs can even kill it.

Having done many plays and worked in front of various types of audiences, I thought I could recognize a laugh line, knew how to build for it, and was able to time it properly. In a scene at a cemetery late one night, in *Dr. X*, where Wayne and Dennis go to see where Bogart is buried, I cast Ian McClellan as an offbeat caretaker. When he is asked by Wayne if he doesn't get lonely in such a place, he says, quite sincerely, "Oh no, these are all my friends." Ian gave me exactly the fey quality I needed. After Wayne and Dennis get his permission to dig up the grave and open the coffin, Wayne looks inside, turns to Dennis and says, "Just as I thought—empty."

The caretaker, standing nearby, peeks into the coffin. Hurt and saddened, he mutters plaintively, "I've been robbed." It was a line I had contributed, and I was sure it would be a great laugh, but when Brynie read it he was equally sure it would fall flat. He could see nothing funny about it. He wanted to cut the line, but I begged him to leave it in for the preview. He did and, naturally, I was waiting expectantly for that line more than anything else in the film. It would tell me whether I knew or didn't know what made an audience laugh.

The film was going well when we came to the graveyard scene. I held my breath. The actor spoke the line, and I waited for the response, but there was silence. I was shocked, my confidence shaken, but a few seconds later a few people down front caught the humor of the line, began to laugh, and slowly it built until the entire house was roaring with laughter. I relaxed. There is more to directing, of course, than knowing where the laughs are, but that is an indication of your knowledge and ability to gauge how an audience will react.

I haven't seen *Dr. X* since that preview, which I enjoyed and both Warner and Foy liked. I knew afterward, despite the fact that it was merely a piece of movie hokum, that I had cause to think that I was on my way to a directing career. All the effects that I had consciously strived for came to fruition.

7
Moving Up

After *Dr. X* was released and I told my friend, Abem Finkle, that I was still being paid only $250 a week, he suggested that I talk to Mike Levee, his agent and Paul Muni's. Levee also represented Greer Garson, Joan Crawford, Claude Rains, and several other big names. When I explained my situation, Levee was polite but said I was not earning enough money yet for him to handle me. I was disappointed, but remembering what Brynie had said when I signed my contract, "Don't bother reading it, they've got you by the balls," I turned my attention to my next film.

Julius Epstein, a writer in the A department, and his twin brother, Philip, also a writer (recently hired), had just done a new version of *Saturday's Children,* based on a play by Maxwell Anderson. It was to be directed by Anatole Litvak and was to star Jimmy Stewart and Olivia de Havilland. For some reason Litvak and the stars withdrew. At that point, I was later told, the Epsteins went to Henry Blanke, the producer, and suggested John Garfield for the Stewart role and me as the possible director. Since the studio needed a picture for Garfield, and the film was to be inexpensive, Wallis, whom I had never met, agreed to let me direct it, even though it was an A film.

It was a good script with appealing characters, warm and human, and the dialog was excellent. I was grateful for the assignment. Blanke was a top producer on the lot and a man of taste. He gave me an excellent cast: Garfield, Anne Shirley, Claude Rains, Elizabeth Risdon, Lee Patrick, Roscoe Karns, and Dinty Moore. I called an old friend, George Tobias, to play opposite Dinty, and they made an amusing and delightful couple. George was placed under long-term contract at the studio as a result of his work.

It is one thing to be friendly with an actor you have known in the past when he was the star of the show and you were just a small-part player, but something quite different when you are suddenly put in the position of directing him. You cannot avoid becoming a little nervous and wondering how he will feel about taking direction from you. I wasn't worried about Garfield. I was older, and in 1932 we had worked together in *Counsellor at Law.* I also had a more important role than he did. But I *was* concerned about Claude Rains, with whom I had worked years before in several plays at the Theater Guild when *he* was the star and I played minor roles. I needn't have worried.

The second or third day of shooting, we were doing a scene in which Garfield, married to Anne Shirley, Rains's daughter, comes home drunk with Roscoe Karns. John was playing it badly, with exaggerated unsteadiness and slurring of words. I was also trying to get him away from the brash character he had played in *Four Daughters,* which was a hit, and had repeated in several other films. This had caused some critics to say he was limited. I don't think John had ever played a drunk before, and I suggested that the secret of acting a good drunk was to try *not* to appear drunk but to reveal it only sparingly. I happened to glance at Claude, who was in the scene. He smiled and nodded to me approvingly. It was a priceless moment for me.

The shooting went well. Blanke was pleased and told me that Wallis and Warner liked my direction. I took the liberty of telling Blanke about a novel I had read years before in New York that I thought would make a great film. It was *The Treasure of the Sierra Madre.* He agreed to read it, and I brought him my copy. He thought it was interesting but told me that Wallis did not like it, so I forgot about it. A few years later, after John Huston wrote and directed *The Maltese Falcon,* he convinced Wallis that he could make a good film out of *Treasure,* and the studio bought the novel for him. Huston won two awards for it, for writing and for directing. I was envious.

During the shooting of *Saturday's Children* I had a distinguished visitor, Sinclair Lewis. He was on a lecture tour, and when I learned he would be staying at the Biltmore Hotel, I left word that Hedda and I would be at the lecture. He invited us to a small gathering of his friends afterward, where we met Sidney Howard, Upton Sinclair, and Max Eastman. The year before, he had sent me a paperback edition of the play *It Can't Happen Here.* On the outside he had written, "To Vincent Sherman, best of directors" and signed it "Sinclair Lewis, Lombardy Hotel, 111 E. 56th St. 10/19/38 NYC." Inside there was a foreword in which was printed the following: "I want to record my gratitude and admiration for Mr. Vincent Sherman who, working with me sixteen hours a day throughout September, 1936, made it possible for me to complete the Federal Theater version." He was happy that I had landed at Warner's and was fascinated by films and actors. I introduced him around, and his visit added prestige to my standing at the studio.

Subsequently, he came to Hollywood several times and always invited Hedda and me to visit him. By then he was divorced from Dorothy. Later, I lost touch with him but heard that he was traveling in Europe and took ill in Florence, Italy, where he died. For days we were depressed. Whenever, and for whatever reason, I have suffered a spell of low self-esteem, his kindness, solicitation, and interest have reassured me. I like to think that he saw something in me that was worthy of his attention.

Saturday's Children opened in New York to excellent reviews. The acting, writing, and direction were praised, and several of the critics pointed out that I had revealed a new Garfield. Archer Winsten in the *Post* was especially flattering, and *Time* magazine went so far as to say that although I was from a small town in the South, I had caught the feeling of New York. I hoped that another A film would soon be handed to me.

But Brynie had no intention of relinquishing me. He had found me, had made me a director, and was already planning several films ahead for me to direct. The first was a remake of *The Great Mouthpiece,* produced by Darryl Zanuck several years before when he was the chief of production at Warner's, prior to Hal Wallis's reign. It was about Bill Fallon, a well-known, flamboyant criminal lawyer in New York who resorted to colorful stunts to free a client. The original had starred Warren William. Brynie had a script ready and wanted George Brent for the remake. George was a leading man in A pictures, and Wallis was reluctant to let him go into a Foy project. Since Wallis had nothing for Brent at the moment, though, Warner okayed it.

The new title was *The Man Who Talked Too Much* (and he did). I was not happy with the assignment, but I had a good cast, including the beautiful Virginia Bruce, William Lundigan, and, to play a small role, Richard Barthelmess. It was easy to see why he had been a big star for so many years. He had a quiet intensity, sharp piercing eyes, and an expressive, handsome face. At the end of the film he sent me a beautiful wallet. I did not tell him that in 1934, although we were never in a scene together, I had played one of his henchmen in a Warner film, *Midnight Alibi,* in which he had starred.

Neither George Brent nor I liked the script of *The Man who Talked Too Much,* but to refuse it meant a suspension—being taken off salary—

so we did it. Brynie and Warner knew that I disliked the project, but weeks later, after the film had been released, Warner stopped me in the corridor of the main building. "You didn't want to make that picture," he said. "But we're going to net over a hundred grand on it." It was not a good film, but it cost only a little over two hundred thousand dollars. Warner Brothers owned sixteen hundred theaters at the time, so they made a profit. A hundred thousand dollars in those days was a respectable sum.

Toward the end of shooting with Brent I first met Bette Davis. I was having lunch at the writer's table in the Green Room of the Warner's commissary when I felt a tap on my shoulder and turned to see Bette Davis standing behind me.

"Are you Vincent Sherman?" she asked.

I nodded affirmatively and rose at once.

"I'm Bette Davis," she said, as if she were unknown.

I nodded again, this time with a smile at her modesty.

"George tells me that he has never worked so hard or enjoyed himself so much," she proclaimed.

I replied that I was equally happy working with George and that he was a genuine professional.

"I was wondering. . . ." she mused. "The studio wants me to do a comedy as my next film. Perhaps you could read the script, and if you like it I'll ask Wallis to let us do it together."

My spirits soared. "It would be a privilege to work with you, Miss Davis!"

She thanked me, then, lowering her voice, added, with a smile and a twinkle in her eye, "They just haven't caught up with me yet."

With characteristic long strides, she returned to her table in the corner of the Green Room. I stood frozen, unable to move. Her energy, warmth, and passion were for me more stimulating than that of any other actress on the screen. The prospect of working with her was overwhelming. Unaware of how long I stood looking after her, I heard a voice say, "You can sit now." Despite the muffled laughter of the writers, when I sat I was a different person. And I suspected that they perceived me a little differently too, for until that moment I was merely a B director. But Bette Davis asking *me* to direct her . . . ?

On the set I thanked George for his kind words and, for the rest of the day, contemplated my good fortune. A week later, the Brent film completed and behind me, I received a script of *Affectionately Yours* from Hal Wallis with a note that this was to be Bette Davis's next film. My heart actually raced as I stretched out on my office sofa to read it. But as I turned each page, the thrill and anticipation of directing a sparkling comedy "starring Bette Davis" gradually diminished and vanished. The script was hopeless; it lacked genuine humor, was "old hat," and it was clear to me that no one could make a good film out of it. What was not clear was my next move. Had Davis read it? What was her reaction? If she liked it, how could I turn it down without offending her? The one thing I did know was that I *would not* direct it, and if I handled the situation diplomatically, the worst that could happen to me would be a suspension of my three-hundred-dollar weekly salary for the length of time it would take to shoot the film, seven or eight weeks. True, I had done the Brent film even though I didn't like the script, but that was much different. No one expected much from a Foy production, but a Bette Davis film with an A budget would be awaited with high hopes.

I decided to ask Henry Blanke, the studio's top A producer, with whom I had become friendly when I was directing *Saturday's Children*, how I should handle it. I respected his judgment. After I told him my problem, he said, "I will talk to Wallis, but don't tell Davis what you think. Wallis would murder you."

It wasn't long before I was called to Wallis's office. He was a formidable executive, and I was in awe of him. I didn't want to antagonize him, hoping that eventually he would ask me to do a good A-budget picture, but I was determined to stand by my decision on this one.

"What's this I hear about your not liking *Affectionately Yours?*" he began as I sat across from him at his desk.

"It's true," I replied. "I don't think it's very good, and it's not my idea of a comedy."

He looked puzzled. "You mean to tell me you'd turn down a chance to direct a film with Bette Davis?"

"That's exactly why I'm turning it down! I'd rather not hear later that you entrusted me with your biggest star and that I almost ruined her."

He stared at me for a long moment, realized, I think, that I was adamant, then spoke quietly but firmly. "All right, but I want you to write her a letter telling her that you think it's a good script, but that you feel you don't have enough experience to do it."

I was appalled and started to protest when he continued. "I have enough trouble trying to get our stars to make pictures without some director telling them not to." I understood his problem but pleaded in vain for him to relieve me of writing such a letter. "You owe it to the studio to help us out," he said with finality, ignoring my plea. The conversation was over. If I refused, I was sure that he'd hold it against me, so I agreed. As I started out he added, "And let me see the letter before you send it."

I struggled to compose a letter that would reveal how anxious I was to work with her and how much I appreciated the opportunity she had offered me but would explain my reluctance to accept the assignment. I finally managed, "I'm sure, with you in the lead, and a more experienced director than I am, it could become a delightful picture, but it isn't exactly my cup of tea, and I fear I won't be able to do it justice. So, please forgive me. I do hope that eventually I will have the pleasure of working with you." I sent the letter to Wallis, expecting him to forward it to Davis. It was late Friday afternoon. I had worked hard on the Brent film and went home hoping to rest on the weekend. When I returned to my office Monday morning, Wallis's secretary, Paul Nathan, phoned to say that Wallis didn't think my letter to Davis was enthusiastic enough about the script, and he wanted me to rewrite it. He felt that Davis would be able to read between the lines and would suspect that I did not like it. Reluctantly, I rewrote the letter, going overboard in praising the script, hoping that Bette would surmise that there was something phony about my enthusiasm. Surely she would realize I couldn't admire a script so much, yet not want to direct it. I sent the letter to Wallis's office and assumed he sent it to Davis.

The obligation fulfilled, I went upstairs to visit the Epstein brothers. When I told them what had happened, they were amused. As it worked out, my plight turned into their advantage; they had just finished writing *The Bride Came C.O.D.*, which James Cagney was to star in, with William Keighley directing, but the production lacked a leading lady. The next thing I knew, Bette was set to star with Cagney.

Although it was not a great success, *The Bride Came C.O.D.* was not a catastrophe. *Affectionately Yours,* which Lloyd Bacon directed, was. I wondered why Bacon had accepted the script. Years later I understood—he was being paid four thousand dollars per week, whereas I was earning three hundred dollars. When you were being so well paid, you felt obligated to do whatever the studio asked.

Bette never responded to my letter, but I was content that we had both avoided a disaster. What puzzled me was that whenever I'd pass her on the lot or see her in the Green Room, she ignored me. No nod or hello or smile—just a turn away, as though I wasn't worthy of recognition. I wondered if she was angry because I didn't accept the script or speak to her personally about it. Or was it possible that Wallis never sent my letter to her? But I could not dwell on it too long. I had to go to work on my next assignment. However, I hoped that someday I'd have a chance to work with her and that she'd change her mind.

Warner hated to spend money on a script and then have to cancel its production because no one in the A department wanted to make it. So he would pass it on to Brynie to see if he could get something out of it. That is how I got my next film, *Trial and Error*. The screenplay was written by Robert Rossen and based on a novel the studio had bought. Foy asked me to read it. I did and felt that, with a little work, we could get a fair movie out of it and make it for a reasonable price.

The story was about a college professor who was dying of some ailment but was determined to make use of his remaining days by saving a young man, who was a friend, from the clutches of an evil woman. He feels justified in causing her death, but when he confesses to the authorities, they hesitate to believe him because he is such a gentle soul and has such a fine reputation. Despite the seriousness of the story, there were some hilarious scenes in it: a psychiatrist questions the professor and ends up a psychiatric case himself as a result of the simple logic of the professor. Thomas Mitchell, recently put under contract by the studio, was cast as the professor; Jeffrey Lynn, his young friend; Mona Maris, the evil beauty; and Geraldine Fitzgerald, Jeffrey's wife. They were all talented and pleasant to work with. After viewing the film, the studio decided to give it a special opening, something very few B films ever achieved. Mitchell became a big booster for me, and I received a call one day from Leland Hayward, who was Tommy's agent. He invited me to lunch at Chasen's and talked about the possibility of borrowing me from Warner's to work for Howard Hughes, taking over the direction of *The Outlaw*, from which Howard Hawks had departed. I was flattered and grateful to Mitchell, but we soon heard that Hughes himself had decided to direct the finish of the film.

Trial and Error became known as *Flight from Destiny*. It was well received and advanced my position at Warner's. I received a call from Mike Levee. He was at the preview, was impressed with the direction, and now wanted to represent me. The deal I made with him was that he would be paid his fee, 10 percent, if and when he improved my contract at Warner's.

The studio had bought a play of Irwin Shaw's that I liked, *The Gentle People*. In addition to warm and amusing characters, it said something that I thought was important: when faced with unadulterated evil, good men must resist, even if it means resorting to violence. It took place during the rise of Hitler and America's isolationism. The locale was Brighton Beach, near Coney Island, which I knew well. I had let it be known that I'd like to direct it, but it was assigned to Anatole Litvak, who had achieved a fine reputation in Europe with *Mayerling*. I liked Tola, as Litvak was called, and thought him a talented man, so I had no resentment.

Foy gave me a screenplay titled *Underground,* an anti-Nazi story about the secret radio in Germany and a family that was torn apart because one of its sons was a loyal Nazi and the other was secretly anti-Nazi and a member of the underground. It was written by Edwin Justus Mayer and Oliver Garrett, and Litvak had worked on it. He had directed *Confessions of a Nazi Spy* as his first film for Warner Brothers, but when it failed to make money, he and Wallis both decided to abandon *Underground.* Again Warner handed it to Foy to see if he could do something with it. Foy read it and thought it would make a fair melodrama and, if made inexpensively enough, that it would not lose money. The studio had already spent a goodly sum on the script, and as always Warner was anxious to recoup something from it, so he okayed the project. That's how it came to me. My disappointment in not getting *The Gentle People* was soon forgotten. I was excited about the possibilities of *Underground.* Brynie was surprised that I liked it and cautioned me. "Don't get your hopes up. Nobody wants to see this kind of picture. Look at *Confessions of a Nazi Spy* and *The Mortal Storm* [a well-made MGM anti-Nazi film directed by Frank Borzage, but also unsuccessful], but if we make it cheaply enough, maybe we'll break even."

"I know those pictures failed," I replied. "But they were downbeat; they left audiences feeling depressed and helpless. *Underground* will give them hope." He listened but was not convinced. I went to work on the script and was given writer Charles Grayson to help me. He accepted and approved all my changes, and we got along well. I should have put my name on the screenplay along with his, but once I had started directing, I no longer took credit for working on scripts.

Information about anti-Nazi activity in Germany was scarce. I dug up what I could and persisted in the belief that there were decent people in that country who were trying to resist Hitler and his gang. (Years later I, along with others, was appalled at how few had the courage to resist and how monstrous was the behavior of the Nazis.) When it came time to cast, I persuaded Brynie that in order to give the film a feeling of truth and reality, we should use as many German refugee actors as possible.

There were a goodly number in Hollywood at the time who needed work. He agreed, mainly because they were not expensive. I pleaded for Philip Dorn, who was under contract to MGM. He was from Holland. I had seen him in one film and thought he was a fine actor who would be ideal for the leader of the underground radio. Foy again agreed, and a deal was made with MGM. A beautiful German girl, Kaaren Verne, was brought to my office by an agent. She spoke English with only a slight hint of an accent and seemed to be a good actress. I cast her immediately as the female lead. In trying to find a young man to play Dorn's brother, a loyal Nazi, I was making a list of possibilities when Foy called to say that Warner wanted me to use Jeffrey Lynn. I was upset. Jeff was a nice young actor and had done a good job in *Flight from Destiny,* but he was very American. I was concerned lest he seem out of place in this cast of European refugees. I pleaded with Warner and Foy to reconsider, but Warner was adamant. I worked long and hard with Jeff, who had a highly emotional role. First, he is shocked to discover that Kaaren, with whom he has fallen in love, is a member of the underground. Then, in an attempt to destroy them, he alerts the Gestapo, but he rescues Kaaren before they arrive. After he tells Kaaren what he has done, she is horrified. He has unknowingly betrayed his brother. He refuses to believe it, but when he hears his brother's voice on the radio as the Gestapo capture him, he realizes what he has done. After the Nazis torture his innocent father and Jeff learns more about their evil ways, he decides to help the underground. He takes up the work of his brother. The best scene in the picture, and a powerhouse for the two brothers, is when the head of the Gestapo finds it difficult to believe that Jeff is so loyal to the Nazis that he would knowingly betray his own brother and has them face each other in his office. Dorn is brought in, bloody and beaten, knowing he will die, but he refuses to believe that Jeff willingly betrayed him. Jeff knows he is being tested and has to lie. He tells Dorn that he considers him a traitor and that's why he exposed him.

Jeff was a New Englander and not used to displaying emotions freely; this role called for an intensity of feeling that was beyond anything he had ever done before. In the scene in which Kaaren tells him he has turned over his brother to the Gestapo and he hears his brother's voice, he stops the car he is driving her away in and is so shaken he can hardly speak. We did take after take as I tried to capture the inner turmoil he needed to show. Then I recalled that gunshots disturbed him. I asked my property man to get me a pistol with six loud blanks. When Jeff saw what I was preparing to do he objected strenuously, which was already a help in stirring up his emotions. Then, as we rolled the camera, I shot six times just a few feet away from him. He jumped with each shot and became unnerved and upset. I yelled, "Action," and he did the scene. I got what I wanted, but his resentment was noticeable. Later, after a visit back home to New England, he told me that his family thought he gave his best performance in *Underground*. I concurred.

The other roles were well cast, and I considered myself lucky to have such a fine group of actors, many of them well known in Europe. Only one role remained to be cast, that of a little old man working in the Gestapo office who pretended to be innocuous and dull but was a shrewd member of the underground. I was looking about for someone to play this role when Bill Jacobs, Brynie's friend and producer of *Underground*, came to the set one morning looking sad and troubled.

"Vince," he began, "I've got some bad news . . . the little old man in the picture . . . Brynie wants you to change the part and give it to a friend of his."

"Who's the friend?" I asked.

"Mona Maris," he replied, hanging his head.

"You gotta be kidding! She's a good-looking, sexy young woman. . . . Besides, she has a Spanish accent! What the hell would she be doing in the office of the Gestapo?"

"I know," Bill said. "I told him you'd hit the ceiling, but he says if he doesn't give her the part she'll cut up all his suits."

"His suits?"

"He's got a few of them at her place, but that's not all. . . ."

"To hell with that. I'll call him."

"Vince, please. I don't like it any more than you do. But he's in a spot and needs help. If not, his wife might find out and he'll really be in trouble. Please, do the best you can."

I loved Bill, who was one of the kindest men I'd ever known, and I reminded myself that Brynie had given me my start at Warner's. Although I considered leaving the picture because of his inexcusable request, I wanted too much to finish *Underground* to give it up. Mona worked hard, gave a good performance, and audiences accepted her in the role even if I didn't.

I have never worked longer hours or more intensely on any film, but I relished every minute of it because I felt that I was helping alert the world to the menace of Hitler and the Nazis. It was also a time when America was still in the throes of isolationism. The America Firsters were dominating the thinking of the country, supported by Father Coughlin and Charles Lindbergh, who were favorably disposed toward the Nazis. The picture was branded by certain politicians as "war mongering," but Brynie got Eric Sevaried to make an appearance at the beginning of the film, substantiating many of the events in it. William Shirer wrote a letter stating that according to his information the brutality shown was mild compared to the truth.

The reviews were smashing, as they say, and business was excellent. The picture wound up doing over $2 million and cost under three hundred thousand, the first successful anti-Nazi film. I received letters and calls from friends and strangers complimenting me. A former writer at Warner's said that he had been in Mexico City when it played there, and the audience rose and cheered at the end. Another friend wrote from New York that she was in the company of Stefan Zweig, the well-known German writer, when the Warner office ran *Underground* and invited him. He heartily approved it.

One morning Jack Benny visited my set and approached me.

"Are you Sherman?"

"Yes, sir," I replied.

"I'm Jack Benny," he said as he extended his hand.

"I know." We shook hands.

"I just wanted to tell you that last night I saw *Underground* at Warner's Beverly Theater, and it's one of the greatest melodramas I've ever seen."

I was overjoyed and thanked him. We chatted for a few minutes, then he left. Moments like that make you forget all the grief you go through on a film. The irony was that Litvak's film, *The Gentle People,* which became *Out of the Fog,* with John Garfield and Ida Lupino, although well done, received little notice, while *Underground* attracted widespread attention, was successful, and became another A film, boosting my stock considerably.

But it was the end of my association and friendship with Brynie. He was proud of having been responsible for bringing me to the studio, but he was also envious that I was doing so well and would most likely be soon leaving the B department. Two incidents precipitated the break. Before *Underground* was released, and just after the final print was ready, I received a phone call late one night from my friend Lee Katz. He wanted to tell me that he had just finished talking to his uncle, Leon Schlesinger, who was in charge of the short subjects at Warner Brothers and was a friend of Jack Warner's. Leon and Jack had had dinner together at the studio, and on the way out Warner had suggested that they look at a reel or two of Foy's latest picture. It happened to be *Underground.* (Warner looked at the rushes of all the A films each day but rarely looked at the B films.) "Just run the first two reels," he said to the projectionist as he and Leon went inside one of the projection rooms. When they saw the first two reels, Warner turned to Leon and said, "Hey, it's pretty good. Let's look at a couple more reels." They did, and finally Warner said to the operator, "Keep running till I tell you to stop."

"We sat through the entire film" (12 reels), Leon told Lee, "and Jack said it was great. I thought you'd like to know because Vince is your friend."

I was grateful for the call and slept well that night. The next morning I was waiting for Brynie to call me with the good news, but I didn't hear from him. Late in the afternoon, I went to his office and was sure he'd say something about Warner's reaction, but he didn't. He talked about another story. Before leaving, I mentioned casually that I had heard Warner ran *Underground* the night before and wondered how he felt about it. Just as casually, Brynie said, "Oh, he thought it was okay." Obviously he did not know about the call I had received. I was miffed that he did not tell me the truth, that Warner was enthusiastic about it. I asked when I might see it, and he said, "We'll run it together in a day or two. I'm busy right now."

I left his office with the feeling that a psychological wall had suddenly risen between us, but I was hopeful that it would soon disappear. On the contrary, the situation was accidentally exacerbated by my discovery the next morning (from one of the editors), that the night before Brynie had run *Underground* for Litvak, no doubt to boast about it and to needle Tola for having given up the film. I was dismayed and angry that he would run my film for another director before he ran it with me. I had participated in the editing, of course, but this was the final print with music and sound effects, and I was anxious to see it. Brynie's action was, I felt, unprofessional and insulting. I was especially angry because he had been skeptical about the success of the film while I was making it, pouring my guts into it, working late into the night, writing and rewriting on the set, trying to make every scene as powerful as possible.

Unable to contain my resentment, I went to his office and said my piece. He made some lame excuse about why he ran it with Litvak and tried to appease me, but I left his office never to return. I had made up my mind that I would not direct another film for him, even at the risk of being fired. He told friends that I was getting "too big for my britches."

In my three years at the studio, I had worked on *Crime School,* a big plus for Brynie, in addition to *My Bill* and *King of the Underworld*. I had written the original story and screenplay of *Pride of the Bluegrass,* had directed *The Return of Dr. X, Saturday's Children, The Man Who Talked Too Much, Flight from Destiny,* which was elevated to an A release, and now *Underground,* also to be released as an A film. I was being paid three hundred dollars a week, far below what I should have been earning, and I thought I should at least be given a little more consideration. Despite his shabby treatment of me, I was still grateful for Brynie's efforts in my behalf at the beginning of my career, and I acknowledge that I learned much from him during our association.

Hedda regretted the breakup because she liked Brynie, but she also understood my feelings. She saw *Underground* at the studio a few days before it was released and came out with tears in her eyes, deeply impressed.

It was not long before Jack Warner invited me to his home in Beverly Hills one morning for coffee. He wanted to tell me that in the future I would be doing A films. Then he took me for a walk over the grounds of his estate on Angelo Drive. "If you'll listen to me," he said, "do the pictures I tell you to do, I'll make you a big director." This was to discourage me from ever turning down scripts in the future. He also told me stories of his early days in Hollywood, of the difficulty he and his older brother, Harry, had getting loans to make films.

"What bank do you do business with?" he asked. I told him. He said, "I used to be with them, but they were ashamed for their customers to see me in the front part of the bank; they always asked me to wait in the rear. Being a movie producer was the same as running a pool room or a whore house. But Gianninni at the Bank of America treated me real nice." Toward the end of our walk, I heard a voice in the distance call out, "Morning, Jack!" Warner turned and waved to a man fifty or sixty yards away who was walking toward us. "It's Charlie Feldman," he said. "He's an agent. Keep away from him." I learned later they were supposed to be good friends.

The next day I was sent a script of *All through the Night*. It was to star Humphrey Bogart, and Jerry Wald was to be the producer. It was the first film, or one of the first films, to be produced by Jerry. Hal Wallis was the executive producer, and the budget was six hundred thousand dollars. This meant that it was an A film and that I was now definitely a full-fledged A director. My salary, however, remained the same, three hundred dollars a week, while several A directors were being paid thousands a week. I was not happy about it, but I was not disgruntled. The fun and excitement of working on screenplays, directing actors, and learning about the technique of film made up for any resentment I felt for being underpaid.

All through the Night was another anti-Nazi film, but vastly different from *Underground* and requiring a completely different approach. The latter had been a grim melodrama set in Hitler's Germany; the former was to be an action comedy taking place in New York. But type casting for directors as well as actors took over, and I had been designated.

Jerry had been a writer at Warner's for several years and was regarded by many as the model for Budd Schulberg's Sammy in his novel *What Makes Sammy Run?* I heard many disparaging remarks about Jerry: that he was a hustler, untalented, and unscrupulous. Also that he once paid Julius Epstein to write for him and then submitted the work as his own. True or not, he was ambitious and enterprising. As I came to know him, I realized that he was well aware of his reputation and was struggling to overcome it. His goal was to win respect. I liked him and sympathized with him.

The screenplay was written by Leo Rosten and Leonard Spigelgass. Rosten had written the brilliant Hyman Kaplan stories, and Spigelgass was an experienced screenwriter. The story was about some Broadway gamblers (Damon Runyon types), led by Bogart, who confront and defeat a bunch of Nazi Bundists who are persecuting loyal German Americans and planning to sabotage the Brooklyn Navy Yard. Although it needed work, I thought it had good commercial prospects: suspenseful action with comedy, usually a sure-fire formula. Also, there were not too many anti-Nazi films being made, and both Jerry and I felt we could say a few things that needed to be said about Hitler and the Bundists. I looked forward to working again with Bogie, who was playing "Gloves" Donahue. He had been slowly moving up in the estimation of producers, directors, and audiences and had been successful in *High Sierra,* directed by Raoul Walsh, and *The Maltese Falcon,* written and directed by John Huston (both turned down by Paul Muni and George Raft). Now, Bogie was being accepted as a leading man and worthy of "getting the girl." In this case it was the beautiful Kaaren Verne, who had played the lead for me in *Underground.* Jane Darwell, who was a hit in John Ford's *Grapes of Wrath,* played Bogie's mother and gave the role just the right touch of warmth and motherly bossiness.

In the story, Bogie has lunch every day with his henchmen at a cafe like Lindy's, and he finishes his meal with a piece of his favorite cheesecake, made by a nice little German baker who is a friend and neighbor of his mother's. Early in the film the baker is being harassed by Peter Lorre, and when he is found dead in the basement of his shop, Bogie's mother insists that Bogie help find the murderer. He and his friends pick up various clues. One leads to Kaaren Verne, a nightclub singer, who was seen at the bakery the day of the murder. After questioning her, Bogie gets involved in the death of Ed Brophy, an employee in the nightclub. He accidentally leaves one of his gloves on the floor near Brophy's body, and the police are soon looking for him. In trying to avoid them and find the murderer and the girl, Bogie and his friends uncover the Bundists, learn that the girl is a hostage, and that the Bundists are plotting to blow up the Brooklyn Navy Yard. After many narrow escapes Bogie and his friends, while still gambling a little on the side, clear up the murder, save the girl, and foil the plans of the Bundists.

Jerry was able to borrow Conrad Veidt from MGM, an actor I had admired for years, to play the leader of the Bundists. To aid and abet him we got Judith Anderson, a great actress, who had recently played Mrs. Danvers in *Rebecca*. We also got Peter Lorre, an unusual talent, and Martin Kosleck, an unappreciated but fine actor. We had several other good actors, some of whom had worked for me in *Underground*. On the American side I had William Demarest, a solid comedian, who was to play Bogie's sidekick, and the ever reliable Frank McHugh, plus Barton Maclane, Ed Brophy, and Wally Ford. A week before shooting was scheduled to start, I received a phone call from Warner.

"Listen, Vince," he began, "I've got two comics I want you to put in the picture."

Before he had a chance to continue, I said, "Mr. Warner, I already have all the comedians I need: Bill Demarest, Frank McHugh, Ed Brophy, Wally Ford—I don't have parts for any more."

"Well, make some parts," he replied, "I'm tired of paying these guys $250 a week to do nothing but sit on their ass."

I started to protest again but knew it was useless to argue with him. "Okay, who are they?" I asked.

"One's a fat guy—a nightclub comic—Jackie Gleason, and the other is Phil Silvers—very funny. Talk to them."

"Yes sir." I hung up the phone wearily and asked Casting to have them meet me in Wald's office the next morning. When they arrived, I explained that there were no written roles for them but that I would try to fit them into the picture. After describing the opening sequence in the restaurant, it occurred to me that Silvers could play a waiter, and Gleason could be another one of Bogie's henchmen. I asked them to bring me in some gags, and I'd try to fit them in. Gleason brought in a page of funny lines, and Silvers, nine pages of jokes. Silvers can be seen briefly in the opening of the film, and Gleason now and then throughout. They were both talented, but because there was not enough work for them at the studio, they were later released from their contracts and went on to become stars and great comedians.

Syd Hickox was again my cameraman, and I warned him we had a long hard job ahead of us: many scenes, sets, locations, actors, and much night work.

The plot was a good one, but it was necessary to reshape many scenes and rewrite the dialog. Bogie had a good sense of what sounded right for him and complained that his dialog was too namby pamby. "It's 'stamp your foot' dialog, Vince. We gotta fix it." And we did, each day and in almost every scene. Because he was going through a difficult period with his wife, Mayo Methot, a talented actress who was hitting the bottle too much, he was often grouchy and irritable. He was also being underpaid. But I tried to keep him happy because he was a good actor and always did his best.

Despite Bogie's complaints and my own changes, trying to improve each scene, I was enjoying each day. I was working with a dream cast; each person was giving his or her all to make a good show. Demarest and McHugh and Peter Lorre often came in with ideas and lines that were better than the script, and I used them. It was the kind of a picture that lent itself to building the suspense and humor of every scene.

Offscene, many happenings also kept things bubbling. Peter Lorre and Kaaren Verne fell in love and eventually got married after Peter divorced his wife, a gracious actress named Celia Lovsky. Bogie and Mayo had a series of drunken brawls. One morning he came in looking awful. I asked what happened. "I came home late last night," he said, "and that bitch of mine locked me out. I had to sleep on the front lawn and damn near froze my ass off." Another time, on a Saturday night, we were shooting on the back lot when my assistant, Bill Kissell, came to me.

"Vince," he whispered, "Mayo is in Bogie's dressing room crying and says she wants to see you." I went in. She was, indeed, crying, but drunk. She threw her arms around me.

"He doesn't love me any more, Vince," she sobbed. "What am I going to do?"

I tried to calm her; I told her she was wrong and assured her that Bogie still loved her. "No, he doesn't," she said. "You've got to talk to him." I tried to reason with her, but she insisted that I talk to Bogie immediately. I found him having a cup of coffee at the snack stand with Bill Demarest. I took him aside.

"Bogie," I pleaded, "Mayo is in your dressing room, crying her eyes out, saying you don't love her any more. For God's sake, go in and be nice to her."

"Fuck her," he exclaimed. "I'm fed up with these goddamned frustrated actresses. All I hear from morning to night is 'Why don't you get me a job?' I've had it." It was not too long before they were divorced.

Lorre was a gifted actor, whom I had admired ever since seeing him in Fritz Lang's great film *M,* made in Germany before Hitler. He was well educated, intelligent, and had been a member of a Berlin theater group that included Hans Eisler and Bertolt Brecht. He was also a wine expert. One of his first films here was Dostoyevsky's *Crime and Punishment,* but because it was not successful and parts for him were scarce, he was reduced to making a series of films for Fox based on the character Mr. Moto, a Japanese detective. From Peter's behavior I surmised that he had given up hope of ever doing serious and meaningful work in Hollywood and had made up his mind to earn as much money as possible, enjoy life, and "make faces." I sensed a bitterness and cynicism hidden inside, which finally resulted in a mockery of himself. Late one afternoon I was shooting a simple scene in which he has to run down a corridor and try to get into a room where Bogart and Demarest have just locked themselves in. Peter draws a gun and shoots at the lock, as Judith Anderson comes down the corridor yelling, "Was ist loss?" Peter replies in German and the scene ends. I called out "Cut," but not "Print," thinking I might be able to get a better take. Peter spoke up.

"That's all, brother Vince," he said. "I can only do this kind of crap once a day. Besides, it's six o'clock. Time to go home."

"Just a minute, Peter," I replied, pretending to be angry. "Don't talk to me about crap—how did you do all those *Mr. Moto*s at Fox?"

"I took dope!" he said without hesitation. We all laughed, and I called it a day.

Months later, Hedda and I were invited to a dinner party at Rudi Fehr's house. He was the editor of *All through the Night* and one of the best. I told the story about Peter merely to provide a laugh.

"But he did," said Rudi. "He took dope all during the making of the series." The laughter stopped. We were stunned.

Toward the latter part of *All through the Night,* we had a scene in which Bogart and Demarest get into a secret meeting of the Bundists by knocking out two members and taking their credentials. When Bogie is called upon to deliver a report, which he knows nothing about, I was faced with the problem of how to get him and Demarest out of their jam. As I searched about for some typically American means of deceiving the Bundists, it occurred to me that they could use good old American doubletalk to stall and then wriggle out of their dilemma. When Jerry told Wallis what I wanted to do, Wallis said he hated the idea; he didn't think it was funny. I was so sure that it would be the most hilarious scene in the film that I blew up and told Jerry that if I could not do this scene, I would refuse to make the picture, and he could tell Wallis how I felt. Jerry assured me that before we came to the sequence, Wallis would be leaving for New York, and we'd do it as I wished. I was appeased.

Bogie and Demarest liked the idea, as did Jerry, and it only added a few extra minutes to the shooting time. Once you're in a setup and the lighting is finished, adding a few lines costs very little. When Wallis returned from New York and we finished the film, we ran the rough cut at his home in the valley. He sat quietly through the running, saying nothing. When it was over and the lights came on, he turned to Jerry and Rudi.

"It's going to be all right," he began, then turned to me. "I thought I made it clear that I didn't like the doubletalk—so why did you shoot it?"

"Hal, I had to have something to get them out of trouble, and it was a chance to build suspense and inject some humor. Please believe me, it will be funny. Just give it a chance."

"Who's running the studio, Sherman—you or me?" he queried.

"You are, Hal, of course."

"I want all the doubletalk taken out," he said as he turned back to Rudi.

Rudi explained that he could take most of it out but had to keep the first line, at least, to make a smooth cut.

"All right, but take out the rest of it," Wallis said. He made a few more suggestions and then graciously offered us a drink. A few weeks later at the sneak preview in Huntington Park, I sat breathlessly waiting for the doubletalk scene. I was fearful that it had been cut so short the audience would not know what the hell was going on and would miss the point. Then came the first line of the doubletalk. It was followed by complete silence for a couple of seconds. It looked as though Wallis was right and I was wrong. The audience didn't think it was funny either. I was miserable, embarrassed, and wanted to crawl out of the theater, when suddenly people began to laugh. In another second or two, the theater exploded with laughter, so much so that the next few lines could not be heard. It simply took them a moment to understand the joke. I was relieved. When the picture ended and we all walked outside to confer, Wallis turned to Rudi. "All right," he said, "put all the doubletalk back in." He didn't even look at me. But he was smart enough to bow to the audience's response.

Judith Anderson, whom I had greatly admired ever since I had seen her for the first time as the queen in John Gielgud's *Hamlet,* was a joy to work with. She brought reality and dignity even to the small role she played in *All through the Night.* Peter liked to tease her and got a big laugh every time he left her dressing room by pretending to zip up his fly. When she found out about it, she went after him with a hairbrush.

A most intriguing actor was Conrad Veidt. I had seen him first in *The Cabinet of Dr. Caligari,* and then in *The Thief of Bagdad* and in other films. I always appreciated the finesse of his work. There was something polished and precise in everything he did. Peter told me that Connie had been a matinee idol in his younger days in the Berlin theater. Girls would be lined up outside the stage door waiting to see him or seduce him. Once I caught a glimpse of his script and was surprised to see, written on each page, details such as "lift pencil," "raise left eyebrow," "smile," and so forth. I became worried and expressed fear that if he predetermined his actions so concretely, it would not leave me much room for creativity. He explained that he always had to know exactly what he was doing in a scene, every detail, in order to be comfortable. I added that I might even have to change his lines occasionally.

"Oh, please, you mustn't do that," he pleaded, "unless you give me the changes the day before." I promised I would do my best.

The night before I was to shoot the big doubletalk scene, which began with Veidt addressing his fellow Bundists, I felt his dialog could be improved. However, I hesitated rewriting it because of what he had warned me about. But I had to do it and worked until midnight redoing the scene—a full page. The next morning at eight o'clock I went to his dressing room, where he was being made up.

"Connie," I began apologetically, "last night I realized your long speech could be better, and I worked on it. Read it and tell me what you think." He was calm, read it through, and turned to me.

"Yes, it's much better . . . but we can't do it today. Maybe tomorrow, but not today, and certainly not the first thing this morning."

I could see that he was angry and adamant. "Please listen to me and don't get upset," I begged. "I have just given the cameraman a setup that will take at least an hour to light and another half hour or more to get all the people in their places and make adjustments. That means you've got almost two hours to study the new scene. What's more, you don't have to do it all in one take. I need only the first part for the opening, then we can cut and pick up for the rest. I must shoot it today. So do me a favor and try to learn it. If not, I'll just have to shoot it the way you've studied it."

He looked at me steadily, and I knew he was furious inside. "You are a terrible man," he said. "I don't think I'll ever work with you again."

"I know how you feel," I replied. "And I can't blame you, but you're a fine actor, and I want to do the best I can for you." I left the room and could hear him growling under his breath. But I had made my point, and I relied on his pride to do the new scene. At ten o'clock I sent for Connie to come to the set for a rehearsal. He arrived, grim but polite. I showed him where he would enter and where to stand as he addressed the crowd of thirty or forty Bundists. I also explained again that I would only need the first paragraph of his speech, but if he wished, he could continue to the end and exit. He nodded, and we began the rehearsal. He read the first paragraph perfunctorily, and I stopped him. We made a few minor changes in lighting and began the first take a few minutes later. I called, "Action." Connie made his entrance, surveyed the crowd, and began speaking. I stood transfixed as he went through his entire speech, letter perfect, and with authority. He then turned and made his exit.

I yelled "Cut and *print!*" He received a big hand from the crowd, which was unaware that he had just been given the lines that morning. I complimented him and thanked him for being such a good sport, and above all such a wonderful actor. Ironically, he boasted about this particular accomplishment more than anything else he did in the film, and on more than one occasion.

"Do you know what this monster did to me?" he'd say and then proceed to go through the entire episode with pride. I think he himself was surprised that he had learned his speech so quickly and done so well. When the picture was finished, he embraced me and said goodbye. I felt that we regarded each other as friends and with great affection. I was sure of it when Louis B. Mayer's office called some time later to inform me sadly that Connie had died while playing golf the day before, and Mrs. Veidt (whom I had not met) wished me to attend his funeral. I could not go because I was shooting a film, but I sent flowers. We had lost a remarkable actor and a gentleman. Recently, I read that Veidt had left Germany because his wife was Jewish.

The picture opened in New York to good reviews, three and a half stars, and healthy business. Some critics said I had stolen from Hitchcock. It was true. All artists, I am convinced, whether consciously or unconsciously, steal from those whom they admire.

After the opening I received a call from Bogie. "I'm sorry if I gave you a hard time, kid, but I was going through hell with that broad of mine."

I told him I understood. I was pleased that he had called and happy that we both seemed to be headed for bigger and better projects. From this point on, Bogie always played leads.

On December 7, 1941, the Japanese attacked Pearl Harbor. President Roosevelt labeled it an "act of infamy" and declared war against Japan. It was not long before Germany was included as an enemy. Despite the America First organization, the country was united.

It was January 1942 when *All through the Night* opened, and it was well received. Needless to say, it was a plus for Jerry Wald and me. It plays often on TV and has become, for some viewers, a favorite Bogart film, along with *Casablanca* and *The Maltese Falcon.*

8

The Hard Way

During the final week of my directing *All through the Night,* Jerry Wald came by the set one morning, obviously keyed up, and hastily told me that the rushes were good. He was about to leave, when I stopped him. I could sense that he was excited about something else. When I prodded him, he admitted it was true. "I've just read the best script ever to cross my desk," he said, "and one of the greatest ever written in Hollywood."

"What is it?" I asked, burning with curiosity.

"*The Hard Way,*" he exclaimed. "Irwin Shaw wrote it, and it's fantastic."

"He's certainly talented," I said. "Is there any chance of my getting a crack at it?"

"I'd like to, Vince," he replied, "but Wyler and Hawks want to direct it. So does Leo McCarey." They were three great directors.

"I guess that lets me out."

"I'm sorry," he said and left.

Several weeks later I arrived at my office one morning to find the screenplay of *The Hard Way* on my desk with a letter attached from Wallis. He wanted to know what I thought of it and asked that I send him a report. It was not "the greatest script ever written," but it was good. If certain changes were made, I thought it would be worthwhile doing and that it could even become a commercial success.

The story was about two sisters who live in a mining town. The older girl, in her thirties, is married to a hard-working but dull miner; the younger one, who lives with them, is eighteen years old and pretty and has some acting talent. When a vaudeville actor, temporarily appearing with his partner at a local theater, falls for the younger sister, the older one sees a chance to promote the romance into a marriage and provide an escape for both of them from their bleak future. She not

106

only arranges the marriage, but she also abandons her husband and manages to go along with the young couple, much to the surprise and disapproval of the actor's partner. Determined to succeed, and ruthless because of past frustrations, the older sister maneuvers to get the younger one into the vaudeville act and finally breaks up the partnership of the two longtime friends. Afterward she gets her sister into a show on Broadway, minus the husband. As the young girl's star rises and her husband's declines, he commits suicide. In promoting her sister to stardom and in trying to satisfy her own ambition, the older sister almost destroys both their lives.

I wrote Wallis that I liked the material and would be glad to direct the film if I could make some changes, which I listed. The next morning I was called to Wallis's office. He greeted me with, "I don't understand you. We have a script here that several big directors want to do, but you have to write five pages of criticism."

Reasonably sure that, contrary to Jerry's statement, Wyler, Hawks, and McCarey were not clamoring to direct it, I said, with a smile, "Well, why not give it to one of them?"

"Because I like you," he replied, also with a smile, knowing that I surmised the truth. Then he picked up my letter. "Let's go over your changes." He agreed with most; others we argued about until we reached a compromise. "All right," he said, "I'll tell Wald you're going to direct the picture and that he should get Shaw in to make the changes."

Later, Jerry called to tell me he was happy to have me on the picture. (What else could he say?) He added that Wallis had sent him my letter, and he thought my ideas made sense. He had also set up a meeting with Irwin for that evening so we could have dinner and talk. I looked forward to it. I had never met Irwin Shaw but had followed his career ever since he burst onto the theater scene in New York with *Bury the Dead,* an antiwar play that had created a stir years before. I was waiting in Jerry's office when Irwin arrived. Jerry rose to greet him, then directed his attention to me.

"Meet Vincent Sherman," he said. "He's going to direct *The Hard Way.*" I rose, ready to extend my hand. Shaw glanced at me without the slightest acknowledgment, as his face registered disappointment. He turned back to Jerry.

"What happened to Wyler and Hawks?" he asked.

"They weren't available," Jerry quickly answered.

"Oh," Shaw muttered. "How about McCarey?"

"He's tied up, too," Jerry replied. He must have sensed my feelings, for he quickly added, "Vincent just did a hell of a good job for me directing *All through the Night,* with Bogart."

Shaw was not impressed (Bogie was not yet the big star). But recognizing his faux pas, and slightly embarrassed, he managed to squeeze out, "Nice to meet you."

I wanted to say, "Go fuck yourself" and walk out of the office. Instead, I swallowed my pride, said nothing, and nodded, but did not shake hands with him. Jerry proposed that we go to the Blue Evening to talk. It was near the studio, mainly a drinking place with a nice bar and a few tables where, if you were hungry, you could also get a steak and french fries. After we were seated at one of the tables and had ordered drinks and food, I began to tell Irwin how I felt about the script. I became aware that he wasn't listening. His attention was focused on two attractive young women seated at the bar. When our drinks arrived, he picked up his glass, said, "I'll be right back," and approached the women. I told Jerry that Shaw's behavior so far was insulting and that I had no desire to continue talking to him. "Don't let it bother you," he said. "He's coming back."

"I thought I knew one of them," Shaw said. He sat down and turned to me. "Now, what were you saying?" I began again to speak, when I realized he was still preoccupied with the two women. Again he excused himself to talk with them. Jerry was apologetic. "Irwin's quite a ladies' man—but it doesn't mean anything."

"It does to me," I said. "He's rude and arrogant, and if I didn't want to finish my drink and enjoy the steak you've ordered for me, I'd leave right now." We waited while Irwin did his best to score with one of the girls. Finally our food arrived, and Jerry called to him. He returned to our table, saw that I was annoyed, and began to ask me questions about the changes. I was no longer interested and answered as briefly as possible. We ate in silence. Jerry concluded the meeting by suggesting that perhaps it would be better just to give Irwin a copy of my letter. I agreed, and the evening ended politely but coldly.

The next morning Wallis called to ask how the meeting had gone. I told him what had happened and added that Shaw was an arrogant prick and I wanted nothing more to do with him. Wallis chided me, said to take it easy and that I shouldn't be so sensitive. Later, Wald called and I repeated my feelings. He agreed that Irwin had behaved badly but argued that we should still try to work with him. Before noon, Wallis called again. "You were right," he said. "He *is* an arrogant prick. He wants ten thousand dollars to make the changes. To hell with him; we'll get someone else!"

The writer I asked for was Daniel Fuchs, who was under contract to the studio and had written several novels I admired (one of them, *Low Company,* I thought would make a good play). He was finishing up a script but would be available in a few days to help me with the rewrite.

One morning, while I was waiting for Fuchs, I received a play from Wallis titled *Everybody Comes to Rick's,* with a note asking me to read it and let him know what I thought of it. Then I remembered that Bob Rossen had asked me a few days before whether I had read it.

"No, I haven't seen it," I replied. "Why?"

"It's a play the studio picked up for thirty-five thousand dollars. It closed out of town before it opened in New York."

"How is it?"

"A piece of romantic crap," he said.

I waited until after lunch to read it, lit a cigar, stretched out on my office sofa, and began. The dialog was only fair, but the background was exotic and intriguing: a north African city with refugees desperately scampering about and unsavory characters engaged in secret activities, some people loyal to Hitler, some to the French. The central character, Rick, an American, runs a cafe called Rick's. He is cynical, disillusioned by the world and by a woman with whom he was once in love but who disappeared without a word and left him embittered. He takes no side in the issues of the day, and when he feels low, he nurses a drink and has his black pianist play his favorite song, "As Time Goes By." One day the woman appears with her husband. They need passports to get out of the country, and she comes to Rick for help. She explains that when she had the affair with him in Paris, she thought her husband was dead. Afterward she learned he was alive and went to him. She still loves Rick, but her husband must be saved. He is an underground fighter and has risked his life to fight the Nazis. Will Rick help or not? (The play, of course, was later transformed into the classic movie *Casablanca*, directed by Mike Curtiz.)

Rossen was right. It was romantic crap, but it had all the elements that used to entice me to movies: danger and intrigue in an exotic setting and a love story with a good situation. I became so excited about its potential that I rushed upstairs to tell the Epsteins about it. I thought it was the ideal vehicle for them. They could give it the kind of dialog it needed to keep it from becoming sentimental. They could make it an adult, timely story set against a turbulent background. More important, the characters were appealing, and I was sure it would be a great success. When I finished my sales pitch, they agreed it was promising but said they were leaving for New York and Washington in a few days and would be gone four weeks.

"Okay, but if I can arrange it, will you do the screenplay?"

"Well, see what you can do about it," was the answer.

It was almost six o'clock when we finished talking. I went to Wallis's office. He was preparing to leave for the day.

"Hal," I began, "I just read *Everybody Comes to Rick's*. It'll make a helluva movie."

Surprised, he said, "No one around here likes it. They think it's a piece of junk."

"It *is* junk but great *movie* junk. And I took the liberty of telling the Epsteins about it. They're willing to do the screenplay."

"They won't do anything. They're going to New York next week."

"I know. They told me. But they've agreed to work on it. If you let me go with them, I promise you that we'll be back in four weeks with a first draft treatment."

"You can't go away. You've got to do *The Hard Way*."

"All right, but will you give me a chance to direct it when they finish it?"

"You're talking about months from now. How can I know what the situation will be? . . . Are you sure they said they'd do it?"

"Definitely."

"Well, tell Irene in the morning, and she'll work it out." (Irene handled the assignments with writers.) After I spoke to her, she had a conference with the Epsteins, and they were set to write the screenplay.

A few days later, Danny Fuchs and I went to work on *The Hard Way*. As it turned out, he was an old friend of Shaw's, but he agreed to the changes that I wanted to make.

According to Jerry, the screenplay was based on a story Jerry had come upon when he was a reporter doing a gossip column in the twenties for the *Daily Graphic*, a New York tabloid newspaper. Jack Pepper, a vaudeville performer, was in the Polyclinic Hospital, recovering from what some said was an attempted suicide, and Jerry went up to interview him. Pepper at one time had been married to Ginger Rogers (who had recently made a hit in a new musical titled *Girl Crazy*). He was a partner of a man named Salt, and they called their act Pepper and Salt. Once while they were playing in Dallas, Texas, Pepper was asked to judge a Charleston contest in which Ginger was appearing. He voted for her, and she won. They met, fell in love, and were married. After they divorced, her career zoomed, managed by her mother, Lela, while Pepper's went downhill. Jerry told the story to Irwin. In developing the screenplay, Irwin changed the story from mother and daughter to two sisters. He also changed the background, fleshed out the characters, and enlarged the love story to include Pepper's partner. (Jerry said he had offered the script to Ginger, who turned it down but observed, "This could be the story of my life.")

What appealed to me was the realism of many of the scenes, especially at the beginning of the story in the mining town. It was also about show business: the struggle to succeed and the frenzied competition it creates. I was particularly interested in the role of the older sister, who epitomized the philosophy that was, and still is, prevalent in our society: look out for yourself and to hell with others. The main thrust of the story, how the older sister escapes her dreary, frustrated existence by exploiting her younger sister, offered rich possibilities for drama.

When it was announced that I was to direct the film, several directors at Warner's wondered why I had accepted it. "It's so downbeat," one of them said. "The older sister is such a bitch," another said. I ignored their reactions because I had begun to realize that I had to make films that appealed to me and hope that an audience would feel the same. I am reminded of what David Lean once recalled that Noel Coward had said to him: "Do what pleases *you,* and if that does not please the public, get out of the entertainment business."

To my surprise, just before we started the film, Warner called me into his office to say that he hadn't realized how little money I was getting ($400 a week) until Jerry pointed it out to him (a likely story!). He proposed that we sign a new deal for another seven years starting at $750 for the first year, going to $1,000 the next, then $1,250, and so on, with $250 raises each year. I thanked him and told him I'd have to discuss it with my agent. (I had three more years on my original contract.) For two years Mike Levee had, presumably, represented me gratis, with the proviso that he would be paid if he bettered my deal. But he said he couldn't because Warner was so stubborn. Now, when Warner's offer came through, I felt I owed it to Mike to tell him. He immediately replied that it was the result of his constant efforts on my behalf. To attach himself more firmly to the new deal, he suggested that I allow him to discuss it with his accountant. The following day he said he would try to get me $1,000 to start and the same for the next two years, which would be a tax advantage for me and would, he believed, make no difference to the studio. He also wanted me to let him handle the negotiations. I took his advice and began paying him his 10 percent.

As Fuchs and I proceeded with making the changes, Jerry and I began casting. Ida Lupino, an English actress who had an excellent reputation as a result of several films at Paramount and had done a good job at Warner's in *They Drive by Night,* was cast as the older sister. I was concerned about her English accent but felt she had the kind of intensity and drive that was needed. Joan Leslie was cast as the younger sister. She was a lovely young actress who had done several good roles at Warner's, including one with Gary Cooper in *Sergeant York* and another with James Cagney in *Yankee Doodle Dandy.* I felt she would be perfect in the early part of our story, when she was supposed to be sweet and innocent, but I questioned whether she would be able to convey the corruption and degradation called for in the latter part. She was too young, and her life experience was limited. When I presented the problem to Wallis, he dismissed me by saying it was up to me to get this quality out of her. (I was not aware that he was preparing to give up his executive producer status for an independent deal at Warner's, which was soon announced.) Joan and I worked hard. It was a difficult, complicated role, and although we may not have succeeded 100 percent, we made a good try. Working with her was a pleasure. Upon reflection, I consider Joan's performance remarkable in that she was barely seventeen years old when we made it. She retired a few years later to become a wife and mother. She is still a very pretty lady and has two grown daughters.

Recently, Joan and I were invited to a showing of *The Hard Way* at the Hollywood Roosevelt Hotel by a group called Cinephile. We had a joyful reunion and were surprised and delighted by the pace and energy of the film and its modernity. The reception was most generous, and afterward Leonard Maltin introduced us to the crowd of over three hundred. We answered questions and later signed autographs for over an hour.

The rest of the cast was ideal. Dennis Morgan and Jack Carson, two friends in real life, played the vaudeville team. Jack played the Pepper role and became the husband of Leslie, Paul Harvey played a producer, Leona Maricle played a playwright, Roman Bohnen was Ida's miner husband, Faye Emerson was a waitress, and Ray Montgomery played a friend of Leslie's. To portray a fading Broadway star who was becoming an alcoholic, I had Gladys George, a superlative actress.

In order to get a realistic look, I wanted to go to Pennsylvania to shoot the mining town, but Warner would not permit us to leave the studio. We compromised and managed to get some footage from a documentary film by Pare Lorentz that gave us the bleak quality of life in such an environment. James Wong Howe was assigned as my cameraman, and he was perfect for the job. After he saw the Lorentz footage, he said he could blend it in with the beginning of our film by setting up smoke pots at the side of each exterior. The black smoke drifting through would match the grimy atmosphere of Lorentz's work. Howe's lighting enhanced the realism of our black and white film.

I insisted that the actors, including the women, wear no makeup during the opening scenes. I wanted the freckles, sweat, and blemishes to come through. At first, Ida hesitated, but she finally went along. After a few days of seeing the rushes, she became concerned because she thought she looked too greasy and messy, and since she was playing a bitter, frustrated woman, began to worry about how audiences would accept her. One day, when I asked her to do something that convinced her she would come across as an unmitigated bitch and that audiences would hate her, she yelled out, "This picture is going to stink, and I'm going to stink in it!" I was confident that what I was striving for was good, and I was not upset about what she thought. But I resented her saying it in front of the crew and the other actors, because we were just getting started, and such a remark from the leading lady would not help the morale of the company.

"Miss Lupino," I said, so that all could hear me, "if you do as I ask, you will probably win some kind of an award for this film." She turned away with a scornful laugh and finally agreed, reluctantly, to do as I asked. From that time on, we were often in conflict. I realized, however, that her fears were somewhat justified, and I explained that I intended to change a later scene and add some lines that would help an audience understand her and even sympathize with her. At times she'd accept my explanation and all would go well, and then suddenly she'd become fearful again.

Midway in the shooting, she received word from London that her father, Stanley Lupino, a well known figure in the theater, had died. She was distraught, and we went through several difficult days with her while we were shooting at an old studio of Warner's in the Los Feliz area, where there was a theater set and stage. In leaping back and forth from the stage to the audience area, where I had set up the camera, I threw my back out and had to be taped up by a doctor in order to keep working. The emotional intensity of the story and my struggle to keep the conflict always at white heat, plus Ida's feelings of insecurity and grief for her father, plus my bad back, caused a strain that often kept us from speaking civilly to each other.

But I still wanted to keep my promise about giving her a scene that would reveal her humanity. I found the moment. She has just schemed to get Leslie into a Broadway show but without Carson, causing a painful rift in the young couple. Dennis witnesses the scene and afterward compliments Ida.

"In a queer, crazy kind of way I admire you," he says. "I like to watch you maneuver. It's like watching the battle games of the Atlantic fleet." He adds that after she has done something particularly mean, he'd like to grab her and kiss her. And he does. Mistaking his compliments for genuine attraction, she responds by dropping her guard; she reveals her yearning for love and affection, returns his kiss with passion, and hopes to make some headway with him. Then he gives her the same line he has fed other girls: "Write me, write me to St. Louis." Furious that she has exposed her softer side, she slaps him hard. Ida played the scene magnificently, and I was certain that the audience would realize she was not just a bitch.

Although Warner complained about my constant rewriting, what he saw on the screen by this time seemed good, so I was allowed some freedom. Of course, you try to get things as nearly perfect as possible before you start, but when you begin shooting, elements sometimes appear that you could not anticipate. If you're smart, you try to adjust to them and make use of them. In one scene in particular I was able to anticipate the need for a change. I look back on it with satisfaction: Jack Carson, playing the Pepper role, is sitting in a dingy little dressing room of a cheap nightclub in Scranton, Pennsylvania. He is depressed because his wife is opening in a Broadway show, whereas he and his partner have gone downhill. We cut to the corridor, where Dennis enters with a girl who also works in the club. As they talk, we hear a shot fired. They rush into the room to find that Carson has killed himself. I felt that Carson's suicide was not properly prepared for and could be made more dramatic. After discussing the scene with Fuchs and suggesting how we might better it, he went to his office and returned two hours later with a scene that was one of the best in the film.

Once, when I was asked to give a talk to a class of forty students about the job of a director, I fumbled about until I began to tell them how we dramatized that situation. It took me an hour to describe the details, but when I finished, the class applauded because it was such a graphic example of how to deliver a scene with maximum effect. We began by shooting over Carson's shoulder as he sits reading a copy of *Life* magazine featuring a cover picture of Leslie, described as a rising

Above, with John Barrymore
in *Counsellor at Law,* 1933

Right, Vincent Sherman,
circa 1940

*All photos are from the
author's private collection.*

With Bette Davis (left) and Miriam Hopkins in *Old Acquaintance,* 1943

As referee between Bette Davis and Miriam Hopkins, 1943

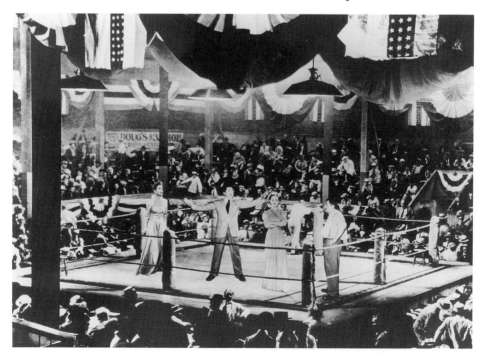

Left, with Ida Lupino during filming of *In Our Time,* 1944

Below, directing *In Our Time.* Ida Lupino on ladder.

Left, with Bette Davis during *Mr. Skeffington*, 1944

Below, with Ann Sheridan during *Nora Prentiss*, 1947

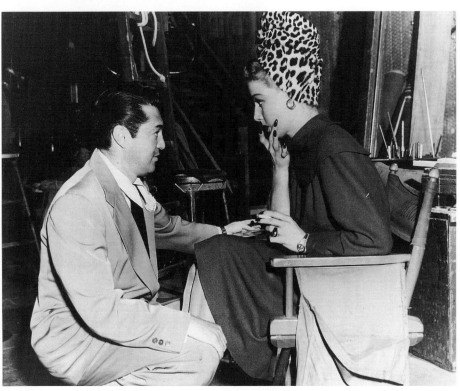

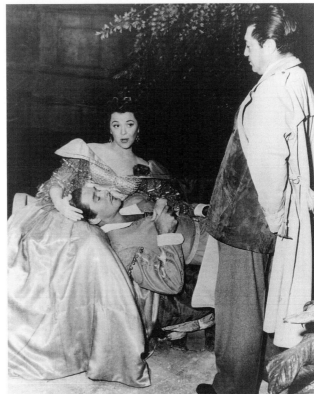

Above, directing Errol Flynn, *The Adventures of Don Juan,* 1948. Jerry Austin at right.

Right, directing Ann Rutherford and Errol Flynn, *The Adventures of Don Juan*

Seated by a huge Technicolor camera with Viveca Lindfors (standing with back to camera), Romney Brent (seated at table), Robert Douglas (standing behind table), *The Adventures of Don Juan*

With Ronald Reagan, meeting British royalty in London, 1949, during the making of *The Hasty Heart*

With wife Hedda and daughter Hedwin, returning to New York after *Mr. Skeffington*

With Joan Crawford
on location for
Harriet Craig, 1950

young star in New York. He gets up as the camera pulls back to a wider angle. We see that he is in his undershirt in a miserable little dressing room, with a Sterno outfit for making a hot drink and a clothesline at the rear, where his washed socks and underwear hang. Obviously depressed, he crosses to a dressing table and begins putting on his makeup. The owner enters and asks where Carson's partner is. Carson replies that Morgan hasn't come in yet. The owner has to tell him that their act isn't working out, and he'll have to let them go. In walks a fellow performer with a copy of *Variety,* the show business paper. He has read an article about Joan Leslie. She's a big hit. He tells Carson he should go to New York and live off the fat of the land. And why not? She's his wife, and he gave her her start. When the owner hears that Carson is the husband of Leslie, he offers to retain him and Morgan, *if he can advertise* that Carson is Leslie's husband. Carson is humiliated and orders both men out of the room. In the corridor Dennis arrives with the girl. As they talk, they hear Leslie's voice from inside Carson's room, as Carson plays one of her phonograph records. After a moment they hear a shot and rush into the room, where they find Carson dead on the floor. The scene ends as Dennis breaks the Leslie record. Carson's suicide, I felt, had been effectively delivered.

One day, while I was on my way to lunch, after we had been shooting for a few weeks, I saw Irwin Shaw walking with Jerry. They did not see me. Later, when Jerry came to the set, I asked him what Irwin was doing on the lot. Jerry regretfully informed me that he had run the first two cut reels for Irwin, who did not like what I was doing with his script and requested that his name be taken off the screenplay. I was upset momentarily, but because I was convinced that what I had shot so far was good, I was not going to allow Irwin or anyone else to discourage me.

Shaw's reaction was not the only negative I had to face. Ida, certain that audiences would hate her, and because of my insistence on maintaining her ruthless drive, didn't even say good-bye to me when the film ended. Jerry, worried by Shaw's withdrawal of his name from the screenplay, as well as Ida's reaction, was depressed. But the climax of negativism came when we ran the first rough cut for Warner at his home in Beverly Hills. He had taken over Wallis's duties and had promoted Steve Trilling, formerly head of casting, as his assistant. When the film ended and the lights came on, Warner uttered a long, mournful sigh. "Boys," he said, shaking his head, "I'm afraid we've got a flop on our hands." I was shocked, especially because, for the most part, I was pleased. I felt we had a film that was realistic, fresh, and unconventional. Jerry was low and glum.

"Why do you say that, Mr. Warner?" I managed to ask.

"Oh, Vince, who cares about these dirty people in the coal mines?" he replied.

I reminded him that what had distinguished Warner pictures in the past was that they dealt with reality. "Besides," I said, "only the first two reels are in the coal mining town."

"That's enough to lose your audience," he replied. "We need to see Ida glamorous before showing the dismal opening scenes." Eventually, we came around to talking about some kind of a prologue, and I suggested that we could begin with Ida, well dressed and beautifully made up, walking dejectedly late at night near the waterfront. She stops as she stares into the East River, then throws herself into the dark waters. This would arouse an audience's curiosity. He liked the idea. I went on. She is rescued, but as she lies in a hospital bed, two police officers try to find out who she is and where she comes from. She is barely able to mutter "Greenhill," as we slowly flash back to the bleak town, and her voice begins to narrate as she recalls her life. After we tell the story, we return to the hospital as she dies. This appealed to Warner. I did not think it was necessary, but I was willing, as was Jerry, to do anything to cheer him up.

The next day I wrote a prologue and epilogue, and Warner approved it. A few days later we shot it. I was able to add an ironic note that related to the title: as the two officers leave the hospital, one of them says, "That's the trouble with them rich ones, they have it too easy all their lives."

Incidentally, the only encouraging word I received before the film opened was from Don Siegel, who shot the montages. He saw the rough cut and told me he thought we had a "damn good film." I was grateful. Don later became a successful director.

Looking back, I think *The Hard Way* was probably the most personal expression of all the films I worked on. It said things about the human condition that are still close to me: that the drive for success in our culture causes us to do things that we might later regret—sometimes too late. I am also most proud of Ida Lupino's performance.

Six weeks later *The Hard Way* opened in New York. I received a phone call from Mark Hellinger.

"Have you heard about the New York reviews of *The Hard Way*?"

"Not yet," I replied.

"They're great. Ida gets rave reviews. One critic compares her to Sarah Bernhardt. . . . Why don't you give her a ring?"

"To hell with her," I said. "She gave me a rough time."

"Aw, come on Vincey, be a good sport." I liked Mark and knew he was friendly with Ida. (Later I learned he was secretly in love with her.) I wanted to please him, so I called. Ida answered the phone.

"Ida, this is Vincent Sherman."

"Oh, darling!" she exclaimed.

From that day on we became good friends and did two more pictures together. The reviews of *The Hard Way* were excellent. All the actors were praised. Carson and Morgan gave outstanding performances, as did Joan Leslie, Paul Harvey, Leona Maricle, Gladys George, Faye Emerson, Bud Bohnen, and the rest of the cast. My confidence was restored and replenished. Interestingly enough, the first two reels of the film, the "dirty people in the coal mines," received the highest praise for its stark realism.

A few months after the film was released, Warner, in a pep talk to the directors and producers in the private dining room, declared, "We don't have to spend three, four hundred thousand dollars to buy a book or a play. We've got people in the studio who can come up with stories that cost nothing and make great pictures." He cited *The Hard Way* as the example. Jerry and I exchanged smiles, remembering when he told us he thought we had "a flop on our hands." Then came the announcement that Ida had won the New York Film Critics Award as the best actress of the year.

Despite the success of the film, Irwin continued for years to express his disapproval. It became sort of a running gag that Fuchs would report to me from time to time as he encountered Irwin. Years later, however, I met Shaw in Rome and we patched things up. To his credit, he admitted that he had been wrong and now appreciated *The Hard Way.*

I must give credit for these successes to Jerry Wald, who initiated the story of *The Hard Way,* to Shaw, who wrote the basic screenplay, and to Fuchs, who made the valuable changes. Peter Viertel did some work with Fuchs, and John Howard Lawson, who was writing *Action in the North Atlantic* for Jerry, helped me with a couple of scenes at the end, for which he received no credit. Leroy Prinz directed the dance sequences and did a fine job; Don Siegel did the montages and Tommy Pratt, the editing. Jimmie Howe was responsible for the camera work. I still enjoy watching *The Hard Way.*

After a revival of the film in 1982, Pauline Kael's 1943 review was quoted in *New Yorker* magazine: "Sharply observed and well acted ... it has unusual authenticity and vitality.... Ida Lupino's English accent comes through at times, but she gives one of the best of her intense, hyper-aware, overcontrolled performances; the conception here justifies much of her tightness and she suggests desperate self-pitying layers under the calculation.... The male leads, Jack Carson and Dennis Morgan are very well directed by Vincent Sherman ... well photographed by James Wong Howe (especially the first sequences in the mill town)." On February 1 and 3, 1991, the film was shown again at the Museum of Modern Art in New York. Pauline Kael's review was reprinted in the February 4, 1991 issue of the *New Yorker*. When Irwin Shaw died, *The Hard Way* was one of the few screenplays mentioned that he had written.

In the picture business you can argue, fight, insult each other, and at times almost come to blows. But if the final result is successful, all is forgiven. Such was my experience with *The Hard Way*, and such is show-biz.

9

Bette Davis

If you are successful in a certain type of endeavor, you are, especially in Hollywood, automatically thought of when a related project turns up. Type casting is the guideline for every job. Thus, after *The Hard Way* and Lupino's glowing reviews, my image changed. I was no longer just a director of melodrama, mostly with men, but was considered capable of handling women and more delicate subject matter. That is the reason, I suspect, that I was chosen to direct *Old Acquaintance*. In fact, Henry Blanke said to me, "You look like a prize fighter, but you are really a sensitive man."

I was on my first layoff—a hiatus between pictures, without pay, usually stipulated in the contract—when I received the screenplay from Wallis's office. It was based on the Broadway play by John Van Druten and was to star Bette Davis and Miriam Hopkins, a successful box-office team the preceding year in *The Old Maid*. Edmund Goulding was again assigned to direct the two ladies. But a note said that Wallis wanted my opinion on the script and even indicated that he was offering to let me direct it. I wondered why, since Goulding was so good at this kind of film and had spent time preparing the screenplay with Van Druten and Leonore Coffee. I was told that Goulding had suffered a heart attack and would be unable to make the film. (Recently, in the Warner archives, a letter from Goulding revealed that he had been irritated by the studio's capitulation to Davis, who wanted Sol Polito as the cameraman instead of Tony Gaudio, Goulding's choice. Whether his heart attack was actual or an excuse to avoid doing the film, I do not know.) I was sorry to hear about Goulding, whom I genuinely admired, personally and professionally.

As for Davis, two years had passed since that day she had tapped me on the shoulder. Her career had taken a big leap forward with *Dark Victory, The Letter, The Little Foxes,* and *Now, Voyager.* But mine had advanced too, modestly, and although the prospect of finally being able to work with her did not have the same degree of excitement as before—I felt that I had learned much in the interim and would be able to contribute as much to her as she would to me—it was still a challenge and stimulating. It also meant that I was now being regarded as one of Warner's top directors.

The screenplay of *Old Acquaintance,* significantly altered from the play, was about the lifelong friendship and rivalry of two women from a small college town, frivolous Millie (Miriam) and down-to-earth Kit (Bette). Kit goes to New York and writes a novel that is praised by critics but is not a commercial success, while Millie remains at home, gets married, and has a daughter. She also writes a novel, which is considered trash but becomes a best seller. Years pass, during which the women go through many stages of jealousy and conflict involving their careers, Millie's daughter, Millie's husband, and Kit's young lover. The two long-time friends are almost torn apart but in the end are reconciled, although left alone with only each other and the memories of their *Old Acquaintance.* I wrote Wallis that the story was pleasant but lightweight, and although I would prefer more realistic material, I would accept the assignment. Preproduction work had already begun: John Loder, under contract to Warner Brothers, was to play Millie's husband; Gig Young, a relative newcomer who had made a good impression in Irving Rapper's *The Gay Sisters,* was selected as Kit's young lover; and Dolores Moran was cast as Miriam's daughter. I preferred Eleanor Parker, but when I suggested her instead of Moran, Warner said to Blanke, "Tell Sherman if she's good enough for Goulding, she's good enough for him!" For a moment I considered testing my strength, but this was my most important assignment to date and a step up into the big league, so I decided it was not worth jeopardizing my position by further arguments. We finished with preproduction, and I met with Miriam to discuss her role. She agreed with my concept and was most pleasant. She was a star and had been in many successful films, including several directed by Ernst Lubitsch, whom I greatly admired. I had not yet spoken to Davis; I learned that she was in Palm Springs resting and that I was supposed to start shooting with Miriam four or five days before Davis arrived. Usually I was given time to discuss the character, makeup and wardrobe with each performer, but because of the sudden decision to have me replace Goulding, and since Davis and Hopkins had already worked together, Wallis saw no need to delay the start. I was not happy about this but again decided not to make waves.

Miriam and I got along extremely well. She was an expert comedi-
enne, and it was a pleasure to work with her. I discovered that she was
from Bainbridge, Georgia, not far from where I was born, and occasionally we indulged in our southern accents. Because I had been an actor, I
sometimes made the mistake of reading a line for a performer the way I
wanted to hear it. (Ideally, a director should explain the intent of the
line and allow the actor to find his or her own reading, but often it was
simpler and quicker to convey the thought by reading the line as I felt it
should be.) In spite of our common heritage, Miriam balked.

"I want you to know," she snipped, "the only other director I'd allow to read a line for me is Ernst Lubitsch!"

"Thank you for the compliment," I replied. "But I have neither his
accent nor his talent!"

The following week Davis paid a visit to the set with her agent, Lew
Wasserman, then head of MCA talent agency. As I finished a scene, I saw
them standing in back at the edge of the set. I walked over, said hello,
and thought surely Bette would refer to our first meeting and say something friendly like "Well, at last we're working together." But she didn't.
As I waited for her to speak before I said anything more, she asked, in a
formal and reserved manner as though we'd never met before, "How are
things going?"

"Very well," I replied. "Why don't you have a look at what we've
shot so far and decide for yourself."

"Oh, may I?" she said, as if I had the power to say no. I was well
aware that this was precisely the reason she'd come to the studio in the
first place. If she didn't like the footage, she had the clout to have me
taken off the film and to ask for a different director. An hour later a
phone call came from the projection room. It was Davis. Her reserve
was gone. Exuberant and enthusiastic, she said she was delighted with
what she saw and asked when I wanted her to report for work. I thanked
her and told her the assistant would let her know. I went home that
night feeling elated and looking forward to the next day.

Bette arrived promptly the next morning, ready for rehearsal. Her
first shot was her entrance in the film, as Kit is discovered asleep on a
train when it arrives in her hometown. I was waiting for her to ask me
how I saw her character, what I thought of her relationship with Miriam,
and how I visualized the entire film. For a while it looked as though she
wasn't interested in my opinion and was going to play Kit as she con-
ceived her. At the last moment she asked me if I had any specific ideas
about her role. I was relieved, since I had a very definite concept of Kit. I

suggested that in contrast to Millie's flighty superficiality, Kit was a relaxed, intelligent, sophisticated, and unpretentious young woman who
looked at the world, and at Millie, with an amused tolerance. She could
see through Millie's often silly behavior yet remain loyal to her because
of their early years together. I added that I felt Kit's personality was very
close to Bette's own. She stared at me quizzically for a moment, and I
thought she was going to say, "How the hell do you know what I'm like?"
But she didn't. I assumed that my evaluation of Bette's self-concept was
fairly accurate. Years later, in a television interview, she was asked if she
had ever played a role close to herself. She named Kit.

I was pleased with her first day's rushes or dailies. Contrary to all
the rumors that she was temperamental, I found her a cooperative, highly
intelligent, and sensitive actress. When I'd ask her to alter a line reading
or a gesture, she simply asked for a logical explanation for the change. In
fact, I enjoyed discussing scenes with her—the intent and psychological
nuances—and felt that we stimulated each other. Uncomfortable watching herself on the screen, she didn't go to see the rushes. When Blanke
came to the set on his daily visit, he complimented everyone. Then he
took me aside. "I don't know what you're telling Bette," he whispered,
"but whatever it is, keep it up. It's the best performance she's given in a
long time. She's simple, warm, and winning. And she's not acting." Later,
I told Bette that Blanke thought she was giving a fine performance, with-
holding his remark about her "not acting."

"That's funny," she chuckled. "I go home every night thinking that
I haven't done anything at all." Tactfully, I indicated that just because she
wasn't playing a highly dramatic, neurotic role didn't mean she wasn't
giving a good performance.

As shooting progressed and the two ladies had more scenes to play
together, I noticed that Miriam became increasingly preoccupied with
where I intended to place the camera. I began also to detect an edge in
Bette's work. When I asked her what was bothering her, she told me
about a conflict that had developed between her and Miriam during the
making of *The Old Maid*.

"You watch her," Bette explained. "She's always pulling little tricks,
trying to upstage me. And she'll do just what she did in *The Old Maid*: as
my character gets older, hers will get younger! You'll see."

Their enmity was well known on the lot, but I hadn't been too
concerned about it. Earlier, when I had discussed the situation with
Blanke, he had advised me to ignore the whole thing and regard it with
amusement as, he said, Goulding had done. Slowly, I began to see what

Bette meant. Although any one of Miriam's actions was trivial, as the days went on her "suggestions" began to mount into a problem. Typically, one day she came to me with an idea. Wouldn't a long cigarette holder capture Millie's superficiality? It seemed appropriate, so I approved the apparently harmless prop. Later I realized I'd made a serious error. At crucial moments in a scene, Miriam would wave the cigarette holder about frantically, drawing attention to herself and away from Bette. Once she went so far as to wave it across the lens and Bette's face while I was shooting over her shoulder onto Bette. When I admonished her, she pleaded complete innocence and, in her sweet southern drawl, said, "Vincent, dear, I was only trying to match up what I did before when the camera was on me."

Each day I'd catch her doing something in a scene to distract from Bette. She'd straighten a picture or rearrange flowers in a vase when she should be concentrating on what Bette was saying to her. Knowing that the eye of the audience always goes to movement, she'd always be ready with some move, until I had to ask her to stand still and stop moving about.

Eventually, her insecurity grew to the point where she tried to influence my staging of scenes. One morning we were about to rehearse a long sequence between Kit and Millie that covered almost five pages of dialog, when Miriam, thinking I was going to put the camera where I was standing with cameraman Sol Polito, made one of her little suggestions. How would it be if I let the two of them feel their way through the scene before I told them when and where they should move? She was hoping, of course, to work out a way for the camera to favor her. Skeptical but curious, I told her that I would be delighted if she and Bette would stage the scene for me. Bette agreed to the experiment. She entered Millie's apartment and, after a greeting from Millie, waited for Miriam to make the first move. But Miriam just stood in the center of the room, her eyes darting back and forth from Bette to me to Sol as we watched the rehearsal. Finally, Bette initiated the action, but each time she would start to move, Miriam would take a parallel step. Whenever Sol and I shifted our position a few inches, Miriam would adjust her stance so that *she* would be in a favorable position. The two ladies played the entire five pages practically riveted to the center of the room. I suppressed my amusement, thanked them, then pointed out that they hadn't made a specific move during the five pages. Bette, realizing it was true, broke into a hearty laugh. Miriam did not find it the least bit amusing. I resumed my job of staging the scene.

As the day wore on, Miriam's insecurity persisted. Bette, usually unconcerned about the camera, began to defend herself. She fought with Miriam point for point to keep equally in view. I was losing my patience with the sparring. In a voice loud enough for everyone to hear, I said, "Ladies, sometimes I feel I'm not *directing* this picture, I'm *refereeing* it!" Bette roared with laughter, which only endeared her to me. Once again, Miriam was not amused. In the days that followed, I was so preoccupied with the conflict between the two ladies that I had no time to think about my growing affection for Bette. I only knew that I felt a genuine artistic kinship with her and hoped she felt the same about me. But I was not sure. She always maintained a cool dignity.

The day for the big scene between Miriam and Bette approached, and as it turned out, the confrontation of their characters bore a resemblance to real life. In the script, Kit finally loses patience with Millie's antics. She grabs her by the shoulders, shakes her violently, then shoves her down onto a nearby sofa, saying, "Sorry, but I've been wanting to do that for a long time," and exits. (In the final film she says only "Sorry" and exits, the rest of the line cut.) I was sure Bette was relishing her revenge. Word about the upcoming scene began to spread around the studio. Stories were also going around about the growing antagonism between the two ladies. Photographers from *Life* magazine asked for permission to come to the set for that day with their cameras. I had no objection, but Warner said it was not his idea of good publicity and denied them access to the set.

The day before we were to shoot the scene, Bette warned me that she was sure that Miriam would try to pull some stunt to avoid doing the scene the way it was written. "The script calls for me to shake her," Bette explained, "and that's exactly what I intend to do!" I reassured her that I would not compromise or hedge the scene. We would play it to the hilt. By now, my sympathies were entirely with Bette. I had seen the pattern in Miriam's behavior. She devised everything she could to take the film away from Bette, including making herself look younger in the film as Bette aged, as Bette had warned me she would do. I spoke to the makeup man. He was trying to control it.

Before shooting began the next morning, I was summoned to Miriam's dressing room. In a pathetic southern drawl, she said, "Vincent, dear, I know Bette is supposed to shake me, but I'd appreciate it if you'd ask her not to be too violent....You see, I slept badly last night, and this morning I have a little crick in my neck." I promised her I would speak to Bette.

When I mentioned it to Bette, she screamed, "I knew it! I knew she'd come up with something!" I calmed her down and told her to do the scene as she felt it and not to worry about Miriam. I rehearsed the dialog and movement very carefully, except for the shaking, praying that we could get the scene with the first take. The moment of shooting came. The camera rolled. All went well until Bette put her hands on Miriam's shoulders. Miriam relaxed her neck so completely that her head began to wobble about grotesquely like a doll with a broken neck. The scene was ridiculous, and as Bette turned to exit, she glanced at me. She was furious. I took Miriam aside and explained that her head wobbling was unnatural and grotesque, that if she would resist the shaking the scene would appear honest. Her reply was innocence personified. "I was only trying to cooperate," she said. After two or three more takes I was finally able to get the scene right.

By the time Miriam was finished in the picture, she and Bette were not speaking to each other. Before she left, however, she said good-bye to me. "I'm sorry if I caused you any trouble," she added. "But because this is Bette's home lot, I was sure you'd favor her over me, since I'm only a guest star." I explained to her that if my own mother was in the film I would not favor her over anyone else. As a director, my job was to favor the film only, not any one player.

Afterward I learned more about Miriam's jealousy and resentment of Bette. Years before, in Rochester, New York, Miriam had been the star of a play called *Excess Baggage,* in which Bette had played a minor role. Later, Miriam played the lead on Broadway in the play *Jezebel,* but it failed. When Bette played the same role in the film version of *Jezebel,* it was a great success, and Bette won her second Academy Award for it. It must have galled Miriam.

At any rate, with Miriam gone, Bette relaxed, and each day was pleasant and satisfying. We had many laughs, and in another two weeks the film was completed. I was sorry to see it end and hoped Bette and I could work together again since I felt there was a genuine bond between us.

I recall only one difference of opinion we had: it was over the last shot in the film. The script called for a tight shot on Bette and Miriam as they offered a New Year's Eve toast to their friendship. Then, according to the script, the camera was to move down to the burning embers in the fireplace and fade out. I felt the camera move was conventional, an obvious ending that had been done many times before. I wanted something that would emphasize the loneliness of the two women. So, as they drank their stale champagne, I proposed to pull the camera back and up as far as the set would permit. (This was in the days before the zoom lens.) Bette, however, preferred the shot in the script. I suggested that we shoot both endings and let Jack Warner make the final decision. Confident that she was right, Bette bet me fifty dollars that Warner would choose the fireplace shot. Equally confident, I accepted the bet. After seeing the rushes the next day, Warner, unaware of the wager, called me to say that he preferred my fade-out. Bette never paid me!

On the last day of shooting, a Saturday, Warner phoned me on the set and requested that, if possible, we finish the film that night, even if we had to work late. I was willing if Bette would agree. (In those days we worked on Saturdays, including almost every Saturday night if there was night shooting. This was so that with Sunday off, the night work would not interfere with the necessary twelve-hour rest for actors between calls.) When I relayed Warner's request, Bette asked, "How late?" I told her it would be midnight or even after. She considered for a moment then, to my surprise, agreed. "But," she added, "I promised my mother I'd spend Sunday with her. She lives on Laurel Canyon, so if you don't mind dropping me off on your way home, it'll save her from having to pick me up so late." I also lived on Laurel Canyon, the Hollywood side. I said it would be my pleasure if she didn't mind riding in my little old Plymouth. Today, a studio chauffeur and limousine would be at the disposal of a comparable star.

We finished the last shot at 2:00 A.M. Sunday. Everyone was tired but relaxed. It had been, except for the tense moments between Bette and Miriam, an amusing, pleasant, and rewarding experience. As we were driving down Ventura Boulevard and approached Laurel Canyon, where a Simon's Drive-In restaurant was still open, Bette said, "I'm starving. Could we stop for a hamburger?" Naturally, we stopped. After the waitress took our orders, Bette turned to me. "Well, Mr. Sherman," she said, her voice lively and enthusiastic, "it's been fun working with you...in spite of the trouble we had with Miriam. But you handled her beautifully, and—I love you!"

"I love you too," I replied, assuming she had tossed the phrase off the way so many people do in our business—a throwaway line that indicates nothing more than friendly approval and is not meant to be taken seriously. Then her voice changed. She became subdued and solemn as she took my hand. "You don't understand...I mean I really love you." To say that I did not understand was a colossal understatement. I was stunned and could not believe that I had heard correctly. How long I paused while trying to think of a reply, I don't recall, but I do remember that I finally muttered, "I'm flattered beyond words."

My shock, when I realized she was serious, was compounded by the fact that not once during the ten weeks we had been working together had she given me the slightest hint that she was interested in me personally. To learn that she approved of my direction was gratifying enough, since she had a reputation for being difficult to please and had worked with several topflight directors, including William Wyler and Michael Curtiz. But to hear her say that she loved me was more than I could have anticipated. Each day that we had worked together, I was drawn closer to her. I enjoyed her sense of humor and hearty laughter, her down-to-earth simplicity and lack of star affectation. She was at the peak of her career, fascinating to watch, possessed of a great vitality and an unusual kind of beauty. She was Hollywood's most provocative actress. In addition, there was something in her eyes that aroused and intrigued me, something sad and unfulfilled, indicating hidden, unreleased pools of warmth and passion.

As we explored the emotions of the characters in *Old Acquaintance,* we had revealed much about ourselves to each other and seemed to be, artistically, blissfully, in harmony. Strangely enough, I had had a premonition long before—from the time I first saw her in *Of Human Bondage* to the films that followed—that if we ever worked together it would be a joyful experience. On several occasions as we were filming, I wanted to tell her how much I admired her and how close I was to falling in love with her. But I refrained—for several reasons.

First, she was married to Arthur Farnesworth, whom I had met and spoken to several times when he came to the studio to pick her up. He seemed to be warm and caring, much better looking than I could ever hope to be, and with his polite New England manners he seemed like a perfect mate for Bette, who was equally New Englandish. And although I was aware that this was Bette's second marriage and had heard the rumor that she had had several love affairs in the past, I had no reason to think that she wasn't happy. Fearful that if I told her how I really felt she might think I was making a pass at her and resent it, consider me arrogant, or reject me and, worst of all, even laugh at me, I said nothing. Second, I too was married—happily—to Hedda, who was modest, devoted, intelligent, and genuinely sophisticated. She had stood by me for thirteen years, in good times and bad. And we had a lovely three-year-old daughter named Hedwin (a combination of the names Hedda and Vincent), whom I adored.

However, what I felt for Bette was something I had never experienced before—a profound kinship of art and soul, a fusion of spirit and emotion. Now, with her declaration of love, I was beginning to think that destiny had taken a hand in our lives. I was stirred and excited, tempted to ignore everything, throw caution aside, take her in my arms, shout for joy, and shower her with kisses. I hesitated because I did not want to behave like some starstruck movie fan. But I did tell her about my attraction to her before we ever met, my disappointment about *Affectionately Yours* (I learned that Wallis had never sent her my letter), and my feelings toward her since we had begun the film—plus why I kept them to myself. We were both amused by our efforts to conceal the truth—our admiration for each other. At that moment, our hamburgers arrived!

While we ate and momentarily relaxed, I asked her about her marriage. She confessed that she was miserable, that "Farney" was sweet but weak and unable to adjust to being "Mr. Bette Davis." He was, she added, equally unhappy, and lately he had begun to drink heavily. I was surprised but relieved to know the truth. I was expecting and waiting for her to ask me about *my* marriage, but she didn't, and that disturbed me. I wanted to be honest with her, to tell her about my dilemma. Instead, she began to talk about some of the amusing incidents that had occurred during the making of *Old Acquaintance.*

It was after 3:00 A.M. when we arrived at her mother's house. We parked at the side of the road and talked for a few minutes about the studio, Jack Warner, and Henry Blanke; then the front door opened, and Bette's mother stepped out onto the front porch in her bathrobe.

"Is that you, Bette Davis?" she called out sharply.

"Yes, Mother," Bette answered calmly.

"Do you know what time it is? Get into this house at once!"

Unmoved, Bette said, "Yes, Mother."

Her mother retreated into the house. I had to laugh. Here was Bette Davis, thirty-four years old, twice married, winner of two Academy Awards, and her mother was yelling at her as if she was fifteen.

"What's so funny?" Bette asked.

"I haven't heard anything like that since high school."

Bette smiled. "Oh, don't mind Ruthie," she said. "She means well."

We talked for a few minutes more, neither of us making any attempt to resolve matters or suggest a course for the future. She had stated her feelings and was, I thought, waiting for me to declare myself. But I was too confused to say anything more than that I was flattered, deeply grateful for her affection, and sincerely drawn to her. After a long pause, she said that it *was* late and that she'd better go in. I kissed her gently goodnight, then gave her another kiss, less restrained.

As I drove home, my mind became a whirling dervish of emotions and questions. If Bette loved me as much as she said, and if I surrendered to my feelings for her, would she ask for a divorce and expect me to do the same? Or was she merely seeking, and would she be content with, a temporary affair? Either way, I felt I was facing the possibility of a momentous change in my life. Divorce or even the rumor of an affair with Bette Davis would catapult me into the news and gossip columns and add a kind of fame and prestige to my name. Was that what I wanted? To become involved with or married to one of the luminaries of tinsel town, find a place in the Hollywood goings-on that Louella Parsons and Hedda Hopper daily publicized to the world? True, I was ambitious, and the glamorous life was enticing, but I was too much of a realist not to know how superficial it was. Instinctively, I rejected it. I wanted to achieve fame and glory through my work, not because I was attached to a famous personality. Those thoughts, however, were of the future. The prospect of being linked with Bette Davis, of holding her in my arms and making love to her was here and now. Both were heady and tempting.

I was in a quandary. But Bette's failure to ask me about Hedda and Hedwin was a major factor. I had introduced her to my wife and daughter once when Hedda brought Hedwin to the studio for a short visit, but it was as though they did not exist or matter to Bette. Did she regard Hedda as merely a simple housewife who would present no problem? Did she think that I would not hesitate to leave Hedda when I had a chance to be with Bette Davis? I had never given her any reason to think that my marriage was not a happy one. Why, then, was she reaching for another woman's husband before she knew his feelings about his wife and child? Her behavior suggested a ruthlessness that I found troubling.

Finally my "Harvey" intruded, that shadowy figure that since my senior year in college had cautioned me to use my head when my heart became excessively exuberant. So, in a vortex of indecision and confusion, I lacked the strength of character to extricate myself. I'd have to wait and see how events shaped themselves.

During the following week Bette gave a wrap party for the crew at a Hollywood nightspot and invited me and Henry Blanke to sit with her. It was an enjoyable evening, capped by her unveiling of a large photo she had had made up of a prize fight ring with Miriam in one corner,

Bette in the opposite, and me in the center as referee. We had a good laugh and made a date to have lunch at the studio a few days later.

The next morning I visited my friends Julius and Philip Epstein, whose office was above mine in the Writer's Building. They had just completed a script of *Mr. Skeffington*. I had read John Huston's version several years before, when he was solely a writer, and I did not consider it a promising project. Having directed *Saturday's Children*, my second film, from a script by the Epsteins, however, had given me great respect for their work, and I asked if I could read *Skeffington*. They gave me a copy, and I finished it that afternoon. I thought it was a brilliant job of storytelling, with great humor, superb dialog, *and* it included an unusual role for Bette. I rushed upstairs to ask if I could show the script to her. The Epsteins agreed, and I phoned her. She too had turned down the Huston version, but she agree to read this one.

She called the following morning. "You're right!" she exclaimed. "It's brilliant. I'd love to do it. I'll call Hal Wallis and ask if we can do it after my vacation." Wallis agreed and named the Epsteins as producers. I was pleased.

At lunch a few days later, Bette told me that she was planning to go to Mexico. She had never been there but had been interested ever since she had played Carlotta, the wife of Maximilian, in the film *Juarez*, starring Paul Muni. I had also recommended a journey there. Then came an unexpected question. "Could you meet me in Mexico City so that we could go on to Cuernavaca, Taxco, and Acapulco for a short stay?" she asked. Until that moment I had never done more than hold her hand and kiss her briefly. Now I had an invitation to deepen our relationship.

In 1942 Mexico was remote and not as popular as today; a liaison might be safe from discovery, and the trip might give us a chance to examine our situation calmly and consider our options without fear. Still, it was a big step, and I thought of what the repercussions might be if we were found out. Already hedging, I said perhaps I could get away for a few days unless Warner insisted that I remain at the studio. I did not tell her that I had never had an affair with a married woman and I hesitated to do so now. It was not that I was so high-minded; it was just that I didn't like the idea of betraying another man. I must also confess that I had no burning desire to just make love to Bette. She was appealing, but the physical act was not really what impelled me toward her. I wanted to hold her in my arms, learn more about her, and tell her more about me. Then we could consummate our feelings. Back in my office I weighed the pros and cons of the situation and recalled that, two years before, I had thought that our meeting was going to lead to something important, but instead it had ended abruptly and left me with the feeling that she had a volatile and unpredictable nature.

The day before Bette was scheduled to leave by train for Mexico with her friend, the Countess di Frasso, I was still uncertain whether or not to accept her invitation to join her there. I knew I would soon have to make up my mind. Once again I reviewed the situation: Bette had been going through an unhappy period in her life and was desperately in need of love and affection. She must have felt that in me she had found a kindred soul. The relationship between a star and her director can become a potent factor in creating intimacy because of the probing of feelings, the warmth and sympathy generated, the trust and reliance developed. I think, too, that initially I earned her respect because I did not attempt to pursue her or make a pass at her. She knew that I was not a Hollywood playboy but a serious, hardworking director who came from the New York theater and had risen quickly from the ranks, qualities that must have appealed to her. So...she thought she was in love. It was ego-satisfying for me, but I wondered whether it was merely a momentary infatuation for her and nothing more. There was only one way to find out—go to Mexico. But should I? I was debating the problem when my dilemma was solved for me. My phone rang. It was Farney, Bette's husband, asking if he could see me in my office; he said he had something to discuss with me. I assumed it was some business matter or that he wanted to ask my advice about a script. I had heard that he was interested in producing a film himself someday. I told him he would be welcome at any time.

A few hours later, in my office, following a moment of small talk, Farney sat, paused for a moment, became tense. Finally he spoke quietly. "Vince, I've been told by friends that you are a decent guy and would not do anything to hurt either Bette or me."

I was immediately apprehensive and made no reply. He continued. "I know Bette is infatuated with you, even thinks she is in love with you. But Vince, you know Bette. She's very emotional and not aware of how bad it could be for both of you if you meet her in Mexico. You're married and so is she, and the press is bound to get ahold of it and have a field day.... So, I'm begging you—don't go! Please don't go to Mexico."

I was dumbfounded. I pretended that his concern was preposterous and asked him who told him all this. He startled me further when he replied that the night before he and Bette had had a fight and that she had blurted out that she was in love with me and that we were going to meet in Mexico. I surmised that they must have had a few drinks before dinner and, in their unhappiness and frustration, were lashing out and trying to hurt each other. Thus, she had exposed what I had thought was our secret.

Farney was such a gentle soul that my first thought was to say something to relieve his agony. I assured him that nothing had happened between Bette and me and that the trip to Mexico was merely conversation. He seemed relieved, and so was I. If I had not considered the possible effects of my trip to Mexico before, the pain in Farney's face made me acutely aware of the damage I might have done to him and others. I also suspected that he had assessed the situation correctly, especially in his reference to Bette's infatuation and emotional excess. When I told him that I understood and had no intention of going to Mexico, he relaxed and, on the verge of tears, expressed his gratitude. In return I asked him to promise me that he would never mention to Bette or anyone else that he had talked to me. "If she finds out," I told him, "she'll end up hating us both." He agreed and said that no one would ever know. We shook hands warmly. He thanked me again and left. I was genuinely touched by his humility and found myself feeling sympathetic. I could never have done what he had done; my pride would not have permitted it. But I could see that he would never have the strength to cope with Bette's powerful personality.

Farney's visit left me shaken. I did not like to think of myself as the subject of a heated conversation between a husband and a wife. And if Bette truly loved me, why would she use me as a weapon against her husband? Nor was I able to dismiss the thought that if I went to Mexico and my wife learned the truth, it might hurt her beyond repair and end our marriage.

When Bette phoned me at the studio several days later from Mexico City and wanted to know whether I was coming or not, I lied. I did not want to disappoint her so soon. I told her I was waiting for an appropriate moment to speak to Warner. In the meantime Jerry Wald requested me for a second film with Ida Lupino, and Warner assigned me to direct her in *In Our Time* with Paul Henreid. When Bette called again from Cuernavaca, I was relieved to have a legitimate excuse not to join her. As always, my work came first and took precedence over everything else. I was also happy to keep my pact with Farney.

I felt sure that after Bette's vacation in Mexico and by the time we were ready to start *Mr. Skeffington* several months hence that her ardor would have cooled and, given the volatility of her personality, her infatuation would have subsided. I felt she'd forget her declaration of love and once again assume control of her emotions. I hoped that by working together in mutual respect and affection we might create a film that would garner Academy Awards for all concerned. I looked forward happily to *Mr. Skeffington*. Neither Bette nor I—nor anyone—could have anticipated what would actually happen.

10

In Our Time

In Our Time **was based** on an original idea of Jerry Wald's as developed by Ellis St. Joseph. The title was an ironic comment on Chamberlain's statement that he was compromising with Hitler and the Nazis only to buy "peace in our time." It was about an English girl (Ida Lupino) who, while visiting Poland with her American employer (Mary Boland), an antique dealer, meets and falls in love with a Polish aristocrat (Paul Henreid). He is equally captivated by her, and they get married. She remains in Poland with him but finds herself in conflict with the feudal thinking of his family. The time is the eve of the Nazi and Russian invasion.

Although it had a number of good scenes at the beginning and received a few favorable reviews, it was not clearly focused, nor was it an ideal subject for film: from midway to the end, it was a series of arguments about the economics and political setup in Poland and was of little interest to American audiences, even though we had the finest cast possible. Alla Nazimova played Henreid's widowed mother; Michael Chekhov played her brother; Victor Francen played a Polish patriot, wealthy land owner, and titular head of the family; and Nancy Coleman played Henreid's patrician sister.

Whatever pleasure I had from the picture was derived from working with the actors. Ida was no longer the hard-driving, ruthless character of *The Hard Way* but a warm, shy, romantic, enchanting young idealist. The range of her talent was immense. Nazimova, with whom I had worked years before when she played the lead in a Theater Guild production of Pearl Buck's *The Good Earth*, in which I played the small role of a Chinese revolutionist, was a joy to direct. She brought to life the confusion and pathos of the aristocracy as it crumbled with the Nazi and Russian invasion. Victor Francen, who once had caused me to weep copious tears in a French film, *The End of the Day* (about an old actors' home), when he delivered a funeral oration about actors at the graveside of Michel Simon, was the epitome of Polish aristocratic hauteur. Michael Chekhov, a nephew of the great Russian playwright, was a fantastic actor and an excellent teacher, as well as a delightful human being. I was fascinated with his technique and watched carefully as he prepared for a scene. Before each take he would walk about, shake his arms as though to loosen up, turn his head back and forth, and hunch his shoulders up and down, all in an effort to relax. Then, as the camera rolled and I called "Action," it was as if he turned on a switch inside and all the elements of his character came together. He sprang to life and became the ironic, philosophical, gentle, sweet uncle. His only problem was the English language. He was not as glib or as facile as he would have liked to have been, but he was a great artist. Nancy Coleman, who was under contract to Warner's, had a most unusual quality and a unique kind of beauty. I thought she had great potential as an actress, but sadly, it was never utilized by the studio. We became good friends, and I still hear from her now and then. She lives in New York and has three daughters. Paul Henreid had scored a hit in *Night Train,* an exciting British film directed by Carol Reed, one of my favorites. Paul was later signed by Warner's and scored a big success in Irving Rapper's *Now, Voyager,* with Bette Davis. Paul also played an important role in *Casablanca.*

Incidentally, that picture, for which I was instrumental in getting the Epstein brothers to write the screenplay and which I had begged Wallis to let me direct, was given to Mike Curtiz. I was disappointed, but Mike was the number one director at Warner's, and I had great respect for him, so I could not object. In a biography of Wallis he says that William Keighley and I turned down *Casablanca.* Maybe Keighly turned it down, but I certainly didn't. Perhaps Wallis felt guilty for not even offering it to me.

Midway through the filming of *In Our Time,* I received a phone call from Bette Davis. She was in New Hampshire at her home, called Butternut, following her vacation in Mexico. She wanted to tell me that she had seen *The Hard Way* the night before at a local theater, liked it, and thought Ida was "excellent."

"Thank you. . . . I'll tell her. She'll be pleased," I replied.

"But I'm jealous," she said.

"Why—what of?" I asked.

"She's working with you and I'm not," she replied.

I was flattered and assured her we'd soon be together again, that the moment I finished *In Our Time* we'd begin work on *Mr. Skeffington.* She said she was looking forward to it. I also told her about the enthusiastic reception of *Old Acquaintance* at the sneak preview and that it was being shown on the Bel Air circuit. This was an exchange of films by top executives of the various studios. They included only the films they were especially proud of. She was happy to hear the news and promised to call me as soon as she returned to Hollywood.

Old Acquaintance was released to generally good reviews and did excellent business. I felt that I had done a skillful job of directing but, as noted before, I was not enamored of it; I considered it lightweight—women's magazine story material. Nevertheless, James Agee wrote in *The Nation*, "The odd thing is that the two ladies, and Vincent Sherman directing, make the whole business look fairly intelligent, detailed and plausible."

With three films in a row that focused on the distaff side of the human condition, and a fourth one, with Bette Davis, in preparation, I was soon called a woman's director. This label clung to me for several years.

The screenplay of *Mr. Skeffington* was a delight: the dialogue was brilliant and the story unusual. It begins just before World War I. Fanny Trellis, an amusing New York socialite beauty, to be played by Bette, lives with her brother, Trippy (Richard Waring), in the family mansion on Fifth Avenue. She is giving a small dinner party for a few friends and admirers when her cousin George (Walter Abel) arrives unexpectedly. She and Trippy greet him warmly. He asks how things are going. Fanny hesitates, but Trippy says he has a good job now—he is working for Skeffington and Company, a successful Wall Street firm. George recalls that it is a Jewish organization, and he's skeptical of Trippy's success. It's obvious George doesn't quite trust Trippy. The dinner is interrupted by a surprise visit from Job Skeffington (Claude Rains), the head of the firm, who informs Fanny and George that Trippy has been writing false orders and has been paid commissions that he is not entitled to. Unless the firm is reimbursed Skeffington will have to go to the district attorney. Shocked and apologetic, George explains that Fanny and her brother are broke and barely able to make ends meet. Fanny is distressed, pleads for Trippy, and begs Skeffington to spare him. Her charm and beauty are so winning that he agrees to forgo his visit to the district attorney. Fanny is impressed by his generosity and his sense of humor.

After he departs, she predicts that he will send her flowers the next day. He does. They meet again and are soon married, although Job knows that Fanny is not in love with him. When Trippy hears the news, he gets drunk because he believes that Fanny married Skeffington only to save him from going to jail. Disgusted with himself and with his sister, he leaves home. Later he joins the French army and is killed in action. Fanny blames herself and Job for her brother's death.

For a while her marriage to Job is shaky, but she becomes pregnant. Afraid that it will affect her beauty, she resents the pregnancy and goes away to have the baby. Skeffington is so in love with her that he tolerates her childish behavior and her preoccupation with her beauty. She gives birth to a baby girl, whom she resents, and returns home. Soon she begins a series of flirtations with various suitors. Job puts up with it for the sake of his daughter. Then Fanny discovers that Job is having an affair with his secretary and divorces him. He gives her a generous sum of money as alimony and goes off to Europe alone, reluctant only to leave his daughter, whom he dearly loves. One of the most touching scenes in the picture is between Skeffington and his daughter, age twelve, as he tries to explain why he and Fanny are having problems.

Years pass. Fanny still tries to appear youthful, but after an attack of diphtheria, she loses her beauty and becomes a recluse. One day George appears and tells her that Skeffington has returned from Europe a broken man, having been tortured by the Nazis, who took everything from him. He adds that Skeffington is downstairs and begs Fanny to see him. She refuses; she cannot bear to have him see her looking so poorly. He pleads with her to forget her lost beauty and do something kind and warm for once in her life. She finally agrees and, fearfully but bravely, goes downstairs. As she enters the living room, where Job is waiting, she steps into a glaring light so that he can see her bereft of her beauty. His hair is white, and he carries a cane. She speaks. He rises from his chair, starts toward her, and trips over a hassock, and she realizes he is blind. Her heart goes out to him. She helps him up and assures him that he is home now and has nothing to worry about. In the past he had said to her that a woman is beautiful only when she is loved. She knows now, and George observes, that to Job she will always be beautiful. End of story.

While doing the final editing on *In Our Time,* I heard that Bette and Farney had returned to Hollywood. I was expecting her to phone me, but she didn't. I hesitated to call her for fear that it might cause a problem. Then came the shocking and tragic news that Farney, while walking down Hollywood Boulevard, had suffered a brain hemorrhage and died shortly thereafter. The newspapers reported that his death was due to an accidental fall during the summer at their home in New Hampshire. I was genuinely distressed and phoned Bette intending to express my sympathy and to ask if there was anything I could do to help, but she was not taking any calls. I understood. There was a quiet funeral service. I sent flowers but did not attend. After trying for several days to reach her by phone and being told that she was still not taking any calls, I stopped phoning.

Two or three weeks later I received word from Warner that Bette had phoned him and said she'd like to get back to work; she thought it would be the best therapy for her. I concurred. He asked me to call her, arrange for a meeting with Orry Kelly to discuss her wardrobe, and make an appointment with Perc Westmore to talk about her makeup.

In view of our past warm relationship, I wondered why she had not called me. If she was genuinely in love with me, why didn't she seek me out for sympathy, or at least respond to one of my several phone calls? The feeling that I had about her unpredictability was revived. Nevertheless, I phoned her home again and gave my name, and this time she took the call. I expressed my sorrow, repeated Warner's message to me, and asked when she'd like to come to the studio. We made a date for lunch the next day. The conversation was short and businesslike, not a word of intimacy. We met in the Green Room and sat at a rear table. She wore dark glasses. Her demeanor was formal, reserved, and I thought I detected a coldness. We spoke quietly, discussed a starting date for *Skeffington,* production problems, casting, and other matters, but not one word personally, as though we'd never known each other. It was a strange experience. I was puzzled but decided that the trauma of Farney's death had so deeply affected her that she could not even mention the closeness that we had achieved in the past.

The meetings with Kelly and Westmore went well. Orry showed us the sketches he had made, from which we selected her wardrobe. Her makeup was to be a demanding job for Perc, not only because of the great number of years covered by the story, but because Fanny was to suffer a bout with diphtheria that would age her twenty years overnight. This was discussed at length. Appointments for dress fittings and makeup tests were finalized, and Bette was ready to return home. I walked her to her car and said good-bye; still not a word was uttered between us personally, but a curious tension lay underneath.

The next day I reported the events to the Epsteins. They made their comments to Orry and Perc. They did not know, nor did anyone else to my knowledge, of my personal relationship with Bette. My anticipation of a happy film was beginning to fade. In addition to Bette's strange behavior, other problems began to crop up: Warner wanted John Loder, who had done a good job for me in *Old Acquaintance,* to play the role of Skeffington. Bette, the Epsteins, and I all wanted Claude Rains for the role, precisely because he was not supposed to be a romantic character. Claude also had the wry and ironic quality called for. Finally, Warner gave in and signed Claude. But a few days before we were to start shooting, he summoned me and the Epsteins to his office.

"Is it necessary that Skeffington be Jewish?" he asked. The Epsteins looked at each other, then at me. We were dumbfounded. We thought at first that he was joking, as he often did, then realized he was serious. We hastened to explain that Skeffington's being Jewish was the heart of the conflict; if that was changed, the script would have to be completely rewritten. That caused him to reconsider. Like most Hollywood executives, he was hesitant about featuring a Jewish hero. He was worried that it would fuel anti-Semitism and the belief that Jews dominated the movie business and were pushing Jewish concerns. The truth is exactly the opposite: Jewish executives have always felt it safer to soft-pedal Jewish issues, and the banks are ultimately in control. When Warner saw and heard our reaction, he finally gave in, and we went forward with the production.

Bette and I spoke briefly a few times, again only about business; there was still never an intimate word. Nor did she ask for a rehearsal or my opinion about how she should play Fanny. I was disturbed and disappointed because I had looked forward to a collaboration in which we would discuss all the artistic problems before we began shooting and come to a mutually agreeable decision. Discouraged, I decided not to argue the point. Imagine my dismay when on the first day of filming, which began in her upstairs bedroom, she read her lines in a voice that was pitched several notes higher than normal. I could not understand why she thought it necessary, nor why she had not had the courtesy to discuss it with me beforehand; to me it was unnatural and unappealing and not my concept of Fanny. When I questioned her, she explained that she felt it made her sound younger and more feminine. I agreed that femininity was a quality that we needed to emphasize, but I indicated that I was not too happy with the high-pitched voice. It seemed false to me; Fanny's femininity and charm should come from within, not from an imposed voice change. She did not offer to change it or even discuss it. I decided I would not make a big issue of it. Gradually, as the day went on, I noticed a distinct change in her attitude toward me. Whereas during *Old Acquaintance* she had accepted and approved everything I suggested, now she questioned and challenged everything. I tried not to worry about it, reminding myself that she was still going through a difficult time, but I hoped that she would eventually relax and become the same delightful, charming person she had been before.

However, as the days went by the situation became more and more tense; whether it was where I was going to place the camera, or the reading of a line, or the staging of a scene, she challenged every step I made. Since I always felt obligated to explain any direction I gave to a performer if he or she asked for it, I often took valuable production time to justify every suggestion I made to her. This happened so much that after a while, when she questioned insignificant details and obviously correct decisions, I wanted to say, "You take care of your acting, and I'll take care of the directing." But I didn't. At last I became so frustrated that I asked Claude, who not only was a friend of Bette's but had also been a close friend of mine for many years, if what I was asking her to do seemed so wrong. He confessed that he did not understand her behavior but assured me that he thought my interpretation of her character and the script was correct. The crew, many of whom had worked with her before, did not understand either. They had never seen her behave quite like this. They asked me repeatedly what was wrong with her. I tried to explain that she was going through a rough time and was not fully responsible for her behavior.

My days were spent trying to avoid confrontations with her. In an attempt to keep the peace, I even resorted to deception: whenever I asked her to repeat a line reading and improve it, she resisted, but I discovered she would accept doing another take if there was a technical problem. So I worked out a secret system with the sound recorder, Bob Lee, whom she trusted, whereby if I did not like her reading of a line, instead of engaging in a long-winded discussion with her, I'd call out to Bob, "How was it for sound?" He'd reply, "I'd like another take if you don't mind; I can get it better." She would do it again, generally better, and it would save me time and energy.

One particular day's argument exemplifies what I was going through: We were doing a scene between Bette and Richard, her brother, in his upstairs bedroom, which is next to Bette's and Claude's. It was just after she marries Skeffington. Her brother hates Skeffington and is violently opposed to the marriage; he reveals his anti-Semitism, then storms out of the room. Bette follows him out to the upstairs hallway and pleads with him to stop, but he rushes down the stairs, throws an angry glance at Skeffington, who is at the bottom, and leaves the house. Claude, seeing Bette distressed, starts up the stairs to comfort her. When he does, she is supposed to turn away and go into *their* bedroom and lock the door, rejecting any sympathy he might offer. We rehearsed the scene, but as Claude started up the stairs, she turned and went back to *Richard's* room. I asked her why she did not go into hers and Claude's room as the script called for. She became defensive and offered several excuses that made no sense to me. I tried to reason with her, but once having taken a stand, she had to stick to it, right or wrong. I knew it was hopeless to continue the argument, but I also knew that in the editing I could remedy the situation. As she turned back, I would cut to Claude before the audience saw which room she went into. I'd keep the camera on Claude as he came up the stairs and went to their room, where the audience would assume she had gone, and where he would find she had locked the door. We rolled the camera, and on the first take, she went to *her* room, as I had asked her to do. I printed the take. My cameraman, Ernest Haller, said, "That was nice of her. She did it like you wanted, after all." I told him that I doubted she was aware of what she had done. He could not believe it. I decided to make sure. I went to her.

"Thank you for going to the right door," I said. Confused for a moment, then realizing what she had done, she gave an embarrassed, nervous giggle and walked away. She could not admit that she had been wrong but instinctively had done it correctly.

Once, while playing a scene with Walter Abel in the study downstairs, where she receives a phone call from one of her admirers, she did not like where the phone was located. She insisted that it be changed. Her reason for it was ridiculous. I pleaded with her to be reasonable and explained that it meant moving a wall and causing an hour's delay. She was adamant. I made the change. Later, when I had trouble making a tie-up shot from that angle and thought she was in her dressing room, I gave vent to my feelings and made an angry remark, threw the viewfinder down, and stalked off-scene. I didn't know she was near the entrance to the set.

"You sonofabitch!" she yelled. "I heard you!" I made no reply, left the stage, and continued toward the men's room, to relieve my bladder and bathe my face in cold water.

I am reminded of two other tense moments. The first one was when the audience first sees her after the attack of diphtheria, when her hair has fallen out. It was one of the few scenes we had not tested. When she appeared in bed, she was wearing a wig, almost bald, with only a few strands of dyed, reddish hair showing. She looked like something to haunt a house. I stared in disbelief at the grotesqueness of the makeup. She realized that I was upset. "Don't worry about it," she said. "My fans like for me to do things like this." What could I say? The second incident was when I noticed that the wrinkles Westmore was putting on her face to age her were becoming heavier each day, to the point of making her appear mummified. To avoid an argument, I spoke to him confidentially and asked him to lighten up on the wrinkles. "That's the way she wants it, Vince," he explained. I told him that even Warner was disturbed by it. He said he would try.

The next morning on the set, I was in my chair looking over the script when I heard her arrival on the stage, always a momentous occasion. The sound of her decisive, clicking heels on the wooden floor filled the stage, came closer and closer, then stopped. I took a sidelong glance and saw her foot tapping the floor near my chair. I looked up.

"How dare you," she said, in a tight, muffled voice, fury in her eyes. "How dare you go behind my back and talk to Perc. Couldn't you talk to me?"

"No," I replied quietly, in an effort to control myself. "I can't seem to talk to you reasonably anymore." We exchanged a few more words. Nothing changed.

After five or six weeks of this kind of strain, going through hell with the constant needless and useless arguments, not sleeping at night, my hair falling out, and more important, not liking what I was getting on the screen with her performance, Hedda questioned me.

"What's going on with you? You haven't been eating, you seem preoccupied, and you look a wreck. What's the trouble?"

I needed to talk with someone, someone I could confide in, so I told her everything: about the night Bette said she loved me, her invitation to join her in Mexico, the visit of her husband to my office and his plea not to go, his death, her strange behavior afterward and, since the start of *Skeffington,* her unfriendly, even hostile attitude.

When I finished. Hedda paused, thought for a moment, then shook her head. "You've got a problem, and I think it will only get worse. My advice for you is to get off the picture, if you can, as soon as possible." I always respected her judgment. She could see through to the heart of a situation almost at once.

The next day I went to Warner's office during the lunch break and asked him to take me off the picture because Bette was displeased with my direction and I was unhappy with her work. He knew about the arguments we were having, had full reports, but pointed out that she had gone through a terrible ordeal lately, and we all knew she was high strung. He asked me to be patient—remain and finish the film. He also requested that I direct a promotional short for the Red Cross, with Bette, the next Sunday. She had agreed to it, and he had set it up with the *Skeffington* crew. Reluctantly, I complied, hoping that by some miracle she would soon change.

At the same time I learned that the Epsteins had become fed up with Bette's petty changes and had told Warner that they would take no further responsibility as producers of the film. As a result, *all* the problems were dumped into my lap.

When Bette arrived on the set Sunday at noon, I suggested how we might do the scene. She wanted a minor change. I agreed—anything to avoid another argument. I do not mind discussion—in fact, I enjoy it. But I do not function well under tension and petty conflict. I have always tried to maintain a relaxed, congenial atmosphere on the set. I want the actors to feel that they are surrounded by friends, that we are all working toward a common goal, and that at all times, anyone (actor or member of the crew) can speak his mind freely. Creativity flourishes best, I think, when there is mutual trust, respect, and affection.

We made the scene, a long shot and a close-up, which took an inordinate amount of time. It was 4:00 P.M. when we finished. I thanked everyone for working on Sunday and sat down in my chair. I wanted to think. The lights were turned off, and I was in the dark, except for one overhead work light. I was trying to figure out how to get off the picture since I saw nothing ahead but more arguments and aggravation. Her petty objection to the simple shoot of a promo was the last straw. I had had it. It occurred to me that I might become ill with my sacroiliac back, from which, since *The Hard Way,* I sometimes suffered. I resolved that I would do something soon, make a move or lift something heavy, cry out in pain, fall to the floor, and be unable to get up, which would make it look legitimate and relieve me of directing the film any longer.

I thought everyone had left the stage, when suddenly I heard footsteps and recognized Bette's walk, again the decisive click of her heels on the floor. I was sure that if I remained frozen she would not see me as she passed, or if she did see me she would ignore me. The sound of her heels stopped. I felt her standing only a few feet behind me; I still did not turn. After a brief pause she spoke, as if she were a New England school teacher demanding an answer from an errant pupil.

"Why are you still here, and why are you sitting in the dark?"

I turned slowly and replied, "Just thinking."

Another pause, and with a slight touch of concern, she said. "Would you like a drink? I have a bottle of scotch in my dressing room."

It was the first intimation since starting the film that she might want to speak to me personally. I hesitated. There was a long pause. "All right," I said and followed her as she went back to her dressing room. Inside, she pulled out a bottle of scotch from a drawer and poured us drinks in paper cups. We sat opposite each other. She lifted her cup, I reciprocated, and we took a drink. I was waiting anxiously to find out why she had invited me. There was another long, awkward pause. Then she began to speak.

"I just want to thank you for not leaving the picture. I know you wanted to, and I don't blame you. I've been a perfect bitch. But I could not help myself. I go home nights and toss and turn in bed, unable to sleep; I can't eat; I feel guilty about what I am doing to you and what I did to Farney."

I stopped her. "Why should you feel guilty about Farney? You did nothing wrong."

Again, a long pause. She looked at me as though she was trying to decide whether to continue or not. Finally, she took a deep breath and began.

"You don't know what happened. On the day I left for Mexico, he took me to the train and helped me on with my things. We had had an argument at home that morning, and he had a few drinks. As I got comfortable in my seat, the train began to move. He started to go, stopped, turned to me, and with a smirk, said, 'Just for your information, Vince is not going to meet you in Mexico. I spoke to him, and he promised not to go.'" She hesitated for a moment, waiting, I thought, for me to reply. But I was so shocked that I couldn't confirm or deny it. "The train was picking up speed," she continued. "I begged him to get off, but he went on, saying he'd had a long conversation with you. I said we'd talk about you some other time but to please get off the train. He lingered and made a few more bitter remarks. I screamed at him to get off before it was too late, and I pushed him toward the platform. Finally, he took the last few steps down and jumped, but by this time, the train was moving rapidly. I ran down to the bottom step, held onto the bar at the side to look back and see if he was all right. He had fallen and was holding his head. I was afraid he was hurt. I wanted to stop the train and get off but was so unnerved I stood frozen, unable to utter a sound or make a move. A porter began to pull me back up into the car and assisted me to my seat.

Gradually, I calmed down, and when we arrived in Mexico City, I called home and was told that he had been shaken up but was not seriously injured."

Again, I tried to comfort her. "It wasn't your fault. You mustn't blame yourself for what he did."

"But don't you see," she said, as her eyes filled with tears, "that's when he hurt his head, which probably caused his death."

I interrupted. "The papers said he had fallen during the summer at Butternut."

"Not true," she replied. This revelation, naturally, was another shock to me. She went on with her confession. "I know I've been taking out my guilt feelings on you. I can't forgive myself. I'm so unhappy—I've been wanting to tell you how sorry I am and how much I appreciate your patience, but I couldn't even do that."

I was grateful for her explanation and was convinced she was telling me the truth. Tears moved slowly down her cheeks, and I was genuinely touched. She had been going through a horrendous experience, the hell of guilt and self-torture. Although it had occurred to me more than once that she was "taking out her guilt feelings on me," I found it difficult to accept because I saw no reason for her to feel so guilty. It also seemed too obvious an explanation. But now she was admitting it. The animosity I had stored up as a result of her treatment of me began to dissolve. I sat next to her, put my arms around her, told her that I understood, and begged her not to worry anymore. I really believed she could not be blamed for her behavior.

I asked her if she'd like to have dinner with me. She said she'd appreciate it. I called my home to say that I'd be late. We went to a quiet restaurant on Ventura Boulevard and sat in a corner where very few diners saw us. As the dinner progressed, the Bette that I had admired and revered reemerged. The bitter tension between us was dispelled, and I began to feel at ease with her for the first time since *Skeffington* had started. The warmth and friendliness that I had once envisioned between us was, at last, becoming a reality.

Overcome by the depth of her pain and the sincerity of her plea for forgiveness, I drove her back to the studio, where she picked up her car and asked if I'd follow her home. I did. It was a large, comfortable house, not far from the studio. She called it Riverbottom. After a drink and more talk, we went to her bedroom, got undressed, turned out the light, and made love. Following a long silence, she turned on the light, lit a cigarette, and went to the bathroom. As she walked away from me, nude, the cigarette in her hand, her two well-rounded buttocks moving in tandem with the Bette Davis hip swivel, I could not help but be amused. I was with her until midnight.

As I drove to my home in Los Feliz, I knew that I had embarked on a complicated affair. It was not the first time I had been unfaithful: once when I was on the road in a play and away from Hedda for several weeks, I had had a casual affair with a young actress who, uninvited, came to my room. When I told Hedda about it, she thanked me for my honesty and promptly seemed to forget it. We made a pact when we first got married, after telling each other all about our past, that we'd always be honest with each other. If either of us misbehaved, we'd let the other know and thereby create mutual trust. We both felt that sex was a human need, like hunger, but not the be-all and end-all in a relationship. If two people genuinely cared for each other, a minor sexual indiscretion should not be allowed to break up a marriage. Since coming to Hollywood, I had only strayed once, again a casual affair, which I told her about, and she seemed to forgive me. But Bette Davis presented a different problem. It was my first affair with a film star, one whom I had admired, was drawn to, and found desirable. It was potentially dangerous to my marriage. She could not be dismissed so easily.

Hedda was asleep when I arrived home. The next morning she joined me at breakfast. "What time did you get home last night?" she asked.

"Late. I didn't want to wake you."

"Well . . . I can guess what happened."

I didn't deny it.

After a pause, she continued, "Of course, that's one way to solve your problem. . . . Just be careful."

I felt guilty but was so amazed by her inner calm that I couldn't think of what more to say. There was no reprimand, no criticism, no fit of jealousy. To this day I don't know how she really felt, whether she was hurt or not, or how much. But I knew, once again, that I was married to an extraordinary woman.

On the set Bette was relaxed and gracious to everyone. So much so that Haller, the cameraman, noted the change. "She's like a different person today, isn't she?"

"Yes, she seems to be," I replied.

Whether it was the psychological relief of her confession or the physiological release of her pent-up sexual energy that was responsible for her changed attitude and performance, I could not be sure. But once again she was agreeable and took direction, and every moment on the set was pleasant. This change can be seen in the park scene, where she and Claude come to see their little daughter, who is with her governess. Walter Abel is with them. He and Claude are both in their World War I uniforms. Bette is light-hearted, tantalizing, and playful—still self-centered but delightfully amusing. She captured the texture I had sought from the beginning—an airy, gossamer quality that would have given the film a better pace and a kind of sparkle. And only I was aware that it was, seemingly, a result of our evening together.

But this euphoria did not last for long: she would be relaxed and pleasant for three or four days, then gradually become tense and difficult again until we spent another evening together. So it went for several weeks. It wasn't long before I began to feel used, as a woman must feel when she learns her lover wants her only for his sexual needs. If it had not been for Bette's seriousness in the matter, the situation would have played more like a comedy by Molnar, the Hungarian playwright, than a ponderous study of a temperamental star for whom sex was an artistic necessity.

Looking back, I suspect that sex had long been a complex problem for her. Coming from a puritanical background, she often relied, I noted, on a few drinks to drop her inhibitions. I recall one particular evening: we were having dinner at Bette's when her mother phoned. Whatever her mother said to her, I only heard Bette reply, jokingly, something about "going to the dogs," which sounded as though she was preparing for an evening of the worst kind of debasement. Once before, when we planned for an evening together, she had referred to it lightly as "going to hell." She was, of course, capable of great passion. Her highly charged, brilliant performances over the years gave proof of it. Yet, because of her repressive nature and her attitude toward sex, I think she rarely allowed herself to indulge her sexuality fully. As a result she was plagued by a misdirected energy that often turned into nervousness, emotional outbursts, and at times cruelty. I say this because she limited her warmth and affection before the deed and afterward seemed only to want to forget that it had ever occurred. It was as though from hunger she had stolen food but felt guilty about it. It's possible that because I was married and had made no commitment to her, her puritanism asserted itself more strongly. Despite these limitations, it would be dishonest of me to say that I did not enjoy being with her. And although I retained some emotional detachment, I was still flattered that she wanted me. I was also grateful to be able to continue the film without too much trouble.

Meanwhile, my life with Hedda and my little daughter was peaceful. Once or twice a week I'd come home late, but Hedda never mentioned Bette, nor did I. Our Sundays were spent pleasantly alone or with friends, and no one knew about my clandestine second life. I cannot say for sure, but I suspect that Hedda, in her wisdom, felt that at the end of the film the affair with Bette would also terminate.

During the last two weeks of shooting, things took a bitter turn: one night, as I was about to leave Bette's house, she suddenly became angry and demanded that I stay the night. I told her that I could not. She continued her harangue, insisting that I get a divorce and marry her. We had discussed it before, and I had tried to explain why I could neither divorce Hedda nor abandon my child. Moreover, the last few months had made it clear to me that although Bette was an exciting, stimulating artist and we had, I think, a genuine affection for each other, marriage was out of the question. I'd be unwilling to contend with her emotional volatility, and she'd be unwilling to live the kind of quiet, simple life that I'd demand. But she did not relent. She got up from her bed and, as I made my way to the front door, followed me, shouting angrily, "You're not going to leave my bed like I was some whore!" I departed quickly. She must have rushed into the dining room, for as I drove away I heard dishes being smashed and her voice cursing me. I dreaded coming to the set the next morning, worried about what she might say or do. But when she arrived she was, to my surprise and relief, calm and relaxed.

The last few days of the film were difficult for both of us. She was in every scene and was tiring; her makeup, as the elderly Fanny, was giving her trouble. The many layers of rubber that Westmore was using on her face, along with the heat from the lights, caused her to perspire freely, which brought on a terrible itching. Toward the end of the day, as we'd complete the last shot, she'd often tear the makeup from her face hysterically.

On the very last day we had a final disagreement during the scene in which she comes downstairs to see Claude and discovers that he has been blinded by the Nazis. It could have been a great moment for her, but I thought it was empty of true emotion and only an indication of what was needed. After the first take, I asked for another. She wanted to know what was wrong. I knew I could not tell her what I really thought as she'd become upset and incensed. So I said simply I felt she could do it better. The next take was still not good, and I was about to ask for another when she protested that she could not do it differently. She was not being defiant but was emotionally drained. I wish now that I had taken the time to let her rest for an hour, talk quietly in her dressing room about what the scene required, and get what I wanted. But I was also drained, physically and emotionally. Our personal entanglement aside, the film was a formidable assignment for her, requiring enormous energy and stamina at a distressing crossroad of her personal life.

When the film ended, we had a wrap party in her large studio dressing room, and I got drunk—the first time in my life. I had to be driven home by my assistant, Bill Kissell. Bette spent the night at the studio.

The next morning when I arrived and tapped on her door, she opened it for me. She was in her pajamas. It was not long before I was in bed with her. Later, we had lunch together, and she went home. During the next few days, I spoke to her several times on the phone. We were both cautious and avoided discussing the future—whether we'd continue as lovers and work together or what.

When I ran the first rough cut of the film, I wanted to make many changes. Her performance was uneven, although there were fine moments and her skill was always present. On the other hand, Claude's performance was, I thought, superb.

A few days later I came upon Bette in the studio as she was about to get in her car. "Well," she said, "I just saw J.L., and he thinks *Skeffington* is great."

"I'm glad," I replied. "There are many good things in it, but I'm not completely happy with it."

"Oh, you're too close to it," she said, and proceeded to tell me that Warner had already decided to do *Stolen Life* as her next film, and we could do it together. At that moment I made a decision that was to end our professional relationship, although I had not intended it to have such an effect. I told her I'd be happy to work with her again if we could have an understanding. She wanted to know what I meant. I explained that it was not possible for me to do good work unless I could do a film as I saw it; we could not both direct.

She took umbrage at once. "Do you want me to be like some little starlet who does everything you tell her to do?"

"I have never asked you or any other performer to do anything that I cannot give you a good reason for," I replied.

She became tense and hostile. "Does that mean you don't want to do *Stolen Life*?"

"Not unless you will let me do it as I see it."

"Okay!" she said, bristling with anger. She got into her car and drove off. I can only think that her ego was such that any hesitation or reluctance to work with her was tantamount to high treason and not to be tolerated. During the following week I was tempted to call her but didn't. I suppose I was unconsciously allowing the affair to end. Shortly thereafter I learned that Curtis Bernhardt was assigned to direct *Stolen Life*. I was neither surprised nor disappointed.

Mr. Skeffington received mixed reviews but was successful at the box office. Despite my reservations about Bette's performance, she and Claude were both nominated for Academy Awards. For some of her fans it has become one of their favorite Davis vehicles. I remember it as a turbulent, frustrating experience; I vowed never again to get emotionally involved with any actress I was directing.

11

Midway

After the heavy going of *Mr. Skeffington,* I wanted a change—something that would be fun to direct and provide laughter for an audience. It turned out to be *Pillow to Post,* a screenplay written by Charles Hoffman, to be produced by Alex Gottlieb. The story was about a young lady whose father sells oil well supplies but because of the war is short of salesmen. She volunteers to help him. He is reluctant to send her into the field, but he has no alternative. She arrives by rail in an oil town where, after seeing a customer, she learns there are no rooms to be had in any hotel or motel, except for servicemen or their wives and families. While waiting at a roadside for a ride into town, she gets a lift with a young lieutenant stationed at a nearby army camp. When he hears her plight he offers to help her get a room by telling the manager of a motel that she is his wife. After registering, he is about to leave when he runs into his commanding officer, who lives in the motel with his spouse and is surprised to learn that the lieutenant is married. The complications that follow, as the young couple have to pretend they are married in order for her to keep the room and for the lieutenant to keep out of trouble with his C.O., offered possibilities for laughs and gags. In the meantime, of course, the lieutenant and the girl fall in love.

I phoned Ida Lupino, told her the story, and suggested she might enjoy doing it. She, too, was ready for a change. She read it and liked it. We talked to Gottlieb, who got an okay from Warner to proceed. I had never done a farce comedy before, nor had Ida, but I was confident we could do it. I had seen her antics when she was in a playful mood, and I thought I knew how to get laughs.

We assembled a good cast: Bill Prince for the lieutenant; Sydney Greenstreet as his commanding officer; Ruth Donnelly as the manager of the motel, with Stuart Erwin as her husband; a gentle, talented black man named Willie Best; also a moon-faced, mischievous little kid whose name I had forgotten—but, when I was doing a TV episode of *Baretta* years later with Robert Blake, he reminded me that he had been the kid. He was, and still is, extremely talented. They were all delightful to work with. Ida was especially winning, and the range of her talent was immense.

The reviews of *Pillow to Post* were only fair, but audiences laughed long and loud, and the film did good business. Ida told me that she received more fan mail from it than from any other film she had ever made. I was gratified later to learn from my cousin Leon Horovitz, who was a captain in General Patton's outfit, that the film came as a welcome relief to American soldiers overseas. Eventually, Ida herself became a director of films and television, one of the few women at the time who was able to break through the gender blockade. She went through some painful episodes in her life, but last year I attended a birthday party for her and found her as bright and amusing as ever. We were good friends, and she was dear to me.

Because *Pillow to Post* did well, Alex Gottlieb, the producer, asked for me when Mike Curtiz turned down doing a sequel to a comedy he had successfully directed called *Janie.* It was also turned down by Joyce Reynolds, the young girl who had created the role and who finally gave up her career in films. I tried to avoid it, but Warner insisted, and the excellent cast finally induced me to do it. Joan Leslie was to play Janie; Robert Hutton, her husband; Edward Arnold and Ann Harding, her father and mother; and Robert Benchley, Hutton's father. Donald Meek appeared in a repeat role, with Mel Torme and Richard Erdman in small roles. A new girl, Dorothy Malone, pretty and talented, made her debut in the role of "the other woman." The film was called *Janie Gets Married,* but the story was less than mediocre, and the film turned out to be a dismal flop.

When I was in the midst of directing it, the war ended, and John Garfield, who had helped create the Stage Door Canteen for soldiers, asked me if I'd direct a stage production of *A Bell for Adano* at the Actors Lab for a group of war veterans. The Actors Lab was a small theater at the rear of Schwab's Drug Store in Hollywood. Leland Hayward, the producer of the play in New York, had given his permission. I told John I'd be happy to do it, even though it meant I'd have to rehearse at night and he'd have to get Jack Warner's approval since I was still under contract. Warner agreed, and it was a rewarding experience for everyone. The reviews were excellent, and the play ran for months. Kent Smith played the lead and was later signed by Warner's to a contract. Other actors also got jobs out of it. During the McCarthy era "red scare," the Actors Lab was accused of being communist led. I was never aware of it, nor did anyone ever interfere with the production.

About this time I read a story, *The Man Who Died Twice,* by Paul Webster, a songwriter. I thought it was a good melodrama and bought it for twenty-five hundred dollars, thinking I might make it sometime in the future, if and when I left Warner's. The trade papers announced the purchase, and the next day at lunch in the executive dining room, where directors had recently been invited to eat for a modest sum, Warner asked me to sit near him. (There was a long table with chairs at each side and one at each end. Warner sat at the far end, where he could observe everyone who entered. Two seats were always left vacant near him for distinguished visitors or whomever he might want to speak to.) He wanted me to tell him about the story I had bought.

He had no patience for a long drawn-out story, so I summed it up as quickly as possible: in San Francisco, a married doctor with two children falls hopelessly in love with a nightclub singer. She is also in love with him, but when he is reluctant to ask for a divorce because he does not want to hurt his wife and children, she can't continue as his mistress and decides to go to New York to pursue her career. He is distraught. Unable to live without her, on the eve of her departure he draws a large sum of cash from his bank account and writes a letter to his wife confessing all, but he can't bring himself to send it. At that moment a patient with a bad heart knocks on his door. Before the doctor can help him, the patient has an attack and dies. The doctor is about to call the police when he realizes the patient is about the same age and height that he is. He sees a solution to his dilemma, exchanges clothing with the dead man, puts a ring from his finger onto the dead man's hand, and transfers his watch. He drives to a cliff, pours alcohol on the man and the car, sets them on fire, and shoves the car over the cliff. He joins the singer as she is about to leave the city, but he does not tell her the truth. She is under the impression that he will get a divorce and they will be married and live happily in New York, where he will continue with his medical practice. For the time being, he explains, until the divorce comes through, he will change his name and they will live in the same hotel but in separate rooms. Later in San Francisco, where it is taken for granted that the doctor died in the earlier accident, his partner learns that he withdrew a large sum of money from his bank account the day before the night of the accident. The police suspect the doctor was being blackmailed for some unknown reason and might even have been murdered. In New York, fear of discovery causes the doctor to restrict his movements. The singer is worried and demands the truth. He tells her. She realizes he will never practice medicine again and she will have to go to work. She gets a job in a new nightclub that her former friend is opening. The doctor becomes jealous and gets into a fight with the owner; he steals a car as the police give chase. He collides with a truck and lands in a hospital with his face burned beyond recognition. The police investigate and learn that he is from San Francisco and his fingerprints were on the can of alcohol that he had poured on the man in the car wreck. They also learn that soon after, at a bank in New York, he had deposited the same amount of money earlier withdrawn in San Francisco. He is charged with murder—his own! Sentenced to death, he can save his life by telling the truth, but he still refuses to hurt his family. He begs the singer to keep his secret. She does, and he goes to his death.

When I finished, Warner thought for a moment. "Could you make it a story for Ann Sheridan?"

It seemed far-fetched. "It's really the man's story, J.L."

"But couldn't you make it her story?" he asked. "If you can and she'll do it, we'll buy it from you and you can make it as your next picture."

I had never considered doing it as an expensive film with a female star, but this was a period when the studio was retrenching and not buying good properties, so I quickly reckoned that I might as well give it a try.

"It might work," I replied, as I realized that I could make the woman's role better and more important. He asked how much I paid for the story, and I told him the truth.

"Okay," he said. "Tell her the story, and if she agrees to do it, we'll give you $7,500 for it. You'll make a fast five grand."

The prospect of working with Sheridan was even more appealing than the "fast five grand," and I agreed. I asked if there were any problems that I should be made aware of.

"No, she wants to work," he said, "but she turned down the last two scripts we sent her, so we had to suspend her. But L.B. Mayer [whom Warner disliked] called me and said Ann's friend, Steve Haneghan [a well-known public relations man], was bad-mouthing us and might buy a few shares of Warner stock so he could attend the next stockholders' meeting and give us trouble. He advised me to make a special effort to put her back to work." I said I understood, and he continued, "Call Bill

Schaeffer [Warner's secretary] in my office. He'll give you Haneghan's New York phone number. She lives with him in an apartment on Park Avenue. See if you can make an appointment with her."

I went into an adjoining room, got the number, and phoned. Ann was most pleasant. I asked her if she'd be available the next evening to talk about a story for her. She said she'd be glad to see me. The next day I flew to New York, and that evening I went to Haneghan's apartment. It was my first time to meet Steve. He and Sheridan were most cordial. I told them the truth about the story and my talk with Warner. I explained that though it was the man's story, I thought we could enlarge the singer's role and make a fairly good movie—one that could become commercially successful. They both sensed that I was being honest with them and gave their approval. Sometimes I lied to the front office to get something I thought was vital for a film, but I rarely lied to the actors and actresses with whom I worked. They had to trust me, and I did my best to deserve it.

Having been saddled with the earthy title of "oomph" girl, attractive, sexy Annie had played various roles in B pictures, then graduated to small parts in A pictures, all the while learning her craft. She became one of the most skillful comediennes in Hollywood (witness her performance with Cary Grant in *I Was a Male War Bride*). She knew how to toss away a line, underplay it with a wry quality, and get the full measure of the laugh therein. She could also play a dramatic role with the best of them. But because she came up from the ranks, her skill was underrated. And what a joy to work with. She was genuine, no affectations and no bullshit; she loved to laugh and have fun and could, when provoked, curse like a sailor on a stormy night. Although many men made passes at her and tried to seduce her, her bedroom eyes causing all kinds of fantasies, to me she was so honest, so lacking in feminine guile, so down to earth, that I came to think of her not as a sexy female but as a good friend or a sister. Hedda felt the same about her.

I had first met Annie when we were both just getting started at Warner's, but for one reason or another I didn't get a chance to work with her. Often, in the Green Room, you could hear her lusty laughter above the noise when someone told her a good joke. And she enjoyed telling a few herself. One day I was having lunch with a friend when Annie passed by, stopped, and leaned over to whisper in my ear: "I had a dream about you last night." Her voice was low and sultry.

"Really?" I queried, anticipating something flattering.

"Yeah," she said, "I dreamt you were a lousy lay."

My face fell, and she roared with laughter as she left the Green Room.

In preparing the screenplay for *The Man Who Died Twice* (later changed to *Nora Prentiss,* the name of the character that Sheridan played), the writer, Richard Nash, and I began to make the doctor and Nora real people, not merely stock characters for the melodrama. The result was that the first two-thirds of the picture became a moving human drama, while the last third seemed, by comparison, phony. I had bought the story originally because I liked the plot, the ironic twist that a man is charged with his own murder, and I thought it would make an effective low-budget film. But as we humanized the people, gave them some depth, the plot became less important. Unfortunately, we were stuck with it and the melodramatic final third. In addition, the doctor's makeup was not as good as it should have been. He was, in my opinion, despite his disfigured face, still recognizable. We should have had a mask made for him that would have changed his face completely and made recognition impossible.

I managed to talk Warner into letting us shoot in San Francisco, which added to the reality of the film. Kent Smith played the doctor and gave an excellent performance, as did Sheridan. She had played this kind of role before, so it was no stretch for her, but she brought it to life. When it was released, the advertising department devised a provocative ad campaign: "Why did Nora Prentiss keep her mouth shut?" Ann went on Jack Benny's radio program and many others in order to promote it. The picture caught on and did better business than expected.

What I got from *Nora Prentiss* was learning how to take cardboard characters and, by examining their motivations and the details of their lives, turn them into human beings. But I also learned that once you have done so, you cannot allow them to revert to the one-dimensional people they were before, just in order to serve your plot. I also learned how to shoot in the middle of a city without letting people know that a film was being made: by concealing the camera in various places; by rehearsing movement and positions with stand-ins while the stars watched from a parked car nearby; or by placing the camera in the rear of a pickup truck where holes for the lens and viewfinder had been cut in flaps at the side.

A successful film, as I have said before, motivates the studio and its producers to look for another vehicle for the same star and director, especially when they get along well. Jerry Wald, as always, was ahead of the others. Shortly after *Nora Prentiss* was released, he informed me that several months before, he had persuaded Warner to buy James Cain's novel, *Serenade,* and would soon have a screenplay ready. "It'll be great for you and Sheridan," he added.

I had not read it but knew about it. "Isn't that the one," I asked, "about a young man who is a singer, made famous by his manager, an older homosexual, but after they become intimate, he loses the masculinity of his voice and runs off to Mexico, where he meets a hooker who restores his manhood?"

"That's it!" he quickly answered. "Dennis Morgan will play the singer and Sheridan will play the Mexican hooker. I talked to Warner, and we both agree it's right for you and Sheridan. What I'd like for you to do is—"

"But Jerry," I interrupted, "how can we possibly do it? You can't even suggest homosexuality in a picture [this was 1946], let alone use it as the basis for a dramatic story."

"I know," he responded, "but don't worry about it. We're changing the manager, the old fag, to a woman."

"So what does one woman do for him that robs him of his masculinity and the other do to restore it?"

"You'll see. I have a good writer working on the screenplay. Warner will let us shoot in Mexico, so I'd like for you to scout locations while we finish the script. By the time you get back, we'll have a completed screenplay." I hesitated and asked if I could read what had been written so far. He begged off, saying that he would prefer I wait. "Come up to the office and I'll give you a copy of the novel. We'll figure out what locations you'll need, and you can arrange to take off for Mexico."

I quickly read the novel. It was well written and confirmed what I had heard about it. I saw no way that the writer could solve the problem. Again I asked Jerry to let me read what had been written so far and discuss it with the writer, but he pleaded with me to find the locations and trust him with the screenplay. Reluctantly, I acquiesced, and together we made a list of possible locations. This was Jerry's tactic to get you tied into a project. Meanwhile, Tenney Wright, the head of production, assigned Don Page to the film as unit manager, Robert Burks as cameraman, and an assistant. Arrangements were made for us to fly to Mexico.

My first visit there had been in 1939. I loved the country and its people, so a return visit, at studio expense, was welcome, although I had a gut feeling it was premature and a waste of money. But Jerry had a theory about the studio; get them to spend enough money preparing a project, and they'd never abandon it. He was often correct.

We had an enjoyable week in Mexico City, marked the possible locations, and spent a lovely evening at the home of Dolores del Rio, that beautiful lady whom Don Page knew from the days when he had been an actor known as Don Alvarado. He had subsequently married and divorced another beauty, who eventually became Jack Warner's second wife. Don was a handsome, charming man, in addition to being a good unit manager.

On our return to Hollywood, Jerry gave me the screenplay of *Serenade*. It was nicely written but unclear about the cause of the singer's breakdown—precisely what I was worried about. After thinking it over, I decided I would have to refuse to do it because I could never explain to the actors or make clear to an audience what the singer's problem was: whether psychological or physiological. Each one would require a different kind of script and would be pale compared to the highly charged premise of the singer's relationship with the homosexual. But the latter was verboten. I knew I'd have to go through a painful session with both Jerry and Warner, but I saw no alternative. The worst that could happen to me would be a suspension for eight or ten weeks.

Jerry's face fell as I told him that I could not make the film, that the story left me confused and bewildered and I would not know how to direct it.

"Warner will hit the roof!" he lamented.

"I know," I said. "You can put the blame on me. But there is an alternative. You have the first draft of a screenplay that I think would make a good movie, and I'd like to do it—and with Sheridan."

Jerry brightened and wanted to know which screenplay I was talking about (he always had a half dozen in the works). "*The Unfaithful*," I replied. "It needs work, but I can see the story, and it won't be difficult to fix. We have the actors here on the lot who would be good for it, so there's no problem."

He was cheered somewhat, more or less agreeable to the idea, and less fearful about breaking the news of *Serenade* to Warner. When he called Warner and said it was important that we talk, Warner was in his private projection room looking at rushes. He asked us to come up at once.

"What's the trouble now?" he said, after stopping the rushes and turning on the lights.

"Vincent doesn't want to do *Serenade*," Jerry said.

"*What?*" Warner yelled. He glanced at Trilling, who was sitting next to him, then back at me and Jerry. "Why not, for God's sake? Vince, you went to Mexico; we spent a lot of money so you could look for locations. What's wrong?"

I knew I'd have to explain my decision carefully, so that he would understand that it was not just for me I was speaking. To make *Serenade* would be a mistake for the studio. I also had a suspicion that Warner did not really know what *Serenade* was about; otherwise he would never have bought the novel in the first place. I took a chance and began.

"Mr. Warner, let me sum up the novel: a handsome young man who has a good baritone voice is discovered and made famous by his manager, a homosexual. But when the singer, out of gratitude, allows the older man to seduce him, he begins to deteriorate, drinks heavily, and eventually loses the masculinity of his voice. He runs away to Mexico, falls apart, and is rescued by a hooker. She nurses him back to health, and after sex with her he recovers his voice. They return to New York. When the old homosexual turns up, she kills him and—"

"Wait a minute!" Warner shouted in disbelief. Then he turned to Jerry. "What the fuck kind of story is that?"

"That has nothing to do with it," Jerry quickly spoke up.

"Jerry," I interrupted, surmising correctly that Warner had neither read the novel nor known precisely what it was about. "That's the novel, that's what the studio bought. It would make a helluva movie if we could do it, but we can't, and the present script will leave an audience confused. They won't know what the problem is. You can't substitute a woman for the homosexual and expect to achieve the same dramatic effect.

Trilling was silent. I was told later that he had had doubts about the project. There was a long pause. Finally, Warner spoke. "What are we going to do about Sheridan?" he asked.

"I have an idea," I ventured. "Jerry has a first draft of a script called *The Unfaithful*. It's a modern story about marriage and divorce. It needs work, but I think it could make a good film and one that Sheridan would like. The plot is Somerset Maugham's *The Letter*."

"But that means we'll have to wait months to get started."

"Not necessarily," I interjected. "If you okay the project, I'll go to work with James Gunn, the writer. We can cast it here in the studio. I'll talk to the actors and tell them the story so that they will know their characters and what happens. We'll start with twenty pages of screenplay, see to it that they have their dialog at least a day ahead, and begin shooting in two weeks."

"Don't be ridiculous," Warner protested. "Sheridan won't start without a completed script, nor will the others."

"Let me talk to her. I'll explain everything, and I'm sure she'll help with the others."

"Okay, you can try, but you're wasting your time," he opined.

Jerry was ready to help in any way he could since it was another Wald project. Back in his office, we jotted down Sheridan for the role Bette Davis had played in *The Letter;* Zachary Scott as her husband, played by Herbert Marshall in the original; Lew Ayres the attorney friend, formerly played by James Stephenson; and we added Eve Arden as a wisecracking friend of Sheridan's.

Afterward, I called Ann and told her what had happened. I assured her that *The Unfaithful* would be a good role for her and asked if she would help me with the other actors. She promised she would. I arranged a meeting in my office, told them the story of *The Letter* and how we were using the plot but changing the background and the intent for *The Unfaithful.* I also explained the problem of getting started in two weeks and assured them they'd have a breakdown of scenes beforehand and dialog at least a day ahead. After Ann told them they could trust me, they agreed to go along.

I had meetings with all the departments involved in the production, and in two weeks we began shooting. Everything went well. There were no delays or holdups. One day Warner called and asked me how I was feeling. I told him I was feeling fine; why was he asking?

"Because if anything happens to you," he replied, "I don't know what we'll do. Nobody knows what's going on except you."

"Don't worry, J.L.," I said, "everything will be all right."

"Are you sure it'll make sense when you're finished?"

I assured him that it would and we'd have a good film. The hours I spent on *The Unfaithful* were unbelievable. After rising at seven every morning, shooting from nine o'clock until six in the evening or after, I'd have a bite to eat at a nearby restaurant and then sit with Jimmy Gunn until eleven and twelve o'clock every night, writing and rewriting and discussing future scenes. On one occasion I had him rewrite one particular scene nine times. He was so incensed with me that he told me later that if I had turned down the ninth version he was going to throw something at me.

We finished the filming at a reasonable cost and with no problems. The actors worked well, and each gave a fine performance. When we took the first cut to Warner's home for him to have a look, he sat quietly all through the running, unusual for him. Then the lights came on. There was a long silence as we waited for his verdict. He excused himself, went to the bathroom, and when he came back, he said to Trilling, Wald, me, and the editor, "Okay, turn it over to music and let 'em get right to work on it." He offered only a few minor suggestions for trims. I was not sure whether he liked the film or was just thankful that, under the circumstances, it was not a disaster. But as we left his home he turned to me. "Come up to my office tomorrow. I want to talk to you."

The next day as I entered his office, completely unaware of what he had in mind, he motioned me to a seat in front of his desk and began.

"Any sonofabitch who can make a picture like I saw last night, without a script, can stay here as long as he likes. Let's make a new deal."

I was relieved to hear that he was pleased and thanked him for his offer, but I wondered if I had not been at Warner's long enough and should move on to another studio. Besides, my contract still had another two years to go.

"Let me think about it, J.L." I suggested.

"All right, but you know, 'the grass is always greener,' or so it seems. Just let me know what you want."

That night I discussed it with Hedda, and we decided that it would be wise to accept Warner's offer since it was well known that if you refused him, he'd give you lousy assignments in the future. It was also true that I felt at home at Warner's. I had been there almost ten years, and we were like a family: every morning in makeup the actors would get together and have coffee and doughnuts or larger breakfasts, gossip, and tell jokes or bitch about the front office. I'd often join them.

What should I ask for? At the time I was earning $2,000 per week, a modest sum compared to the salaries of other directors at major studios. Based on the profitable returns of the films I had made, I decided to ask for a five-year straight deal, no options, with four weeks guaranteed vacation each year, and starting at $2,500 per week, with $500-a-week raises each year, going to $4,000 and continuing to the end of the contract. When I presented the deal to Warner, he replied, "You've got it." I called Hedda to tell her the news; I also called Sheridan to tell her how happy Warner was with the film and thanked her for her performance and cooperation.

The Unfaithful was well received, and Sheridan was happy. We saw each other socially many times afterward but, to my regret, did not get a chance to work together again. But I can never forget her, her warmth, her love of life, and her laughter. I am reminded of one of the hilarious stories she told me: she was in Casablanca on a USO tour with Martha Raye and Ben Blue when they heard about a nightclub that featured two female dancers who, while undulating their nude, bronzed bodies as they moved in a circle around the dance floor, inserted lighted cigarettes in the lips of their vaginas and were so amazingly developed in that area that they were able to draw smoke and expel it as they danced. Wanting to see the show, but not wanting to be seen going into the place, Ben Blue sneaked them in through a rear door and found a booth that was in a dark area. When the two dancers appeared and began their act in a follow spotlight, Ann and Martha hid their faces behind their napkins, except for a slight space to peek through, and they watched with fascination. Ben sat near the edge of the booth and looked on nonchalantly until the dancers came near their table. Then, as they puffed their cigarettes lustily, Ben leaned forward with a cigarette in his hand and said, quite casually, "May I have a light, please?" Martha screamed hysterically and Ann burst into uncontrolled laughter as they both ran from the place.

Several years after Sheridan and I had both left Warner's to freelance, as happens so often in our business, we began to lose touch with each other. Hedda and I were in Europe when we heard the news of Ann's untimely death from cancer.

It is not easy to know what people are like inside since most of us tend to hide our true feelings, but I always felt that Ann was not driven to become a big movie star. It slipped up on her, and she went along with it. She was no intellectual, but she had good sense and a keen instinct about people and events. For a short while she enjoyed the advantages of being in the limelight: money, glory, and pleasant work. Coming from a humble background, she gained inner satisfaction from being a star, and it bolstered her modest ego, but I always felt that she would have preferred being a housewife with a loving husband and children. She was a grand girl, talented, and a joy to know and work with.

12
Errol Flynn

With the completion of *The Unfaithful* and my new contract, I took a few weeks off to relax at home with Hedda and Hedwin and the recent addition to our family, my son, Eric, who was born June 29, 1947. We had hoped for a boy and felt doubly blessed because he seemed to be a perfect baby: he was in good health, rarely cried, slept well at night, and played in his pen quietly for hours. We had sold the house in Los Feliz and bought a three-acre place in Van Nuys on Chandler Boulevard. It was an old New England type of farmhouse, which had five deodar trees on a huge front lawn, a large backyard, twenty walnut trees, grapevines, a swimming pool, stables, servants' quarters, and two garages—all for twenty-six thousand dollars.

The first Sunday there, I took Hedwin, nine years old, and Eric, only a few months old, to the pool. It was a warm day, and the water was cool and refreshing. Hedwin was swimming up and down the length of the pool as I was dunking Eric under the water to get him used to it. Hedda came outside to join us and watch. We were happily enjoying our lives. Suddenly, and for the first time since we'd come to Hollywood, I became conscious of the fact that this pool, this big house, the trees, and this piece of land were mine. Until that moment, although I had been gainfully employed for the past ten years and knew that we were reasonably secure economically, I had never had a feeling of owning anything, of possessions, and certainly had never dreamed of being able to afford a swimming pool or any other luxury.

"It's the strangest thing," I said to Hedda. "I just realized that all this belongs to me, to us. That I have a family, and the future looks good."

"We've been very lucky," she said.

I nodded and silently thanked Providence.

Back in the studio, I was talking to Jerry Wald about doing *Johnny Belinda,* which he was preparing, when I was summoned to Jack Warner's office.

"Errol Flynn has asked for you to direct his next film, *The Adventures of Don Juan,*" Warner said. "Here's a script; read it and we'll talk."

I was surprised because I barely knew Errol and had never been associated with his kind of film. Besides, Jean Negulesco, a colleague, had been working on *Don Juan* for some time. I learned later that it was Sheridan, a good friend of Flynn's, who had recommended me to him. He had been complaining to her that Raoul Walsh, with whom he had made a half-dozen successful films, had double-crossed him in the front office (meaning with Warner). He had made the same complaint earlier about Mike Curtiz, who launched him on his career. Ann told him that I would play straight with him. That's why Negulesco lost *Don Juan,* got *Johnny Belinda* (and did a good job), and Jane Wyman won an Academy Award—while I got Errol.

He was Warner Brothers' biggest moneymaker but at times became the studio's biggest headache. Women and liquor were the devils that tormented him. He could not resist a pretty girl and was constantly besieged by dozens of them wherever he went. He enjoyed drinking as a release from inhibitions, and his escapades were widely publicized. "In like Flynn" became the metaphor for his life. He had reached the peak of his career and was approaching the descent when I was chosen to direct him. For years he had wanted to do *Don Juan,* ever since he saw John Barrymore, whom he admired, play the role in the first film version. Three or four writers and several directors working with Jerry Wald, who was producing it, had spent months and thousands of dollars trying to come up with a screenplay that would be worth making. But they had failed. The studio had just about given up hope of ever doing it when George Oppenheimer, an experienced screenwriter, delivered a script that was finally approved.

It was to be a big production. Enormous sets had been built, and hundreds of expensive props and costumes were being made. In the past I would have been pleased to get such an important assignment. But time, life, drinking, and women had taken their toll on Errol, and he was no longer the dashing young man. Nevertheless, I thought it would be good to do a Flynn picture and try the action and adventure genre. I went to my office immediately to read the script.

George Oppenheimer's name had been on so many scripts at MGM, usually as a final collaborator, that when he was introduced to Dorothy

Parker, that witty lady is rumored to have said, "You mean 'and George Oppenheimer'?"

The screenplay of *Don Juan* was literate and had been written with charm, but it was not what I had envisioned as a vehicle for Flynn. It was like a Disney product, lightweight, humorous, and more like a film for children than for the fans of Errol Flynn. While I sat in my office thinking about what could be done to make it a viable project, my secretary announced that Oppenheimer was waiting to see me. I asked him to come in. He had just been told that I was to do *Don Juan,* and he wanted to have a few words with me about it. George was a sophisticated, articulate, urbane, effete intellectual. He wanted to apprise me of what he was trying to accomplish and hoped that I would agree with his intentions. "This is not a typical Flynn picture," he began. "It's a fairy tale and must be handled delicately, like a piece of Venetian glass."

I wanted to say, "I agree with you, and that's what worries me." But I restrained myself and said I'd certainly keep his words in mind. Late that afternoon I had a meeting with Warner and Jerry Wald in order to give them my reaction.

"The writer says it's a delicate fairy tale, and he's right. If it was a Disney project for children, I'd say 'Good,' but it's Flynn, and I think we need more conflict, action, and humor."

Warner immediately spoke up. "He's right. Errol has got to be either fighting or fucking."

"Moreover," I added, "he is no longer the young lover. He's getting on in years, and I think we have to be conscious of it and perhaps even allude to it humorously." Jerry and Warner thought it a worthwhile suggestion. I asked if we could get another writer for the job because I sensed that George would be reluctant to make changes. Jerry suggested Harry Kurnitz, a writer who had recently been signed by Warner's. He was also from MGM, where he had written many screenplays. I had met Kurnitz in the dining room and listened to some of his stories. He had a dry wit and was a most amusing character. I thought he was a good choice to do the rewrite.

Kurnitz hesitated because he and George were old friends, but he finally agreed that the script needed work and could use a tongue-in-cheek approach. Oppenheimer was disappointed, of course, but he had given us the basic story. Kurnitz set the tone for the picture when he wrote a bit of narration for the opening: in a "March of Time" stentorian voice, a narrator proclaimed that for centuries man had been climbing ever upward and onward in his quest for knowledge, and in England another man was climbing, hand over hand, ever upward and onward, in his search for love. We gradually revealed Errol climbing to a lady's balcony. This approach to the story suffused the film and gave it the humorous quality I felt it needed.

Especially delightful was a scene that Kurnitz wrote after we had discussed a finish for the film: Errol and Alan Hale, his friend, are on a country road, leaving Madrid on horseback, after a turbulent experience in that city. Flynn vows that from now on he is going to renounce adventure and romance and devote his life to serious study. A stagecoach approaches. It stops and a pretty young woman (Errol's wife at that time, Nora Eddington) leans out to ask if this is the road to Madrid. Flynn confirms that it is, and as she leaves she gives him an inviting smile. For a moment he is torn, then decides to pursue her. When Hale tries to stop him and reminds him of his vow to study, Flynn replies, "There is a little of Don Juan in every man, and since I *am* Don Juan, there's more of it in me." He gallops after the stagecoach, and this gave us a perfect ending. The opening and closing set the tone for the picture. In between, I injected as much action and humor as possible.

At the same time I became concerned about the many stories I had heard about Errol: that he was given to drinking on the set, causing delays, and often scheming to get out of work. Raoul Walsh, whom I genuinely admired as a director, cautioned me to be on guard with Errol.

"He's a tricky bastard," Raoul said. "Once we were shooting on a Friday afternoon. He complained of stomach cramps and fell to the floor in agony. He begged us to call for an ambulance to take him home. We did, and as we put him in the ambulance he said he didn't think he'd be able to work the next day and to please let him rest. I told him not to worry. Later, I learned that he had arranged with the ambulance service to drive him to San Francisco that night so that he could see a football game the next day. So watch him." I assured Raoul that I would.

Don Juan was to be in color and the most expensive film I had made so far. Its budget was well over $2 million, a huge sum at the time. The color was of the three-strip type developed by Technicolor. The camera was a big and cumbersome box. I was apprehensive about the entire project and was aware that it would be compared to *Robin Hood*, which had been a great success. Unless I did it well enough, I'd be in trouble.

Edward Carrere, the set designer, was an ingenious artist. He realized that to build a separate set for every room in the palace of the king and queen of Spain would cost a fortune, so he built a series of gray walls and columns, two huge doors, and two stained glass windows, which we shifted about and, with different lighting, converted into the throne room, the king's study, the queen's chapel, the fencing academy, the king's minister's office, various corridors, and the great reception hall with its huge staircase. It was so vast that it occupied a full stage and required 110 electricians to light it.

Together with Jerry, Trilling, and Warner, we cast the major roles: Viveca Lindfors as the queen with whom Don Juan falls in love, Romney Brent as the ineffectual king, and Robert Douglas as the king's evil minister. Alan Hale was to play Leporella, Don Juan's servant, and Ann Rutherford, a young lady smitten with Don Juan. Also in the cast were Robert Warwick, a fine actor with whom I had acted years before in the Barthelmess film, and Jerry Austin, a clever dwarf.

My next task was to confer with the man who was to help me with all the dueling and sword fights, Freddie Cavens, a great fencer and instructor who had worked with Flynn before, and in years past with Douglas Fairbanks. He was picture wise and most cooperative. His son assisted him and was equally helpful. I knew nothing about fencing but told him what I'd like to see on the screen. He and his son not only helped me stage the fights but also did a magnificent job of presenting an exhibition of fencing with boys in the academy where Don Juan teaches. At the end of the film we had a sensational final duel between Flynn and Robert Douglas on the staircase in the great hall. Errol wanted to make a leap from midway up the staircase to the floor below in order to finish off Douglas, but we had trouble finding a double willing to try it. Frank Mattison, our unit manager, said there was only one man in Hollywood who could do it, Jock Mahoney. We called him. He studied the task and agreed to be the double for a hefty fee. The next day I had two cameras ready to photograph him. It was a spectacular leap. I should have shot it in slow motion, to show Mahoney sailing through the air, but I didn't, and every time I see the film I want to kick myself.

My first meeting with Errol was in the costume department. Leah Rhodes had designed some beautiful jackets for him, which came down to a few inches below the crotch line. He wanted them shortened so that the jackets only partially covered his crotch. To keep him happy, we did as he asked, although we had trouble occasionally, especially in side angles: the protrusion was too pronounced, and we had to change the lighting or else I had to stage the scene differently. I asked him once if he could help us in some way.

"What do you suggest, Vince?" he asked.

"Perhaps you could do what I've been told ballet dancers do: pull your thing up and put a piece of tape across it, then put on the jock strap or the cod piece."

"My dear boy," he said, "I've done many things for Warner Brothers over the years, but I'm damned if I'll tape up my cock for them."

The truth is that in the beginning he was most cooperative. He made only one minor request: "My left side is my best side, so whenever you can I'd appreciate it if you'd photograph me from the left." I did.

During the first week of shooting I learned that Errol had a stand-in for his stand-in, and on each of his films he had a coterie of coworkers: several stunt men whom he liked, Sol Gorse and Don Turner, in particular. I knew them, and they were good and reliable performers; he also had various extras and bit players, as well as horsemen and wranglers, who worked on his films. In return he extracted favors from them. One morning I wanted to pick up a shot in the palace and asked my assistant, Dick Mayberry, to get the beefeaters ready. Dick took me aside and whispered that they would not be available until later.

"Why not?" I asked. "Weren't they called?"

"Yes," he said, "but they're cleaning Errol's tennis court this morning."

"And the studio is paying for it?" Dick nodded. I learned that Warner's often indulged Errol in his extra perks. He was also devilish: we were working in a Spanish inn, and a beautiful young girl, who was playing the daughter of the innkeeper, was serving Errol and Alan Hale. She was under contract to the studio, and this was one of her first roles. After we made the master scene, Errol asked me about her. I wondered why.

"She's beautiful," he said, "I'd like to take her to bed. Tell her that I like her and think she could become a star and asked you to make a close-up of her. Then if I score I'll help you get her into bed." I agreed that she deserved a close-up, but my interest went no further. I have no idea whether he seduced her, but I'm sure he tried.

For several weeks at the beginning, he worked hard, was always on time, and we got along splendidly. One morning I was rehearsing a bit of swordplay with two actors when he came to me and put his arm on my shoulder.

"You little bastard, I really love you," he said. Curious, I turned to him. "You know what I mean," he quickly added. "I love working with you." I told him I felt the same about him, and at that time I really did.

"I can love a man," he said, "be a good friend. But I don't trust women." We began to talk, and since he was so friendly, I asked him about his background, his mother and father and his life before he became an actor. He said he loved his father, who was a marine biologist at the Scripps Institute at La Jolla, but when I asked about his mother, I was shocked to hear him refer to her as "a cunt." It was the first time I had ever heard a man speak of his mother so harshly. As for his past, he told me one story that I think is worth repeating. He was in Sydney, Australia, and was broke; he needed a job desperately, when an employment agency sent him out on an interview to some place at the end of a streetcar line. After a half hour of travel he got off, walked into a junkyard, and asked a man who seemed to be in charge about the job.

"See that big pile of bottles?" the man said, pointing to a huge mound of empty bottles nearby. "Some have had vinegar or wine in 'em—you throw them on that pile to your right—the others have had petrol in 'em—throw them to the left; they gotta be washed differently."

"But how can I tell which is which?" Errol asked.

"You smell 'em!" the owner said and walked away.

"How did you make out?" I asked.

"Okay," he said. "Of course, after I smelled a few hundred bottles I couldn't tell the difference. So I just put some on one pile and some on the other. That evening when I took the trolley back home I noticed two women giggling as they looked at me. When I got home and looked in a mirror, I saw a dirty ring around my nose." He also told me a sad story of how he passed a restaurant several times when he was hungry and saw in the window a plastic replica of a blue plate special. The first money he got, he went in and ordered the dish, but it was disappointing. He said he learned two lessons: things are not always what they seem to be, and the anticipation of getting something you've always wanted is often more exciting than getting it.

Before making *Don Juan,* Errol had played the lead in a remake of *Escape Me Never,* a lightweight romantic comedy with Ida Lupino and Eleanor Parker. It was released in New York a few weeks after we began shooting. A friend had told me about some of the reviews, which were unkind to Errol. They said that unless he was on a horse, doing a western with a gun in hand, or playing a swashbuckler wielding a sword, he was a total loss in a film. One morning, I went to his dressing room to speak about an upcoming scene and saw the New York reviews on his table. As I entered, he asked in a lighthearted manner, "Have you read the reviews of *Escape Me Never*?" I told him I had not. "They really let me have it," he added, with a bitter chuckle.

"Why should you care what they say?" I interjected. "You can do things on the screen that no other actor can do."

"Like what?" he asked.

"Errol," I replied, "you are one of the few actors who can wear a costume as if you really belonged in it. And you have a grace and manner and style that no one can match. You handle a sword as if—"

"So what? What's that got to do with acting?"

I tried to explain that it was all related to acting and that he should not demean what he possessed, but it did not console him. I realized then that he wanted, more than anything, to be thought of as a good actor, but to cover his hurt, he pretended most of the time that acting and his career didn't mean much to him. I became aware for the first time that I was dealing with a man who was far more sensitive and complex than I had ever imagined. His devil-may-care attitude was merely a protective coating.

From that day on he began to drink again. He would come in one minute before nine in the morning (to avoid any legal trouble), his face swollen, looking like a skid row bum.

"What do we do today, chum?" he'd ask. I'd tell him, and he'd say, "You get things ready, and I'll soon be with you." He'd go into his dressing room, and a doctor from Glendale would soon arrive. Two hours later Flynn would come out, all dressed and smiles, his eyes flashing and his step lively, as though he was on some kind of high. I never found out what he was being given, but it was obviously some kind of stimulant. His health was deteriorating. Often while doing a scene requiring swordplay, after only ten seconds of dueling, he would have trouble catching his breath. I'd have to cut, let him rest, and whenever possible, cover the action with doubles. He was not really a good fencer, but he was so graceful he could make an audience think that he was a master of the craft.

With each week conditions got worse instead of better: once I had to do a scene with Errol and Robert Douglas in which Douglas proposes that Flynn work with him in his evil plans. Originally, Douglas was to be seated, and Errol was free to walk about the room as Douglas made his proposal. But the morning we were to shoot, Errol arrived with a terrible hangover and was unable to stand, so I had to reverse the scene: have Errol sit as Douglas walked around. I also had to shoot one line at a time with Errol, who couldn't remember more. On location one afternoon, as Flynn and Hale were escaping on horseback from the guards of a jealous husband and were mistakenly greeted by a royal group of soldiers come to escort a young bridegroom to London, the sunlight faded quickly, and we had to do the close shots and dialog in the studio. By the time we arrived, put the saddles on two ladders, and got Alan and Errol on them, they had had a few drinks and I was forced to have a prop man kneeling at the side of each to keep them from falling off. Even while slightly inebriated, they had such a delicious sense of fun and projected such humor that it was difficult to get angry with them.

One Saturday night Errol invited my wife and me to have dinner with him and Nora. They had a lovely home at the top of Mulholland. As we entered the living room, he greeted us warmly and gave us a drink, and we were soon joined by a sweet and pretty little girl about three or four years old.

"Deirdre," he said, "meet Mr. and Mrs. Sherman. He's directing Daddy's picture." She graciously shook hands with us. "Now," he continued, "come here and let Daddy feel your little titties." Hedda was shocked, but Errol's manner was so playful, so utterly lacking in prurience, that no one could take offense. Nora soon joined us and was most friendly. Later we went to Ciro's for dinner, where we ran into Mickey Rooney with his then current wife. He was sitting at a table next to us, and we had an evening of fun and laughter. Hedda thought Errol was one of the most delightful and attractive men she had ever met.

Twice during the making of the film, which took almost nine months to complete, Errol told us that he was ill and had to take time off to recover. The first time, we had to shut down the production for several weeks while he went to the desert to rest. This was legitimate, and he came back refreshed. The second time he "fell ill" was phony; we learned later that a helicopter had landed on his tennis court, picked him up, and taken him to La Jolla, where he joined his father in a short expedition to the waters off Baja California to photograph the mating of the whales.

When he returned from the second illness, we were supposed to complete a sequence in a large fencing academy where Don Juan was employed by the queen to teach youngsters. Such a long time had elapsed between the first scene and the second that some of the boys had grown out of their costumes, which had to be altered. Each day Errol provided us with an amusing experience. Once, two coarse-looking but sexy young women appeared on the set, guests of Errol's. He barely acknowledged them but told them to sit. Soon after, he asked me what I planned to do when we finished for the day. I asked why, and he replied, "I've got these two girls—maybe you'd like to come up to the dressing room with me afterward and get your joint copped."

"Errol, . . . when I'm finished shooting for the day, I'm so tired I just want to go home, have dinner, and get into bed. I don't know how you can even contemplate anything else."

"Oh, I just lie there and read the trades while they work on me," he said.

Even with all the delays and problems he caused me, I could not get angry with him. He was, I felt, a deeply troubled soul who was suffering from a variety of complexes—at times, a kind of arrested development, which manifested itself by his attempts at childish humor and games. One time my assistant told me that Errol had asked to speak to me in his dressing room. I went in and found him sitting, completely nude, except for a small towel over his lower section. He started asking me questions about the scene we were to shoot. As I was answering him, he slowly removed the towel and my eye was caught by an enormous phallus, twelve inches long, nestled between his legs. I stared in amazement, and he roared with laughter. He had had Westmore, of the makeup department, fashion it for him out of plastic material.

"Let's get Alan Hale in and try it on him," he suggested. Alan was called, arrived, and stood in the doorway as Errol began: "Alan, Vince and I have been talking about the scene and we were wondering if there was another way we might do it?" As Alan started to offer a suggestion, Errol again slowly removed the towel from his lap. Alan glanced down and with hardly a blink said casually, "I'll take a pound and a half." We laughed, and that was Errol's fun for the day.

A man who has the classic Don Juan complex is supposed to be unsure of his masculinity and need constant reassurance, so he attempts to seduce every woman he comes in contact with. I suspect Errol was a victim of this kind of anxiety—especially toward the latter part of his life—which was probably brought on by his drinking. Also, I think that his basic distrust of women, and perhaps even secret hatred of them, often motivated his desire for oral sex; he gave me the impression that he considered it a form of debasement for a woman.

Only once during the production did I lose my patience with him, although there were times I thought I could no longer take the endless delays. I had caught a bad cold and was running a fever but thought if I was careful it would soon disappear. I dressed warmly, took aspirin, and reported to the studio. When Errol arrived I told him I was not feeling well but did not want to hold up the shooting because we were already so far behind schedule. He looked worse than I did; he went to his dressing room, and his doctor arrived. At 9:30 I was ready to shoot and asked Dick to tell Errol. He did, and I waited for one hour for him to come out. When he didn't, I became so angry that I told Dick I could wait no longer but would have to go home. He should call production and say that I was ill. I left the set and drove home. As I arrived, my wife came out to tell me that Errol had just called to say that he had had no idea I was so ill and was sorry if he kept me waiting. I returned the following day, and we continued working.

Afterward, Jerry told me that when I went home, Warner called Walsh to take over, but Errol objected, and the set was closed for the day. Jerry also thought that Errol felt guilty and would behave much better for the rest of the film. He was right. Errol did not hold us up any longer. Still, I was happy when *Don Juan* ended. At least a half dozen times during the filming, Warner phoned me to protest the delays, and his anger grew with each day. "You tell that son of a bitch that he's costing us a fortune, and I'm not going to put up with it." After the fourth or fifth call, I was so tired of hearing his complaints that I spoke up. "Mr. Warner, I have to work with Errol, and my job is to get a good performance out of him. That means I have to keep on friendly terms with him. You are the one who pays his salary, and you are the only one who can discipline him. Why don't you talk to him?"

"I will. . . . I'm not afraid of him." He hung up. But I recall only one occasion when Warner phoned Errol on the set. Whatever Warner said, Errol's replies were not polite.

At the end of the film, we ran a rough cut for Errol, and he was pleased. He thanked me for my help and gave me a gold cigar cutter. When I showed it to Raoul Walsh, he was surprised. "He's the tightest bastard I ever worked with," he said.

Although *Don Juan* had been an ordeal for me, I learned much from it: the value of color (it was my first), as well as which colors blended and which ones clashed; how to plan and execute duels, stunts, and various types of action sequences; and the technique of pageantry. More important, I came to know an unusual and interesting man. Looking back, I feel sure that Errol wanted more than anything else to be respected as a serious artist, which, except by a few ardent fans, he never achieved. Yet, he was a much better actor than he was ever given credit for. Today, however, his performance in *Robin Hood* is appreciated.

In my effort to understand him and the cause of his self-destructive habits, I questioned a friend of his, who told me that Errol had once suffered a mild case of tuberculosis and had a heart condition, which led him to believe that he was destined for a short life. If true, it could be the reason for much of his behavior. But I suspect that part of his attitude was the result of a cynicism that he developed toward Hollywood and the life he saw around him. Recall his early struggle to make a living and achieve recognition, then his meteoric rise to stardom, with men clamoring to get close to him and women trying to get into his pants. It is not easy to handle such a great change or to know the feelings of a young man who, from being a nobody and penniless, suddenly becomes famous and in a relatively short time is being paid five thousand dollars a week. There has to be a feeling of guilt, a doubt that he is worth so much. And hidden deep inside, from earlier years, a nagging touch of low self-esteem.

He has been accused of being bisexual and having affairs with men, which I doubt. But if he did, it was only because he was ready to try anything once. True, there is in the Don Juan character an incipient homosexuality, but he was certainly not a practicing homosexual. As for the allegation that Errol was a Nazi spy, William Donati has written a refutation of the charge in a book titled *My Days with Errol Flynn,* coauthored by Buster Wiles. I must add that I never once heard Errol make a racist or unkind remark about any ethnic group. He knew that I was Jewish, and his relationship with Jack Warner was a love-hate affair.

With all the grief and cost overrun on *Don Juan,* the moment Warner saw the first rough cut of the film, he took out a page ad in the trade papers complimenting Errol on his performance. The picture opened in New York to good reviews and was a moderate success in this country, but a huge success in Europe, where the Don Juan legend is more familiar. I was told that at one time it was playing at five different theaters in Madrid.

Errol had been discovered at Warner's. They made him an international star, and his pictures earned millions for the studio. He was also paid one of the highest salaries in Hollywood. He lived an uninhibited life and died at the age of fifty, looking years older. I was directing a film at Warner's when J.L. invited me to join him and a group from the studio who were going to attend the funeral service at Forest Lawn. A limousine drove us over. When we arrived I noticed dozens of benches on the outside of the chapel, where they were expecting an overflow crowd. But the vast public that Errol attracted in his heyday, both to his films and in person, had not yet shown up. Inside, not even the chapel was filled. Only a small gathering of studio executives and a few producers, directors, and actors who had worked with him, plus a handful of friends, were in attendance.

Warner delivered the eulogy. It was short and dignified. In his heart, although he fought with Errol constantly, I think he admired him, with his free spirit and defiance of convention. He referred to him as "the

Baron." When we came out, the extra benches were still empty. I felt it was a depressing end to a glamorous and exciting career. But I don't think it would have depressed Errol. It would have confirmed his cynical attitude toward Hollywood, a fickle public, and justified his contempt for the myth of being a movie star.

13

London

Big sets, crowds, costumes, sword fights, stunts, and the palace intrigues of Don Juan had preoccupied me for months, and I longed for a simple story that explored only the human condition. I remembered that the studio still owned *The Hasty Heart,* a play they had bought months before that I liked. When I asked Trilling why it was not being made, he said there was a feeling that no one wanted to see a war film. I tried to convince him and Warner that *The Hasty Heart* was not a war play but a human story with the war merely as a background. I begged them to let me make it, but they turned me down. Instead, I was asked to do a film that was later titled *Backfire.* I had read the original story when the studio first bought it, but I found it confused and pointless, and I vowed to keep far away from it. Tony Veiller was the producer. I told him how I felt, and he agreed that work on it was necessary. He was putting two bright writers, Ivan Goff and Ben Roberts, on the screenplay, and I would have a chance to talk with them.

That weekend I invited Goff and Roberts to my house to see if we could simplify the story and make something out of it. They were intelligent and talented, but after several hours of discussion, I concluded that it was an impossible task and that I would have to withdraw from it. I advised them to do the same. Their answer was that they were just getting started, needed the job, and would have to do the best they could with it. When I told Warner I could not do it, he urged me to reconsider. "I know it's not a great story, but I've got six actors sitting around doing nothing but picking up their checks. I have to put them to work; so do me a favor: make the picture and do the best you can. I'll do you a favor sometime."

The actors who were "sitting around doing nothing but picking up their checks," who finally appeared in *Backfire,* were Edmund O'Brien,

Gordon MacRae, Virginia Mayo, Viveca Lindfors, Dane Clark, and Richard Rober, all talented and anxious to work. I could appreciate Warner's problem and said, "I'll do it, but it'll put me into a hole, and I'll need something to pull me out. If you let me direct *The Hasty Heart* afterward, you've got a deal."

He thought for a moment. "All right, but you'll have to make it in London. It won't cost as much over there, and maybe we'll get our money back." This was the period of blocked funds—pounds earned by American pictures that could not be taken out of England but could be used for productions in England. I was happy to get a story that I liked, for a change, and I looked forward to my first trip abroad. As for *Backfire,* despite the fact that Goff and Roberts did a noble job with the screenplay, and the actors were good, and we even received fair reviews, my prediction was correct: it was not a success.

The day after I finished it, Warner called me into his office to talk about getting *The Hasty Heart* started. "You'll make it at ABPC [Associated British Pictures Corporation] in Elstree. It's just outside of London. We own 40 percent of the company; we're supplying the script, the director, and some of the actors; they'll supply the studio, the production facilities, and the rest. They'll release it over there; we have it here. We don't want to spend more than $1.2 million on it, and we want to get started as soon as possible." It was always this way: pressure to start, and the moment you started, pressure to finish, then pressure to start another. I had only two requests: instead of flying, I wanted to be allowed to go by train to New York and by boat to London, which would give me a few days of needed rest. He agreed to both.

Before I left, he gave me final instructions: "ABPC is being run by a lawyer, Robert Clark. He's smart but doesn't know much about making pictures. Just don't let him interfere. If he gets in your way, let me know or talk to Jackie [Warner's son]. He's in London and can help you. Use him as much as possible." I was glad to hear Jackie would be available.

The Hasty Heart was set in a hospital in Burma during World War II. In one of the wards several young men are recovering from wounds: two Englishmen, an Aussie, an American who volunteered, and a Basuto African. An English nurse looks after them. The colonel in charge, after a brief inspection, tells them that he is assigning a young Scot to their ward. He was wounded the day the war ended, and they had to remove one of his kidneys. He has recovered from the operation but can only live a short time with the remaining kidney. He hasn't been told the truth yet and has no family, but the colonel wants him to spend his last days among people who will be sympathetic. They seem like a warm and friendly group, and that's why he has selected them. They understand and promise to do their best. The American is skeptical. His grandfather was a Scot and impossible to live with.

When Lachie, the young Scot, is brought to the ward, he is angry because the colonel will not let him go home or tell him why he is being kept in the hospital. The men understand, but he is a pain in the neck; he resists their efforts to be friendly and reveals his distrust of people and alienation from the world. They are ready to give up, when the nurse pleads with them to be patient. Eventually, after their repeated efforts to win him over, Lachie succumbs, and his attitude changes. He responds to the men, falls in love with the nurse, and proposes marriage. She agrees, and for the first time in his life, he is happy and at peace with the world.

Then the colonel is ordered to tell him he can either go home or remain in the hospital. He demands to know why he is suddenly given the choice, and he is told the truth, that he does not have long to live. When he learns that the men already knew, he is convinced that they were friendly to him only because they pitied him and that the nurse agreed to marry him for the same reason. He becomes hostile and bitter again, tells them off, and decides to return to Scotland. Only when he is given proof that they had genuinely come to like him, and the nurse explains that there is pity in every woman's love and that if he leaves, he faces dying alone, does he reconsider and decide to remain.

I asked Warner who he had in mind to play the Scot.

"You'll find someone over there," he casually replied. I was amazed that the most important decision—who would play Lachie—was so lightly dismissed. However, I was so excited about seeing London that I gave it no further thought. Hedda was also looking forward to joining me with the children as soon as I got things organized.

In November 1948 I left Los Angeles. Four days later I was in a stateroom on the promenade deck of the *Queen Mary*. The first night out, as we ploughed through heavy seas, I thought of how my parents had crossed the Atlantic years before in the steerage section of an old ship and how their son was now traveling. I marveled again at the change that had taken place in one generation and wished they could see me now.

The nights and days passed quickly. I did little more than eat and sleep and think about *The Hasty Heart*. We landed at Southampton, where I was met by Jackie Jr. in a limousine. He could not have been more gracious. On the drive to London, while he was giving me a rundown on ABPC and describing life in England, I caught glimpses of the countryside that reminded me of the novels of Thomas Hardy. As we approached London, I saw streets and buildings that recalled Charles Dickens. I was put in a room at the Berkeley Hotel near Piccadilly until a suite at the Savoy would be available.

That evening Jackie and his wife took me to dinner at Les Ambassadeurs, a club where, I was told, one could eat better than at most restaurants. Soon I was to discover that the food situation in London was dismal. Everything was rationed, and what was available was of poor quality. English cooking, at the time, was bland and dull. Potatoes and brussels sprouts were a daily offering, and the bread tasted like a combination of sawdust and cornmeal. Only when I was invited to someone's home did I have a really satisfying meal.

The effect of the war was still visible: a pile of rubble near Piccadilly where once had stood a house of worship; a building at a corner standing alone, all the buildings around it having been blown away; and here and there fire-gutted homes—grim reminders of a tragic time.

Soon after my arrival I went with Jackie to the Warner Brothers offices in Wardour Street where I met Arthur Abeles, a handsome young man who had once been an actor in a Warner Brothers film in the thirties. He was in charge of distribution and was obviously a success at his job. Afterward I was taken to Golden Square to meet the executives of ABPC, including Robert Clark and Warner's American board member C.J. Latta. I also met a debonair gentleman named Alex Boyd, who was a kind of liaison between the Americans and the studio. They were all gracious and courteous, and I found Robert Clark, whom Warner had cautioned me about, to be a charming Scot with a droll but delightful sense of humor. He assured me that he was ready to help me in any way possible. My next meeting was with Bob Leonard, the casting director for ABPC, whose office was in London. It was through his efforts that I was able to find the actors I needed. We became friends.

In good weather, Elstree was a forty-five-minute drive from London, and I enjoyed the ride out, where I saw another part of London and its suburbs. The studio was small but well organized. I met Vaughn Dean, the production manager, Terence Verity, a talented young scenic designer who was to do the sets for *The Hasty Heart,* and a few other members of the staff. I soon became aware that many of them were Scots. Their soft burrs were not always easy for me to understand. The same was true of the Cockney accents of many cab drivers and workmen, but I gradually became attuned to the different rhythms and accents.

Within a short time after my arrival, I was shifted over to the Savoy

Hotel, where a suite that had been occupied by George Cukor was to be mine for the next few weeks. My first day was an embarrassment. I moved in just before noon and quickly put my things away; after lunch with Bob Leonard I returned around four in the afternoon. When I went to hang up my jacket, I found that my two suits and my dinner jacket were missing, along with two pairs of shoes. Alarmed, I called frantically downstairs. They calmly suggested that probably the valet had taken them to "tidy them up a bit." I felt foolish.

My second faux pas was the next morning. I decided to have breakfast in my room. I ordered an egg with bacon, toast, and coffee. When the waiter entered, dressed in livery, he spread a white linen cloth on a table and offered me a serviette. He brought an enormous silver tureen to the table and lifted it to reveal a sad looking little egg and two shriveled slices of bacon. I could not help but laugh at the incongruity of such an elaborate service for such a pathetic bit of food. He was offended, and later I understood why. The English people had gone through hell during the Battle of Britain and were still suffering from the effects of the war. For me to find such a shortcoming amusing was neither polite nor in good taste.

Here I must make a confession: prior to my stay in London, although I had sympathized with the British during their brave resistance to Hitler and his Luftwaffe (ably described in radio broadcasts by Ed Murrow), I had no particular love for them. I had the impression that they were haughty and snobbish, lived off the exploitation of their colonies, and still foolishly supported their monarchy. But as I worked with them and came to know them, I made a complete turnaround. I found them to be loyal, courageous, and perhaps the most civilized people on the face of the globe.

Once I was settled at the Savoy, it was arranged for me to meet the press, during which time I was asked to talk about plans for *The Hasty Heart*. I had by then been informed that Warner was sending over Ronald Reagan to play Yank, the American in the film, and Patricia Neal, a Broadway actress under contract to the studio, to play the English nurse. I learned also that before my arrival a test had been made and sent to Hollywood of Gordon Jackson, a young Scot, as a possible Lachie. I was waiting to hear Warner's reaction and to see the test myself as soon as it was returned. The meeting with the press went well, and I met several London film critics—an intelligent, dignified, knowledgeable group.

Following this, a cocktail party for me was arranged at Elstree to meet all those who would be involved in *The Hasty Heart* and some of the actors under contract. Before the party I received a long distance call from Warner telling me that they had seen the test of Gordon Jackson and found him to be a very good actor, but he asked me to try to find someone more likely to become a young leading man. Later, when I saw the test, I realized that he would have been perfect as Lachie but was basically a character actor. At the party, while I was at one end of the bar talking to Robert Clark, I spotted a nice-looking young man at the other end, and I wondered if he might be an actor.

"Yes," Clark answered. "He's under contract to us."

"How is he—has he done much?"

"He's played a few small roles. We pay him forty pounds a week. [The pound was worth about $2.80 then.] Would you like to meet him?" I said I would, and he sent someone over to fetch Richard Todd. I asked him if he knew *The Hasty Heart*. "Yes, indeed," he said, with a slight Irish lilt. "I once played Yank in a little theater production. Would you be thinking of me for a part?"

"Possibly. Do you think you could do Lachie?" I asked.

"Oh no, the man you want is Gordon Jackson. He's a real Scot and a fine actor."

"Yes, he's very good, but why don't you come to my office here at the studio tomorrow, and we'll talk about it." I liked Todd's look. He was short of stature but had a good, strong quality, and there was something fresh and attractive about him. The next day, after reading a few scenes with him, I felt that he could play Lachie. I had him coached by a Scot for a few days on his accent, then made a test and sent it to Burbank. Soon I received another call from Warner. He approved of Todd.

My days were filled with casting and production problems and a few minor changes in the script, with which Tom Morrison, a writer for ABPC, helped me.

Two weeks before we were scheduled to start, Ronald Reagan and Patricia Neal arrived. Both were given suites on the floor at the Savoy that I was on. I was pleased to see them and thought they'd be ideal for their roles. I had known Ronnie for years, but it was my first meeting with Pat. She was not only a lovely young woman but also, as I soon learned, a fine actress.

One evening I had dinner with Reagan, and we spent some time talking about the past. He had recently been divorced from Jane Wyman, and I could sense that he was deeply hurt by the way things had gone for him, both in his career and in his personal life. He and Jane had had various problems that they were unable to resolve, and she had asked for the divorce. As for his career, he was unhappy with the roles he was being given and had hoped to play Lachie in *The Hasty Heart,* but Warner had assigned him to Yank. I tried to comfort him by telling him that some of his problems with Jane were common to many marriages and that I was sure he'd eventually meet a woman with whom he'd fall in love and be happy. I also tried to convince him that the role of Yank was a good one. He seemed inconsolable, and I was genuinely sorry for him. To me, he had been a most likable human being and a pleasant, agreeable actor. He was also, for years, a fellow Democrat and a strong Roosevelt supporter. As we talked, however, I began to detect a change in his political beliefs, a shift to the right. He knew my feelings, which were to the left of center, but for the moment we were tolerant of our differences.

Before production started, I was invited by Danny Kaye, whom I had met at Warner Brothers when he was making *The Inspector General,* to a party celebrating the unveiling of his wax figure at Madame Tussaud's gallery. Many film and stage stars were there. Danny's picture *The Secret Life of Walter Mitty* had been playing for six months in London, and I was told that he was so popular he could have been elected to public office.

One evening I was having dinner at a cafe with Peggy Henderson, who was in charge of wardrobe, and said that I could not understand why Americans complained about the London weather. I was comfortable wearing my California clothes. But after dinner we had to wait outside an unusually long time for a taxi, and a cold dampness crept through my thin underwear. I was seized with a violent chill. My teeth were rattling when Peggy dropped me off at my hotel. I rushed upstairs and got into a hot tub. The next day I purchased some "woolies" at Simpson's and prepared myself for the coming winter. I also found an apartment in a building at Edgeware and Marlyebone that would, I thought, be good for my family.

We began shooting a few weeks before Christmas. The cast consisted of Alfie Bass as the orderly, Marion Crawford and Ralph Michael as two Englishmen, John Sherman (no relation) as the Aussie, Orlando Martens as the Basuto, and Anthony Nichols as the Colonel, in addition to Todd, Reagan, and Neal. Arrangements were made for a chauffeur to pick up Reagan and Neal at the Savoy, then Todd at his digs, then me at the apartment. We rode together each morning to the studio.

The first day of shooting, we began rehearsing at 8:30 with Alfie Bass, the orderly, making an entrance in the hospital ward to wake the men, who were still asleep in their beds. Alfie was a bright young actor who quickly grasped what I wanted, and I gave him the freedom to improvise and add any English phrases that fit the scene. A half hour later, when the long sequence was well rehearsed, I called for a finder, gave starting marks for the camera, suggested the lens we should use, where to lay the dolly tracks, and when to make a move. The crew stood by, silently watching. When I finished, there was no comment; no one asked any questions or made any suggestions. They set about to do as I wished, but I was not sure whether they approved or disapproved, or if their silence was English reticence. It was a sharp contrast to Hollywood, where I'd be inundated with questions and suggestions, whether accepted or not. I did feel, though, that I was on trial, that everyone was questioning why an American director had been sent over to do a film about a Scot. It was understandable, but I could do nothing about it except direct the film to the best of my ability.

At ten o'clock, after the lighting was completed and we had had a final rehearsal, I turned to my assistant. "I think we can try a take now." Just then all the lights went out except for a work light high up above.

"Did a transformer blow?" I asked him.

"No . . . tea, governor," he replied. And then I learned that every morning at ten a woman brought a tea cart in. All work stopped while the crew had their hot tea and a sandwich, which took about twenty minutes. The same routine took place around four in the afternoon. I was surprised that no one asked the director if they could stop. My assistant took me aside. "The electricians are tough, mostly reds," he whispered. Reagan thought such behavior was rude and inexcusable. I withheld my comment for the moment. Later, I learned more about the unions, the workmen, and their relationship to the studios.

Meanwhile, I participated in the tea drinking and ordered a cheese sandwich. The tea was good but the sandwich was a heavy biscuit with a slab of cold, hard cheese inside. I wondered how the men could eat it. After a while, when the weather really got bitter cold, I was one of the first to inquire about the tea wagon. I also learned to eat and enjoy the cheese sandwich. It stuck to your ribs and helped withstand the chill of winter. The first week of shooting went smoothly except for one day when Pat Neal got terribly upset. It was my fault: I had been told that a nurse in the British army was an officer, a member of the QAIM, or Queen Alexandria's Imperial something-or-other, and that although she might be friendly and joke with the men, she would also, in contrast to an American army nurse, be more reserved. It was this quality that I wanted to get from Pat, which was a subtle and difficult shading. After several scenes, during which I cautioned her and repeated a few takes, she broke down and began to cry, saying she could not give me what I wanted, and that I should find an English girl to do the part and let her go back to Hollywood. We stopped shooting for an hour while I tried to assure her that she was doing a fine job and that perhaps I was overemphasizing the importance of the matter. She calmed down, and I discovered she was highly sensitive and a little insecure. (I learned much later that she was also lonely for Gary Cooper, with whom she had fallen in love while they were shooting *The Fountainhead,* although he was married at the time.)

We continued shooting, and after the film was released, she was pleased with her performance and thanked me. Pat went on to give many fine performances, including her role in *Hud,* for which she was given an Academy Award. Her life has been filled with tragedy, but she has faced it with courage and guts. I have always admired her.

Just before Christmas, Hedda arrived with the children. For the first few weeks they were thrilled, and I was happy to have them with me. Hedda got ration books and learned where to shop for various items—a different store each for vegetables, meats, canned goods, and bakery products. I understood why England was said to be a nation of small shopkeepers. We were allowed only a small amount of meat per week, but Hedda managed to make a delicious stew and different kinds of soups, so that I had a hot meal waiting for me every night when I came home. We were also lucky enough to find a sweet little woman, Peggy O'Neill, whose husband was a postal carrier, to clean the apartment and help with the children.

On Saturday nights Hedda and I went to the theater, which we both enjoyed immensely. We saw some good plays and some fine acting, and we enjoyed the routine of the ushers serving hot tea and biscuits at our seats between the acts. One of the memorable evenings was when we saw *The Browning Version* and *Harlequinade,* written by Terence Rattigan, whom I later met. They both starred Eric Portman, who gave great performances.

On Christmas day we had a party at our apartment, which was attended by Ronnie, Pat, Richard, and other friends. Robert Clark sent a greatly appreciated case of Mumm's champagne. The rushes of the first week's work were sent to Hollywood for viewing. Satisfied with what he saw, Warner cabled that it was not necessary to send any more.

Everything was moving along smoothly: the crew was polite and dignified, carried out every order I gave, and accepted without ever a question every suggestion I made, but I was still uncertain how they felt about me. One day, two of the property men had to move a heavy table. Without thinking about it, I gave them a hand to hurry things along and made a joke about having a union card. When I returned to my chair, Wilkie Cooper, the cameraman, with whom I had become friendly, leaned over and whispered to me. "That was very smart of you."

I didn't know what he was talking about and looked at him questioningly. "What do you mean?"

"Helping the boys with that table. . . . No English director would do that."

"Why not?" I asked, and he went on to tell me about class differences in England, which I had heard about but had not yet come upon. To me such feelings were strange. I have respect for anyone who does his or her job well, whether it's sweeping the stage or the most highly skilled technical work. If I ever lose respect for a person, it is because he or she is a bad worker with no sense of responsibility. But all the people on *The Hasty Heart* did their jobs well and conscientiously.

The winter of 1948-49 in London turned out to be one of the worst in over twenty years. Each day it seemed to get colder and colder, with the fog heavier and thicker. On several occasions, when we were shooting in the compound and it was supposed to be suffocatingly hot, the actors were dressed only in their shorts, but it was so cold that they all wore heavy bathrobes while rehearsing. As soon as we were ready to shoot, they slipped them off. We quickly sprayed perspiration on them and rolled the camera. Often, when we had a long take, I could see the goosebumps slowly rise on their arms. The moment the take was okay, they got back into their bathrobes, and there were no complaints.

It was a different story with me and Hedda. The children became ill with bad colds. I tried to find grapefruit or oranges for them, but citrus was scarce. Finally, I was able to buy some oranges on the black market (the first and only time I ever did) through one of the members of the crew. But to this day I do not know whether it was the shortage of food, or the weather, or my preoccupation with the picture that produced the friction that eventually arose between me and Hedda. Toward the end of January, with the children still indisposed, Hedda became irritable and nervous, and the arguments between us increased. At last she decided to return to the warmth of California and the comfort of our home in Van Nuys. I was sorry to see her and the children leave, but under the circumstances, I thought it best.

Despite all the problems, the film went well. The actors were a joy to work with. I was confident we'd have a good picture.

In the past I had learned that each film dictated its own style. In *The Hasty Heart,* Lachie's conflict was not only within himself, but also, and primarily, with the men in the ward. The more I kept them apart, yet in the same frame, the greater the tension, and more effective the film became. It was for that reason that I gave Lachie a bed in the foreground away from the others, but I could still hold him and the men in the background together in the same shot.

My relationship with most actors had always been good, and although the scripts I was assigned to do were often less than what I would have liked, the performances were always credible, and I was never ashamed of any of them. Unfortunately, toward the end of *The Hasty Heart,* I encountered a situation that was disheartening. All through the shooting I had tried whenever possible to feature Reagan—first, because he was doing a good job, and second, because I knew he was unhappy and I wanted to cheer him up. Then came the day for his big scene. Lachie, after he learns that the men knew he was going to die and thinks that's why they were nice to him, becomes embittered and flings away a string of beads that Blossom (the black Basuto) has made for him. Ronnie, fed up with Lachie's behavior, grabs him by the arm, twists him around and lambasts him for his ornery behavior. He angrily points out that the Basuto did not know he was going to die because he doesn't understand English. He made the beads for him because he liked him. It was a well written scene with a long speech by Ronnie, delivered in heat, and it was a climax in the film. He delivered it letter perfect, as usual, but as he rattled it off I suddenly felt it was a memorized speech and lacked the inner truth necessary. When he finished and the take ended, there was silence, a tense moment. I think he was expecting everyone to applaud. When they didn't, he was disappointed. He also looked at me questioningly, wondered why I had not yelled "Print!" and, as I usually did, complimented him. I was trying to think of how to tell him what I thought without hurting him, because most actors want and need approval and are hypersensitive to criticism.

"It was very good, Ronnie," I said for all to hear. "But I have a suggestion." Then I took him aside and quietly told him I thought that the speech was a little too rapid, that perhaps he could break it up a bit, get more out of it, without losing its dramatic build. I did not want to say that in places I felt it was just words without emotion. He seemed miffed and said he didn't think he could do it any better. I said I was willing to print the take for him to look at with me, but I'd like for him to try it again. He agreed reluctantly but always behaved like a true professional. After two or three more takes, I had what I thought was a good scene—not as good as I would have liked, but I did not think it wise to keep repeating it. From that time on I sensed a change in Ronnie's feelings toward me. It's possible that he was also annoyed with my attitude toward the crew, with whom I had become friendly and he disapproved. But now and then during the shooting, I was able to talk to some of them and learned why they felt and acted as they did.

"I guess we *are* a bit tough," one of the electricians said. "But you don't know what it was like in the past. We'd get up at 5:00 A.M., travel an hour and a half or two by bus to get to a studio where we had been told there was work, and then when we arrived we would be told there was *no* work. It was a wasted day and wasted money for bus fare. Now the shoe is on the other foot." I asked about their wages and learned they were much below the scale of the Hollywood workmen. I do not mean to imply that the men were mistreated at Elstree. I'm sure that management was as good as at any other studio, if not better, but like all studios, they were out to make a profit, and certain practices were followed.

When we finished shooting, Ronnie, Patricia, and I decided to give a farewell dinner party for the cast and crew and for several executives, including Robert Clark, Vaughn Dean, and Alex Boyd. At the end of the dinner, speeches were called for, and good feelings were expressed all around. A spokesman for the crew, in a Cockney accent, concluded with, "And I just want to say that if management treated us like Mr. Sherman did, there'd never be any problems between us." He got a big hand and sat down. I appreciated his kind words but regretted any embarrassment to the management, who had treated me so well.

Before the evening was over, I was presented with an antique Scottish "skene-dhu" (a small double dagger once used at banquets) that I still treasure. Attached to it was a silver heart with the following engraved on it:

> Here's tae ye
> Wha's like ye
> Damned Few
> And They're A' Deid

Ronnie and Pat returned to Hollywood, and while I waited for the editor to prepare a final cut, I had a few days off. Jackie Warner and Barbara were going to Rome for a short visit and invited me to join them. I was ready for a change.   Rome, the eternal city, was glorious. I felt comfortable and at home with the Italians at once. They were warm and friendly. We stayed at the Hassler Hotel at the top of the Piazza de España and went to dinner the first night at Paseta's in the Piazza Navona. As we entered, I saw to my right a large table laden with a variety of mouthwatering hors d'oeuvres. I could not believe it—in Italy, which had lost the war, there was so much to eat, but in England, which was triumphant, there was so little. I never learned why, but that night I ate like one who had been starving for six months.

As we were leaving, I saw Cheryl Crawford, my friend from the Theater Guild days, at a table. It had been years since we had last met. We talked for a few minutes, and she asked if I'd like to go with her the next day to a party that a friend was giving for Tennessee Williams. I was grateful for the invitation and met many people there, including Williams. However, at most parties, including this one, you rarely get to know anyone, and the conversation is given to small talk.

That same evening, as I returned to the hotel, I heard a voice cry out, "Hello, Mr. Sherman." It was a young lady who had once been a student in a class in which I delivered a series of talks on directing. She was just passing the hotel when she saw me. She had been in Rome for several months working in the film industry but was free at the moment and offered to show me about Rome. Since I wanted to give Jackie and his wife time to be alone and a break from having to drag me along everywhere they went, I accepted her offer, and for the next two days she took me to various places that I wanted to see. She also told me about a film that she thought was great but had flopped in Italy. It was called *Bicycle Thief,* directed by Vittorio De Sica, a well-known actor. I told Jackie about it, and through the Warner Brothers office we were able to get a print. I thought it was great. It had been made, according to my friend, for eighty thousand dollars. When I asked whether she could explain why it flopped, she replied that Italians thought it was a commonplace story that they came upon every day. Not so for America, I thought, and I urged Jackie to buy it for the studio. If Warner's did not want it, I thought he and I should buy it together. Jackie found out that it had already been bought by someone in New York.

I was especially interested to learn that many of the actors in it, including the man who played the lead, were not professionals but had been picked up by De Sica on the streets. Before we left Rome, I realized that almost everyone in the city had acting talent. I had never seen so much open expression of emotion. Rome was a casting director's delight. As for *Bicycle Thief,* it received great reviews in America, won awards, and then returned to Italy, where it was acclaimed and did good business, but only after the rest of the world had appreciated it.

Back in London, I saw the first cut of *The Hasty Heart* and made a few changes. Then a telegram arrived from Warner. He wanted me to return to Hollywood as soon as possible; they needed me at the studio for another film. I gave my notes for music and sound effects to the various departments, discussed the main title and other needs with Jackie, and prepared to leave. Because I was only a short distance from Paris and had never seen it and had no idea when and whether I might return, I was anxious to spend the weekend there. But when Jackie relayed my desire to his father, a cable came back saying that I could see Paris some other time and to hurry back to the studio. This was, I thought, unreasonable. I had brought the picture in for eight hundred thousand dollars, almost four hundred thousand less than Warner had originally intended to spend; endured a gruesome winter; and never once gone to Paris, even though my old friend, Jean Negulesco, who was in London directing *The Mudlark,* flew there every weekend to eat a good meal.

Jackie was sympathetic and said go ahead, take two days and say nothing about it. I followed his advice and bade goodbye to all those who'd been so kind to me. At the airport Friday evening, as I was boarding the plane for Paris, I came upon John Huston, whom I had not seen since he had left Warner's. He was to direct *Quo Vadis* for MGM and was on his way to Paris to examine the various studio facilities. We sat together and talked about the old days at Warner's. I was carrying the gift presented to me at the dinner in London, and John was curious to see it. As we passed through customs in Paris, the inspector asked me about the gift, which was in a leather case. I told him it was an antique, which was duty free. He looked it over and was ready to let me through when John spoke up. "Hey, that's beautiful. It must be very valuable." With that, the inspector said I'd have to wait. John went on through, grinning like a naughty boy. It took me another twenty minutes to get cleared, but John was waiting for me. A car sent by MGM was there to pick him up. He drove me to the Prince de Galle Hotel and then went to the George V, where he was staying. As it turned out he did not direct *Quo Vadis.*

I have been asked many times about why John left *Across the Pacific,* with Humphrey Bogart, Mary Astor, and Sydney Greenstreet, which he had been directing while he was still with Warner's, and how I happened to finish the film. One morning as I arrived at my office, a phone call came from Warner. He wanted me to go down to the set of *Across the Pacific* and have a talk with John, who was leaving the film the next day, and take over the direction.

"Why can't John finish it?" I asked.

"He has to go into the army," Warner replied.

"I can't believe the army would not allow him to finish the film," I said.

"It's not only that," Warner added. "The poor guy is having other troubles. His wife comes in one door as Olivia de Havilland walks out the other, and sometimes he doesn't know what he's doing. Get a script from Wald, see the film, and take over in the morning."

I called Jerry, who said the script was on its way and he was arranging for me to see the film shot so far. He also suggested that I have a talk with John. It was about 10:30 when I walked down to the stage where John was shooting. Arthur Edison, the cameraman, and Lee Katz, the assistant director, were having a cup of coffee as I entered. On the set, Greenstreet, Astor, and Bogart were standing around reading sheets of paper.

"What's going on?" I inquired. "Warner wants me to take over tomorrow and says the army won't let John finish the picture." They shrugged and smiled. I asked, "What are they doing now?"

"Going over some new dialog," Lee informed me.

"Have you shot anything this morning?"

"Not yet," Arthur replied.

At that moment, John happened to look back, saw me, and motioned me to come forward. I said I'd return after he completed the scene.

The assembled footage, about an hour and fifteen minutes, was ready for me to look at. I thought it was an interesting story, the actors were good, and the situation was intriguing up to that point, but the denouement was yet to be shot. I had lunch and at four in the afternoon went back to the set to see John. He and the actors were still reading the new pages.

"Haven't you made a shot yet?" I asked Lee. He shook his head. I thought it best that I leave because I felt tension gathering. In my office I read the script and thought the latter part undistinguished and ordinary melodrama, though the rest was a promising film. While I was thinking about what might be done to improve it, I received another call from Warner. It was now five o'clock.

"They've been screwing around all day and haven't made a shot," he said, obviously annoyed. "I told the assistant to send everyone home and you'd start fresh in the morning."

"J.L.," I said, "I ran the cut film and think it's pretty good, but the last part of the script could be improved."

"Vince," he interrupted, "we're already way over budget. I'm sick of all the delays and don't want to spend any more money on it. Just get in there in the morning and finish the damn thing!"

I knew from past experience that when he was in that mood, it was impossible to argue with him. So, the next morning I checked a jungle setting that had been built on one of the stages, where a small plane was waiting in a cleared area and a machine gun was in place nearby. When the actors arrived, they had learned their lines, and I proceeded to shoot the scene. For the next ten days I shot the balance of the script, with only minor changes, as quickly and as best I could. I did not ask for or want any credit for it.

Word that John had left the picture before finishing it soon circulated, and several reporters called to ask what had happened. I could only tell them that John had to go into the army. Later, in his autobiography and in several interviews, John treated the entire episode as a joke. He said that before he left he had arranged to have Bogart so thoroughly tied up that no one could get him out of it. He added that I was assigned to the task but was less than successful. No doubt John was capable of playing such a prank, but I do not think he was engaged in one at that time. Instead, I think he realized that the denouement was not up to the first part and did not, at the moment, know what to do with it. In that situation, and under emotional pressure from his romantic entanglement, he used the army as an excuse to get away.

I always envied John's charisma, his ability to seem superior to and above any film he was working on and his use of silence to indicate deep thought. Often, though, I suspected he had nothing to say. Once I invited him to address a class on motion picture directing and was shocked at his lumbering delivery and lack of articulation. I know he was loved and admired by most of the people he worked with and made some great films—he might even have been a genius—so my comments are probably prejudiced, and I am a victim of the green-eyed monster.

It was quite late when I checked into the Prince de Galle Hotel, so I decided to go to bed and get up early the next morning, Saturday. I slept well and at nine o'clock walked over to the Champs Elysées, picked up a copy of the *New York Herald Tribune,* and sat at an outside cafe table, where I ordered a cup of hot chocolate and a brioche. It was Easter morning. The sun was shining, the trees were filled with green leaves, and I thought the Champs Elysées was the most romantic and beautiful street in the world. Paris seemed to be exactly as I had imagined it. At that moment I felt that I was exceedingly lucky and that life had been good to me.

After a second brioche and chocolate, I walked all the way down to the Place de la Concorde and into the Madeleine district, bought perfume for Hedda, and had a delicious lunch in the Bourse area. On Sunday I visited Notre Dame and walked about the Left Bank, saw Napoleon's tomb, and went to the Rodin museum, which Hedda had mentioned as one of the places she remembered best when she was in Paris years before. After being stopped several times by men selling jewelry or "French postcards," I asked one of them how he knew I was an American. He pointed to my shoes.

Late Sunday afternoon I took a plane to New York and stopped over for a day to rest and visit the Warner Brothers office, where I had lunch with Larry Golub and Ben Kalmenson, the head of the sales department. The following day I left for Hollywood.

When the print of *The Hasty Heart* arrived in Hollywood and Warner ran it, he decided that he wanted a new music score and a few changes in the cutting, all minor, but it gave him the feeling of creative participation. I understood and did not object. The film opened in London first, and we received a half dozen cables telling us about the successful premiere. The audience stood and cheered, Richard Todd was acclaimed a coming star, and the picture was doing sensational business. I was credited in London as producer as well as director, but when it opened in Hollywood, Warner took my name off as producer, indicating that he had produced the film. I was not too disturbed.

Later, Todd was nominated for an Academy Award as Best Actor, and from forty pounds a week he went to fifty thousand dollars for his next role, in the Twentieth Century–Fox film *A Man Called Peter.* His letters to me expressing his appreciation were touching, and I kept them for years. (They were destroyed along with other memorabilia when Hedda and I were living at Ojai, California, years later and our study was flooded.)

In 1950, while I was preparing *Harriet Craig* for Joan Crawford at Columbia on a loanout from Warner Brothers, my producer, Bill Dozier, greeted me one morning with a front-page article in the *Los Angeles Times* saying that I had been given the National Film Award in London. Robert

Clark accepted for me, and several years later, while there, I picked up a silver statue. What pleased me most was that I was told the award came as a result of a poll taken by the *London Daily Mail,* asking its readers which film in 1949 they thought was the best. I was running against *The Third Man,* one of the really great melodramas of all time, directed by Carol Reed, for whom I had enormous respect. In Hollywood I was not even nominated by the Academy, a fact that was noted by Lowell Redellings, motion picture critic of the *Hollywood Citizen News.*

Years later, when Reagan wrote a book called *Where's the Rest of Me?* in which he talks about all his films, he said that *The Hasty Heart* had a wonderful script, a fine cast, an unusual set, and a great performance by Richard Todd. He mentions almost everyone connected with it except the producer-director. I can only think he never forgave me for trying to improve his performance.

With Reagan's second presidential election victory and approaching inauguration in 1985, I received a phone call from Ted Koppel's secretary. They had seen *The Hasty Heart,* thought Reagan was excellent, and wanted to ask questions about him. Having once been a newspaper reporter, I knew he was hoping for something controversial, but I told him that Ronnie had been affable and professional. He wanted to know if he had ever expressed any political ambition.

"No," I replied, "and I feel that he must wake up now and then and say to himself, 'My God, I'm president!'" He wanted to know if I'd come on television and say that. I begged off. He asked what I thought was Reagan's best performance, and I said, "As President."

The ability to deliver a speech and to make it sound as though he had written it and believed every word of it was something he developed over the years as an actor and while stumping for Barry Goldwater and other Republicans. He was, in my opinion, elected because of the power of TV, and his popularity and approval by the vast majority of Americans, despite his many gaffes and questionable decisions, is a tribute to his skill. It would not surprise me if, in the future, other actors decided to enter the political arena.

Recently, I learned that Ronnie had let it be known he was suffering from Alzheimer's disease. Despite my opposition to many of his political decisions, I was saddened. It took guts and courage to make such an announcement, especially when his memory, which he prized, had been so outstanding; he was what we call a quick study and could learn long speeches with ease. I recall a scene in *The Hasty Heart* in which he had to recite all the books of the Bible. I staged it precisely so that an audience would know that it was not a cheat, the camera never leaving him, and he did it perfectly on the first take. I hope that a cure or treatment will soon be found for his ailment and that he will enjoy many more years of life.

14

Joan Crawford

She was the ultimate star—magnetic and glamorous. She had won an Academy Award for her performance in *Mildred Pierce* and had replaced Bette Davis as Warner's number one female. I had never thought of her as a great actress, but she was certainly talented and had a vivid personality, and I admired her drive and determination to better herself. So I was not unhappy when told that my next assignment would be to direct Joan Crawford in *The Victim,* to be produced by Jerry Wald.

Her career had been well publicized. There were many sides to her personality, none of them all white or all black, but varying shades of gray. I knew a little of her history through fan magazine gossip: that she came from an extremely poor family, was probably born out of wedlock, had worked as a servant in a girls' school in order to get an education, and had eventually left and become a chorus girl in a Chicago nightclub. She was at the nightclub when J.J. Shubert offered her a job in a New York musical. There Harry Rapf, a producer at MGM, saw her, and she was signed to a contract for seventy-five dollars a week. Hollywood was the first stop on her road to success. Filled with ambition, energy, and vitality, she was determined to live life to its fullest. Until then she had been deprived—a nobody, rejected, humiliated, and hurt. She loved to dance and went nightly to the Cocoanut Grove. She fell for Michael Cudahy, a rich playboy, won Charleston contests, and was the life of the party wherever she appeared. Her secret goal was to become a great dancer and a big star, and in her early years she did everything possible to get publicity and attract attention. But she soon realized that to become a star she would need more than publicity and would have to be able to do more than dance. She would have to learn how to act and improve herself—her mind and her manners.

She got her first big acting break in a film called *Our Dancing*

Daughters, but she was still regarded by the Hollywood elite as a pushy, ambitious little dancer who was ready to do anything to get ahead. She pretended to ignore such criticism but secretly took it to heart and made up her mind that someday she would cause her critics to eat their words. After the picture was released, she was on her way and achieved her first goal: people began to know and acknowledge Joan Crawford.

In those days the mark of success and recognition in the Hollywood social world was to be invited to Pickfair, the home of Douglas Fairbanks and Mary Pickford. But even as Crawford advanced toward becoming a star, she still was never invited. It only intensified her determination to get there one day. About that time young Douglas Fairbanks Jr. was acting in a play at a Hollywood theater. Joan went to see it and afterward went backstage to tell him how much she liked his performance. They soon began seeing each other, even though Fairbanks Sr. and Mary Pickford tried to discourage it. Finally, Doug Jr. and Joan were married and became the best known and most romantic, fun-loving, young couple in Hollywood. She now became a guest at Pickfair, presumably having achieved social status. She had scored her second victory along the road to success, although she was never comfortable at Pickfair.

She and Doug Jr. enjoyed several years of fun and laughter, but as her career advanced, she wanted more: to develop herself artistically and culturally. She was looking for identity, dignity, and importance. Then, because of her rapid rise to stardom and the resulting competition between her and Doug, plus, according to her, her desire for a more serious life, they drifted apart and were soon divorced.

It was not long after that when she met the man she thought would be able to supply those new needs and wants, Franchot Tone. He was from a fine family back east and was a member of the Group Theater, which had recently created a cultural stir in New York. She embraced the theater world that he introduced her to, and she met many famous people in the world of the arts. She and Tone were married, and she had achieved her third goal—a cultural and artistic patina. She respected Tone, his superior education, his social standing, and especially his acting ability. But none of these made one successful in films. Tone was a good actor but never a star. Soon word began to spread that he and Joan were having trouble because of his lack of success, and one day when she discovered him with a starlet in his dressing room, their marriage ended.

By now she felt secure in her position, not only at MGM, where her name was linked frequently with Clark Gable, but also in the picture business overall. Her last contract at MGM was for over $1 million for five pictures. She was shrewd and made a careful study of Hollywood. She knew what made it tick, and she was prepared to use her knowledge wisely to sustain her place in it as long as possible. She was friendly with Louella Parsons, Hedda Hopper, and many other newspaper people, and she had an instinct about publicity—how to get her name in the papers, or how to keep it out when necessary.

At last she thought she had everything she had ever wanted, except children and a family. But she wanted them without the burden of another romance or volatile love affair. So she adopted a child—a daughter, Christina—followed soon after by a son, Christopher, and baby girls, Cathy and Cindy. For a while she was content, but she was not used to living without a man, and children needed a father and a home. To round out her life, she decided that she must have a husband—someone who would be a companion, an escort, and a loving father for her children. She met Phillip Terry, an actor recently put under contract by MGM, and found in him what she thought she needed. He seemed ideal; he was comfortable and comforting. They were married. But it was not long before she realized that "she mistook peace of mind" for love. Their marriage was short-lived.

About this time her career began to falter. After several films that were box-office flops, she, along with several other stars, including Katharine Hepburn, were referred to as "box-office poison." She and MGM parted company, even though she had been there seventeen years. Subsequently, she signed a contract with Warner Brothers for much less money than she had earned before.

The story of *The Victim* was based on the life of Virginia Hill, a young girl from a poor family down south. She ran away to Chicago while still in her teens, where she got a job as a "cooch" dancer in a sideshow at the Chicago World's Fair of 1933-34. There she met an accountant who fell in love with her and introduced her to members of the mob for whom he worked. Eventually, she cast him aside and became the mistress of Joe Adonis, a New York gangster who was said to be a relative of Frank Costello and high in gang circles. After several years in New York living a life of luxury, she was allegedly sent to Las Vegas to spy on Bugsy Siegel, the man largely responsible for establishing that town. He was suspected of cheating the organization, and they wanted the truth. She went there to make a play for Siegel and, if he was guilty, to expose him. The mob would do the rest. Instead, she fell in love with him and was living with him at the time he was shot and killed.

It was in many ways typical of many of Crawford's early vehicles at

MGM, portraying the struggle of a woman from rags to riches, and the wages of sin. But I hoped we could bring something fresh to it. Jerry Wald had asked Harold Medford, a writer under contract to the studio, to do some work on the treatment, but he informed me that he was bringing out Jerry Weidman from New York, a well-known novelist, to do the screenplay. When Weidman arrived, a meeting was arranged with Crawford, Wald, Medford, and me to discuss the story and come to an agreement about the way it should be developed.

We met in Crawford's dressing room on the Warner Brothers lot, and it was my first glimpse of her in person. She was still an attractive and formidable woman, and although I have always admired strong women and shied away from clinging vine types, her reputation was such that I made up my mind I would never get personally involved with her.

Following a general agreement about the story, Weidman was to retire to his hotel and begin work on the screenplay. As the pages came in, Medford and I would review them and confer. What I did not know but found out later was that Wald had told Weidman to write the screenplay as he saw fit and not to consult with Medford or me. By this time in my career, I wanted to work closely with the writer and prepare a step outline with him, in which each scene would be thoroughly discussed, so that we could deliver the story in the most exciting form possible. In this case I thought I'd just wait to see what Weidman came up with before lodging any protest.

Within ten days he sent in seventy-five pages of script, an unheard-of amount of work in such a short time. I thought the dialog was excellent and the scenes good, but I became alarmed because the story had hardly started and we already had over half a script. At this rate we'd wind up with more than three hundred pages. When Wald asked me what I thought, I told him my worry about the length. Medford's reaction coincided with mine. I wanted to talk with Weidman to see if we could get the pages down to an acceptable length, so that we could tell the full story in 125 to 140 pages. But Wald did not want to stop Weidman and insisted we let him continue writing. I sensed trouble ahead. In those days, the desired length of a film was between one hour and forty minutes and two hours. To go beyond that, you needed an unusual story or one with epic qualities or great production values. As Harry Cohn, head of Columbia Pictures, once said, "After an hour and forty-five minutes my behind begins to get tired." I have come to appreciate his statement. There is no reason, in my opinion, that you cannot tell the average story in two hours. Past that, you are asking for physical and mental concentration that tends to diminish as you continue.

I had not spoken to Crawford since our first meeting. She phoned to ask if I had read the pages. I said I had and was worried. She was surprised. She said Jerry had told her that I thought they were great. She knew nothing of my complaint and was beginning to worry about my judgment. Angry because Jerry had lied to her, she demanded a meeting and expressed her feelings to him and Weidman. So did I and Medford. Weidman listened and said he would compress whenever possible from that point on, but he asked to be allowed to finish the script before making changes. We agreed but informed him that meanwhile, Medford and I would be trying to condense the first batch of pages.

During the meeting, when Joan was not looking at me, I had a chance to observe her carefully and realized that even though she was still attractive, she could never be made to look like a young girl trying to escape from a dreary home life, which was the basis of our story. There were lines in her face, crow's feet around her eyes, and her neck was beginning to show wrinkles. This preyed on my mind, until Medford and I had a talk with Wald, who finally agreed that we had better take this into consideration and devise a different opening for our film than had been written. At the same time I began looking for locations and preparing the production.

When Weidman finished the script, it was, as I had feared, over three hundred pages. There were many good scenes, but now we had to cut them down. Weidman felt he had done his job and wanted to go back to New York. He did not want to spend time with the tedious business of cutting and compacting. Besides, his contract time had been used up. Crawford insisted that Wald now turn over the script to me and Medford for the final draft. She indicated that she had confidence in us. Weidman returned to New York.

Our first task was to devise an opening that would set up Crawford's role believably and would state the theme of our film. I recalled a conversation I had once had with Sinclair Lewis, who told me how he happened to write *Dodsworth*. His first wife was Grace Hegger, who not only was socially ambitious but, as she approached fifty, began to worry about no longer being attractive to men. She felt that once a woman passed fifty it was the end of her sexuality. Not that she was unfaithful to Lewis or contemplated unfaithfulness, but she enjoyed having men pay attention to her and flirt with her and wanted to cram in as much excitement as possible before it was too late.

Medford agreed that this was a good thrust for our story, and together we wrote an opening that revealed Crawford, a housewife, married to a worker in the oil fields, living a dull, drab life. She has a son about seven who craves a bicycle. She buys it for him and is berated by her husband, who says they can't afford it. He demands that she take the bike back. She pleads with him not to disappoint the boy, but he is angry and stubborn. The boy is up the street from his house showing his new bike to friends when the father orders him back home at once. He starts back and is run over and killed by a passing truck. With his death, Crawford has nothing to keep her in this dismal atmosphere or with this dull husband. She leaves him and her mother and father, with whom they have been living, and goes to New York alone, determined, while she is still young enough and has her looks, to find a better life. We sent the opening to Crawford. She liked it. From that time on she phoned me almost daily about some story point, or she came to the studio to talk about her wardrobe. Gradually, she revealed many of her past experiences and much of her present thinking. She pretended to love Hollywood, but I could detect a healthy cynicism. However, behind a facade of toughness, I sensed an incurable romanticism. She was still looking for her Prince Charming. I hoped we could capture some of this in our film.

One morning, after some wardrobe tests, she suggested that we run *Humoresque,* which I had not yet seen, so that we could discuss the various hair styles she might use. I made arrangements for us to have dinner first. With the help of a few martinis, she volunteered a little more about herself and confided that she was looking forward to our working together. She tried to get me to talk about Bette Davis, but I avoided it. Later, we went to the projection room at the lower end of the Warner lot and began running *Humoresque.*

She looked ravishing, and I thought the film was well done in every department. Midway, when I complimented her on a very sexy scene, she took my hand, held it against her breast, and soon followed it by placing her other hand on my knee and moving it up my leg. I was stunned but aroused. Before I could say or do anything, she stood up, raised her dress, and quickly pulled off a pair of silk panties she was wearing. I had never encountered such female aggressiveness and thought mostly of one thing—lock the door to the projection room before anyone might drop in and see us. As I rose to go to the door she put her arms around me and held me close. I urged her to let me go so I could lock the door, but it didn't seem to matter to her. She pressed her body against me, and we kissed as I stole a look up at the projection booth to see if the operator could see us. He could not. Finally, after I pleaded with her, she released me, but I discovered that there was no way I could lock the door from the inside. Oblivious to possible discovery, she was ready for me to have her on the carpeted floor. I persuaded her to restrain herself and wait until the picture was over and we could go to her dressing room. She relented, and we resumed watching *Humoresque*. Needless to say, my concentration was impaired during the rest of the film. I realized that she had been stimulated by her own eroticized image and that I was confronted with a female who went after what she wanted and was masculine in her approach to sex.

I also wondered why she thought I was available. For all she knew, I might have been happily married and not interested in sex with her. Or was it possible, despite my efforts to keep it quiet, that someone had whispered to her that Bette Davis and I had had an affair and she was out to accomplish what Davis had not: have me get a divorce and marry her? Or was she simply concerned that I had not made a pass at her or indicated that I desired her? Was she testing me or herself? She had told me about her childhood, and I was fascinated by the similarity of the emotional problems that she and Bette Davis had: a father who deserted the family early, which, for a young daughter, can be an even greater rejection than for the wife and can result in an undying hatred and distrust of men. Was she, like Bette, unconsciously seeking first a father, then a lover and, once having gotten him, intending to get even with all men by emasculating him? Although they came from different backgrounds—Bette from a middle-class, strict, puritanical New England family, and Joan from a lower-middle-class midwest family—in my opinion they were, despite their intense dislike of each other, sisters under the skin.

The truth was that I had no great urge to have an affair with Joan. I was turned off by the gossip of all the men she had gone to bed with, plus her reputation of being possessive and callous. Moreover, when I returned from London, I was determined to spend more time with my children and mend my relationship with Hedda. But Hedda and I were both headstrong; she was not ready to forgive me for my criticism of her in London, and I felt that if she cared enough for me she would have tried to please me. For the sake of the children we were pleasant to each other, but there was a gap between us that prevented any closeness from developing; she withheld her affection and only grudgingly permitted a resumption of our sexual relationship. I became resentful and vulnerable, which weakened any resolve I might have had to avoid becoming involved with Crawford. Joan, too, was at a vulnerable time in her life;

she had just broken up a long-standing affair with Greg Bautzer, a handsome and successful attorney. I took the path of least resistance. By the time we got to her dressing room, the sudden rush of passion that had overcome her in the projection room had subsided, and our lovemaking was anticlimactic.

Before we started the film, I had dinner with her at Don the Beachcomber, where she had a special table reserved in a secluded corner. We also ate once at her home in Brentwood on Bristol Avenue. It was a movie star's palace: a circular driveway with two Cadillacs in the garage, a small entry hall as you opened the front door, and to the right, a large living room done in white by her friend Billy Haines, a former star at MGM and now a successful decorator. To the left were a comfortable den and bar, a breakfast room, and a large formal dining room. A huge kitchen, a pantry, and a laundry room, plus maid's quarters, completed the ground floor.

Outside at the rear were a large patio, a huge swimming pool, and beautiful grounds with trees and flowers along carefully groomed pathways. To the right as one came out of the house was a small building that was her projection room. I met her children: Christina, thirteen years old, Christopher, ten years old, and Cindy and Cathy, three years old. They were charming and polite; they bowed and curtsied but seemed a trifle stiff and unnatural. I was introduced as Uncle Vincent.

After they were sent upstairs to bed, we had dinner. It was just for the two of us, but it was quite formal. Joan waited for me to pull back her chair before she sat and thanked me for opening her serviette and handing it to her. The table was laid out with expensive silverware and dishes and an elegant candelabra. I had been in a few wealthy homes in the past where everything was beautifully arranged, but none surpassed this one. The excellent dinner was served by a gracious woman dressed in a black outfit for evening. I sensed that everything was the best that money could buy and that Joan had made a study of social behavior. I was particularly intrigued that, coming from a poor and humble background, she would insist on things being so correct. But perhaps that was the answer. Someone more secure would be less interested and insistent.

After dinner she took me on a tour of the house, showing me her upstairs living room with several large closets—one for shoes, with a hundred or more pairs neatly arranged; another, cedar-lined, for her fur coats; another for suits and dresses. Adjoining was her bedroom, with a king-sized bed at each end, both with silk sheets and pillow covers and beautiful comforters. Everywhere we went, we were followed by her white

French poodle, Cliquot. Her children's names all began with C, and so did her dog's.

The tour over, I was prepared to go home, when she said she was going to take a shower and get to bed. She invited me to join her. I hesitated, but the excellent dinner, the good wine, and the luxurious surroundings added to Joan's seductive manner and were too enticing to resist. We got undressed in the bathroom. Her body was well shaped and her breasts firm, even at her age, but she was much shorter than I had thought. It was the way she carried herself that made her appear taller. She saw me staring at her and waited for me to speak. I complimented her. She was pleased, smiled, and said modestly, "But I've still got to lose a few pounds."

In the shower her sexuality became rampant. There was a built-in place to sit. She pushed me down to it and lowered herself onto my lap. The warm spray from the shower covered our bodies as we made love. When I commented about her lustful behavior, she replied, "The ideal wife is a lady in the living room but a whore in bed." I was with her until midnight, then went home.

Hedda sensed what was going on. "Have you been sleeping with her?"

I admitted that I had. She hesitated for a moment. "Are you in love with her?"

"No." And she knew I meant it.

"Well," she sighed, "I suppose it's too much to ask of any man that he turn down a chance to sleep with Joan Crawford."

I marveled at her lack of jealousy, her acceptance of a situation that not many women would have tolerated. I realized once again that I had an extraordinary woman for a wife. To this day I am not sure whether she was hurt and resented it or felt secure in the knowledge that I genuinely loved her and would never leave her, which I once told her in the midst of the crisis with Davis. I meant that, too. In spite of the friction between Hedda and me, I could not erase those early years, the closeness and love and respect we felt for each other. In fact, I told Joan how I felt about Hedda and, although she seemed to accept my loyalty to her, as Hedda seemed to accept my relationship to Joan, she was curious to meet the woman who had such a hold on me.

At the end of the second week of shooting, Joan gave a lavish party on Saturday night at her home and invited me and Hedda. A large tent had been put up in her backyard. Charcoal burners were placed all about to provide heat for the guests. It often gets chilly in southern California at night, no matter how hot it is during the day. The place was crowded with celebrities, including Louis B. Mayer, Joan's old boss at MGM, and her new boss, Jack Warner. Hedda and I knew only a few of the guests, but Joan introduced us all around. It was a lovely evening. When we got home Hedda said, "She's still a stunning woman, and strangely enough, there's something about her that I like and admire."

"I'm curious," I replied. "What is it?"

"She's gracious and considerate, and if you can see beneath the Hollywood crap, you can detect a woman who refused to become a loser, who pulled herself up from nothing and made something of her life."

I agreed with her. Moreover, I enjoyed every moment working with Joan. She took direction easily, agreed with everything I suggested, and even anticipated almost every move or idea I offered. I had never worked with anyone who was so keen, so knowledgeable about filmmaking.

The first bit of personal trouble I had with her came when we went on location to Palm Springs. She arranged through the studio to get us booked into the Racquet Club with a room for me next to hers, which I did not discover until we arrived. There was also a connecting door between us. It bothered me that she had done this without telling me, but I said nothing. One day Hedda decided to drive down with Freda Lerch for a visit. Freda was an old friend, formerly Willy Wyler's secretary and script supervisor. Freda was curious about Crawford. We were shooting outside when they arrived, and I took them over to a shady spot where Joan was sitting so that they could say hello. Joan was polite but withdrawn, not her usual gracious self. I invited them to have lunch with us, and they wanted to use my room to freshen up. I was disturbed lest Hedda find out that it was so close to Crawford's room. She knew that I was having an affair with Joan, but I did not want it to be so blatant as to embarrass her. Fortunately, the connecting door was locked, and I heard nothing from Hedda about it. The moment she left, Joan turned on me angrily and said I should not have allowed her to come. I pointed out that I did not know she was coming; even so, how could I tell her not to come? She was my wife. It was the first argument we had had since the film began, and I did not like what I sensed: Crawford's need to control. Was this why she seduced me so soon after we met?

That evening, instead of having dinner with me, she ate in her room alone and kept the door between us locked. I thought it just as well since I was annoyed too and determined not to let her take control of me or of the film. After dinner she took a walk with Steve Cochran, a tall, handsome, sexy young actor who was playing the Bugsy Siegel role in the film. She was no doubt attempting to make me jealous and punish me. The next day I did not even mention it. She was aloof during the shooting, but as the day ended she asked if we could have dinner together. I knew I had done the right thing. As long as I held the reins tightly, all would be well, but if I relinquished control, I was certain there would be hell to pay.

That night we talked. She wanted me to get a divorce and marry her. I reminded her that I had told her from the start that although Hedda and I had some problems, I still loved her and could never leave her or my children. If she could accept that, we could continue to see each other, work together, and give each other as much pleasure as possible. When she learned that Hedda knew about our relationship, she could not understand her lack of jealousy or how she could permit it. She was convinced Hedda did not really love me but was merely holding onto me for other reasons. Nor could she understand how Hedda could still occasionally come into my bed. She vowed that if she ever found out that I was unfaithful to her with anyone besides Hedda, that it would be the end of us! I assured her that I had no interest in anyone else. She calmed down and we finished shooting in Palm Springs without any further problems. I could not refrain from being amused at the situation: a wife could accept sharing her husband with another woman, but the other woman resented sharing the husband with his wife. Perhaps it was the difference between love and possession.

Back in the studio, while we were completing the interiors, Joan made arrangements to spend from Monday night to Friday in her dressing room, which was the size of a small apartment. Friday night she'd go home for the weekend. This made it more convenient for me to see her at the end of the day since I lived only a few minutes away from the studio.

I have often been asked how we kept our affair out of the gossip columns. The truth is that about the same time, several stars, important and married, were rumored to be having torrid affairs that the press was protective about: Gary Cooper and Patricia Neal, Victor Fleming and Ingrid Bergman, Errol Flynn and Patrice Wymore, Alan Ladd and June Allyson, John Huston and Olivia de Havilland, Ida Lupino and Helmut Dantine, and perhaps others.

Since Hedda had met Joan, any resentment she might have had toward her seemed to have dissolved. She felt that our affair would come to an end when the picture was finished, that it was a temporary affinity created by the nature of our work, and that if a husband and a wife really loved each other, it was wrong to allow a sexual indiscretion to break up a marriage.

I must also mention a phenomenon that the layman is unaware of: in the course of communicating with each other about the emotional demands of a role, a director and his star often and inevitably reveal things to each other that sometimes they never reveal to their spouses, things that move them to tears or laughter. A good director will try to get to know everything he can about his star, male or female, in order to help him or her summon up the feelings called for by the script. This kind of rapport between a male director and his female star over the length of the film, sometimes many months, can lead to a closeness that is difficult for either to resist. It is the same pattern, I'm sure, that causes some women to fall in love with their analysts.

With the completion of the picture, I felt much as Hedda did, that it would mark the end of the affair with Joan. I asked Warner if I could take a few days off to rest. He agreed, and I had proposed taking Hedda and our children for a short trip somewhere when Joan called and said it was important that she talk with me.

Columbia Pictures had submitted a script to her to start in a few weeks, and she wanted to have me read it. If I liked it, she'd talk to Harry Cohn, head of Columbia, and Bill Dozier, the producer, about our doing it together on a loanout from Warner's. I told her I would be glad to read the script while I was away with the family. She begged me to postpone my trip and give her a few days. "We'll take a drive up to Carmel. You can relax and read the script there and we can discuss it." I asked if she couldn't wait until I returned, and she said they had to have a yes or no by Monday morning. It was now Thursday. I said I'd call her back. After explaining the situation to Hedda, I asked if she'd be upset if I left on Friday and returned Monday morning. I explained that it was not a pleasure trip but business and promised that the moment I returned we'd go to Yosemite for a week. She did not object.

The next day, while Joan drove us to Carmel, I read *Lady of the House.* As soon as I got through the first twenty or thirty pages of the screenplay, I realized that it was a remake of *Craig's Wife,* a play written by George Kelly and made into a film with Rosalind Russell twenty years before. When I finished it, I told her she would be foolish to do it. Not only was it dated, but also I felt audiences would not respond to it even if an attempt was made to update it.

"Can't you figure out something to do with it?" she begged. "Warner's has nothing for me at the moment, and I could use the money."

She was getting two hundred thousand dollars a picture. I pleaded with her again not to do it and said I would not touch it even if she felt she had to do it. She was disappointed. But she had reserved a suite with a fireplace at the inn, and at sundown she had it lit and ordered a delicious dinner with a bottle of wine sent to the room—all of which was, of course, conducive to making love afterward. The next morning I read the script a second time but still could not see any way to make it work and get a good film out of it. When I returned home and told Hedda that I had turned down doing the picture, she took it for granted that the affair had ended. So did I.

A few days later Rudi Fehr, the editor of *The Victim,* was ready to show me his first cut. We made a few changes, then ran it for Warner, Wald, and Trilling. They seemed happy, and I suggested a new title, *The Damned Don't Cry,* from an old novel that Warner's had bought years before but never made. Everyone agreed it was appropriate and a better title than *The Victim.* I called Joan to tell her the reaction. She was pleased.

Meanwhile, she turned down *Lady of the House,* and I took time off to be with Hedda and the children. Two weeks later Trilling phoned me. "How would you like to go back to work?" I told him I was rested and ready.

"Good," he said. "We just made a deal for you to direct a picture at Columbia with Margaret Sullavan."

It was the first time I was to be loaned out, and I was interested. Sullavan was a fine actress and had an unusual voice and quality. "What's the picture?" I asked.

"I haven't read the script," he replied, "but the title is *Lady of the House.*"

"Oh, shit!" was my response. I told him briefly about my talk with Crawford and asked, "What happens if I turn it down?"

"Gee, Vincey," he said, "we've already made the deal for you—twelve weeks, and you start next Monday. If you refuse to do it, you'll be breaking your contract, and you don't want to do that." I certainly didn't. I was being paid $3,000 per week, and my next raise was to $3,500, and after that to $4,000. I learned later that Columbia had paid Warner's $60,000 for my twelve weeks, which gave Warner's a profit of $20,000.

Monday morning, I reported to Columbia and Dozier's office. He was easy to talk to, intelligent, and knowledgeable about films. I told him about my experience with Joan and my feelings about *Lady of the House.* He listened politely and explained that Cohn had always wanted to remake *Craig's Wife* and had asked him to produce it. He suggested that I reread the script and, since I was committed to doing it, make notes about any changes I might have in mind. I was given an office and went to work.

That afternoon I was told that Harry Cohn wanted to see me. I had heard many stories about him and was curious to meet him. As I entered his huge office, he was seated at the far end at an enormous desk with all kinds of buttons and phones. His face was grim and slightly terrifying. I recognized a fighter, tough and with sharp eyes, that verified his reputation.

"I hear you don't like this project," he began.

"Right," I said. "I don't know why you spend money borrowing me for something that I am not enthusiastic about, when I think I'd be better suited for something else you have."

"What are you talking about?"

"*Born Yesterday*," I replied.

He stared at me for a moment, then asked why I was right for it. I told him that I understood the people, I thought it was a good play, and I felt I could give him a hit film. He thought for a moment. "I'll let you read the script. Tell me what you think."

I was elated. A script was sent to my office. It was written by my two favorite screenwriters, Julie and Phil Epstein, but as I read it I had reservations. In their effort to take it out of the one set—a hotel room—it was confined to on the stage and open it up, I felt that they had lost some of the dramatic tension of the play. The next day when I went up to see Cohn and gave him my reaction, he replied, "I paid the Epsteins a hundred thousand dollars for that script. Now you're telling me to throw it away?"

"No—not at all!" I explained. "They're two of the best writers in Hollywood. I'm only suggesting that you don't lose the tension of the play and only go out of the hotel when there is a need and a definite advantage."

He listened quietly and said he'd think about it. Meanwhile, he asked me to concentrate on *Lady of the House* and give it my best shot. I promised him I would. I can't explain it, but there was something about Harry Cohn that I liked. I sensed a vulnerable human being underneath his gruff exterior, and I learned later that I was correct. When George Cukor directed *Born Yesterday,* I was happy to see that he did what I think I would have done.

The following day I received an urgent call from Joan. She was upset. "You're a fine friend. You ask me to turn down *Lady of the House;*

then you accept it." I tried to explain what had happened, but in vain. She called Dozier, whom she knew, and said she would now do the film since I would be directing it. In short order, Cohn arranged for a loan-out of Crawford from Warner's, and Sullavan was put into another film. I always suspected that Cohn and Dozier maneuvered the whole thing.

After intensive examination of *Lady of the House,* I proposed a series of changes, which Dozier accepted. I asked for James Gunn, with whom I had worked on *The Unfaithful,* to help me with the rewrite.

By now, having been to Crawford's house several times for dinner and having observed her behavior, I realized that in many ways she was the embodiment of Harriet Craig, the character she would play, in her obsessive attitude toward her home; her distrust of men and her desire to control; her power of manipulation; and her concept of the proper way for a man to behave toward his wife, including opening doors for her, pulling back a chair for her to sit, and being careful not to spill cigarette ashes on the carpets. I tried to capture these traits in the film, and although they were a critical comment, she never once objected. So I was never sure she was fully aware of what we were doing.

During my visits to her home, I was also able to watch her conduct with the children, especially Christopher and Christina. I liked them both, but she'd often humiliate one or the other in front of guests. When I suggested that maybe it would be better to wait until the guests departed before criticizing them, she said, "I'm going to teach them how to grow up to be ladies and gentlemen!" I withheld any further comment for a long time.

The actual shooting of *Harriet Craig* (as the film was eventually titled) was enjoyable and rewarding. I was working with a fine cameraman, Joe Walker, who had been Frank Capra's man on the great films he made at Columbia. Joe flattered me constantly by asking me to look through the lens after he had lit a scene and before we shot it to see if I could find anything that he could improve. At first I thought he was merely being complimentary—but he was serious; he told me he thought I had a good eye.

I felt that I was at the peak of my ability as a director and had control of every phase of picture making, if only I could get the kind of scripts I needed.

Joan made arrangements while shooting, as at Warner's, to spend the night in her dressing room at Columbia, where she had a small kitchen and a bath. Sometimes I'd take her out to dinner or she'd have it sent in and I'd join her. We put aside any personal problems for the sake of the film, and we all enjoyed a smooth and satisfying production that both Dozier and Cohn were pleased with.

Vi Lawrence was the editor on *Harriet Craig,* one of the few women in Hollywood doing such work. She had cut some of Columbia's best pictures, and I soon learned why. She always knew what I was trying to accomplish in every scene, knew where to go for action and reaction, and had a sense of rhythm, pace, and construction. After viewing her first cut, I gave her a few notes, and the final film was all I could have hoped for. The reviews were good, and it did much better business than I expected. Joan gave one of her best performances, and I received many compliments.

When I phoned Trilling that I had finished, he told me that Warner's had bought *Goodbye My Fancy* for Crawford to star in and for me to direct. It had been a hit play in New York, with Madeleine Carroll and Sam Wanamaker, and was written by a friend, Fay Kanin. The screenplay was being prepared by Ivan Goff and Ben Roberts, also two old friends. I was sent a copy of the play; I enjoyed reading it and looked forward to directing it. On the surface it was a comedy, but underneath there was a love story that was seriously concerned with academic freedom. Joan was to play the role of a liberal congresswoman who is invited back to her old college to deliver the commencement address. As a student, she fell in love with a young professor and was out too late one night but refused to name him and was expelled. He is now the president of the college. Her return brings up old issues and new ones.

When I called Trilling to tell him I was pleased and would be glad to report back as soon as I had had a short rest, he said they were looking forward to seeing me. He asked me how things had gone at Columbia and told me they had heard that I did a good job. I learned later that Jerry Wald was on the phone every day with Cohn, who gave him a report, and Wald in turn relayed the information to Warner, who was not speaking to Cohn. It was well known that Warner and Cohn hated each other.

After I returned to Warner's, Jack asked how I liked working for "that no good s.o.b." I told him we got along fine. Jack then proceeded to vilify Cohn, saying he was a disgrace to the community, contributed to charity only what he could take off his taxes, and was crude and vulgar. As for Cohn's taste, I must say that although he could at times be crude and vulgar, when it came to films his taste was impeccable. He often surprised me by suggesting a cut when he thought a line or a piece of business was not in good taste. When I left Columbia, Harry Cohn let

With Ava Gardner on the set of *Lone Star*, 1952

Directing Clark Gable and Lionel Barrymore (seated) in *Lone Star*

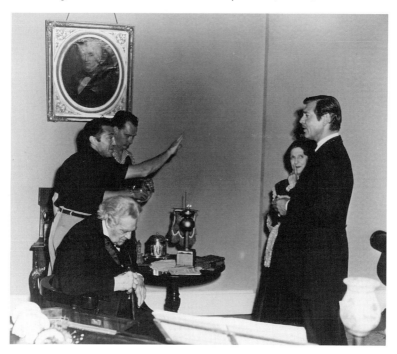

Directing Rita Hayworth, *Affair in Trinidad,* 1952

Directing Glenn Ford and Hayworth in *Affair in Trinidad*

On location in Africa with Darryl F. Zanuck for *The Naked Earth*, 1958

Adjusting Juliette Greco's
wardrobe in *The Naked Earth*

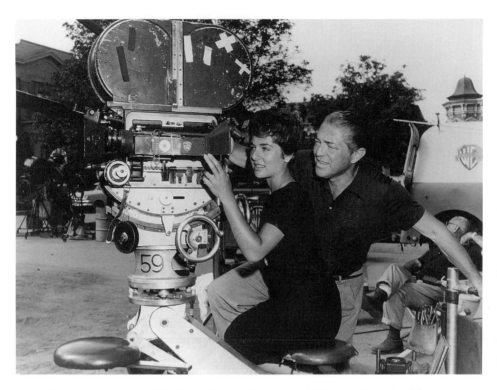

Showing daughter, Hedwin, the outdoor set at Warner Bros. backlot for *The Young Philadelphians*, 1959

With Diane McBain (left) and Carolyn Jones on the set of *Ice Palace*

With son, Eric, and Robert Ryan in Alaska while filming *Ice Palace*, 1959

With Debbie Reynolds, *The Second Time Around*, 1961

With Carroll O'Connor, *The Last Hurrah*

With Mark Harmon and Morgan Fairchild, *The Dream Merchants*

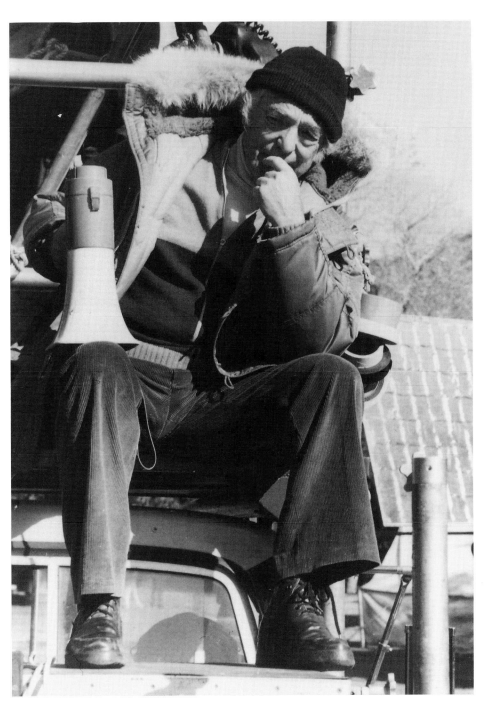

Directing

With Meta Wilde and Donna Cameron in 1994

Cosimo, Eric, and Vincent Sherman, with Chris Stanfield
at 1995 Telluride Film Festival, Telluride, Colorado

me know there would be a place for me there if and when I ever left Warner's. I was grateful to him.

Even though everything went smoothly during *Harriet Craig,* I was exhausted at the end of the film. Joan asked me if I could take a couple weeks off and drive with her to Lake Louise in Canada. She needed a vacation, had heard it was beautiful, and had always wanted to go there, but not alone. I told her I would have to think about it. I really did not want to be away from Hedda and the children for such a long time, but I asked Hedda how she felt about it.

"Well, you certainly need a rest, so it's up to you. I don't care, but I'm glad you asked me." I think she knew that no matter how far I strayed I would always come back to her. Joan had been kind to me in many ways and continued to tell me how much she loved me and how grateful she was for all my help on *Harriet Craig.* She showered me with gifts: money clips, a gold watch, cuff links, initialed linen handkerchiefs from Charvet and Fils, silk pajamas, tailored jackets from Carol Stoner, silk ties from Sulka, and a Stereo Realist camera that I still use. I begged her to stop and explained that it was embarrassing for me. She replied, "It gives me pleasure, so why should you mind?"

As we drove to Canada, we registered under fictitious names in motels along the way and ate in quiet places. Joan was careful to avoid being recognized; she wore dark glasses and a bandanna around her head. Everything went well until we came to a small town somewhere in the state of Washington late one afternoon and decided to spend the night. We checked into a motel and ate early in a restaurant where several young people who were obviously movie fans spotted her and later followed us to the motel. They must have called the local newspaper. A few days later the story was back in Hollywood: Joan Crawford was seen in the company of a man at a motel, where they were registered under a fictitious name as man and wife. This prompted Harrison Carroll, the gossip columnist, to call Hedda and ask whether I was home. When she said I was away for a short vacation, he asked whether we were getting a divorce and whether I was with Crawford. Hedda said she knew nothing about it and hung up. When I called home from Seattle, she was upset and so was I. As long as my relationship with Crawford was confined to the studio, she could tolerate it, but when it became public, she was distressed.

The journey to Canada was not a happy one. I soon became aware that Joan was still hoping it would bring us closer together and cause the rift in my marriage that would finally pave the way for divorce. When I realized this, it had the opposite effect and caused me to retreat further from her. We cut short our stay in Canada and returned to Los Angeles. I apologized to Hedda for the embarrassment that I had caused her and promised that it would not happen again.

Reporting back to Warner Brothers, I was given the completed screenplay of *Goodbye My Fancy,* asked for a few changes, and began casting. Robert Young was set to play Joan's secret love before he became president of the college. He was ideal, but when Warner cast Frank Lovejoy as the newspaper reporter who was currently in love with Joan, I balked. Frank was a good actor and a friend, but I did not think he was right for Joan. Their chemistry did not seem to ignite. Blanke, who was producing the film, agreed, but our protest was ignored. Frank was under contract, and Warner was adamant that we use him. Eve Arden played Joan's secretary and provided the laughs. A new girl, Janice Rule, formerly a dancer and recently signed by the studio, was cast as Robert Young's daughter. It was her first film and a difficult role. For some reason, perhaps her youth, Joan took a dislike to her, and whenever I spent an extra moment to talk with her, Joan became suspicious and jealous, which made it difficult for me and for Janice.

But the major problem I had was Jack Warner himself. During the second or third week of shooting, Trilling called to say that Warner wanted me to keep away from any close-ups of Joan—she was "getting too old"—and to do only full figures or knee figures of her.

"Does that mean no close-ups of anyone in the picture from now on?" I asked.

"No, just keep away from Crawford."

I tried to explain that it was a ridiculous order: how could I make close-ups of the others and not Crawford; she would be the first to know, and how could I tell her what Warner said? In addition, how could the picture be cut smoothly without her close-ups? Steve had no answer. Nor did I. It was the first time Jack had ever interfered in such a manner. I told Steve I would handle the situation as best I could. Wherever possible, I compromised and only made close-ups that I deemed absolutely necessary.

Added to my problems were Joan's jealousy and animosity toward Janice, for which there was no cause, except in her own mind, and her frustration with me because I still refused to get a divorce and marry her. Time and again I tried to reason with her, but it was hopeless. She was in a vortex of insecurity from which she could not seem to escape.

One Sunday when I was going to the Academy to see a film that Hedda had no interest in, Joan asked me if I would stop by her house to talk about a scene we were to do on Monday. I went. She was in the kitchen when I arrived, preparing lunch for the children. Christopher did something that displeased her. She began to scold him, and I could see his eyes fill with tears and humiliation. I begged her to stop. She turned on me.

"Don't you ever interfere between me and my children!" she yelled.

I apologized but said I could not stand to see the boy hurt and warned her that he would hate her for it. She became livid.

"I told you once before, I'm going to teach them how to be ladies and gentlemen, and if you don't like it you can leave right now!"

She crossed to the kitchen door, opened it and indicated for me to go. I had no desire to remain. But just as I got to the doorway, she stuck her foot out and tried to trip me. I stumbled and almost fell but caught myself and impulsively swung around and slapped her so hard that she fell to the floor—the first and only time I have ever hit a woman. The irony was that, although I was defending the children, Christina rushed to Joan to help her. I continued out the door and went to the Academy, where I tried to forget the incident and enjoy the film. In a way I was relieved. Our relationship was becoming painful and abrasive, and I felt this would surely end it.

A half hour later, over the loudspeaker in the theater, a voice said, "There is a phone call for Vincent Sherman in the office." It was Joan, crying, asking me please to forgive her. I told her to forget it and that I would see her on the set tomorrow. I had a strange feeling that in some perverse way she had enjoyed the episode.

I finally managed to finish the film, although under stress. It was a good picture—well acted, well written, and well directed, with some fine scenes and genuine emotion. It still is, for that matter. But it was not a success. The romance between Joan and Frank Lovejoy, as I had predicted, did not work. Furthermore, the subject matter of the piece was too political and too intellectual for Crawford fans, and she could not lighten the texture of her performance. The truth is that neither Joan nor Bette Davis had the kind of light touch necessary for comedy.

When the picture was finished, Trilling called me into his office to tell me that Warner was displeased with the fact that I ignored his order not to shoot close-ups of Crawford. His name was on the outside of the studio, he said, and unless I could follow orders it would be best for me to leave. I was hurt and angry that after all the years of my devotion to the studio and all the films I'd given them, he'd want to get rid of me so abruptly. Besides, I still had almost two years to go on my contract. My pride was such that I called my agent, Arthur Park, at MCA, and told him to get me out. I did not want to stay where I was not wanted, nor did I want any of their lousy money. Arthur correctly advised me to cool off and said he would try to work out a settlement. Eventually he did. When I told Joan that I was leaving, she was sorry to see me go and said they would have liked to break her contract too, but she was going to stay until the end and make them pay her. It would be years before I learned the real reason I had been encouraged to leave.

I saw Joan a few times afterward, but our relationship had deteriorated beyond repair. One night she asked me to come for dinner; we had an argument about something or other, and she said we were finished. I agreed and left. When I got home, Hedda was in bed watching TV, with a bowl of grapes by her side. She turned to me as she ate a grape.

"Your girlfriend called and said she was sending you back to me."

"And what did you say?" I asked, amused at her casualness.

"Nothing . . . just 'Thank you,'" she replied, as she popped another grape into her mouth. I had to laugh again and thought to myself that I was married to a truly unusual woman. That night I begged her to forgive me for the grief I might have caused her, and I took her in my arms.

A few nights later I was awakened by a phone call at 2:00 A.M. It was Joan. Her voice was barely audible.

"Good-bye, Vincent," she said, and I heard the phone drop. I became alarmed and pleaded with her to pick up the phone and talk to me, but there was no answer. I told Hedda I was worried and had to find out what was wrong. I got dressed quickly and raced madly from the Valley to Brentwood, rang the front doorbell frantically, got no answer, and went to the kitchen, where the cook finally opened the door for me. I rushed up the back stairs to Joan's bedroom. She was lying on the bed in her nightgown, the phone still dangling near the floor, and there was an open bottle of sleeping pills on the night table. I had no way of knowing how many she had taken or whether she was faking the whole thing, but I thought it best to get her up and walk her about. She was groggy, and it took me some time to get her out of bed and on her feet. I had the cook make some hot coffee. After I had worked with her for an hour, she seemed all right. I begged her to be sensible and try to understand that I cared about her but could never leave Hedda or my children. I also reminded her again that I had told her this when we first met. She calmed down. It was almost 5:00 A.M. when I got back home.

The day I left Warner's was one of the saddest I can recall. I had spent over fifteen years there, and my heart was heavy. But I took with me many memories. Joan made one more film at Warner's, then she too departed. Although none of the three pictures I made with her were smash hits, they were respectable productions, and I was pleased with her work and mine.

Fortunately, after leaving Warner's, she had a big success with *Sudden Fear,* an excellent melodrama directed by David Miller. She followed this with a semimusical, *Torch Song,* at MGM, directed by her old friend Chuck Walters. A year later she made *Johnny Guitar,* with Nick Ray directing, and *Female on the Beach,* directed by Joe Pevney. After those came *Queen Bee* at Columbia with Randy McDougall; *Autumn Leaves* with Robert Aldrich; another film with David Miller, in London, *The Story of Esther Costello;* and afterward *The Best of Everything* for Jerry Wald at Fox. These were followed by a series of low-budget horror films with William Castle, when she finally met and married Alfred Steele, the head of Pepsi Cola, and began a new career as the promoter of Pepsi. She traveled all over the globe to help open new plants. Before her marriage to Steele, she had never traveled by plane. Now she went everywhere. I should add that she was introduced to Steele by an old friend of mine, a college mate from Oglethorpe, Earl Blackwell, the founder of Celebrity Service. . . . Small world!

Her life with Steele, I was told, was far from tranquil, despite her declaration that it was perfect. After his death she was soon separated from Pepsi Cola, where, I understand, she had made some enemies. Not long after that she was cast, along with Bette Davis, in *What Ever Happened to Baby Jane?* I sent her some flowers on the first day of shooting and wished her good luck. She phoned to thank me. As we talked she said, "Oh, here comes Bette, why don't you say hello to her." I wanted to tell her that I didn't think it was a good idea since Bette was angry with me for a letter that I had sent to the *Los Angeles Times*, criticizing her and Paul Henreid for a TV interview they had given. During the interview they had denigrated the work of Irving Rapper, who had directed *Now, Voyager.* But before I had a chance to speak, I heard her say, "Bette dear, it's Vincent Sherman; he'd like to say hello." Then to me she added, "And thank you for the flowers." It was Joan's way of telling Bette that I had called and sent her flowers. I was surprised that Bette took the phone. She said, "Hello," in a flat voice, and I could only reply, "I'd just like to wish you good luck on the picture." She said, "Thank you," and obviously handed the phone back to Joan. I was annoyed with Joan and cut the conversation short.

When she was about to start her next film for Aldrich, *Hush, Hush,*

Sweet Charlotte, also with Bette, I read that she had suddenly taken ill and was in the hospital. Again, I sent her flowers and wished her a speedy recovery. She phoned and asked if I would come to see her. The next day I was there. She confided that there was nothing wrong with her and that she was merely trying to get out of doing *Sweet Charlotte* because Bette was maneuvering Aldrich to reduce her (Joan's) role down to nothing. After we talked for a few minutes, she got up from the bed, walked over to the door, locked it, and asked me to get into bed with her. I was astonished but tried to please her.

When she returned to New York, we corresponded frequently. She even used to write to Hedda, and she always sent me Christmas greetings and a telegram on my birthday. The last time I spoke with her was after I had written to say that I was not going to attend the presentation of the Life Achievement Award to Bette Davis because of the way she had treated her devoted friend and admirer, director Irving Rapper. Betty Barker, a charming lady and Crawford's secretary for years in California, called me to say that Miss Crawford wished to speak to me and wanted to know if I would be home during the next half hour. I told her I would, and soon a call came from Joan in New York.

"Vincent, darling," she said in a low, controlled voice, "I'm so happy you're not going to the dinner for Bette. She's such a bitch. She made my life miserable on *Baby Jane.*" I assured her I was not going. She added, "Don't let anyone change your mind." I sensed she was under some kind of strain.

"Are you all right?" I asked.

"Yes, darling. Goodbye and God bless."

It was the last time I was to hear her voice. A few days later I received in the mail a photograph of her, obviously touched up, which radiated modesty, sweetness, and a soft, gentle, retiring quality—none of the traits for which she had ever been noted. It was inscribed, "To Vincent—with constant love—Joan." A note was enclosed saying that I could tear it up if I wished. It told me something about her state of mind. She would never have written such a negative, self-deprecating note years before. It was not long after that I was shocked to hear she had died. I called Betty Barker to ask if there was anything I could do to help. She told me that she was getting ready to fly back to New York with Christina. I asked her to tell Christina that I was ready to help in any way possible and would call her when she returned to California.

An announcement about Crawford's will was puzzling. She had cut Christina and Christopher out completely and left whatever remained of her estate, which was small compared to what she had earned over the years, to the young girls, who were now married and had had a good relationship with her.

Within a few days I was approached by NBC to do a story on Joan for TV. I said I could not before talking with Christina. We met in the Valley at a restaurant and chatted for three hours. She was shocked to learn that she had been cut out of Joan's will and did not know what was meant by Joan's statement that "she would understand." She had been under the impression that their relationship was better than ever. They had spoken frequently on the phone together and were most friendly.

When I told her about the NBC interest, she explained that for some time she had been working on a book about her relationship with Joan and would prefer to complete it before any other story came out. There was no vitriol in her voice toward Joan, but she was trying to recapture her experience of growing up. I gave up, for the moment, any notion of writing about Joan.

We spoke of Joan's last days, and I suggested that perhaps two things contributed to her death, which some say was caused by cancer: one was a party given for Rosalind Russell in New York, which Joan attended. She wore a wig that was too wiggy, and her body had grown heavy. She also had a few too many drinks. Newspaper photographs were taken at the party and some of them printed the next day, and Joan was revolted by her appearance. I saw one or two of them, in which she looked more like an overdone madam than the ex-glamour queen. According to some reports, she vowed she would never again appear in public. Because she considered her beauty and attractiveness her main attributes, their loss now meant that she had little to fall back on. Another factor in the gradual lessening of her desire to live was, I suspect, the absence of things to do. For years she had been accustomed to making up a list each day because her schedule was so full. Now that the time had come when there was no need for such a list since publicity and newspaper people were not calling and she was not slated to make any films or TV programs, this realization of having nothing to do the next day—no objective for tomorrow—must have tormented her.

As I look back on her life, I see a spirited young girl determined to rise above the bleak future that lay ahead of her and meet the challenge to become somebody. But in striving to achieve her goals, she often did things she was not proud of, and which left her with a residue of guilt. When she got what she wanted, it did not provide the satisfaction she had hoped for.

While working on this chapter about Joan, I received a call from Shaun Considine, the author of a Streisand biography. He was working on *Bette and Joan: The Divine Feud* and asked me for some information about them. When I told him that I was writing an autobiography, he was most gracious and offered me the following: in a past interview Crawford had said, "There were only two directors from the fifties and sixties that I respected—Vincent Sherman and David Miller. They answered to themselves and not the money men." I thanked him for telling me.

There are those who think that we are each responsible for the choices we make during our lifetimes, ignoring the pressures that society subjects us to. Some of us, who have not been prepared to cope with the problems we encountered, are tossed about like leaves in a summer storm, helpless to control our destinies. Joan Crawford unquestionably made some decisions that were less than noble—but how many of them were free from the pressures that our culture and society imposed on her? The same, most likely, could be said about Bette Davis. They were both remarkable women, dynamic and fascinating, so alike in their struggles to achieve recognition—clawing their way to the top in a man's world and industry, and staying there—and in their desperate, futile searches for happiness.

There were, of course, differences. In life and offscreen, Bette was simple, forthright, honest, and unaffected. The moment she began playing a role she became actorish and theatrical. Joan, on the other hand, was simple, forthright, honest, and unaffected when playing a role, but in life she was exactly the opposite: actorish, theatrical, and affected. Bette dressed poorly and never seemed to care much how she looked, whereas Joan was always well dressed and highly conscious of how she appeared. Bette never thought of herself as being beautiful or attractive, whereas Joan was sure of her beauty and dedicated her life to taking care of it. Finally, I think sex for Bette was a biological need, while for Joan it was, primarily, an ego trip. Each one left her mark on the world, and I consider myself privileged to have known them, worked with them, and loved them, in my fashion.

15

Freelancing

It was the first time in fifteen years that I had been unemployed. I felt a touch of insecurity, but after a few days at home, being able to sleep late, becoming friendly again with Hedda, playing with the children, catching up on back reading, and doing a few neglected chores, I began to enjoy myself. But the break from work did not last long. My agent, Arthur Park, called to ask if I'd be interested in doing a western with Clark Gable. Would I ever! I had had, for a while anyway, a surfeit of women's pictures. A western with Gable was a welcome prospect.

A script titled *Lone Star* soon arrived. It was about Texas, naturally, and was written by Borden Chase, whose name had been on several westerns, including *Red River,* an excellent Howard Hawks film. The story began with Gable, a soldier of fortune, arriving at night at the home in Tennessee of the retired Andrew Jackson. Jackson (played by Lionel Barrymore), with whom Gable once served, wants him to go to Texas and find Sam Houston and convince him of the importance of bringing Texas into the union and of resisting those who are opposed to the project, led by a wealthy and powerful Texan (Broderick Crawford). Gable accepts the mission out of his friendship for Jackson. On the way to Austin he helps rescue a white man from an attack by Indians. The man is Broderick Crawford, his potential enemy, who, at the moment, is duly grateful. When he asks Gable what brings him to Texas, Gable says "business." They ride into Austin together, where Crawford introduces him to Ava Gardner, the editor of the local newspaper and the woman he hopes to marry. She, like Crawford, is opposed to statehood. But she is attracted to Gable, and he to her. Crawford considers Gable a friend until he learns the truth of his mission to Texas. The conflict between them grows, exacerbated by his jealousy about Ava's feelings for Gable. It ends in a battle between the pro- and antistatehood forces, led by Gable and

Crawford, respectively. The antagonism between them is finally resolved by Sam Houston, who points out the threat from Mexico. Crawford is won over, and he and Gable join to fight Santa Ana.

The subject had promise, but the screenplay was poor—the writing pedestrian, the characters superficial, and the dialog juvenile. I told Arthur that although I'd like to work with Gable, the script was bad, and I'd have to turn it down. He urged me to meet with the producer, Z. Wayne Griffin, and Gable and tell them my feelings. I agreed and met them at MGM, where the picture was to be made.

Gable was as handsome offscreen as on, and when I told him I remembered seeing him in New York in a play, *Hawk Island,* before he came to Hollywood, we reminisced about the theater and established a genuine rapport. Griffin was tall and good looking, a socialite and intelligent, but with limited experience in the picture business. I gave them my reaction, tempering my criticism because they obviously thought the script was good. After listening to my ideas about a rewrite, they thanked me and said they'd "mull it over." I made it clear, however, that as much as I'd like to work with them, unless it was rewritten, I could not do it. A few days later Arthur called to say that I could forget about *Lone Star* because Howard Hawks had agreed to direct it. Hawks was an expert filmmaker, and I could only conclude that he would know what to do with it.

Two weeks later I received a phone call from Arthur saying that the deal with Hawks had fallen through and that Griffin and Gable would like to talk with me again. (Later I heard that Hawks had said no one could make a picture out of the script.) They felt that by turning it down initially, I had proved I was not a whore (a director who accepted any script just for money) and respected my integrity. They also agreed now that it needed work. I went once again to MGM.

Griffin had already spoken to a woman who had written the screenplay for a film about Sam Houston some years before and who was supposed to be capable. We discussed in greater detail the changes I thought necessary, which Griffin and Gable both approved, and I agreed to direct the film.

MCA decided that my freelance salary was to be seventy-five thousand dollars per picture, a respectable figure at the time. I was satisfied with the deal and wanted to meet the writer and talk with her, but Griffin said he would relay my suggestions and wanted me to start preparing the production: look for locations, start casting, discuss the sets, and so forth. I hesitated because I always felt that the story was the first and most important factor to be considered and that no amount of production or clever shooting or casting could save a poor story. But Griffin assured me that he understood my objections to the screenplay and would convey my thoughts to the new writer. I mistakenly agreed.

A meeting was set up for me with Hal Rosson, the cameraman. We were to start looking for locations. Meanwhile, a friend cautioned me about Rosson. "He's Gable's favorite cameraman, and if you're not careful, he'll take over the picture." He added that on the MGM lot they referred to him as "little Napoleon." I had no fear of anyone taking over from me. On the contrary, I had reached a stage of security that caused me to look forward to a challenge from someone or to any interaction with a person from whom I could learn something new.

Early one morning I met Rosson at the studio, where a car and a man from the location department were waiting to drive us to various areas in the San Fernando Valley that might suit our needs. Rosson was a few years older and a few inches shorter than I, but well built and ruggedly handsome. I could sense that he was self-assured and knew his job. He had once been married to Jean Harlow, and he was a fixture at MGM. He was polite enough when we were introduced, but as we drove to the first location, he read the morning paper and said very little. Once or twice I tried to start a conversation with him, but he seemed distant, so I did not persist. After we arrived at the location and I appraised it, I asked for his opinion of the area.

"It's up to you," he said. "If you like it, I'll shoot it."

I had hoped for a more friendly response and perhaps a suggestion for a better spot since he knew many of the MGM locations. But he seemed reluctant to open up, so I said I would think about it and make up my mind later. After two or three days of his reticence, during which we had to decide whether we could shoot day for night in some places, and I got only his cryptic, "It's up to you—if you like it, I'll shoot it," I called him aside.

"Hal," I began, "the only reason I'm doing this picture is because I wanted to work with Gable and do a man's picture for a change. But I've got a tough job ahead of me, and I'm going to need all the help I can get. It's a lousy script and—"

He interrupted. "Excuse me, what did you say about the script?"

"I said it was lousy. The producer has promised to rewrite it, but—"

Again he interrupted.

"I guess I owe you an apology. The producer told me that you said it was a great script, and all I could think was that if you thought it was great then you didn't know much. I'm sorry." We both laughed and shook hands. "Don't worry," he said, "I'll help you any way I can."

From that moment on he was like a different man. He became warm and friendly. We kicked around some ideas and traded thoughts about picture making. We were two old pros stimulating each other. He was a tremendous help all through the film. He did a splendid job, and we had a happy company. I learned later that at the end of the picture, he went up to the front office and told one of the MGM executives (when they were considering who would direct *Plymouth Adventure* with Spencer Tracy, a technically difficult film dealing with ships) that, with the exception of Victor Fleming, I knew more about making pictures than anyone he'd worked with. I was naturally flattered and grateful, but Dore Schary, who was in charge of the studio at that time, and whom I knew from New York when we were both struggling, decided to have Clarence Brown direct the film. It was not a successful venture, through no fault of Brown's or Tracy's—just a dull story.

Having scouted various locations for *Lone Star,* I finally decided, and Rosson concurred, that apart from one section of the story that would have to be made on location by a second unit, we could do almost everything on the backlot at MGM and save money.

My attention was then given over to casting. One afternoon, while talking to Lionel Barrymore in the wardrobe department, where he was being fitted for his role, I received a call from my secretary telling me that Ava Gardner was waiting to see me. I said good-bye to Lionel, with whom I had had a pleasant chat about his brother John, who had died several years before. In my office, Ava was sitting in my chair at my desk, her feet on top, perusing a script of *Lone Star.* She was dressed in a pair of blue jeans, a man's shirt, and a pair of loafers. She looked up as I entered. After I introduced myself, she spoke.

"You've got a pretty good reputation, Sherman—what are you doing this piece of shit for?"

I smiled. "You're right," I explained. "But I've just left Warner's, and my agent recommended that I do it for various reasons [to establish my freelance salary and to do a western]; I also wanted to work with Gable. Besides, they've promised to rewrite it."

"I know," she nodded understandingly. "They always give us the same old crap—they'll rewrite it—but they never do. I'm not right for this part, anyway. I can play hookers, fallen women, and such, but a newspaper editor . . . me? . . . Hell, I don't look like I've ever read a newspaper, let alone edit one."

I adored her immediately. She reminded me of Ann Sheridan—modest, honest, down to earth, and a with great sense of humor. I assured her that she underestimated herself. After we talked for a while and I explained how I saw the role, she relaxed and agreed to accept it. She was without a doubt one of the most beautiful women in movies, and her unaffected behavior was refreshing. At the moment she was involved with Frank Sinatra, and I was told they were having problems. Sinatra was at the lowest point in his career in Hollywood. He had just made a film at Universal that was a dud, and the talk was that you couldn't give him away. One day as I was rehearsing a scene with Gardner and Gable, I saw Sinatra standing far back at the rear of the set. I motioned for him to come forward, but he signaled that he preferred to remain in the background. I can only surmise that his ego had been so badly bruised that he didn't want to face people. I knew the feeling and was sympathetic.

Broderick Crawford, I thought, was excellent casting for the role of Gable's opposition, as was Beulah Bondi as Andrew Jackson's mistress. Among others in the final cast were Moroni Olsen as Sam Houston, Ed Begley as a senator, and those wonderful old-timers, William Farnum and Russell Simpson. In addition, I was lucky to have William Conrad and Trevor Bardette in smaller roles, plus James Burke, who had worked for me in *All through the Night.*

Meanwhile, I was told that months before, Gable and MGM had come to a parting of the ways. Several directors on the lot had turned down *Lone Star,* feeling that Gable was washed up. (His pictures since he got out of the army had been less than box-office smashes.) *Lone Star* was to be an independent production, with Gable as a partner. Griffin had been about to take it elsewhere when some executives at MGM, who felt a loyalty to Gable, decided to make and release the film through MGM.

In the midst of preproduction I was forced to take a few days off for a minor operation. When I returned, Griffin informed me that Gable had received a call from someone who warned him that I was a "red" and sent Griffin a list of my activities. I asked if I could see the list.

"It's confidential," he said. "Clark likes you, Vince, and so do I, but he's upset."

I asked again if I could see the list. He finally showed it to me. It was, as I recall, from *Red Channels,* a famous anticommunist journal that purported to contain the name of anyone who had ever been associated with or sympathetic to the Communist party. I went through everything, affirmed those organizations that I had joined and helped, and denied those that I had not. As for being a member of the Communist party, which the list strongly hinted at, I categorically denied it.

"Okay, we don't want to lose you," he said. "So would you object to signing a loyalty oath?"

"I don't approve of loyalty oaths, nor do I think they mean a hell of a lot. If a man was a traitor, he'd be the first to sign. But if it will make you and Gable feel better or reassure you that I am not a red, I'll sign it. . . . And I appreciate your leveling with me." Subsequently, I went up to Eddie Mannix's office, where I signed the oath. He apologized for the necessity of it but explained why the studio had to have it: there was a threat of boycotting any picture made by a red or whoever was even suspected of being sympathetic to the Soviet Union, although that country had only recently been our ally. It was the last I heard of the matter until eighteen months later.

While eagerly waiting for the new script, I was dismayed to hear that the woman they had engaged to do the rewrite had proved unsatisfactory, and they had let her go. I did not even have a chance to meet or talk with her. Instead, Griffin brought back Borden Chase to rewrite and asked me to talk to him. I spent several disagreeable but revealing hours with Chase as he spewed out his so-called super-Americanism and his vicious antidemocratic and antiliberal sentiments. He felt Roosevelt was a traitor and that Hollywood was infested with communists. He must have known my liberal background and might have been baiting me, but I said very little and just let him rave on. I was, however, amused when this great patriot proceeded to tell me that the founding fathers never intended for the United States to be a democracy, but a republic, which was a completely different form of government. He also informed me that in the past, during the period of *Lone Star,* large numbers of people in Texas never wanted to join the Union, and that even today many Texans would prefer not to be a part of the United States. He went on to explain that in a republic only a select few, because of their wealth, intelligence, and background, would be able to vote and govern the country, and the ignorant and poor masses would have no power at all. I asked him if he approved of the republic idea, and he said he did, wholeheartedly.

In addition to his political beliefs, which I found distasteful, he was an unappealing human being who was later accused of incest with his stepdaughter. What amused me about him was that he seriously considered himself to be an important American writer, when the truth was that he was nothing more than a hack. He plotted his projects mechanically: get two men who love the same girl in conflict about a big issue, have a fight here, a chase there, and a final big confrontation when the two men are reconciled. He thought the best love story was about two strong macho men. Women were merely sex objects.

He was a member of the Motion Picture Alliance for the Preservation of American Ideals, headed by Ward Bond, Roy Brewer, Morrie Ryskind, and John Wayne. It was obvious that Borden had been told that I found fault with his script, and naturally he did not approve of me as the director. I kept our conversations as far from politics as possible and stuck to a discussion of the characters, especially how to give them some depth, which he seemed to have little interest in, and he quite likely didn't even know what I was talking about. Finally, a few scenes were improved, but only slightly, and I resigned myself to doing whatever I could to reduce the corny dialog and make the story work. Griffin had heard that I was constantly rewriting scripts on the set, and he was apprehensive. But as he saw each day's dailies and received reports from Gable, he relaxed and allowed me to make changes. Still, I could not make a silk purse out of a sow's ear.

Before we began shooting, Griffin cautioned me to be mindful of Gable's creeping Parkinson's disease. It caused his head to shake if a scene ran too long or if he became tense or tired. Whenever it did happen, which was not too often, I found a reason to cut the scene or change some bit of direction so that he would never become self-conscious about it.

I'm sure I'm not the first director to report that it was a distinct pleasure to work with Clark Gable. He had to be told only once by the assistant that we were ready for him. He appeared dressed and made up, knowing his lines, and ready to rehearse and shoot. He never once objected to any direction I gave him, whether it was when and where to move, or the reading of a line, or any piece of business that I gave him. Sometimes, during a rehearsal, I would sense that a certain line bothered him. "Clark," I'd ask, "if that line doesn't seem right, what do you feel like saying?" His reply was, "Could I say . . .?" And he'd almost always improve the line. As I think back on his behavior, asking "Could I say . . .?" when he was referred to as the king at MGM, I realize how privileged I was to work with him. He was, like Errol Flynn, a much better actor than he was ever given credit for.

In addition to his gracious and charming modesty, he had a wonderful sense of humor. One morning as we finished shooting on the outside, and I returned from a quick lunch in my office (most of the time I enjoyed having lunch with Gable, Tracy, and Cedric Gibbons at their special table in the MGM commissary), I found Clark sitting at the entrance to the stage, smoking a small Robert Burns panatela cigar, as was his habit after lunch.

"How're you doing?" I asked.

"Oh, man, I'm beat," he replied.

"I don't understand," I said. "When we work outside, I can go for hours. The fresh air is so invigorating. I get tired when we work indoors on the stages, where we have such lousy air."

"Well, you're still a young man," he observed.

"Aw, come on, there's not that much difference in our ages," I suggested.

"How old are you?" he asked.

"Forty-six."

"I'm past fifty," he replied. "They say life begins at forty, but they've got no fucking slogans for after fifty."

The shooting of the exteriors occurred during the month of June, when there was almost always a heavy haze in the morning that did not clear up until noon. This hinders shooting in black and white until the sun comes out (though it's often ideal for color). I was losing two and three hours of work every day and falling behind schedule as we sat around becoming bored and enervated. At Warner's I had often been accused of being slow, which I felt was unjustified. I wanted to dispel the notion, came up with an idea, and approached Rosson.

"What would happen," I proposed, "if we rehearsed the full sequence thoroughly so that we were absolutely sure of what we wanted to do. Then, instead of shooting normally, beginning with the longer shots, we proceed in reverse, start with the close shots using artificial light and work backward until we have normal sunlight for the longer shots?"

"You've got a hell of an idea," Hal replied. I assembled the cast and explained what we were going to do. We began, and later, the unit manager, Sergei Petchnikoff, and Joe Cohn, the head of production, came to the set. When they saw the lights, they asked Howard Koch, the first assistant, if I was shooting a night scene. Howard explained what we were doing, and Cohn became worried. He was concerned that it might mean a lot of retakes and reminded me that no one was forcing me to shoot in reverse. I assured them there would be no problems. And there weren't. We saved several days of shooting time.

I do not remember a time when I enjoyed directing a film more than *Lone Star*, despite the poor script. The second unit work was skillfully done by an old-timer, Johnny Waters, and Hal Rosson's brother, Art. We had a great crew, set designer, and music score, and we had Ferris Webster, an excellent editor. The picture received fair reviews and did good if not great business. Griffin and Gable were happy with the results.

When we were finished, they invited me and Broderick Crawford to have dinner with them one evening at Chasen's—just the four of us. We ate and drank and laughed until quite late. It was a release from the usual tension of filmmaking. I must have had one drink too many and challenged Crawford to a brawl (which I don't remember), took a poke at him, and drove my fist through a wall, which in turn brought Gable and Griffin into the fracas. The next morning I woke up in Brod's apartment, my right hand bloody and swollen. Brod said I had been too drunk to drive home the night before, and he had called my wife, who asked him to let me sleep over at his place. I learned later that our melee cost Griffin several hundred dollars.

An amusing incident happened in connection with the filming of *Lone Star.* In a scene following what was obviously a night of love with Gable and Gardner, I shot an added scene that revealed Ava walking happily down the street the next morning, singing to herself. Schary did not think it was good for a laugh and thought it even in poor taste. I tried to point out that it had been good for a laugh since pictures began and was legitimate. It was cut. When I told the story at the lunch table to Tracy and Gable, Tracy observed, "Since Schary took over, there's no fucking in MGM pictures." At the preview I was lucky. Although the shot of Ava walking down the street was cut, when she entered the interior of her newspaper office I had her overlap the happy walk and singing, and with only a few feet of film, the audience responded with a hearty and welcome laugh.

Before I left MGM, a friend loaned me his advance copy of *The Caine Mutiny* to read. After reading it, I immediately advised Gable and Griffin to buy it, but they were discouraged when they heard that the navy would not give its approval or cooperation if the film was made.

Another friend, who ran a bookstore, told me about a great book called *From Here to Eternity.* I got a copy, read it, and was making inquiries about it when it was announced that Sylvan Simon at Columbia had bought the rights to it. Simon was, at the time, Harry Cohn's executive producer. I phoned Sylvan to ask who was going to direct it.

"I'm hoping to do it myself, Vince," he responded. "I'm tired of being an executive and want to get back to the set."

I could understand his feelings and wished him luck. It was not long after that he died suddenly. I called Harry Cohn to express my sympathy and learned that *From Here to Eternity* was a long way off since the army objected to it. But Cohn wanted to talk to me about something else and asked that I come to see him the next day.

"How would you like to make Rita Hayworth's first picture now that she's left Aly Khan?" were the first words that greeted me as I entered Harry Cohn's office.

"Who wouldn't?" I replied. She had been one of the hottest stars in Hollywood when she married the prince. Her picture in a black negligee on the front cover of *Life* magazine a few years before had sent many a man into an erotic reverie. "Have you got a story for her?" I inquired.

"A great story."

"Could I see it?"

"I'll give you the first twenty pages of screenplay. Go into the little office, read it, and tell me what you think."

I took the twenty pages, and after a few minutes of talk about my experience at MGM with Gable, went into the little office—a small adjoining area to the left as you entered Harry's much larger office. The story began in Port of Spain on the island of Trinidad, a British colony, where a young man, an American painter, has been found dead. There is talk that it was suicide, but the inspector of police suspects foul play. Together with the American consul, he informs the dead man's wife (Rita Hayworth), a dancer in a local nightclub, of the tragedy and questions her. She is shocked and says she knows nothing because she and her husband have been at odds for a long time. When the inspector (Torin Thatcher) suggests that Mr. Fabian (Alexander Scourby), a wealthy, mysterious resident in whose company she has often been seen, might know something, she is resentful. She says that he is merely a friend who bought several of her husband's paintings. Upon further questioning in the office of the inspector, who now has evidence that her husband was murdered, he insists that she knows more than she is telling him. She walks out in a huff. Meanwhile, Glenn Ford, to be cast opposite Rita in the hope of repeating their success in *Gilda,* is flying to Trinidad in response to a letter from his brother (the dead painter), who has written that he is in trouble. End of the twenty pages.

"What do you think?" asked Harry.

"It's a springboard," I reported. "What about the rest of it?"

"Would you like to make it?"

"Sure, if the story is good."

"You'll love it. I'll pay you your price, and you can start today, right now." He extended his hand. "Is it a deal?" With Harry, a handshake was a deal.

I hesitated for a moment and finally shook his hand. I had already alerted Arthur Park that Cohn wanted to see me and he might expect some kind of an offer.

"Now go downstairs to Virginia Van Upp's office. You know her, don't you?" I nodded. We had met the year before at the home of composer Lester Lee, my neighbor in Van Nuys. "I'll tell her you're going to direct the picture. . . . Oh, do you know Bert Granet?" I said I did, and he added, "Good, he's the producer. They'll tell you the rest of the story."

As I left his office a cool wind passed over me—or had I only imagined it? I became concerned. It had all happened too fast. Why was I chosen to direct the film when almost every big director in town would, I thought, have been happy to work with Hayworth? She had been a star before she married Aly Khan and now, as a princess, with all her publicity, she was even more glamorous and valuable.

Virginia Van Upp had worked on *Gilda,* expertly directed by Charles Vidor and beautifully photographed by Rudy Mate. It had been a great success, and Van Upp became, for a while, Cohn's executive producer. She left Columbia later but was now back writing the screenplay for Rita's return to the screen. Rita had been away three years.

Bert Granet, whom I had met some time before, was an experienced producer and a nice man. He and Virginia greeted me as I entered her office. After a few minutes of badinage about directing a princess, I said, "Well, I guess Harry told you, I read the first twenty pages of screenplay, and he said you'd tell me the rest of the story."

Virginia was a buxom lady in her latter forties with a mop of flaming red hair. She was seated on a low sofa surrounded by piles of typewritten pages. In her hands was a pad and pencil. Bert was in a chair across from her, and I took a seat between them. Virginia squirmed a bit and turned to Bert. "Bert," she said, "I've been working all morning on this scene, and I'm a little tired. Why don't you tell Vince the story?"

Bert seemed surprised. "Virginia, it's your story," he replied. "I think it would be better if you told it." As they discussed who would tell me the story, I had a sinking feeling in the pit of my stomach and a premonition that something was not right. At last Virginia agreed to start, with Bert promising to fill in whenever necessary. Two hours later, I had heard not one story but four or five, as the line would go along in one direction, then branch off to another, return to the original, and branch off again.

Anyone who has worked either as a director or as a writer knows that when you have too many stories, you are in trouble; it means that you don't have one good one. When they finished, I asked if I could read the original story.

Virginia found a copy. "It won't do you much good," she said as she handed it to me. "We've changed so much of it." I said we'd talk again tomorrow. Bert left the office with me. As we moved down the corridor, he spoke quietly, confidentially.

"You have no idea what you've gotten yourself into," he said.

"Tell me, for God's sake," I pleaded.

"When Rita came back, Cohn had to get something ready for her, so he called Virginia. She whipped up a yarn that Cohn bought. Now they're in trouble. I'm getting off it, and I'd advise you to do the same."

"But I just got on. Besides, how can you get off? You're the producer, aren't you?"

"Not really," Bert replied. "I signed to produce Garson Kanin's film with Judy Holliday, when Cohn asked me if I'd pitch in and give him a hand with the Hayworth project. I sense big trouble ahead, and Cohn will be looking for someone to blame, so I'm getting off." I hated to see Bert leave since I felt he would be a help to me as a producer, but he was adamant.

That evening I read Van Upp's original story, a thin morsel with nothing substantial to feed on. I slept little that night and went to the studio early the next morning. A large, sumptuous office on the ground floor was waiting for me. No sooner had I settled in than a call came from Cohn.

"Come upstairs. I want to talk to you." I went up and was promptly admitted to his office. He was sitting behind his desk, a smoldering coal ready to burst into flame.

"I don't like a quitter," he said. When I pretended not to know what he was talking about, he continued. "Granet just walked off the Hayworth picture."

"Well, Harry," I replied, "he's worried, and you can't blame him. You said you had a story, but at the moment there's not much to work with."

"Don't you think I know it?" he quickly admitted. "Listen, Rita came back unexpectedly. I had no warning, and according to the terms of her contract, I had to put her back on salary or lose her. I didn't have anything for her, so I called Van Upp. She concocted a story that I thought might work, and I paid her fifty thousand dollars for it, but she's drinking and having trouble at home. Hayworth has been drawing thirty-five hundred dollars a week for the past sixteen weeks, and New York is screaming for me to get something started. That's why I called on you. I know you can help me out. Will you do it?" I had never seen the imperial Harry Cohn so abject, so meek, so disturbed. I was genuinely touched and didn't remind him that he had literally tricked me into my deal with him.

"All right, Harry," I said. "I understand the situation, and I'll do the best I can."

"Good. Get yourself a writer, and I'll find a way to let Van Upp go. And listen, just get me twelve reels of film, an exotic background, a love-hate relationship, a few good dance numbers, and we'll go to the post. Okay?"

"Okay," I said, and he shook my hand again.

"I knew I could count on you," he replied.

It had all happened so fast that I could hardly believe it. As with *Lone Star,* when I allowed my admiration for Gable and my desire to do a man's picture as well as establish my freelance salary, to sway me to do a script that was not good, so now, with Rita Hayworth, because she was an exciting star and a glamorous personality, I had accepted a project that was doubtful and risky. I suppose I also enjoyed the challenge and had begun, mistakenly, to think that I could make almost any story work. Overconfidence can become a dangerous flaw. I phoned Jimmy Gunn, the writer who had worked with me on *The Unfaithful* and *Harriet Craig.* He was free and delighted to work on a Hayworth project. I sent for a print of *Notorious,* the excellent melodrama Hitchcock had made with Ingrid Bergman, Cary Grant, and Claude Rains. In it Bergman, whose father has been a Nazi, in order to prove her loyalty to the USA, agrees to marry Claude Rains, suspected of being a big wheel for the Nazis, and to spy on him. I stole from it: Rita's passport is taken from her by the inspector. She will not be able to leave Trinidad unless she can prove her innocence, and the only way she can do that is by becoming intimate with Scourby and finding out what he is up to on the island. Glenn arrives and is shocked to learn of his brother's death. He is at first suspicious of Rita, then thinks he made a mistake and is drawn to her. But soon he becomes suspicious again as she tries to cooperate with the police, thus establishing the love-hate relationship. The inspector forbids Rita to tell Glenn what is going on, and Glenn decides to conduct his own investigation into his brother's death.

As Jimmy and I were discussing the story, which had no foundation, I hit upon the idea that Scourby was working with the Russians, who were anxious to establish a base in the Caribbean for an eventual attack on the United States, never dreaming that later, in reality, there would be the Cuban missile crisis.

While we were working out the details, Cohn asked me to come to his office. He wanted me to meet Rita. She was simply dressed, seemed shy and apprehensive, and said little. She was still beautiful, but her face was pale and slightly drawn, and I sensed that she was sad and depressed. I tried to cheer her up by telling her how much I enjoyed her work, especially in *Gilda,* and that I hoped we could duplicate its success. Cohn asked me to tell her a little about the story. I improvised a few scenes and tried to assure her that we were working hard to give her a good film. She seemed to relax, and after she left the office Cohn cautioned me, "By the way, don't give her too much dialog. Give it to the other people and let her react. She's a great reactionary type."

A few days later he called to say that he was arranging for Rita to have a special interview with Louella Parsons. They'd meet in my office in the afternoon. We'd have a drink with them, and after a few words with Louella about the film, we'd leave them alone to talk.

"Order some liquor, hors d'oeuvres, and flowers," he added. "And charge it to the studio. You know, give the whole thing some class. I'll also make arrangements to have pictures taken."

The day of the interview, Rita arrived dressed in a pair of blue jeans, a man's shirt, and scuffed loafers over bare feet, with her hair simply brushed back and no makeup. A few minutes later, Cohn brought Louella into my office. He was all smiles as he saw the flowers on my desk and coffee table and took note of the tray of hors d'oeuvres and the various bottles on a small bar that I had requested. Then he looked at Rita and his face fell. After I welcomed Louella and she greeted Rita, I poured drinks for everyone, and they engaged in a round of questions and answers: how Rita felt about her return to California, going back to work, and so forth. Soon Harry and I excused ourselves and went up to his office.

"How do you like that broad?" he said. "I arrange a special interview for her that's going to be read and seen by millions of people, and she comes in dressed like a peasant—worse, like something the cat dragged in." No pictures were taken. I could only think that Rita had little interest in gossip columnists and publicity.

When I asked Cohn if plans had been made for Rita's dance numbers, he told me that the studio had engaged Valerie Bettis, a dancer who had made a hit in a New York musical, to work with Rita, choreograph the dances, and even play a role in the film if there was something suitable. I had seen Bettis perform when I was in New York on a business trip a few months before, and she was sensational. When she arrived, I told her the story, as far as we had developed it. We got together with my neighbor, Lester Lee, and his collaborator, Ned Washington, who were to do the music and lyrics for the picture. We discussed the kind of dance numbers that would be needed, and I soon realized that Valerie was not only talented but also intelligent and articulate. Lester and Ned went to work, and Valerie began exercises with Rita. After a few days, Lester and Ned came up with the first number, and Valerie started rehearsals. A short time later she came to see me.

"I think you'd better come to the stage and see a rehearsal of what I'm planning to do, and also what my problem is," she said. "Rita has been away from dancing for several years, and her body shows it."

"What do you mean, exactly?" I asked.

"To put it bluntly, she's become flabby in places, and we'll have to work hard to get her firm again. I don't know if she's willing to do it or is up to it."

"Do you want me to talk to her?"

"Not yet—I think she realizes what she has to do, but I'd like for you to have a look at what I'm preparing."

The next day I watched a rehearsal. I could see what Valerie meant. Rita was in a black leotard, perspiring freely, and while her figure was still good, there was a flabbiness about her thighs. But I thought Valerie was moving in the right direction, and the dance numbers promised to be exciting. I assured her that she'd have ample time for rehearsals since we were weeks away from a completed screenplay.

Valerie and I became friendly, and she was a frequent weekend guest in our home. Hedda and Hedwin found her to be a stimulating artist and were intrigued by her.

Late one afternoon, as Gunn and I were trying to complete a scene, my secretary announced that Rita was in the office and would like to see me. I rose to welcome her, then told her that Valerie was happy with her and that I thought the dance numbers would be great. I added that she was looking better every day. She seemed pleased and wanted to know how the screenplay was coming along. I told her we were working day and night to get it done. When Jimmy said something about having dinner, I suggested that if she did not have a date, perhaps she would join us. To my surprise, she said she'd like to, and we went to Lucy's, for years

a well-known Italian restaurant near Paramount Studios. After a pleasant meal during which Rita said very little but occasionally hinted that
she was nervous about facing the camera again, I assured her it was a
natural reaction and she should not worry—we'd go slowly until she felt
at ease. Jimmy sensed that she wanted to say more and excused himself,
saying that he would take a cab back to the studio and try to finish the
sequence we had been working on. I promised to join him shortly.

During the next half hour Rita relaxed and began talking about
the years she had been away from Hollywood, some of which were painful. She confessed, somewhat bitterly, that when she had married Aly
Khan, she had almost three hundred thousand dollars, but when she left
him, she had nothing. He had spent not only his money, but also most
of hers. (I remembered that when I was in London in 1948-49 and having a suit of clothes made in Savile Row, I had been told that the Aga
Khan had shut off all credit to his son.) She also revealed that Aly had a
print of *Gilda* and would often run it before he'd make love to her, which
caused her to wonder if he had married Gilda and not her. I soon gathered that she was lonely, insecure, and anxious to unburden herself. I
wanted to hear more, but I was also impatient to get back to the studio
to help Jimmy.

"Rita," I said, "I've enjoyed talking with you, and I hope we can do
it again soon, but I do have to get back to the studio to work on *your*
picture."

"You're bored with me, aren't you?" she said ruefully.

"Oh my God, no! Please don't think that." I tried to assure her I
was not—and I really wasn't. I was just worried about finishing the
screenplay because the whole studio seemed to be waiting. But she was
not convinced.

"I can always get a man," she said with a slightly bitter smile, "but I
can't seem to hold him."

In those few seconds I thought I caught the sadness of her life: Rita
Cansino, an uneducated Mexican girl, whose father was a dancing teacher,
had become a beautiful and desirable movie star. She had married several times, once to Orson Welles, and now was the ex-wife of a prince
who was the son of one of the world's richest men. She was alone, fearful
of the future, and seeking a friend. The world would not have believed
it. I probably should have spent the rest of the evening holding her hand
and letting her talk, but my preoccupation with the film took precedence. We drove back to the studio, where her secretary, a nice young
woman, was waiting to take her home.

In a few more weeks we had completed a first-draft screenplay, and Cohn suggested that I get Oscar Saul, a writer whom I had known in New York and who was at Columbia, to help polish and spice up the script. Oscar was a talented man with a genuine sense of humor, and we worked well together.

While he was doing the final rewrite, I asked Cohn if there was any chance of shooting the film in Trinidad, and he explained that it would be too expensive. I asked if I could at least pay a visit to the island to get a feel of the place, and he agreed. I left on a Friday, flew to Miami, where I spent the night, and departed early the next morning for Port of Spain. I took my camera and made color shots of exteriors and interiors to bring back and give to the art director, Walter Holscher, who later did a great job of duplicating the atmosphere of Trinidad. It was a beautiful island with lush tropical vegetation, colorful streets, and calypso bands. The Columbia representative there met me and was most helpful. I spent one evening with Geoffrey Holder's brother, who had a small dance group. He was a talented and gracious young man, and his group performed several numbers that were unique. I would have liked to bring them to Hollywood to appear in the film, but Cohn would not go for it. I was in Trinidad only three days, but I was able to get a feeling for the place and, with the help of the art director, recreate its ambiance.

On my return Oscar gave me several scenes that he had rewritten, and they were greatly improved. Rita had worked hard, her body had firmed up, and she was in good spirits and as sexy and beautiful as ever. I looked forward to starting. Only once was I disturbed. Late one night as I was about to leave my office, the phone rang. It was Rita calling. She had had a few too many drinks.

"I've got a problem," she muttered. "My brother says if I don't get him a job as an actor in the picture, he's going to picket the studio with a sign saying he's my brother and I refuse to help him. . . . What'll I do?"

"Tell him to leave you alone," I replied instantly. "You've got a tough grind ahead of you and can't be bothered. If he wants a job, tell him to call me."

"Thank you," she said. "Do you know Charlie Feldman?"

"I've met him. . . . Why?"

"I just kicked him in the balls and sent him home." She hung up. I never heard from her brother, nor did she ever mention the phone conversation or Charlie Feldman again. Neither did I.

We needed a title for the film, and one evening while I was having dinner at home, my daughter, Hedwin, who was listening as I told Hedda how we were finishing the screenplay, suggested that we call it *Affair in Trinidad*. I thought it was good, exotic and erotic. Cohn agreed, and so it was called.

With Rita and Glenn heading the cast, Scourby playing the main villain, and Thatcher the inspector, I had George Voskovec and Karl Stepanek, two talented refugees, play Scourby's associates. Bettis played Voskovec's wife; Steven Geray, the nightclub owner; and Juanita Hall, Rita's maid. I also had several other good actors in smaller roles. Joe Walker was again my cameraman. He was not only a first-rate artist but also modest, and he made my work a pleasure. Joe lived past ninety and was credited with many improvements for cameras and lenses. He also had a great crew, which enabled me to make the film on schedule. Sam Nelson was my capable assistant.

During the first weeks of shooting, Rita was nervous, but I understood and spent extra time rehearsing with her. Her confidence returned, and each day she improved. Like Ava Gardner and Ann Sheridan, she was a better actress than ever given credit for. But what was remarkable was to see how her eyes lit up and her body became electrically charged the moment she was called upon to dance.

My editor was Viola Lawrence, the same talented lady who had cut *Harriet Craig,* and whom I trusted. The rushes looked good, and Cohn called me often to tell me he was pleased. Only once was I disappointed with him. It was during the second week of shooting. Rita was uncertain about an upcoming scene, and I said we'd talk about it at the end of the day. I finished with her about 5:30 and had another shot to make. She asked me to drop by her dressing room afterward and left the stage. A few minutes after six, I was in her room. It was upstairs in another building, and it was the first time I'd ever been there. She offered me a drink, and as we began to talk her phone rang. She answered it. After a pause, she said, "Yes, he's here." She extended the phone to me. "It's for you."

Following my "hello," a female voice said, "Just a moment." Then I heard Cohn's voice: "What are you doing in her dressing room?" I was so stunned by his question that I replied simply: "We're discussing tomorrow's work—why?" There was a pause. "Nothing—I'm sorry." He hung up.

I was puzzled. Rita took the phone back and said, "It was Harry, wasn't it?"

"Yes, he wanted to know what I was doing in your dressing room." She smiled.

I became angry. "He's got a helluva nerve, and I'll tell him."

I started to reach for the phone, but she stopped me. "Don't let it bother you. Whenever I'm on the lot, his spies tell him every move I make. He's so jealous he can't see straight."

"Jealous? I don't understand. Is there something I should know?"

She smiled and told me a story I had never heard, how when she first came to Columbia, Harry had fallen in love with her and at one time proposed marriage. She had turned him down. Ever since, she said, he had always been curious about any man she spoke to and jealous of any man who came close to her. It told me something about Harry that only made him seem human and vulnerable. I never referred to it again, nor did he.

When we completed the shooting and ran the first rough cut at Cohn's house one night, I had a chance to judge it properly. It was not a very good or important picture, but I thought it was fair entertainment and the best I could have done under the circumstances. Cohn was pleased and asked me to come to his office the next morning. Ben Kahane, Columbia's vice president and a respected member of the film industry, was there along with Irving Briskin, the head of Columbia's TV division and former B picture producer. As I took a seat, Cohn said, "I want you to know how much I appreciate what you did for the studio with the Hayworth picture."

"It's nothing to be proud of, Harry," I replied.

"Don't worry, we'll do all right with it. And I know the nights you sat up putting it together." He turned to Briskin. "I want you to give this guy a check for ten thousand dollars as a bonus."

I was speechless. In all the years I had worked at Warner's, Jack Warner had never offered me a bonus, although he had often expressed appreciation of my work by increasing my salary, provided I signed a new contract extending my services. After recovering, I managed to say, "Harry, that's the nicest thing that's ever happened to me, and I thank you."

"Okay," he said. I rose and started out, thinking the meeting was over, when he stopped me.

"Wait a minute, I'm not through with you yet," he said in his gruff manner. I turned back, wondering what he had in mind. "I'm also giving you 2 percent of our share of the profits. Rita's company, Beckworth Corporation, owns 25 percent, and we own the rest."

I could not believe it. "Harry," I said, "again I have to tell you that I am not only grateful, but touched. I just hope you do well with the picture."

"You will too," he said. "I'll see you at lunch."

I gave little thought to the percentage because I had heard about such deals, and no one to my knowledge had ever received anything for their points. But for Harry Cohn, the man almost everyone in Hollywood hated, to treat me with such kindness moved me. Back in my office, I called my wife to give her the good news, and she said I'd be foolish not to try to remain at Columbia. But they made only a few pictures each year, had no directors under contract, and had only three or four producers, so what did I have to offer? I began to examine my storage bin of ideas for films that I had gathered over the years and remembered a story about the copper wars in Montana that I thought could be woven into another project for Glenn and Rita.

At lunch I told Cohn that I had an idea I'd like to talk to him about, and he asked me to come to his office the following morning. Late that afternoon, Rita dropped by to say hello and chat. I poured us a drink and told her how pleased Harry was with the film and that I was sure he'd run it for her as soon as the music and sound effects were finished and an answer print was available. She didn't seem concerned, and I had a feeling that for the moment she was bored by pictures.

She said she was anxious to get away from Hollywood and was planning to go to Mexico for a vacation. I heartily approved. It was the first time we had relaxed and talked personally since that night at Lucy's before the film started. I asked her if she had a dinner date and, if not, would she like to have dinner with me at an Italian restaurant on Gower Street near the studio. She said she would and asked if I'd drive her home afterward so she could let her secretary go for the night. I agreed. She called her home and I called mine. We enjoyed dinner, and afterward I drove her to a house in Beverly Hills that she was renting. When we arrived, she invited me in for a nightcap and asked if I'd fix us a drink while she went upstairs to see her children and kiss them goodnight.

Ten or fifteen minutes later she came downstairs in a bathrobe, barefoot, and her hair hanging loosely about her face. I handed her a drink, and she sat at one end of the sofa. I sat at the other.

"Would you mind if I put my feet up?" she asked.

"Of course not," I replied. She lifted her legs and they came to rest in my lap. I put my drink down and began gently massaging her feet. She relaxed, closed her eyes, and muttered, "Oh yes . . ."

As I looked at her, whatever sophistication and sex emanated from her screen persona, she now seemed an innocent child. I sat quietly watching her until she opened her eyes. "Thank you so much. You're very kind."

We talked a while longer, then she said, "Now I think I'll take a warm bath and go to bed." She got up, and I was prepared to leave when she turned to me and said, "Would you like to come up with me?"

Could any man refuse? I doubt it. Anyway, I couldn't. I went into the bathroom with her and drew her bath while she brushed her hair. Then she slipped out of her robe. Her body was voluptuous and firm. I helped her as she stepped into the tub, and I bathed her as I would a child. She seemed to crave tenderness, to be starved for it. I had never seen such a peaceful, contented look on her face. My heart went out to her. After a while she said she'd better get out before she fell asleep in the tub. I draped a huge towel around her, and, as she stood still, I dried her. Afterward, she slipped into a silk nightgown, and I walked her to her bedroom. She crawled into the bed and slid between the covers. Any carnal desire I might have had melted away as I observed her innocence and vulnerability. She looked at me for a moment. "Don't you want to lie down with me for a while?" she asked.

"I think I should go home and let you sleep," I replied. She seemed hurt. I got undressed and lay next to her, held her in my arms for almost an hour, then we made love. The next day she came to my office and said, "I don't know why I'm going to Mexico. I don't really have anything there. I'd rather stay here if I could see you."

I realized then that she was desperate for someone to love and cherish her, someone she could talk to and be herself with, someone whom she could rely on who was not just looking for a toss in the hay. Again my heart went out to her. I put my arms around her. "Rita, darling," I began as gently as possible. "You're a lovely, talented lady, and it would be easy to fall madly in love with you, but I'm married to a remarkable woman who has been a devoted wife and companion for many years. We also have two beautiful children, and it would be unfair of me to allow you to count on me for the love and care you need and deserve. Go to Mexico, try to have fun, and know that I will treasure every moment I've spent with you." There were tears in her eyes as she kissed me goodbye. I did not see her again. But I was pleased to learn that when John Kobal was going to write about her, she suggested that he talk to me.

Affair in Trinidad opened to mild reviews but excellent business, and I was surprised to receive statements from Columbia over the next few years, reporting sales and expenses and checks for my percentage. The film cost a little over $1 million dollars and grossed over $6 million, a respectable sum in 1953. My checks amounted to well over fifteen thousand dollars. It was not the money, but the consideration Cohn revealed that to this day prompts me to defend him whenever I hear someone badmouth him. Later, when I was talking to Fred Zinnemann, he agreed that Cohn had also treated him decently, and Dan Taradash was equally impressed with Harry's humanity.

The same afternoon that I said goodbye to Rita, I told Cohn about my idea for a story set in Montana at the time of the discovery of copper, and how we could use the plot of *Gilda* for it. He considered it for a moment and said, "Listen, . . . why don't you stay here? We'll work out a deal for you to produce and direct, and you can get a few projects going." It was precisely what I wanted to hear him say, and we worked out a deal whereby I would have a nominal drawing account while I was preparing projects and then my salary plus a percentage of the profits for any film I produced and directed.

In addition to the story of the copper wars, I came across a western about a doctor in a cavalry outpost who had been disgraced in his profession but, through his efforts in promoting understanding and peace with the Indians, had redeemed himself by saving his post from annihilation.

With two stories in the works and a good relationship with the head of the studio, I was happily looking forward to the best years of my life. In fact, Harry had taken to calling on me for my advice on various studio matters. Should he make the deal with Broccoli and Allen to do a film in London with Alan Ladd? I urged him to accept. Would I look at the rough cut of *Salome* with Rita, which Buddy Adler had produced following *Trinidad* and which William Dieterle had directed? Would I suggest how to improve the dance numbers that had been staged by Valerie, but which Harry was not yet satisfied with? (This was an embarrassing task, since Adler was humiliated, and Dieterle had been a director at Warner's when I started; in addition, Valerie was a friend.) But I sat one night for several hours with Buddy and made suggestions for changes. Valerie accepted them, Cohn approved them, and they were later filmed. During this period Cohn invited me and Hedda for dinner at his home and to a charming party that he and his wife, Joan, gave for many of their Hollywood friends.

One morning he summoned me to his office. "I've just signed your old friend, Jerry Wald, as executive producer," he said. "He's through at RKO and going to start here next week. I'm going to let you two run the studio."

I knew that Cohn was constantly in touch with Jerry, who was having trouble at RKO, where he had moved after leaving Warner's. But what Cohn did not know was that Jerry and I had come to a parting of the ways. I had made six pictures for him at Warner's, and we had presumably become close friends, when he went to RKO and formed a partnership with Norman Krasna. He had never mentioned a word to me prior to the announcement, and I was hurt. Nor did he say good-bye when he left. Several months passed and I still had not heard from him, when I was told that he was having trouble with Howard Hughes and could not get a picture started. Finally a call came, and he said he wanted to talk to me. He asked me to leave Warner's and join him and Krasna. No specific deal was mentioned, but he indicated that we might work out a small sum up front and a percentage. Before I left, I was convinced that Jerry was simply trying to get me to commit to a picture for little money. I turned him down.

I did not tell Cohn any of this. Instead, I said that Jerry was an energetic, prolific, and hard-working producer, and I hoped all would be well. Nor did I tell him that although I admired Jerry's ambition and his casting and promotion ideas, he was no help when it came to developing a project with a writer and director: he had no patience with the probing of character or digging into the guts of a story, qualities I think an executive should have.

When Jerry arrived, I sent him a note of congratulations and wished him well. I also offered my cooperation. He phoned to thank me, and we made a date to talk in a few days. When we met, he was cordial, but he picked up a sheet of paper from his desk and said, "Vincent, I've gone over the program of pictures in preparation and decided that we have too many westerns scheduled. I want to drop your western. I like your idea of doing a remake of *Gilda,* except I'd like to switch it from the past in Montana to the present in Tangiers and make someone like Lucky Luciano the villain."

My immediate reaction was negative. "If you make it modern and set it in Tangiers, I see no difference from *Gilda,* which was modern and in Argentina. The point of a switch, I've always thought, was to change the background and the period."

"Well, that's how I see it, and I would like for you to try it my way. Besides, why do you want to be a producer? You're a director, and I've got some projects I'd like for you to direct." I hesitated about giving him an immediate reply but sensed that we were on a collision course.

"Let me think about it," I said and returned to my office. That night I discussed the situation with Hedda. I told her that I found myself in an awkward position: when Jerry was a producer at Warner's and came up with a foolish suggestion, I could tell him straight out and he'd back off. Now that he was the executive producer, I could not argue with him as I had before. Also, I did not want Cohn to think that I approved of what Jerry was doing with my two projects, but I could not go behind his back and criticize. I saw no alternative except to ask for my release.

The next day I wrote a short letter to Cohn stating simply that I did not agree with Jerry's plans for the remake of *Gilda* or canceling the western, but that as executive producer he was entitled to put his program to work. I thought it best, however, that I leave. Cohn was surprised and said he thought Jerry and I were friends. I said we were, but I could not go along with his plans this time. Harry gave me my release, and we parted amicably. Jerry put Al Hayes on the rewrite of *Gilda,* but it was never made.

Two years later Jerry was finished at Columbia and went to Twentieth Century–Fox. During those two years I suffered a harrowing experience, and Hollywood went through one of the most shameful periods in its history.

16

Red Scare

While waiting for MCA to come up with a job offer, being anxious to work and make a good film after the two profitable but mediocre projects I had recently done, I went through my memory file of stories that I liked but had not yet made. I recalled *Ghost of a Chance*. It had been submitted to Warner's while I was still under contract there.

It was about a young New York street hoodlum, full of hostility, who is sent to prison for five years because of a petty crime. His cell mate is an old man who was once a famous tap dancer but who, in a fit of jealousy, killed his wife and is now in prison for life. The old man (an ideal role for James Barton) recognizes the self-destructive drive in the young man and decides to save him by teaching him how to dance, so that he will have a profession when he gets out and won't waste his life in bitterness. At first the young man refuses, but he is finally won over. When they are free from prison duties, they spend countless hours together; the old man teaches him everything he learned in his thirty years of show business. As the young man acquires the technique, he reveals a furious energy, the result of his hostility. The old man tries to change this but gives up after realizing that it is the young man's rage that makes his dancing so unique and powerful. He expresses the pent-up anger and frustration of the dispossessed.

When the time comes for the young man to be released, the old man gives him the name of an agent in New York, but he advises him to change his name and say nothing about his life in prison. The agent gets the young man a tryout in a musical, and the producers are so impressed by his dynamic quality and highly charged dancing that he is given the lead. During rehearsals, word of his talent spreads quickly up and down Broadway. Excitement about him builds, as does the mystery of his past. He falls in love with the leading lady, about his own age and recently widowed. She has a small daughter, age five, whom he adores. His reticence to talk about his past and his struggle to keep it a secret, for fear of losing the woman he loves and her daughter, who are slowly changing his attitude toward life, provide the drama. He sends the old man weekly reports of what is happening, and as opening night approaches, the old man, in failing health, is anxious to see his protégé before it is too late. He escapes from prison, makes his way to the theater, and manages to see the first performance from a niche in the second balcony, unaware that the police have traced him to the theater and surrounded it. He watches with satisfaction as the audience applauds his handiwork. When the curtain falls, the young man is given an ovation. The old man rejoices. When the lights come up and the police enter, he is found dead. The young man reveals his identity, his past, and his debt to the old man. He also wins the love of his leading lady and her daughter.

Ghost of a Chance was written by Ned Young, whom I had never heard of when I read it in 1950. I had asked Trilling and Warner to buy it for me. They said they would if they had Gene Kelly under contract, but since they didn't, they turned it down. I then phoned the author's representative at MCA, Ned Brown, to ask about the price. If not too high, I would have considered buying it myself. He told me that it was already sold to MGM, as I recall, for twenty-five thousand dollars.

Since five years had passed and nothing had been done with it, I thought MGM might be willing to sell it and that I could persuade Universal to buy it as a vehicle for Donald O'Connor, who was a good dancer and popular at the time. I met with Arthur Park and told him the story, which he thought was great. He was surprised to learn that his agency had sold it. He was also enthusiastic about my idea of talking to Universal about it. I added that, however, there might be a stumbling block: the author, I had heard, had recently appeared before the House Unamerican Activities Committee. Arthur immediately assured me that neither he nor I need be concerned because such matters were strictly a question of studio policy.

The next day he called to say that MGM was willing to sell the property for a reasonable sum and that Ed Muhl, the head of Universal, wanted to talk with me. An appointment was arranged, and I met Arthur and his associate, Herb Brenner, at Universal. Before we went in to see Muhl, I again mentioned the advisability of telling him about Ned Young, but they both said it was neither my responsibility nor theirs. Muhl was excited about the project and suggested that I buy it from MGM since I could probably get it for less than Universal could. They would then buy it from me, and we could work out our deal—a salary and a percentage. Within a few days, because it was complicated for me to buy it and then sell it, Arthur arranged for MGM to sell it directly to Universal. He also worked out the deal for me.

I had counted on producing and directing the film myself, but Muhl explained that studio policy required one of their producers to supervise the project. However, he said I could choose one from their list. I chose Stanley Rubin, with whom I had worked when I was directing a show after the war for the navy at the Los Angeles Memorial Coliseum. That night Stanley called me at home to thank me. He had read the story and thought it was sensational.

Before we could begin work, contracts had to be drawn with MGM and Universal, which would require a couple of weeks. It suited me because I wanted to go to New York for a visit. When I returned, Muhl assigned me an office and told me that, on thinking it over, he felt the character of the street hoodlum was much better for Tony Curtis than for O'Connor. I could see his point, but what about the dancing? He had talked to Curtis, who would start taking tap dancing lessons immediately. By the time we were ready to shoot in ten or twelve weeks, he'd be ready to go. That day at lunch in the studio restaurant, Tony Curtis came to my table and told me how thrilled he was to be doing the story. He said he'd work day and night to prepare for it.

The next morning when I arrived and picked up a copy of the *Hollywood Reporter,* there was an item in the gossip column that read: "The story Vince Sherman is set to direct at Universal was written by one of the most obstreperous witnesses ever to appear before the HUAC." An hour later, Arthur called to say the shit had hit the fan. Muhl vowed he knew nothing about Ned Young and was upset. I reminded Arthur of my advice, but again he said it was not his or my responsibility to bring it up. I asked him if Muhl wanted to cancel the deal. He said no, but he'd come talk to me.

In my office, he explained that Universal did not want to lose me or the deal, but it was essential to get Young's name off the script; otherwise they might have trouble releasing the picture. Did I know Young personally? Could I ask him if he'd agree to remove his name so that I could make the film? I told Arthur that I had met Young only once, in 1953, when MCA brought him to my office at Columbia as a possible writer on the western I was preparing. Otherwise, I had never spoken to him. As for me asking him to remove his name from the script, I refused. If Universal wanted to ask him or offer him money to do it, that was up

to them and to him. Arthur said Universal could not do it, but maybe I
could. Again I refused; it would be insulting to ask anyone to take his
name off something he had written; and if I did ask, he'd be justified in
telling me to go to hell. I added that I would not hold Universal to the
deal; if they wished, I'd go home and forget the whole thing. Arthur said
he'd talk to Muhl and get back to me. He called later to say that Muhl
was grateful for my cooperation but asked to cancel the deal.

When I told Hedda, she was furious—with Universal, MCA, MGM,
and me. She said that the studio had made a deal with me and should
honor it. She was always more practical and businesslike than I. I made
decisions from emotion, she from her head.

A few days later Arthur called to say that MCA was sending me a
script about the Lewis and Clark expedition to explore the Northwest. It
also featured the story of Sacajawea, the Indian girl who acted as a guide.
I had read the Lewis and Clark journals and thought a film would be
possible. It was a Pine-Thomas production for Paramount and was to
star Charlton Heston. But I found the screenplay dull. If they were willing to rewrite it, I said, I'd be glad to talk with them. The answer was no,
so I turned it down. Arthur reported that Lew Wasserman, the head of
MCA, had said, "Tell Vince they are not paying his kind of money often
these days and for him to make the picture." I told him that if Lew asked
me to do a good script for half my salary, I'd prefer that rather than my
full salary for a bad script. The picture was made by someone else but
was a dismal failure.

Not long after, Arthur called to say that he was having a problem
concerning me: someone at Universal had said that I was supporting
communist writers and buying stories from them. I told him it was a lie
and asked if my accuser would name any story that I had bought other
than the one from Paul Webster, a songwriter, years before. He added
that the same person had said I was a well-known red. I liked Arthur. He
was a decent man, but I thought the problem had developed because of
the way MCA had handled the situation, not making it known that I
had suggested telling Muhl about Young and thus letting my enemies
think that I was trying to pull a fast one, doing a film written by a communist. I felt that Wasserman and MCA should step forward and protect me. They didn't, and I asked for my release.

I signed with Sam Jaffee (not the actor), whom I had known for a
long time and who was Bogart's agent. Sam checked and learned that I
was on a gray (not black) list. He advised me to talk with Ward Bond,
who was on a committee of the Motion Picture Alliance for the Preser-

vation of American Ideals and could probably get me cleared. He made an appointment for me, and I went to Bond's home. He kept me waiting for an hour. After I explained what had happened at Universal, he said there were other things against me. I asked what they were, and he said he was not at liberty to tell me. I asked if there was anything else I could do to clear my name, and he suggested that I talk to Roy Brewer, also a member of his committee.

When I reached Brewer and pleaded my case, he informed me that, according to their information, although I was not a card-carrying communist, I was high in the echelons of the party and exerted influence. It was ridiculous, and I asked him to put me in front of my accusers. He said he could not because it was confidential. I left his office realizing that I was caught in a Kafkaesque situation and that there was nothing more for me to do except perhaps hire a lawyer and go to court. I discussed that course with the Jaffee office, and they said it was futile. One of their writers, F. Hugh Herbert, who had also been in trouble, had tried it and accomplished nothing. The committee would deny that they were preventing me from working, and there was no way I could prove it. Nor would the studios admit that there was a gray list or even a black list.

I was appalled that this organization and small group of men who wrapped themselves in the American flag but were flouting the very principles for which it stood could wield such power and decide the fate of others. The whole town was infested by the lies and innuendos that were being circulated. True, I knew many of those who had been named as communists, and I had contributed to various organizations that were opposed to Hitler, Mussolini, and Franco, but I supported them because I thought they deserved it and not because communists may have supported them. I read the *People's World* occasionally and subscribed to the *New Masses* magazine, but I also listened to Father Coughlin and read *Mein Kampf* to learn the thinking of both the right and left. Admittedly, I was a Roosevelt Democrat who leaned to the left. I was branded by the right as a "premature antifascist," a "fellow traveler," and a "pathologic liberal." But I was not a communist, nor did I approve of their policies or tactics.

I wrote Jack Warner to ask if he could find a picture for me to direct and didn't even get a reply. I went to see Harry Cohn, who called Ben Kahane, his vice president, into his office and asked him to speak to Ward Bond on my behalf. Ben did, in my presence, but nothing helped. Despite all my efforts to clear my name, I did not work for a year and a half. Finally, I gave up hope of ever being employed again in Hollywood.

Hedda and I were thinking about moving to New York, where I might find a play to direct, when Bill Josephy, an agent I knew, stopped me on the street in Beverly Hills to ask what I was doing and whether I was being represented. I told him I was free, but that no one in Hollywood would hire me.

"I'm with Kurt Frings," he said. "We have calls for directors to work in Europe. Come on up to the office with me." I met Frings, a pleasant man, who was handling Elizabeth Taylor at the time. He gave me a book to read at once, *The Fair Bride,* by Bruce Marshall, and asked me to call him the next day.

It was a strange story, the locale Spain: A young priest, disillusioned with Franco and the church, deserts his calling to help the loyalists, who, he feels, are fighting for the people. He is befriended by a prostitute and falls in love with her. Later, he becomes even more disillusioned with the loyalists and feels he made a mistake in leaving the church. He returns to the fold and is forgiven for his temporary lapse. It is not long before he is given an important task. A relic, the petrified finger of one of Christ's disciples, must be removed from a church and kept hidden from the communists, who are seeking it as a symbol of their success. He vows to guard it with his life, but he is captured. How can he hide the relic? Where can he put it for safekeeping? There is only one place—you guessed it—up his rectum. At that point I stopped reading. I knew it was not for me; I saw problems ahead with the Catholic Church (a priest who defects and has an affair with a prostitute), the Johnson office (which succeeded the Hays office as watchdog for the picture business), censorship, liberal groups, and the HUAC. I had enough trouble politically and didn't need any more. So, no matter how anxious I was to get back to work, I'd pass it up.

Josephy called and asked me to meet him the next morning at the Beverly Hills Hotel so that we could talk to Geoffredo Lombardo, the Italian producer who was going to make the film. I said I'd be there but hesitated to tell him what I thought. Bill was waiting at the entrance when I arrived. He had some news for me. Victor Mature, who was being considered for the priest, had just finished a film with Tony Mann directing and had requested that Mann be hired to do *The Fair Bride.* Bill hoped I was not disappointed. I confessed that I was relieved and told Caesar Gerosi, who was assisting Lombardo, about the problems I foresaw in doing it. He told me that Lombardo nonetheless wanted to meet me and would give me a commitment to direct another film, based on a novel by Verga, for fifty thousand dollars and three hundred dollars a week expenses while making it.

I met Lombardo and told him I would accept his offer, contingent upon the script. He said he had hired an American writer to do the screenplay and would tell him to send me the first forty pages as soon as possible. We shook hands, and I left. I felt relieved; at least I would be working, and it was a chance to see Rome again. The following morning I was having breakfast when Gerosi called to say the deal with Victor Mature and Tony Mann was off, and they'd like to talk with me again about doing *The Fair Bride*. Again I told Gerosi that it was not for me. He said, "I understand your objections, but we have an idea how to make the priest's affair with the prostitute easier to handle—what if we get Dorothy Dandridge (a beautiful young African American actress) to play the part?" I couldn't believe it and had to control myself to keep from becoming hysterical with laughter. I realized he must have thought that sex with Dandridge would be more acceptable and less offensive than with a white girl. I did not ask for an explanation. I just said no, I could never do *The Fair Bride*!

Two weeks later I received the forty pages and a synopsis of the Verga novel. It was about a young girl whose mother dies, and her father remarries. The stepmother is evil and favors her own daughter, about the same age. The father is blind to his daughter's plight. In desperation, she runs away and enters a convent. Before taking her vows, she comes home for a visit and meets a young man who is engaged to the stepsister. He falls in love with her instead and is ready to break off the engagement. Scolded and vilified by the stepmother, the girl returns to the convent and dies of a broken heart.

It was so old-fashioned, so downbeat, so steeped in religiosity that I tried to call off the deal. But Lombardo wanted me to come to Rome to talk. I went. When he was satisfied that I was not trying to get out of the deal because I had a better offer (his first thought), he proposed a different story. It was similar to *Five Star Final,* made years before by Warner's, and was about the callousness of the press as they dig up an old story about a young woman, unmarried, who became innocently involved in a scandal. Now she is happily married and has a ten-year-old daughter. The revival of the story threatens to destroy her, her husband, and her daughter. It was nothing new, but certainly better than the other stories they had offered me, so I agreed to make it. Besides, in 1955 Rome was a dream city. I felt a genuine kinship with the Italian people. To sit in an outdoor cafe during the summer and listen to "Arrividerci Roma," eat Italian food, and drink good Italian wine was a joy. It helped me forget what was going on back in Hollywood.

One weekend I was taken to Amalfi, where I had the pleasure of meeting and talking with Vittorio De Sica, his beautiful mistress, and their two lovely children. At dinner one night in Rome I also met, through a friend, Yves Montand and his wife, Simone Signoret. I also met a fine French actor, Charles Vanel, who was to play a role for me in the film. Signoret berated me and all other Hollywood professionals for permitting the rise of McCarthyism. I tried to explain that we were in the grip of a wave of reaction and that nothing more could be done at the moment; I was myself a victim. She refused to listen to any excuses. She and her husband, who were said to be communists, later broke with the left and denounced the Communist party.

While preparing *Scandal in Milan*, the title of our film, I brought my family to Rome. My daughter was seventeen years old, my son eight. I looked forward to a few happy weeks before shooting began but, as in London, Hedda complained about the apartment I rented and the young lady I engaged to drive her and the children about town. She became cold and distant. She and my daughter were also having problems. Only my son and I had fun. After four weeks they returned to California. Hedda may have been going through menopause, which I was unaware of at the time but was told later by a doctor.

By the time production began, I had assembled a good cast: Martine Carol in the lead, Gabrielle Ferzetti as her husband, Vittorio Gassman, a reporter, and Vanel, the editor. I also had a talented child actress. Carol and Vanel spoke their lines in French, Ferzetti in Italian, and Gassman in English. It took a little time for me to get used to this, but I learned that most films were dubbed with different voices in the language of the country where they were to play. So it didn't matter what the original soundtrack was. (The first time I heard John Wayne speaking Italian in a John Ford western, I almost fell out of my seat with laughter.)

Although the shooting went smoothly, when the film was completed, Lombardo wanted to add several scenes, heavily laden with sentimentality and religious elements. I thought they would hurt the picture and refused to shoot them. After I left Rome, an Italian director shot them. I never saw the final film.

On my way back to California I stopped off in London to see whether it was possible to get a directing job. Arthur Abeles, with whom I had become friendly while making *The Hasty Heart*, asked me to read a first-draft script he had an interest in. It was *The Naked Earth*, written by Milton Holmes and Harold Buchman, two Americans who were in London at the time. It was the kind of material that appealed to me, a simple story about a man and a woman in Africa who marry because of a need for each other and eventually discover love.

I suggested that we give the script to Robert Clark, the head of ABPC, who had been friendly to me. He liked it and said that with me directing it he would be interested in producing, provided I could get my name cleared. I hoped that by some miracle the situation in Hollywood would soon change.

Back home, Bill Josephy greeted me with the news that Raymond Massey had requested me to direct him in a film about John Brown, the antislave fighter, to be made at Allied Artists. We went to see Steve Broidy, then head of the studio. He said that as much as he would like to hire me, he couldn't. I was still on a gray list. He even admitted that he had turned down Marcel Hellman in London, who had asked for me to direct a coproduction of a film with Dana Andrews to be made there. But, he added, what he was telling me was confidential, and if I repeated his words he would deny them. As we left his office Bill expressed surprise that Broidy would reveal such information—that we could sue him. I said I wouldn't think of it. The man was decent enough to tell us the truth, and I appreciated it.

Not long after, Bill left the Frings Agency and joined Martin Baum at GAC (General Artists Corporation). I asked Frings to cancel my contract. I was sure that my career in Hollywood was finished.

One friend called to say that if I wanted to get cleared, I should say that I was once a member of the Communist party but had resigned. What, I asked, should I say if they asked me to name names? He said, "Just name those who have already been named." I thought about it and decided it was absurd. Why should I say I was a member if I never was?

During this period, Hedda's attitude toward me changed. She became sympathetic and supportive, and we began once again to live in relative harmony. Fortunately, we were not desperate for money. Hedda's management of our business affairs had been careful. But my hopes of again functioning in my profession were bleak.

Out of the blue, Arthur Park, my former agent, phoned. He said he had not been able to sleep nights knowing that I was not yet cleared, so he had taken steps to help me. He was a Republican and had worked to elect Donald Jackson, a congressman who was chairman of the California HUAC. After Park told him my situation, Jackson said they had no wish to hurt an innocent person, and if I was willing to talk with one of their investigators they would try to clear things up. Arthur gave me

Jackson's phone number. I called him, and he told me to get in touch with a man named Wheeler. I phoned Mr. Wheeler and made an appointment to have lunch with him at the Roosevelt Hotel. I told him the complete story of the Universal deal and answered various questions about my background. He summed up the situation: MGM saw a chance to get rid of a hot property and Universal to get a good story at a reduced cost, but when it blew up, they left me holding the bag. He asked if I would come to his office and make a statement. I did, and he said if a problem arose at any studio, they should be told to call him. I thanked him for his courtesy and left. Arthur thought he had the possibility of a job for me, but it did not work out. Nonetheless, although he had indirectly been the cause of my trouble, he was also responsible for helping to clear me.

With my name removed from the gray list and my right to work established, I notified Abeles in London and asked him to let me know if and when he was prepared to do *The Naked Earth*. He wrote that they had completed the final draft of the script but had not yet worked out a deal with Robert Clark. Meanwhile, I phoned Harry Cohn to tell him the good news and asked if I could talk with him about a novel that I thought would make a good film.

"When do you want to come down?" he asked.

The following day I was in his office. He greeted me warmly and asked about my experience in Rome and how I got cleared. I told him all and mentioned the possibility of directing *The Naked Earth* in London. Then I told him the story of *Walk with the Devil* by Elliott Arnold, which I had read several years before and tried to buy, but it had already been optioned by Mark Robson. Now it was free.

After I finished, Cohn asked, "How much can you get it for?"

"Ten thousand. I've already talked to the author."

He thought for a second. "We'll buy it." Then he asked what kind of a deal I wanted. I told him—no salary, just an office and a writer to help me prepare a screenplay. If, after it was completed, he decided to make it, then I'd want my salary and a percentage. He agreed, and I went to work on the screenplay.

After two or three weeks I received a call from Cohn to come to his office. He informed me that Robert Aldrich had been directing a film for Columbia called *Garment Jungle,* which had been written and was being produced by Harry Kleiner, but he (Cohn) was not satisfied with several scenes, and as soon as the picture was finished, which was only a few days off, he wanted me to retake them. I balked because no director wants to replace a colleague. I did not know Aldrich personally, but I considered him a capable director.

"Can't you explain to him what you want?" I said.

"We're not speaking," he replied. "If you won't do it for me, I'll have to get someone else. But they're delicate scenes, and I'd rather have you do them."

I recalled Harry's kindness to me and said, "Okay, Harry, you've been a friend, so I'll help any way I can." He said he would let me know as soon as the shooting was completed.

A day or two later, on a Friday, I was awakened at 6:00 A.M. by a phone call from Jack Fier, head of production, who said that Aldrich was ill and Cohn had instructed him to ask me if I would please go to the studio and pick up where Aldrich had left off the day before. I said I would. At the studio I read the scene to be done, talked with Joe Biroc, the cameraman, and the script supervisor, who explained that they had made a master shot when Aldrich said he was not feeling well and had better go home. I phoned Aldrich. He thanked me for taking over, said he hoped to be back by Monday, and briefed me on what shots he'd like to have me do to complete the sequence. I followed his instructions. The scenes were between a new and lovely young actress, Gia Scala, and Robert Loggia, from New York, in what I think was his first film role. I enjoyed working with them and shot some additional sequences. When the day ended, I said goodbye to everyone and thanked them for their cooperation, assuming that Monday morning Aldrich would return.

Saturday morning I received a call from Cohn to come to his home near the Beverly Hills Hotel. He was going to run the dailies of what I had shot, having put a rush on them. Lillian Burns, his assistant, was there, and so was Harry Kleiner. After the running, Cohn turned to Kleiner and Lillian. "I want Sherman to finish the picture," he said. Then to me, "You will report to the set Monday morning and take over." I started to protest, but he stopped me. "Please—I need your help. I'll take care of everything. Read the script and look at what we've shot so far, so you'll know what to do."

I went to the studio with Kleiner and saw the rough cut. The story was about the conflict between two partners, Lee Cobb and Robert Ellenstein, in the dress manufacturing business in New York's garment district. Cobb is opposed to letting the union into the shop; he has worked hard all his life to build a business and does not intend to allow outsiders to tell him what to do. His partner favors the union. Cobb has hired Richard Boone, the leader of a goon squad, to keep the union out. The partner hates Boone, who eventually engineers the partner's death in an elevator accident. Cobb is a widower and has a son, played by Kerwin Matthews. The son is inclined to favor the union and dislikes Boone. Cobb does not suspect Boone is guilty of his partner's death, and when the accusation is made, he refuses to believe it. When he confronts Boone and learns the truth, he tries to get rid of him but is himself killed. The son takes charge of the business and fires Boone, who refuses to be dismissed and even demands a share in the business. Boone and the son fight, and the son is eventually victorious.

After viewing the assembled footage, I was disturbed by certain elements but said nothing at the moment. Monday morning I was on my way to the set when I was told that Aldrich was already there. I went to my office, called Jack Fier, and said I would not go to the set and embarrass Aldrich. Besides, I had been told that everything would be taken care of. A short while later, Fier called to say that Aldrich was off the film and had merely come to say good-bye to everyone. When he left, I went to the set and began shooting the last few scenes to be made. I could feel resentment from some of the cast and crew. It was natural. They liked Aldrich and saw no reason why he should be removed, even though it was well known at Columbia that Aldrich and Cohn had not been getting along. The relationship between Kleiner and Aldrich was not a happy one either. In such circumstances it is not easy to make a good film.

At any rate, I did the work scheduled for that day and was asked to come to Cohn's office. He asked what I thought of the rough cut and the script. Kleiner and Burns were present. I pointed out that I was confused by Lee Cobb's character: if he knew that his partner had been killed by Boone and did nothing about it, he was monstrous and irredeemable. If he did not know or even suspect Boone, he was stupid. For a moment Cohn made no comment, then suddenly hit the desk with his fist.

"I knew it!" he yelled. "I knew there was something wrong with the damned picture. That's it!" I began to apologize for stirring up a hornet's nest. Cohn stopped me. "Keep quiet, you said enough." For the next two hours we discussed how to resolve this story point and other questions that were raised. "We can't go on until we straighten out this mess," Cohn concluded, then turned to me. "How long will it take you and Kleiner to rewrite what we've discussed and go through the film to see what has to be reshot and what can be saved?"

I wanted at least a week, but Cohn said he could give us only three days. Kleiner and I went to work at once, and I called in Lee Cobb. We had not spoken in years. He had made a big hit in the New York theater with his role of Willy Loman in Arthur Miller's *Death of a Salesman.* He had had a promising career in films when he was ordered to appear before the HUAC, where he admitted to having been at one time a member of the Communist party. He also named names. He was now in his first role in a picture since his clearance. As he entered Kleiner's office, I could see he was uncomfortable when he learned I was taking over the film. I told him my feelings about the story and his character. "Did you or didn't you know that Boone had caused the death of your partner?" I asked him.

He blew up. "I asked Aldrich that same question, and he said, 'Yes and no.' How the hell could I play yes and no?"

I told him we would fix that and other problems. He shook my hand as in the old days when we were close.

"I can't tell you how happy I am that we're going to work together again," he said and left. While Kleiner was rewriting, I sat with the editor and saved every foot of film possible.

During the first few days of shooting, Cobb could not have been more gracious or cooperative. For that matter, so was the entire cast. They soon realized that we were only trying to improve the picture. On the thirteenth and last day of shooting, Cobb disagreed with something I asked him to do and began to argue with me. He resisted everything I suggested, reverting to his old ways, but I fought him and insisted that he do the scene the way I wanted. He left at the end of the film and didn't say good-bye. He had behaved badly once before and repeated it this time. He was talented but stubborn and filled with his own importance.

I had reshot in the thirteen days almost 70 percent of what Aldrich had shot in thirty-one days. He had made many good scenes. I only tried to straighten out the storyline, which he and Kleiner had had disagreements about. When Cohn saw the new rough cut, he called me to his office and thanked me. "What can I pay you?" he asked. "I can't give you your full salary. We're already way over budget." I told him he didn't have to pay me anything. He had given me a deal on *Walk with the Devil,* which had put me back in business, and I was grateful.

"No, no," he said. "You saved the picture for me, and I want to pay you something. Suppose I give you a thousand a day for the thirteen days; would you be willing to accept that?" I said it would be fine. From being idle to a thousand a day was welcome.

At the same time, I received word from Abeles that he had worked

out a tentative deal with Clark for *The Naked Earth,* but before signing it
he thought I should come to London and discuss it. I asked Cohn if he
would permit me to take a leave of absence, promising that the moment
I finished *The Naked Earth* I would return and continue with *Walk with
the Devil.* He agreed, and we shook hands.

Hedda and I had not yet come back to each other with the warmth
and closeness we used to have, but we had achieved a kind of truce that
allowed us to live without too much pain. I promised to bring her and
the children to London as soon as I could.

A few days after my arrival in London, a letter came from the Directors Guild saying that they had received word from Aldrich that I had
behaved in an unprofessional manner with regard to *Garment Jungle.* I
sent back a long, detailed reply explaining every step of what had occurred. I never heard anything more from either Aldrich or the Guild.
When *Garment Jungle* was released, I was surprised to see that I had a
solo credit on it. I was perfectly willing, and had suggested, that Aldrich's
name be first and mine second. But I was told later that he did not want
his name on it. It should have been, since he deserved credit for many
good and effective scenes. But he had been hurt, and I can only assume
that his pride was at stake. Aldrich went on to make many successful
films, including *The Dirty Dozen,* which I thought was an excellent job
of directing. *Garment Jungle* got favorable reviews and did good business. My consolation was that I had helped Harry Cohn, who had helped
me.

My enthusiasm for *The Naked Earth* was enhanced by the prospect
of shooting the exteriors in Africa. I had always yearned to visit the dark
continent; I felt the same kind of excitement about seeing new places
and people as when I was a boy. But the deal that Clark and ABPC had
offered to finance the film fell short of what Abeles and the writers had
hoped to get. They were waiting to talk with me about it, since Clark was
my friend. The day after my arrival in London, I ran into Bob Goldstein,
who was in charge of the London office of Twentieth Century–Fox. He
was curious to know what I was doing in the city. When I told him, he
asked if he could read the script, and if he liked it, maybe he could offer
us a better deal than ABPC. I reported the conversation to Abeles, and
he sent Goldstein a script. Within twenty-four hours he called and, indeed, made us a better offer. I was reluctant to take the project away
from ABPC but had to admit that the Fox offer was an improvement,
and they could also give us better distribution worldwide. However, I
asked that I be allowed to make the film at the ABPC studios with the

same crew I had while doing *The Hasty Heart.* Fox and ABPC were agreeable to the arrangement.

When it came time to discuss my personal deal with the project, I had the choice of receiving a salary or becoming a partner with a one-third share in the profits, plus my expenses. I foolishly opted for the latter.

While waiting for contracts to be drawn, I began studying the screenplay and thinking about casting. The story centered on a young Irishman who goes to Africa at the turn of the century to join his friend and partner, who has gone ahead of him and bought a piece of land on which they hope to grow tobacco and make their fortunes. The climate is ideal, and African labor is cheap and plentiful. On a stopover in Marseilles, his partner has written, he picked up a young woman who, fed up with her life as a lady of easy virtue, offered to go with him to Africa to help with the work and provide his other needs in exchange for part of his share of the tobacco crop. When the young Irishman arrives at the farm in Africa, he is shocked to learn that his friend has died of a fever and the woman is ill. Refusing to accept defeat, he decides to stay and try his hand at developing the farm. Meanwhile, he nurses the young woman back to health and plans to send her back to France on the first boat available. However, the elderly white missionary slyly suggests that it is important for a man to have a woman and hints that he should consider keeping her; she is young and strong and could be a good worker and helpmate. The young man is inclined to agree, but when the Father asks him to marry her, he balks. The Father explains that he has spent years preaching marriage to the Africans, and it would be unseemly if he and the woman lived together in sin. Reluctantly, the young man asks the woman to stay, offering to marry her and give her the same share of the tobacco crop as his partner had promised. She is not especially enamored of the young Irishman but accepts his offer because she has nothing better to go back to. Their getting together is just a business deal and a need for each other. He is impulsive and emotional; she is practical and realistic. They argue about everything, but through hardships mutually faced, they fall in love.

I felt that out of this story I could get a film similar to some of the French and Italian classics that I had seen in the thirties, which were down to earth, dramatic, and filled with honest humor. Moreover, the story especially appealed to me because it followed, to some degree, the pattern of my own marriage: Hedda and I worked together, raised a family, and loved each other, despite my lapses of unfaithful behavior. We also argued incessantly.

When their first crop of tobacco fails after months of hard work, and she becomes pregnant but loses the baby, the young man begins to earn money hunting crocodiles. The skins have suddenly become popular in Europe, an influence of the actress Sarah Bernhardt, who has her shoes, belts, and handbags made from them. On the verge of breaking up, and still arguing, they finally decide to remain together and make another attempt to grow tobacco.

I wanted to submit the screenplay to Richard Todd, whom I had found when I directed *The Hasty Heart,* but my partners leaned toward Richard Burton. I thought Burton would be fine. He turned it down, but he sent me a nice note.

Since *The Hasty Heart* Todd had appeared in several films, including the successful *A Man Called Peter* for Twentieth Century–Fox and an English war film that did well. I sent him the screenplay, which he liked, and we soon made a deal with him. For the woman, several actresses came to mind, but Goldstein suggested that we use Joan Collins, who was under contract to Fox. She was a possibility, but she turned us down because, we were told, she did not want to leave Armand Deutsche, whom she expected to marry. She never did.

Meanwhile, I had to find locations in Africa. We needed a river with a large open field nearby, where we could construct a small house and lay out the tobacco farm, a place for the missionary, a river with crocodiles, and a huge waterfall, where the Africans toss two evil white traders to their end.

Research revealed that Murchison Park in Uganda was our best bet for crocodiles, and it also had a waterfall. A scouting trip was arranged for me, a production manager, and an assistant. Entebbe was our destination. As we flew from London, I was tingling with excitement in anticipation of seeing Africa. Passing over the Egyptian desert, I saw far below a camel caravan as it moved over the sands. It conjured up ancient times and trade routes. We stopped at Khartoum to refuel, and although the airport was a dismal little building full of flies, the name alone evoked mystery and adventure.

Uganda was under British rule. Its capital was Kampala, a good-sized town not far from Entebbe, where we landed. We stayed at a nice English hotel in Entebbe, which overlooked Lake Victoria. (Uganda later became notorious under Idi Amin, and Entebbe was the site of the daring Israeli raid.) The next morning we hired a car and drove to Murchison Park, a couple of hours away. It was a game preserve supervised by a game warden. There were lions, elephants, water buffalo, hyenas, baboons, and monkeys scattered throughout the park, plus hundreds of small deer-like animals called impala, which were beautiful to watch as they hurtled gracefully over the land. At noon we arrived at the park headquarters. The log cabins for guests, the kitchen, and the dining area were large enough to house and feed our crew and actors. A small bar was there as well.

After lunch the game warden, an accommodating Englishman, took us for a journey up the river in a small launch. On the banks were dozens of crocodiles sleeping and sunning themselves with their mouths wide open. They ranged in length from a few feet to twenty feet or more, and we were told they sometimes lived to more than a hundred years old. I was fascinated to see now and then a bird perched on the inside of a croc's mouth and pecking away at its teeth. The warden explained that the croc has no tongue, cannot masticate its food or clean its teeth after eating, and relies on the birds to keep them clean by pecking at the particles of food lodged along the jawline. "Doesn't the croc ever close his jaws down on them?" I asked.

"Never," the warden replied. "His tick bird is too important to him. They have an agreement between them. The tick bird gets food and keeps the croc's teeth clean. Many animals have their tick birds: the elephant can't extract bugs from its ears, but its tick bird can. You can often see the bird sitting serenely atop the elephant."

As we plowed slowly up the river, a hippopotamus would observe us, only its little pink ears and head visible, incongruous with its enormous body when it surfaced. The crocodiles were so still they seemed lifeless. I wanted to see if I could get them to move, so at one point when we were near the bank, I banged on the side of the boat. The warden yanked me back.

"You can lose an arm like that," he warned me. "Crocs are very fast; they can grab your arm before you know it or pull you overboard and drown you." He went on to tell us more about them. "They are considered vermin in Africa and are one of the few animals that will actually go after a human being. Unless surprised, wounded, or threatened, most animals will hardly ever attack a human, but the croc will. The problem at the moment is to preserve them because they are being rapidly depleted. Native poachers are killing them for the prices their skins bring."

I was curious about what the crocs fed on, why it was so important to preserve them, and how they lived side by side so peacefully with the hippos in the river.

"Crocs feed mostly on the larger fish in the river. If they didn't, the larger ones would soon multiply and gobble up all the smaller fish. That's how the balance of nature prevails. Crocs will also sometimes kill a small impala."

"How do they do that?" I asked.

"Animals come to the river in the early morning and late afternoon to drink. The croc lies stealthily in wait just below the surface of the water near the shore, looking pretty much like a floating log. When the impala is drinking, the croc whips his tail around, knocks the legs of the impala out from under him, grabs him with his powerful jaws, and drags him to the bottom of the river, where he drowns him, then anchors him and waits for him to putrefy before attempting to eat him."

"And the hippos—what do they feed on?" I asked.

"Mostly plant life at the bottom of the river," he replied. "They submerge, walk about, eat, and stay under as long as fifteen or twenty minutes sometimes. We don't yet know how. They seem to be gentle but occasionally get angry—although I've never seen them fight with a croc, only another hippo."

We soon reached the base of the falls, docked the launch, and walked to the top. It was a drop of several hundred feet. There was also a road from the camp to the falls, so that we could reach the location in half an hour's drive.

As we came down from the falls and started back toward the launch, a huge elephant was feeding at the side of our path.

"We'd better circle around him," the warden said.

"Is he dangerous?" I asked. The warden nodded. "But they seem so gentle, those in the circus, anyway," I added.

"Those are Asian elephants," he answered. "They are easily disciplined, but not the African elephant. They're difficult and unpredictable. There is only one place where they are trained in the Belgian Congo. They haul heavy logs." We took the warden's advice, made our way back to the launch in a wide circle, and returned to the camp.

We had our crocs and the waterfall; now we needed to find a second river with an open field nearby where we could construct a small house and plant the tobacco crop. We also needed a location for the missionary's house and a place of worship. To cover Uganda by car would take days, so it was decided that I would fly around with a young man who had a small Cessna for hire that would cover the territory in a short time. I was about to give up when I spotted an open field at the edge of Lake Victoria, only a few minutes from our hotel. If I photographed it properly, the audience would see only a body of water and not know whether it was a lake or the edge of a wide river. We landed, and when I drove the production manager and my assistant to it and told them what I had in mind, they agreed that I had hit upon a practical solution.

Back in London, after briefing everyone on what I had found, my decisions were approved. A budget was prepared, and we continued casting. I was delighted to learn that Finlay Currie had been signed to play the missionary and Lawrence Naismith to play one of the two villainous white traders.

Darryl Zanuck, the former head of Twentieth Century–Fox Film Corporation, had relinquished his position in Hollywood, left home, and sought a different life in Paris, where, attracted to a young singer and actress, Juliette Greco, he hobnobbed with intellectuals and artists at the Cafe Deux Magots. He was still a large stockholder in Twentieth Century–Fox and now and then would individually produce a film. When he heard of our need for a leading lady, he suggested that we use Greco, who had made a good impression in his production of Hemingway's *The Sun Also Rises.* After it was screened for me, I decided she would be ideal: she was sexy, had an earthy, peasant quality, was French, spoke English well enough, and seemed to be a good actress.

When Goldstein told Zanuck how I felt, he suggested that I hop over to Paris and come to the George V Hotel, where he had a suite, and he would introduce me to the lady. I had never met Zanuck but was looking forward to seeing him and Greco and talking about the script, because I thought he might have some worthwhile suggestions. When I arrived, he informed me that she was indisposed and would not be able to see me, but he assured me that she would be perfect for the part. He was pleasant enough but seemed distracted, and after a short visit I left, puzzled as to why he didn't phone me in London with the information instead of having me come to Paris and waste a day. I never found out. At any rate, I returned to London and after a few days left for Africa without seeing my leading lady. However, she accepted the role, and her measurements were sent to London, where her wardrobe was prepared.

Terence Verity, who had done the sets for *The Hasty Heart* and had become a good friend, was engaged to do *The Naked Earth,* and by the time I arrived in Africa, everything was ready. It was my intention to shoot all the exteriors there and only the interiors at ABPC in Elstree. Another member of the *Hasty Heart* company to join us was Orlando Martens, who had played the Basuto, Blossom, and was cast as an African in *The Naked Earth.* John Kitzmiller, an American black actor who had been working in Rome, was engaged to play a good role. Erwin Hillier, a favorite of Michael Powell's, was hired as our cameraman, and the crew was made up of many of those hardworking, loyal chaps who had helped me on *The Hasty Heart*. I had an excellent assistant, Phil Shipway, and his ex-wife, Maggie, held script.

Before I left for Africa, I was in Goldstein's office to say good-bye, and as I was on my way out he introduced me to a young man who was anxious to become an actor in films. He was handsome and rugged but looked more like a stevedore than an actor. He wore a dark suit and a working man's shoes and seemed modest and dignified. His name was Sean Connery.

In Africa we took the company (without Greco) immediately to Murchison Park and began shooting as soon as possible. Our transportation was, unfortunately, poor: old Land Rovers, trucks and jeeps, and a few Volkswagen buses and pickups (the best available in that area). One day at the waterfalls, in order to finish a sequence, we had to work late and were returning to camp as it was getting dark. The game warden had warned us not to work too late because it would necessitate using our lights to drive back, which disturbed the elephants. I was riding with my assistant and an African driver in a small car when the motor stopped and we couldn't get it started again. We decided to get into the first transport that appeared. Soon a VW pickup truck came along carrying several members of the crew and two Africans at the rear, their legs dangling from the truck bed. I was offered a seat in front with the driver but declined, choosing to ride between the two Africans. They were pleasant fellows and spoke a few words of English. Our driver was rushing to get back to camp before it got too dark. We were moving along the small dirt road at about twenty or twenty-five miles per hour when he stopped. I turned and asked why.

"Elee-fant," he replied and pointed ahead.

A behemoth was feeding at the side of the road about fifty yards ahead. I approved of the driver's decision, remembering what the game warden had told us. The driver cut the motor, and we waited ten or fifteen minutes, hoping the animal would move away, but he was in no hurry. It was getting darker by the minute, and we'd have to use our lights.

"Ay tank we better take chance and go," our driver said, and we all agreed. He started the motor, stepped on the gas, and we moved forward. I was facing the rear and expected to see the elephant momentarily as we passed him, but he didn't appear. As I turned again to ask what happened to the elephant, he loomed up, like a giant locomotive, running at the side of the road, along with us, angry as hell, his ears spread wide and trying to catch up with us. He was traveling at least twenty-five miles an hour, and we were barely a few feet ahead of him. He leaped to the center of the road so he could make better time and was closing in on us. I yelled to the driver to go faster, but his foot was already pushing the accelerator through the floor. The two Africans and I drew our legs up quickly and moved away from the rear, as far forward as we could get. We were scared shitless as the elephant came within a few feet of us, then began to fall behind as we slowly pulled away. I was careful not to work too late in the park again. It's no fun being chased by an angry African elephant.

Each day something happened that etched itself into my memory. Once at the falls I had a dozen Africans, tall, strong, and handsome, carrying supplies for two villainous traders, and I asked them to sing a song as they marched, one they would normally use on such a trek. They did, and we recorded it. When they heard a playback later, the first time they had ever heard their voices reproduced, they shouted and gesticulated like delighted children.

After ten days we moved to Entebbe and prepared to work at the tobacco farm. Juliette Greco arrived, accompanied by Harold Buchman, one of the writers, who told us that everyone was pleased with the rushes so far. Juliette was a warm and friendly young woman, anxious to do a good job. She was, like every artist, a trifle nervous at the start. Her English was halting, not as glib as I'd hoped. But I felt she'd improve each day, and she did.

We had a happy company. Todd and Greco worked well together, and the Africans were cooperative. Finlay Currie, who played the missionary, was in his early eighties but robust and energetic, a fine actor and a delightful man to have around. In between setups, he'd play old music hall songs for us on a small organ that we had rented for his place of worship. Entebbe is near the equator, and the heat was unbearable at times, but our first-aid lady saw to it that we took our salt tablets.

One morning Juliette informed me that Zanuck would be paying us a visit. He had phoned the night before to say that he would arrive by plane with Paul Mantz, the well known flyer for studios in Hollywood. They were photographing different areas that Zanuck planned to use in *Deluxe Tour,* a film that he was preparing but never made. Juliette did not seem pleased, and I wondered why.

"He's spying on me, that's why he's coming," she answered and then invited me to have dinner with the two of them that evening.

"I appreciate your thoughtfulness, Juliette," I said. "But I think Mr. Zanuck would prefer to have dinner with you alone the first night of his arrival. . . . Maybe tomorrow night."

That night when I entered the dining room, he was at a table with Juliette and his son Dick, who was on the expedition. I went over to say hello and told him how nice it was to have him visit us. I invited him to the location the next day. We were shooting the exterior of the farm-house when he arrived alone. Someone took a picture of us as we talked. I told him about some of the production problems but said that I was happy with Juliette's performance. He asked if I had seen any rushes, and I explained that I had not because we were trying to save the expense of shipping them back and forth.

"That's ridiculous," he said. "You've got to be able to see what you've been shooting." Two days later, we received twenty or more cans of film, and he arranged for us to view them at a Fox theater in Kampala late one night after the last showing of their current film. A rented limousine picked him up, along with Juliette and me, and drove us the twenty miles. The rushes looked good, and he was more than pleased with Juliette's performance; he thought it would make her a star. The following day, while I was discussing a setup with the cameraman, Zanuck came again to the location. I saw Juliette talking to him, then noticed that she angrily walked away, leaving him standing alone on the field. She crossed to John Kitzmiller and started laughing and joking with him. I called her aside. "It's none of my business, Juliette," I said, "but I don't think you should walk away from Zanuck and leave him standing alone in the middle of a field."

"But why does he have to come to the location? He knows I don't like it."

"I can't answer that. I only know he is responsible for your being in this film, and I think you owe him a little respect." She went back to him, and after a few words he came over to me to say good-bye. She then walked him to a car that was waiting for him, and I went back to my job.

We had assembled a group of twenty or thirty Africans for a scene at the edge of the water, and I was trying to tell them what I wanted them to do when Zanuck's plane buzzed us as he left Entebbe. The Africans panicked and scattered. It took us a half hour to coax them back.

After completing the location work, I returned to London, well tanned and ready to do the interiors at Elstree, which were mostly with Juliette and Todd. Toward the end of our schedule, Robert Clark told me that Jack Warner was in London and was due at the studio the following day. Warner also sent word that he wanted to see me and would come down to our set. It was the first time I had spoken to Jack since leaving Warner's over three years before. He was jovial and greeted me warmly. I introduced him to the crew as "my former boss" and then he whispered that he wanted especially to meet Zanuck's girlfriend. She was in her dressing room. She came to the set and was pleasant, but Hollywood big shots did not impress her, and she soon excused herself and went back to her dressing room.

Warner took me aside and said that as soon as I finished the film, he'd like for me to come back to Warner Brothers. "Your old home, Vince." I thanked him and promised to go out for lunch when I returned.

In the meantime I brought my family over. We took an apartment near Victoria Station, and every Saturday we enjoyed walking a few blocks to shop at Harrod's. It was a pleasant visit. After a few weeks, they toured Europe and then returned to California.

At the end of the shooting, and after a look at the first cut, I felt that we had a good picture and began to work with the editor to make a few changes. I had no sooner started than Zanuck announced that he was coming to London to take over the editing. Since he wasn't even the producer in charge of the film, I was dismayed by his behavior. According to the Directors Guild contract with producers, I had a right to make a first cut, but he ignored it. He sensed that I was unhappy and wrote me a letter saying that John Ford allowed him to cut his films, so why shouldn't I? Later, I was told this was not true. What disturbed me more than his taking over was seeing the first reel of his cut. It was edited as though it was intended to be a fast-moving melodrama rather than a simple, realistic love story that depended for its success on its characters and their struggle to conquer the African background.

I protested to my partners (the writers and Abeles), who were equally unhappy, but they asked me to remain calm because Zanuck had the power to give the film special attention, and if we made trouble, he might have it buried. Nor could Goldstein or Joe Moskowitz, a vice president of the company from New York, say anything. Zanuck was still important at Twentieth Century–Fox. My suspicion was that he was having trouble with Greco and was intent on showing his power. Grown men in high positions, dynamic in business, often lose their sense of proportion and behave childishly when it comes to women.

Although I was miserable about what was happening, I did not feel like getting into a battle with Zanuck because I knew it would be useless. Despite the poor editing, *The Naked Earth* received good reviews, including one even from the *New Yorker.* However, because it was an English production, it had no real promotion in America and did little business. I was never paid one cent for my one-third of the profits. My total pay covered only my travel and living expenses, ten thousand dollars. But I saw Africa and was on my way back to Hollywood, where I hoped to fare better.

17

Back to Warner's

Before discussing a return to Warner's, I felt that I had a moral obligation to talk with Harry Cohn. He had bought *Walk with the Devil* for me, and I had agreed to prepare the screenplay gratis. If a definite job was offered me at Warner's, I thought Cohn would not object if I took it as long as I promised to work on the screenplay on my own time. I phoned for an appointment and learned that he was in Arizona resting and would return in a few days. Then came the news that he had died of a heart attack.

His body was brought back to Hollywood and the coffin taken to one of the stages at Columbia Studios, where the funeral service was held. A large crowd gathered to pay their respects. A comedian was heard to say, "Give the people what they want, and they'll come." But I was sad. I sat alone and thought about the stories Cohn had told me of his early life: his struggle to survive in the Hollywood jungle, how many people disliked him, and how few knew of his good qualities. In my opinion he was a soft, sentimental man who, aware of his weakness, overcompensated by becoming too hard and too tough. In fact I once said to him, in describing a character in a script, "He's like you, Harry. Everyone thinks you're a sonofabitch, when the truth is you're a softie." Oscar Saul was present and later said he was afraid Cohn was going to hit me, but he didn't—he just listened. I was also told that one Christmas he gave a party in his office for longtime employees, and a nice little Jewish tailor raised his glass and proposed a toast.

"Here's to your newborn son, Mr. Cohn," he said. "May he grow up to be like his father." Cohn knocked the glass from his hand and said, "His father has no friends."

With Harry gone, I felt no obligation to return to Columbia, which was in an unsettled state. I called Warner to let him know I was back in town. He invited me for lunch the next day, and I was warmly greeted by many former coworkers. Nothing had changed. Jack told a few jokes at lunch and gave me a cigar, and Trilling asked me to come with him to his office to discuss a deal. Having been briefed by Warner, he offered me a one-year contract at less than one-third of my former salary. I was outraged, turned it down, and was ready to walk out of his office when he stopped me: "Vince, you may not get a film off the ground within the year."

"But suppose I do. You expect me to work on a script and direct it for a thousand a week?"

"No, of course not. If you do a film within the year, we'll add a fifty thousand bonus. How would that be?"

"That's a little different. Let me think about it. And what property are you planning to offer me?"

"We have a very good novel called *The Philadelphians.* I'll get you a copy. Read it, and we'll talk about it."

I read it, could see a film in it, and after a discussion with Hedda, decided that I would accept the Warner offer. I was given an office and a secretary in the main building, and within a few days I felt as if I had never left the studio. I soon learned that several writers and producers had tried to come up with a satisfactory script of *The Philadelphians* but had failed.

The novel was a complicated, sprawling story that covered three generations of a poor Irish immigrant family struggling to achieve respectability. It centers about a young woman whose husband, a member of a prominent Main Line family, commits suicide on the night of their marriage because he "can't love a woman." It drives her into the arms of a former suitor, an Irishman, who becomes the father of her son. But she clings to the Main Line family's name, both for herself and for her son. The son's development and rise in the legal profession, his discovery of his real father, and his conflict with Main Line society provided the drama.

Jimmy Gunn, the writer, was available, and I thought he was well suited to help me get a first draft because, coming from a good San Francisco family, he knew what it meant to belong and also to go against the mores of the best families. Within a few months we had a workable screenplay. It was sent to Paul Newman, who was under contract to Warner Brothers. I had first seen him in New York several years before when he appeared in William Inge's play, *Picnic.* Later, he was signed to a long-term contract by Warner's and made *The Silver Chalice,* which I had not seen but was told he hated. After that he made a hit in *Somebody up There Likes Me,* directed by Robert Wise, on a loanout to MGM. I thought he'd be right for the son and was pleased at the possibility of working with him. Within a few days his agent, my old friend Arthur Park at MCA, informed me that Paul did not like the script. I explained that it was a first draft only and that I was not averse to making changes. I suggested that Paul come in and discuss it with me. The next day he arrived, and I listened to his complaints. He was unhappy at Warner's and anxious to get out of his contract. I felt that this colored his attitude toward the script. Nevertheless, I promised to consider his criticism and try to improve the screenplay.

A short time later he agreed to do the film and recommended Barbara Rush to play opposite him. I was grateful because she gave a fine performance. An agent brought Robert Vaughn in to read for the part of Chet, Paul's Main Line friend. I had never heard of him but thought he had the right quality for the role. He was later nominated for an Academy Award as Best Supporting Actor in the picture. In addition, I was lucky to have a wonderful cast of older players, all from the theater: Billie Burke, Otto Kruger, John Williams, and Frank Conroy, together with several younger but excellent performers, including Alexis Smith, Brian Keith, Diane Brewster, Robert Douglas, Richard Deacon, Fred Eisley, Adam West, and Paul Picerni. I also had a great crew, led by Harry Stradling, an outstanding cameraman.

Directing the film was a happy experience. Paul was a gifted actor and gave a fine performance. He does not regard the film with favor, but audiences liked him, and the film was successful. His friend Stewart Stern helped us by rewriting and improving several scenes.

Stern, whom I did not get to know well at the time, was recently invited to the Florida Film Festival to speak about writing for films. I was also invited there to speak about directing. He was working on a biography of Paul Newman, and we talked for hours. He is a sensitive, thoughtful, talented, and compassionate human being, and I look forward to anything that he writes.

I was especially delighted to work with Billie Burke. She was seventy-five years old, and although still energetic and beautiful, she was having trouble remembering her lines. In a scene with Paul, when I realized she was struggling to remember the exact words of the script, I whispered to her, "Billie, you know what the scene is about, use your own words and don't worry about what's written." She took my hand. "Oh, you darling boy." I alerted Paul, and they both played the scene with such give and take that it got big laughs, and often applause, from the audience. Paul was not at the preview, but Stewart was present and told me later that he was surprised and delighted with what he saw. I later received a letter from Billie thanking me for reviving her career; she also sent an autographed copy of her book, *With a Feather on My Nose,* which I treasure.

During the shooting Warner was in Europe, and one morning we heard that he had been in a terrible auto accident the night before and might not live. For weeks he was in a hospital, but finally he recovered. Before he returned to Hollywood, I completed the film, and with the help of Bill Ziegler, the editor, we got it down to two hours and twenty minutes running time. Trilling was worried, fearful that Warner would raise hell because we had not kept it under two hours. Normally, I also objected to overlong films, but because of the nature of the story, I begged him to preview it before making any further cuts. If Warner was angry, blame it on me (I was also the producer, although never credited). We previewed the film at Huntington Park, California, and although Warner also questioned the length before he saw it, he came out of the theater all smiles. When I suggested a few trims he said, "Don't gild the lily. You heard the audience. They loved it, so leave it alone and ship it." Trilling was relieved.

It was finally titled *The Young Philadelphians.* Not long after, Paul bought his way out of his Warner contract. He has since made many good and successful films (although there are others I don't understand why he even accepted). He is undoubtedly one of our most talented actors and a socially conscious, fine human being. I feel sad, however, that he has not stretched his talents or reached his full capacity as an actor by undertaking heavier assignments in the theater. For example, I feel he might have done Romeo or Hamlet successfully.

After the preview, Warner Brothers paid me the promised bonus, and I was immediately assigned to *Ice Palace,* the novel by Edna Ferber. I was not too happy, having heard that several writers and producers had attempted a screenplay but had been unsuccessful. It was about a conflict between two men, one who loved Alaska and one who loved money. The latter was using mechanized fishing boats to catch salmon and endangering the future of the area. Dorothy Parker in reviewing the novel said the two men were "crashing bores." She might have added, so was the rest of the novel. When I questioned why Warner ever bought it, I heard this story: that even before the film *Giant,* also a novel by Ferber, was completed, Warner realized he had a big hit in the making, and "Swifty" Lazar, Ferber's agent, told him that Ferber was at work on a new novel "bigger than *Giant.*"

"How can it be bigger than Texas?" Warner asked.

"Alaska!" Lazar replied. "And it's called *Ice Palace.*" Warner bought the rights to it before reading it and paid four hundred thousand dollars.

When I protested that I did not want to work on it, Trilling said, "But Vince, you're so good at this kind of story. Look at *The Young Philadelphians.*" I explained that the latter was about human beings; *Ice Palace* was about salmon. Then Jack pleaded with me to make it, pointing out that they had sunk over a half million in it and had to find a way to recoup at least part of it. I was still reluctant to do it.

A few days later Trilling called. "I have an old friend of yours in the office. You worked with him on *Garment Jungle* at Columbia. He has an idea of how to do *Ice Palace.* I'm sending him in to see you." Harry Kleiner and I had gotten along well on the rewrite of *Garment Jungle.* He agreed that *Ice Palace* was not a good novel but thought he could make it work. He was also looking for an assignment. He gave me his thoughts on the subject, and although I was dubious about any writer being able to make a good screenplay out of this one, I did not want to stop him from getting a job and agreed to work with him. Henry Blanke was made producer—it was always pleasant to work with him.

One day a phone call came to my office. My secretary was at lunch, so I answered it. A woman's voice said, "May I speak to Henry Blanke?" I replied, "He's not here at the moment, but how are you, Bette Davis?" She asked, "Who is this?" I told her and she shouted, "Oh, my God!" We talked pleasantly for several minutes, and I asked her if she'd like to come out to the studio for lunch one day. "I'd love it," she replied, and I promised to call her soon. But I became so bogged down with *Ice Palace* that I forgot and never called.

When Kleiner and I finished the first draft, I thought it was as good as we could do but still not worth making—it would be an expensive production. Warner, however, was ready to go forward with the project. At that point I made a mistake. I said to him, "You will not even be able to get a decent cast for it."

"If I do, will you make it?" he asked.

I said I would, confident that no topflight actors would be willing to do it. A few days later he summoned me to his office.

"Here's your cast," he said, and then read off the following names: Richard Burton for the lead, Robert Ryan for the second role, and Carolyn Jones for the female lead, with Martha Hyer as the second lead—all good performers. I was caught. Later, when I told Burton that he had double-crossed me by accepting the role, he explained that because his last few films had not been successful, Twentieth Century–Fox, to whom he had been under contract, had released him. Warner's offered him $125,000 for six weeks' work. "I knew that no director could make it in six weeks and would be lucky to make it in twelve. I needed the money, so I took it," he said. He had figured correctly. As for the others, Robert Ryan, a solid actor and superior person, was no longer a young leading man, so he accepted. Carolyn Jones and Martha Hyer were happy to be playing with Burton and Ryan. I suppose, too, that after *Garment Jungle* and *The Young Philadelphians,* my reputation had been somewhat revived. For Burton's friend, I had Jim Backus, an amusing man and reliable performer. His wife and son were played by my good friend Sheila Bromley, who had become a fine actress, and my own son, Eric, who was twelve years old and did a good job, praised even by Warner. The other players, Karl Swenson, George Takei, and Barry Kelly, contributed their talents along with Shirley Knight, Ray Danton, and Diane McBain—the latter three under contract and just getting started. I also brought from Alaska three native Eskimos, a man and two women, who were seeing Hollywood for the first time.

Burton was not only a good actor, but also a delight to be around. He had a magnificent voice, which he relied upon too much at times, and would recite Shakespeare at the drop of a hat. Now and then he'd reveal his potential by playing a scene so well that I was sure it came from some heartfelt moment in his own life. He enjoyed drinking and often drank too much. He had a great sense of humor and attracted women, young and old, as I had never seen before and have never seen since. I am happy to have worked with him—also Ryan, Backus, and Carolyn Jones, who are gone now.

The shooting of *Ice Palace* was in color and called for location work in Alaska: salmon canneries, fishing boats, ice and snow, bears, and dogsled teams. We also had to do some flying and landing on skis, a hazardous task. We worked often in thirty-degrees-below-zero weather and were kept from freezing by parkas, boots, wool underwear, sweaters, fur-lined gloves, knitted caps, and hand warmers.

Before I was halfway finished with the film, Warner wanted to sign me for an added three-year term and a boost in salary. I held off because the studio was retrenching, making fewer films and buying few new properties. Also the business was changing. Television was taking over what might have been successful small films in the past. Costs were mounting, and I was sure that my future would be confined to rescuing old and tired properties.

Ice Palace was well photographed by Joe Biroc, and we had an excellent crew. The performances and production values were good, and we did the best we could to make it worthwhile—but the basic story was nothing more than a glorified soap opera.

Afterward, Burton went to New York to play in *Camelot,* which gave his career a boost and led eventually to his playing in *Cleopatra,* where his affair with, and eventual marriage to, Elizabeth Taylor put him on the front pages, and he became a big star again.

My reluctance to sign a new deal was soon justified: I was sent a novel, *Fever in the Blood,* as my next film. It was about a judge, a man of integrity, who resents the shenanigans of an ambitious district attorney and decides to fight him. It was reminiscent of many other films; in addition the judge was an old man, at a time when youth-oriented pictures were taking hold. These factors made the film's commercial prospects seem dim. When I told Trilling I did not want to do it, he informed me that Roy Huggins was to be the producer, and since we were friends, Warner thought that I'd be glad to direct it.

Roy, whom I had met at Columbia Studios, was a successful producer of TV at Warner's, having created *Maverick, Hawaiian Eye, 77 Sunset Strip,* and other series, including *The Fugitive.* Weeks before, Trilling had called to tell me that Roy was reluctant to do any more TV and wanted only to produce films (which I was aware of). He asked if I thought Roy would make a good producer.

"Look at his record," I replied, and added that I felt sure that if given a chance, Roy would prove to be as successful in pictures as he had been in TV. Unfortunately, he was made a producer at a time when Jack Warner had become cautious and fearful and the studio was suffering from a loss of vitality. I went to Roy's office to talk with him and learned that no one had told him I was assigned to the film. He was pleased to hear that we might be working together but angry that it was not even discussed with him. I couldn't blame him, but I explained that the feelings of producers and directors had often been ignored at Warner's. It was, as they say, par for the course. I also told him that I considered *Fever in the Blood* an old-fashioned story with dismal prospects for the future. He agreed but said he would try to update it wherever possible; he would begin by making the judge a younger man. Harry Kleiner, who had done the script of *Ice Palace,* was to write the screenplay. He felt that together we could make a respectable film, and I accepted the assignment.

Soon we were told that Efrem Zimbalist, Jr. would play the judge, and Jack Kelly, who had been in *Maverick,* was cast as the district attorney. Although the rest of the cast included Angie Dickinson and Don Ameche in good roles, plus Herbert Marshall, Carroll O'Connor, Parley Baer, and Jesse White in smaller parts, the fact that Zimbalist and Kelly, as the two leads, were known primarily through TV would, I felt, cause audiences to regard the film as merely an enlarged TV program. This, together with the familiarity of the story, despite the good performances of all the actors and a skillful job of producing, writing, and directing, doomed us from the start. Had Roy not been the producer and a friend, I would have refused to make it. The result was that although we worked hard and there were many good scenes of political drama, it was not enough to make it a hit. The elements of success are usually built into a property, either in freshness of theme or unusual characters and situations, neither of which we had.

Before *Fever* was released, the studio sent me another novel, *Gown of Glory.* It had been sitting around for years, and although it was a pleasant little story of a small-town minister, I was certain it would be a disaster as a film. I had been promised viable projects when I returned but so far had been given properties that others had been unable to lick or that were dated and hopeless. I wrote a letter to Warner (which is probably in the archives) asking for a release from my contract, which still had some months to go. He granted it, and we parted amicably. Huggins also soon left to become head of TV at Fox.

Within a short time my agent, Martin Baum, phoned to say that Bob Goldstein, now in Hollywood and in charge of production at Twentieth Century–Fox, wanted to see me. He offered me a deal to produce and direct pictures, with a drawing account while preparing projects, then my full salary if and when I made a film. I accepted his offer and persuaded Fox to buy, for a modest sum, an amusing play, *Drink to Me Only,* by Ira Wallach and Abe Ginnis. I thought it could be developed into a good comedy. The studio also agreed to hire Gabby Upton to work on an original idea I had for a film. I had just completed a first draft of the two projects when Goldstein called me to his office.

"We have a problem," he began. "Debbie Reynolds has a contract with us. It's a pay or play deal. We either have to make a picture with her soon or pay her five hundred thousand dollars. Jack Cummings is the producer of a script that we think might be good for her, and she's agreed to do it. We were going to assign Bob Parrish to direct it since he too has a picture contract with us, but he's been preempted to do a film in London. When we asked Debbie who she'd like among our directors, she asked for you. So we'd like you to postpone any further work on your projects and start preparing *Second Time Around* for Debbie. We'll pay you your salary for directing it." It was nice to know that Debbie, whom I had never met, had asked for me, but I was concerned about *Second Time Around*. A few days before, while I was having dinner at Danny Fuchs' home, he had received a phone call from Parrish, his friend, who said that he was trying to find a way to get out of doing a dreadful script at Fox called *Second Time Around*. I did not tell this to Goldstein, but I was fearful of what lay ahead. I went to Cummings's office to pick up a script, and he insisted on telling me the story. I thought it trivial and, except for the fact that Fox had to pay Debbie five hundred thousand dollars, I wondered why anyone would want to make it. After I told Goldstein my reaction, he asked that I get a writer of my own choice to work with me and do the best I could with it. I liked Goldstein, who had been kind to me in London, and felt I could not turn him down. I also liked Debbie Reynolds's work and hoped that we could get a film that was at least entertaining. Cummings was reluctant to hire another writer because he didn't think the script needed work, but I was able to convince him that it did. I asked for Oscar Saul, who had helped me on the Rita Hayworth picture.

The time of the story was early in the century. In New York, a young mother (Debbie) with two children, whose husband has gone west for his health, is worried and decides to join him. Until she knows exactly what the situation is, she leaves the children with her mother-in-law. When she arrives, she learns that her husband has died and his body is being shipped back east. Short of funds, she gets a job working as a farmhand for a widow, Thelma Ritter. A neighbor, Andy Griffith, finds her attractive; so does Steve Forrest, owner of the town's gambling casino. She soon learns that the town is dominated by a corrupt sheriff who has everyone cowed. She decides to fight him, runs for the office of sheriff, and is elected. She cleans up the town and sends for her children.

We inserted as much action and humor as possible into the script, and in a few weeks we had a workable screenplay. Before we started, I was told by a few friends to be careful of Debbie, that she was a "tough little cookie," despite her sweet girl appearance, and would try to tell me how to make the picture. I had heard this kind of talk before, about stars, producers, and even cameramen, but had rarely encountered the predicted difficulty. As for Debbie, I can only say that never have I worked with a brighter, more cooperative, or more knowledgeable actress. She never once intruded during the preparation of the script or tried to make any change just for her benefit, and she insisted on doing many of her own stunts that other lesser performers would have refused to do. She was always on time, took direction beautifully, and worked like a Trojan to help make the picture a success.

Before the picture was finished, Goldstein was replaced by Pete Levathes, who had been in TV advertising in New York. After a satisfying preview at a Westwood Theater, Levathes sent for me. He said he was not in a position to renew my option, which was coming up, but he asked me to remain on a week-to-week basis. I thanked him but explained that if, after the rescue job I had done on *Second Time Around,* the studio was uncertain whether they wanted me, I would prefer not to remain. He understood, and a short time later I departed.

A phone call soon came from Debbie Reynolds inviting me and my wife to a dinner party at her home in Beverly Hills. She was married to Harry Karl at the time. When we arrived, I was surprised to see Bette Davis among the dozen or more guests. She was distant and somewhat cold when we said hello. At dinner, Debbie, knowing that we had worked together, seated us next to each other, and although I made an effort several times to speak with her, she remained aloof. I could not tell whether she was uncomfortable to be sitting so close to Hedda and me or was angry that I had never called her. It was a painful session, which I'm sure Debbie was unaware of.

For a long time I was disturbed about my relationship with Bette Davis—unfortunately, she died before we might have had a reconciliation. But shortly after her death, in November 1989, I received a phone call from her secretary and friend inviting me to a memorial service for Bette to be held at Warner Brothers studios. I was surprised and asked her if she was aware that Bette and I had not been on friendly terms lately. She replied that I was mistaken—Bette had spoken very highly of me. I was pleased and attended the service. It was a moving tribute.

In the meantime, a short time after the dinner at Debbie's, I received a phone call asking me to come to Levathes's office. He told me that *Second Time Around* had opened to surprisingly good business, one of the few Fox releases that was doing well, and offered me a contract for another year. I returned, hoping to get back to the projects I had been working on. But it was a difficult period for the Hollywood studios and especially for Fox, which had not yet been able to come up with a successful TV program and had spent millions on *Cleopatra,* which was not doing as well as expected.

I was just getting started on my new contract when Bill Self, in charge of TV at Fox, having replaced Roy Huggins (who had had bad luck with several series he started), informed me that the studio would soon close, and everyone would be laid off except those under contract (which included me), who would have to be paid. A small contingent, however, would be moving to the old Western Avenue lot where an attempt would be made to activate TV. He asked if I'd be willing to help out by taking charge of some projects that were being developed. I had no wish to be paid for doing nothing and agreed to help. A group of us, including Self, Hal Kanter, Paul Monash, and me, were given offices at Western Avenue. Frank Glicksman, who was a reader at the time, accompanied us. I began working on the material I inherited, none of which I had any great faith in. Meanwhile, Pete Levathes was replaced by young Dick Zanuck, and the Twentieth Century–Fox studio in Beverly Hills closed.

Bill announced that we would be going to New York to meet with network and advertising bigwigs in an effort to get things moving, but the trip was less than successful. I attended a meeting where Richard Zanuck was present and an attorney suggested that perhaps Fox should be liquidated and the Western Avenue lot turned into a supermarket. Richard strongly opposed the idea. Subsequently, we heard that Darryl Zanuck had told the networks that unless they gave Fox a commitment for a TV series, they would not get any of the past Fox films to show. The result was that *Peyton Place* was accepted as a possible series. The studio reopened. Paul Monash prepared an hour pilot, which Self offered to me to direct, but I did not care for it. It was done by another director, but the network turned it down. They suggested that it be rewritten as a half-hour show. This was approved, made by still another director, and became a success. I did direct a comedy pilot with Shirley Temple and one with Gary Lockwood, neither of which were picked up.

During this period I got to know Frank Glicksman and found that our tastes were similar. Frank later became producer of a series based on *The Long Hot Summer* and asked for me to direct several episodes. While doing one of them, I received a phone call from Henry Weinstein in New York. He had been a producer at Fox when Goldstein was in charge. Henry was now associated with Ely Landau and Oliver Unger Productions. He was aware of the work done on *Second Time Around* and recommended me to his bosses as a director for *Cervantes,* a film about the life of the great Spanish author who wrote *Don Quixote.* He said he was sending me a script based on a novel by Bruno Frank, which he thought could become a worthwhile project and which would be made in Europe as a coproduction.

The prospect of doing a motion picture about Cervantes was like manna from heaven. I approached the script with reverence and great hopes but was deeply disappointed. When Henry phoned for my reaction, I thanked him for recommending me but said I could see no way to do the present script. He knew it needed work and asked me to talk with Oliver Unger, who would be coming to Hollywood in a few days. Oliver was a pleasant, soft-spoken gentleman. I liked him. As we had lunch together at the studio, I told him that a rewrite was useless; he needed a new writer and a new approach. Unless that drastic step was taken, I could not commit myself to the project. He said he'd think about it and left. A week passed, and Henry phoned again to tell me that both Landau and Unger had come to the conclusion that I was right, and they were talking to David Karp, a writer, about doing a new script. Before they made a decision, however, they wanted me to come to New York to talk with Karp and see if we all agreed with his approach. If we did, they wanted me to go to Madrid with Henry and Unger to meet with the European producers, who had the final say in hiring a director. Naturally, they would take care of my expenses.

I had read one of Karp's novels and thought he was talented. The prospect of going to Madrid was also appealing since I had never been there. By this time my daughter, Hedwin, had married and was living in New York, and my son, Eric, was at Yale. Hedda and I were alone, and she was looking forward to a vacation in New York while I went to Madrid.

David Karp was a good writer. He read the novel, and since the producers wanted to concentrate on the young Cervantes, he felt that the story should deal with his idealism and disillusionment—with women, the church, war, and life in general. I thought Karp was on the right track.

When Oliver, Henry, and I were about to go through customs, Henry discovered that his passport had expired and he'd be delayed a few days. On the plane, I learned from Oliver that Michel Salkind and his son, Alex, had initiated *Cervantes*. Michel was in his eighties and had an impressive list of credits: Orson Welles's *The Trial, La Maternelle, Maedchen in Uniform,* and several other well-known films. *Cervantes* was to be an expensive production, with a colossal naval encounter between the Christians and the Turks in the sixteenth century, known as the Battle of Lepanto. Over three hundred ships were involved, and more than thirty-five thousand lives were lost within a few hours. Cervantes enlisted and was wounded. Taken prisoner by the Turks, he became a slave and spent five years in Algeria before returning to Spain.

As we approached Madrid early the next morning, Unger said that a reservation had been made for me at the Palace Hotel, and if I would come to the lobby at 11:00 A.M., Alex Salkind, Michel's son, would arrive with several investors, including the Italian and Spanish producers, to talk with me. He also asked me not to say anything about a new script being written because it might frighten them. "All they really want to talk about are the production problems," he added. After checking into the Palace Hotel and having a hot shower, I had breakfast and went to the lobby—an enormous room on the mezzanine. Soon, four little men led by Alex Salkind, who was in his forties, came up the broad stairway. They found me, and after introductions Alex began to question me.

"How long do you think it'll take you to make the picture?" I wanted to say it all depends on the new script, but, mindful of Oliver's request, I refrained.

"It's hard to say," I hedged. "There are certain improvements we hope to make, which may add or subtract from the number of days."

"We understand," Alex said. "All directors eventually make little changes, but based on what is now written, how long do you think?"

"Well . . . I haven't made a breakdown—that is usually the assistant's job—but if you'll get me a typewriter and give me until tomorrow afternoon, I'll try to give you an idea of how long each scene should take. Of course, a lot depends on your cameraman. The Battle of Lepanto depends on how much I will have to shoot and how much is done with miniatures."

"We'll get you a typewriter, but how long would *you* want to do your part of the battle? Could you do it in four weeks?"

"If you tell me you can only afford four weeks of shooting, I'll adjust to it. But I will need at least two ships, one for the Christians and one for the Turks; stuntmen, firepower, and powder men for the guns and cannon; and good fencers and swordsmen, plus equipment to produce smoke and flames. And we should have two or three cameras available to save time."

They looked at each other, smiled, and nodded. After a bit of whispering between them, they rose, thanked me and promised to send a typewriter at once. In a few hours I was in my room typing away at a breakdown of the present script. Oliver called to say that Alex had told him the meeting was a success. The following day, after reading my breakdown, they felt that I knew the problems involved, was a serious director, and that they could rely on me. I learned too that they had seen Errol Flynn in *The Adventures of Don Juan*.

Weinstein arrived the next day, and he, Unger, and I went to Paris, where we met Alain Delon and discussed the possibility of his playing Cervantes. He was interested, but his schedule was uncertain.

Back in New York, I wanted to remain in the city to work with Karp, but the producers felt it best that I return to California and wait for the script to be finished. They also assured me that a contract for my services would be forthcoming. Several weeks later the script arrived, and I was encouraged. I thought that Karp had done a good job, although I felt we still needed some work. Contractual arrangements having been worked out, plans were made for me to go to Madrid, scout locations, discuss casting, and make final preparations for the production. Karp and Weinstein would come later for last-minute changes. I had high hopes for *Cervantes*. I thought it would appeal to young and old alike and become both a commercial and an artistic success because it dealt with the disillusionment of youthful idealism and had a good love story and a famous sea battle.

Hedda accompanied me to New York, where she was to wait until I completed the scouting tour and found us a suitable apartment in Madrid. She had been depressed and gloomy of late, and I hoped that a change of scenery would be good for her. In the interim, she'd have a few weeks to see friends and be with Hedwin. Eric would also be nearby at Yale. At the airport in New York, while I was waiting to catch my plane for Madrid, we got into an argument about some trivial matter, and she ended by telling me how unhappy she had been with me lately and how much she hated having constantly to adjust to my needs, likes, and dislikes. She found it abrasive and nerve-wracking and was convinced that living alone was preferable. I left New York depressed, upset, and uncertain about how to handle the situation.

The making of *Cervantes*, later titled *The Young Rebel*, was the most bizarre, exasperating, incredible, and often hilarious experience I have ever had. To describe it in detail, along with my own behavior during the months of production, would require an inordinate amount of time and space.

In Madrid, offices had been set up at Sevilla Studios, and I met, for the first time, Miguel (Michel in France, Mischa in Russia, where he was born) Salkind, who was pixieish, cultured, delightful, and the father of Alex. We were simpatico immediately. He liked the new script, and soon a scouting trip was arranged with my assistant, Julio Semperi, a treasure, and Enrique Alarcon, a brilliant set designer, plus a Spanish director whose name escapes me, to help in any way possible.

As we traveled through the south of Spain, I often felt we were in California—the oleanders, the fruit trees, and the vineyards were so similar. And why not? The Spanish settled California and brought with them the plants from their country. We selected Granada and the Alhambra for various scenes in Algeria, the town of Denia for the arrival of the slave ship, and Cartagena for the Battle of Lepanto. Everywhere we went, the people were warm and friendly.

Gradually, from my traveling companions and others, I began to pick up bits of information about European film producers, especially how they operated and raised money. They sold rights in various countries; obtained government help and concessions, as well as credit from suppliers; and enticed individual investors and speculators. The Salkinds were known to be experts in the field. But I also gathered that there were still many facets of *Cervantes* that were not yet settled, particularly with regard to finances. This was confirmed when we returned after a week of scouting and Miguel gave me only part of my expense money—and I learned from my agent in California that my contract had not yet been signed by Unger-Landau. Nevertheless, I went to the studio daily and continued to prepare. Every few days, Miguel would open the door to my office and introduce a stranger to me and Julio, then pointing to the sketches of sets, props, costumes, photos of locations, and so forth posted on the walls, would say, "You see, everything is moving ahead, on schedule." I soon realized that these were prospective investors, and that it was important for them to see me and my assistant at work.

Henry Weinstein arrived with David Karp. We discussed script revisions and finally came to a general agreement.

What seemed to be holding up the financial arrangements was the lack of a leading man and woman. Before final commitments were made, backers wanted to know who was going to play young Cervantes and the woman he falls in love with. Weeks went by as negotiations with Alain Delon and Ava Gardner took place. I had visited Ava with Weinstein and Karp when they were in Madrid, and after we talked to her about the lead, she said, "Look, Vince and I are old friends. We'll talk tomorrow and I'll let you know." The next day I went to her apartment, and when the maid let me into the living room, Ava was dancing wildly in the center of the room, barefooted, her hair flying about, as two musicians played a flamenco song. Several guests, whom I did not know, were seated about and applauding her. When she finished the dance, she rushed to greet me, introduced me, and poured me a drink. She was loaded and feeling high. I knew there would be no serious discussion about *Cervantes* or anything else. She just wanted to dance, have fun, and forget whatever was troubling her. She sat with me for a moment, took another drink, leaned toward me, and whispered, "Why is it all the nice men are married?" I was trying to think of an answer when she got up abruptly and began to dance again. So it went for the next hour: another drink, a few quick words as she sat next to me, then another dance. Finally, she turned to her guests.

"Now, I've got to talk to Vince." They thanked her, and after the maid paid off the two musicians, they all departed. Then Ava sat down once again with me. She was perspiring, dried her face with a large kerchief, and was about to speak when the front doorbell rang. Surprised, she turned toward the entrance. "Who the hell is that?" The maid opened the door and admitted a tall, dark, nice-looking young man. He stepped into the living room. We were sitting at the far end. "Buenos noches," he said, bowing politely.

Ava turned to me. "What the fuck does *he* want?"

"I imagine he has a date with you."

"Oh, shit! I don't even remember his name. I'm sorry, Vince." I rose to go. "I'll call you tomorrow," she said, and I left.

The next day she called, apologized, and asked me to come for dinner. We had a pleasant evening. She was sober and told me that although she had done the same type of role before, the producers had offered her $150,000 to play the courtesan and she could use the money. We talked about the old days in Hollywood. I detected a nostalgia and a lost soul underneath. By the time I left, I felt sure that she would be in *Cervantes*. A few days later she called. She was angry and said that her European agents had screwed things up for her and she was not going to do the film. I tried to find out what had happened, but she seemed upset and reluctant to talk. Her last words on the phone were, "I'm sorry Vince, I'm sure we'd have had fun." I never learned the truth. This was followed by the news that Delon wanted too much money up front, and he too was out.

Soon after, Salkind informed me that Gina Lollobrigida was available, and he wanted me to go to Rome to speak with her. He asked also that I contact Sam Arkoff, the head of American International Pictures, who was at the Excelsior Hotel and had been sent a copy of the screenplay. He might be willing to invest in the production. I was happy to do both, although I doubted that *Cervantes* was the kind of film that Arkoff would like to invest in. I was right. He was a realistic businessman, and I liked him. We leveled with each other. He said he'd be interested in a swashbuckler film with lots of action and comedy, but *Cervantes* did not appeal to him. I explained that although I hoped to inject more action and comedy wherever possible, our story was about young Cervantes and his idealism, how it is almost destroyed, and yet how he clings to his faith in humanity. Arkoff said he'd think it over.

I had dinner with Lollobrigida. She was as beautiful as ever, liked the role of the courtesan, and indicated she would be happy to do it if the financial arrangements were right.

Back in Madrid, Salkind was pleased about Lollobrigida but unhappy about Arkoff. And there was still no sign of a leading man. I was becoming concerned, because my money for expenses was falling further behind, and I received word that although my contract had been signed, no salary checks had yet arrived.

Meanwhile, Hedda was becoming impatient. My daughter wrote that she was also becoming a problem—did nothing but sit around the hotel all day or come to her apartment and complain about everything. I replied that I was sorry, but the production was still uncertain and I might be coming back any day.

At one point, Weinstein and Unger came to Madrid and informed me that in addition to the difficulty of getting a well-known young leading man, the Salkinds were still having financial problems, and they thought it best to postpone the picture. I felt sure that if postponed, it would never be made, and this was my last chance to get a feature that would not only appeal to the youth of the world but achieve some distinction and inform audiences about how and why *Don Quixote* came to be written. I sensed too that unless it was made, I would never be paid, and my time would have been wasted.

When it seemed that the project was hopelessly mired in a financial morass and would never be done, I was suddenly told that Horst Buchholz would play Cervantes, Lollobrigida the courtesan, Louis Jourdan would play Cardinal Acquaviva, and José Ferrer would play the important role of Hassan Bey, the cynical ambassador from the Ottoman Empire. Smaller but meaningful roles were to be played by Paco Rabal and Fernando Rey, two fine Spanish actors. A half dozen other performers and genuine artists were cast in smaller roles. I never found out how or why the situation changed so abruptly, but now we had a starting date, and there was a mad rush to get things ready. I had to make many last-minute decisions. I also had to decide what to do about Hedda. I knew that I would not be able to handle her downbeat mood and hostility toward me, that I would have limited time to spend with her, and that she didn't speak Spanish. I also knew that I'd need peace and quiet at the end of a day if I was to do a good job of directing. I made a decision that was self-protective. I discouraged her from coming and wrote to Hedwin and Eric explaining the situation and asking them to forgive me and adjust as well as possible.

As in Rome, we began shooting at noon and worked straight through until nine o'clock at night. My cameraman was a friend of the Salkinds, brought from Paris. He had photographed Orson Welles's *The Trial* and *Chimes at Midnight*. I had a good cast, a good staff, and a good crew and was looking forward to a happy production. But from the day we began to shoot until we finished, I was never sure of what awaited me when I arrived on the set. My assistant would schedule a sequence, and I'd prepare for it the night before, only to be told the next day that because of a delay with costumes or an actor or set decorations or props, or some other problem, I'd have to do a different sequence. I soon realized that I'd better be prepared to do any sequence in the picture at a moment's notice and be able to adjust to any problem.

One morning I had to do a scene in a wooded park area, where a group of well-dressed men and women are seen riding wildly on horseback, Lollobrigida with them, as they leap over a hedge. Her horse balks, rears, and almost throws her, when Buchholz, in a carriage on his way to Rome with Jourdan, for whom he works as a secretary, sees it and, in a chivalrous move, leaps out to help her. I had asked for horses that could jump and a good stunt double for Gina. My assistant had made the request, but when it came time to shoot, I was told that only one or two horses might be able to jump. Also, they could not find a female who could ride and jump, so they sent a man to double for Gina. He was short and heavy, and even though we put a costume and a wig on him, he looked absurd. I had to place the camera so far away that the shot was ineffective, and what should have been a good scene was flat and dull.

Once, Alex's wife came to the set and made some derogatory remarks about the actors, and they refused to go on as long as she was present. I had trouble getting her to leave. Several times during the shooting, an actor would refuse to go on because of not having been paid. One day I was to shoot a scene with Louis Jourdan, who was playing the cardinal, and with an actor who was due in that morning from Rome to play the pope. The night before, I had blocked the action for Louis and the cameraman in the pope's quarters. The moment I arrived the next morning, Louis came rushing from makeup, visibly upset.

"Have you seen the pope?" he asked. "He must be seven feet tall. I can't possibly stand next to him. It would look like Mutt and Jeff." I told him not to worry; I'd stage the scene differently than planned. He calmed down. I kept the pope seated the entire time Louis was in the room. But in the midst of shooting, Louis stopped and called me aside. "Vince, I can't do it, I can't go on, it's impossible. You can't see it because his back is to the camera, but the man doesn't understand a word of English. He gives me no reaction. He only knows that when I stop, he speaks. I'm talking to a blank wall. Please help me." I shot only the beginning and end of the scene, cut, and then read the pope's lines in English for Louis's close-up, then his lines in Italian for the pope's close-up. (We always had on hand scenes in Spanish, Italian, French and English.)

On several occasions the camera broke down and we had to wait while it was being repaired, and once or twice we ran out of film because a previous bill had not been paid. In some scenes I had one actor speaking Spanish, another French, and another Italian. Although I knew a smattering of each, it was sometimes difficult to convey my thoughts to the actors. Fortunately, Jourdan, Ferrer, and Buchholz spoke English. Because José Ferrer had to leave by a certain date, I had to revise a sequence in order to get him finished, and do the same with Gina. I kept my cool and adjusted to most of the problems, but then came the move to Cartagena and the Battle of Lepanto.

Originally, I was promised four weeks to shoot the spectacle, but halfway through the schedule Michel approached me with a downcast face. "Vincent, my friend, I have some bad news. Due to various expenses and some financial problems, we will only have enough funds for three weeks." By this time I was immune to bad news and replied sadly, "Well, if that's all you have, we'll do the best we can." The following week he approached me again, depressed, his face filled with shame and regret, to say that, due to unforeseen circumstances, another week would have to be shorn from the Battle of Lepanto. From four weeks I was now down to two. But I was so drained of energy and weary of the daily struggle to make a good film that I threw up my hands and accepted my fate.

When I had completed most of the film, before departing for Cartagena to shoot the greatest naval battle in European history, I received word from Paris, where Michel had gone to raise more money, that there had been a miscalculation and I would have to do the Battle of Lepanto in *one week only*. I was ready to commit mayhem, but there was no one around I could vent my anger on or bludgeon. In Cartagena I discovered that the two practical ships that had been prepared for me (replicas of ancient sailing vessels constructed over motorized barges) had been damaged by winds buffeting them about and needed repairs, which required two days. This meant that I had less than a week to accomplish what I needed. Then I asked to speak to the stuntmen and learned that instead of ten or twelve, which I had requested, I had only two. I was bitter and disgusted, but I blamed no one but myself for having gotten involved in such a mess.

However, the crowning blow was yet to come: I had, early on, warned Salkind that we would need men on the two ships who would know how to handle the long oars and row in unison and that, to save time, they should be practicing before I arrived. Otherwise there would be a costly delay. Salkind assured me before I left Madrid for Cartagena that I had nothing to worry about; he had made arrangements with the Spanish navy to get me fifty men. They would know how to row, fight, and do whatever I might require. I was relieved. Sure enough, the fifty young men were in costume and waiting at the dock when we were ready to begin. We took off from the Cartagena harbor and had gotten past the breakwater and out to the open sea when a mild breeze came up and our ship began to dip and roll a bit. I was standing on a raised area in the stern, where I had a bird's-eye view of the entire deck. Suddenly, I became aware that several of the so-called navy men had crossed to the rail and were leaning over and struggling to throw up. They were seasick!

"Julio!" I yelled to my assistant, who was nearby. "What the hell is going on? If these men are in the Spanish navy, why are they getting seasick? I am no sailor, but this mild roll does not bother me!"

Julio was also puzzled and moved down to the deck to talk to the men. He soon returned. "It's true," he said. "They are in the Spanish navy, but they are raw recruits from farms and villages, and this is their first time out to sea."

I threw up my hands again. "That means they won't know how to row, either!" Julio nodded. "It's like a bad dream," I said and began to consider ways and means to do what was required. I shot the close-range fighting scenes with two stuntmen who put on different clothing, wigs, beards, and moustaches at least half a dozen times and died differently each time. Everyone cooperated to the best of his ability, and I called on every shortcut and cheat that I had learned over the years to come up with enough footage to make a reasonably exciting battle. So instead of four weeks, the Battle of Lepanto was shot in three days. I don't know how long it took to make the miniatures, which were done after I left Spain.

To be fair to the Salkinds, the lack of sufficient funds was the basic cause of all our problems. I do not know the final cost of the film, but it was, I think, a little over $2 million. Today, with the great number of sets, locations, and the huge cast, plus the time of shooting, it would cost $20 or $30 million, even on an independent basis.

As I began the editing, I sent for Hedda and took a hotel room for us. She fell one day while visiting an American friend and smashed her knee. She underwent an operation and was hospitalized for ten days. When she was able to move, I took her back to New York, where she waited at our daughter's place while I went back to Spain to finish the editing.

After the first cut in Madrid by Margarita Ochoa, a talented lady, the film was shipped to Paris, where the Salkinds had made arrangements for the final work: dissolves, dubbing, music, and sound effects, minus the miniatures. I went to Paris. Landau and Weinstein flew in from New York to see how the film looked in its rough cut. They were happy with the result and complimented me. Soon after, I left Paris and returned to New York, and from there with Hedda went to California.

Later, I was told by Unger that Salkind had made certain changes in the cutting after I left, and that they had made a deal with Arkoff and American International to release the film, but that Arkoff had also made changes. I went to New York to see the final version. In the attempt to preserve only the action sequences, the film had been botched, with the result that it was neither an action picture nor the story of a human being. Motivations had been cut, transitions eliminated, and shifts from one place to another unexplained. I wrote a long letter stating my objections and asked that my name be removed from the film. I do not know if it was ever released theatrically in the United States, but many months later it was shown on television with a few changes and my name still on it, and it received a few surprisingly good reviews. If it had been left as I first cut it, I think it might have had a chance. But it was bungled, alas, by the input of too many others. The Salkinds and Unger-Landau eventually paid my salary and expenses.

I returned with Hedda to our ranch at Ojai. We had sold our home in Van Nuys and bought a seven-acre place near Lake Casitas, eventual site of the 1984 Olympic rowing events. It was a quiet life, just what I wanted, but lonely and not pleasant for Hedda, although she settled in and the tension between us subsided. We'd drive occasionally to Ojai or Ventura for dinner or sometimes to Los Angeles to see a film. I was resigned to working on the ranch, reading, and perhaps now and then working on a screenplay, but I was convinced that my days of directing features were over. I was past sixty and had not had a really good film since *The Young Philadelphians.*

To my surprise, one day I received a phone call from my old friend Frank Glicksman, who was now a TV producer at MGM.

"I'm doing a series called *Medical Center,*" he said. "How would you like to do an episode?" I hesitated for a moment, since I thought it would only confirm the end of my career as a picture maker. But I respected Frank, and I knew he felt the same about me.

"Okay," I replied. "I'll try one, and we'll see how it goes."

18
Twilight Years

The challenge of episodic television, to bring to life in a few minutes a dramatic situation that will grab and hold an audience for an hour, was stimulating. As skillful as I thought I had become in directing films, I still learned from doing television. The small screen dictates a minimum of production or background shots and impels you to get to the faces of your actors and the heart of scenes as quickly as possible and to avoid unnecessary moves, details, and complicated setups. The added value for a director is to shoot an episode one week and see the result soon after. If you are open-minded you can learn why you succeeded or failed to accomplish what you were aiming for.

Working with Frank Glicksman was a pleasure. His associate, Al Ward, was an experienced writer who later became co-producer of *Medical Center.* They were joined eventually by Don Brinkley, who became the principal rewrite man for the series. We had a mutual respect for each other, and the series ran for seven years. I directed thirty-five or forty episodes, several of which I thought were bold and superior. I worked with many talented actors: Diane Baker, Cyd Charisse, James Daly, Robert Douglas, Chad Everett, Harry Guardino, Salome Jens, Steve Lawrence, Gary Lockwood, Vera Miles, Lois Nettleton, David Opatashu, Linda Purl, Robert Reed, Pippa Scott, Peter Strauss, Barry Sullivan, Jessica Walter, and Dana Wynter.

I was also called to do other TV episodes: Roy Huggins's *Baretta* with Robert Blake; several episodes of *The Waltons,* including the opener; also *Doctor's Hospital; Executive Suite; Westside Medical;* and *Trapper John, M.D.* I worked with Linda Carlson, Ellen Corby, Will Geer, Larry Hagman, Elisabeth Hartman, Greg Harrison, Michael Learned, Rita Moreno, John Randolph, Mitchell Ryan, Pernell Roberts, John Saxon, Sylvia Sidney,

James Slater, William Smithers, Richard Thomas, and Ernest Thompson, who became a successful writer.

Several friends asked if I did not feel that doing TV was a come down for me. Of course, I would have preferred directing a good film, but having reached my sixty-second birthday and lacking a big hit immediately behind me, I did not expect to be offered one. So my reply recalled the moment in London when I asked an actor who had been playing leads in the theater if he did not object to playing a small role in a film. His answer was, "My profession is acting. If I am offered a role in a respectable production, whether small or large, I will, if I like it, accept it." I thought that was a healthy attitude and felt the same about directing.

As I became busy with TV, Hedda decided we should move back to the city and soon found us a house in Malibu. During a hiatus in 1971 we took a trip to the Orient that brought us closer together; I was not preoccupied with a script and was able to give her some attention for a change. I tried to make her happy. She relaxed, enjoyed the new sights, dropped her defenses, and we became intimate again.

After *Medical Center* ended its run, Martin Baum, a great agent, phoned and asked me to rush to a projection room at Metromedia studios to see a few reels of a TV Movie of the Week, *Lady of the House,* with Dyan Cannon and Armand Assante. It was shooting in San Francisco and being directed by Ralph Nelson. For some reason, the producers were unhappy and decided to make a change. They wanted a director who was "experienced enough to take over immediately, get things done, and keep on schedule." Marty recommended me.

I did not know Nelson personally, but I had respected his work ever since I saw *Lilies of the Field.* As always, I was reluctant to replace a fellow director, but I was told that a change would be made whether I accepted the assignment or not. After viewing the assembled footage and hearing the rest of the story—based on the life of Sally Stanford, once the operator of a bordello—I agreed to finish the film, provided I could talk to Nelson first.

It was 9 P.M. when the producers asked me to fly to San Francisco at midnight. I rushed home, had a bite to eat with Hedda, packed a bag, and a limousine picked me up and took me to the airport. I read the script on the plane. At 2 A.M. I was in a motel room, and at 7 A.M. I was on the set ready to shoot. Dyan and Armand were cooperative, and we worked well together. When I finished, Baum told me that the producers sent him a case of champagne as a gift for recommending me. *Lady of the House* was well received. Ralph Nelson and I met later at the Directors Guild, had a pleasant conversation, and agreed to share the credit and residuals.

Soon after I received another call from Baum. Carroll O'Connor had asked if I was available to direct him in a remake of *The Last Hurrah* as a Movie of the Week for NBC. I had directed Carroll in two films at Warner's several years before and thought he was a fine actor. When he became such a great success as Archie Bunker in *All in the Family* I was sure he had forgotten me. So his inquiry was a pleasant surprise. I was curious, however, as to why he agreed to remake a film that with Spencer Tracy in the lead and John Ford directing had not been a success. Later, I realized that Carroll saw it as a chance to get away from Archie. He wrote the screenplay and gave an excellent performance, along with half a dozen other actors, including Mariette Hartley and Burgess Meredith, who were both nominated for Emmy awards.

Because the story is basically a character study and lacks strong dramatic action, it was only a mild success. I suspect, too, that audiences were hoping to see Archie Bunker as the Irish politician. Once an actor has created such an overwhelming success in a role, it is difficult to change his image. (Chaplin faced the same problem.) In real life, Carroll is as far from Archie as anyone could get. He is most intelligent, well read, liberal-minded, sensitive, and a pleasure to direct. Eventually, he managed to overcome Archie with his TV series *In the Heat of the Night.*

Following *The Last Hurrah,* I was offered another Movie of the Week, *Women at West Point,* for CBS, with Linda Purl, Andrew Stevens, and Jameson Parker, who gave good performances. We made the entire film at West Point, received great cooperation, and I was pleased with the result.

Next came an offer to direct Harold Robbins's *The Dream Merchants.* Milton Sperling was the executive and Hugh Benson his producer. It starred Mark Harmon and Morgan Fairchild, and I was given a good cast: Eve Arden, Kaye Ballard, Red Buttons, Robert Culp, Howard Duff, José Ferrer, Vince Gardenia, Carolyn Jones, Brianne Leary, and Jan Murray. It was a story of the early days of picture making. Critics have never been kindly disposed to Robbins, but audiences seem to enjoy his work and no doubt he "laughs all the way to the bank."

No sooner was *The Dream Merchants* finished than I was asked to direct a Movie of the Week about Humphrey Bogart. The script was well written by Dan Taradash, but casting someone who would be acceptable as Bogart was the major problem. I was told that the producers were negotiating for John Cassavetes. I did not know him personally, but I thought he was a fine actor and would be excellent as Bogart. I accepted the assignment.

During the first week, when my principal concern was the casting, I was told that the producers had been unable to reach Cassavetes. Baum suggested that maybe I could speak to him and gave me a phone number to call. I phoned, gave my name to someone, and, sure enough, John came to the phone. He was most pleasant, said that he would be happy to work with me (I had the pleasure once of directing his talented and charming wife, Gena Rowlands) but that he had promised Lauren Bacall, a good friend, that he would turn down the role if offered to him. I wondered why Bacall was so opposed to John doing it. He did not tell me, but he had made a promise and could not break it. I could only think that perhaps Bacall wanted to do her own version of Bogart (which was understandable). Someone suggested that I talk to the actor who played Bogart in the Woody Allen film *Play It Again, Sam.* I did, made a test that was satisfactory, and was ready to go forward with him when the New York office of CBS turned him down. Because I had always been careful in casting, I was annoyed that my wishes were ignored.

After sitting around for days, seeing other actors, none of whom seemed right, Philip Barry Jr., the Hollywood producer for Charles Fries, executive producer of the Bogart venture, received instructions from CBS to come to New York with me to look for someone who would be right for the Bogart role. I had gone through the list of New York actors, saw no one that I thought was right, and felt the trip was not necessary. Nevertheless, I went.

After several days of interviews, I was asked to make a few tests of actors the New York office thought were possibilities. I returned to Hollywood. Weeks had gone by, and I was restless to get started. Again I asked for the actor I wanted but was ignored. Finally, word come from New York that they had selected the actor for the Bogart role. He was a nice man and a good actor, but I did not think his personality was right for the role. I called Baum and wanted to get off the project, but he pointed out that it would be awkward for me to leave after being on the project for so long. Moreover, CBS had already paid me $10,000 in overtime, which meant I would be receiving $60,000 for the project. Also, I would not be wise to antagonize the network. "Do the best you can and we'll have another assignment before this is released," Baum counseled. I followed his advice.

Neither the script, direction, nor production was strong enough to overcome the mistake of casting, despite my efforts and those of the actor who played the role. I was depressed. It was one of the few times that my advice about casting had been so completely ignored. I was also seventy-five years old, had spent forty years in the business of entertainment, and had little hope of being offered a script that would inspire me. When I discussed it with Hedda, she suggested that maybe I should rest for a while, take a nice long vacation, and afterwards try to work on an original idea or look for a novel. "We don't need the money," she said. "We have enough to live on—so let's have some fun for a change." I thought she was right. We took a trip to the Greek Isles and Israel, visited our daughter in New York, and began to spend more time with our grandchildren in Los Angeles.

We saw friends and family, caught up on back reading, attended showings of films at the Directors Guild and Academy theater, and enjoyed the California sunshine. I worked on a screenplay. Hedda became increasingly tired at the end of each day and subject to dizzy spells. At first, we thought it might be because of improper eyeglasses. When that proved false, we had her ears tested, but there was nothing wrong there. Her blood pressure was high but not alarming. Then I noticed that her abdomen had become distended. We went to a hospital for a liver scan and were told that her problem was caused by her liver.

A visit to a specialist was a disaster. He turned to Hedda and said, "Your liver is scarred, and it's irreversible." The blood seemed to drain from her face. When I asked him what could have caused it, he replied bluntly, "It's cirrhosis, probably brought on by alcohol." He was surprised when I told him that Hedda was not a drinker and only occasionally had a cocktail or a glass of wine. He asked if she had ever had hepatitis or had a recent blood transfusion. We could think of neither, and he concluded by saying, "Well, all I know is that the liver is scarred." Not a word of hope or encouragement.

I had been told that this doctor was an expert in his field, but I wanted to tell him he knew nothing about the human heart and mind. He gave us a prescription, and we left his office, two of the most depressed human beings imaginable. From that day on, Hedda's strength, courage, and will to live seemed to wither away, and her condition deteriorated.

I phoned my daughter, who was a psychologist at the Institute for Rational Emotional Therapy in New York. She took a leave of absence for three months and came to California with her husband, son, and daughter to be with Hedda during the summer. When she arrived, Hedda made her promise that she'd go back to New York in September and not delay the children's education.

We knew that death was approaching, but I never spoke of it to Hedda. Neither did Hedwin or Eric. I hoped that it could be postponed for a long time to come. Meanwhile, we concentrated on making life as pleasant as possible for all of us. The summer passed quickly. Much of the time Hedda rested in bed, but often she would get dressed and join us at meals and attempt to be cheerful. Other times she would sit outside alone and remain silent for long periods.

Then came the day that she was no longer able to get up and move about. Our doctor increased the amount of sedative prescribed to alleviate her pain. For weeks we took care of her, made her as comfortable as possible. She was grateful. When she could no longer even take a sip of water, the doctor said she'd have to be fed intravenously and ordered an ambulance to take her to St. John's Hospital in Santa Monica. I went along in the ambulance. For eighteen days her pain increased but she was kept sedated and alive, although most of the time only semi-conscious. Now and then she'd nod or half smile when I whispered in her ear. They put a cot in the room, and Hedwin and I took turns staying with Hedda from seven in the morning until ten at night, when a private nurse took over.

On the first day of September I insisted that Hedwin do as she had promised: go back to New York with the children. With tears in their eyes and sadness in their hearts, they kissed Hedda goodbye and left. September 9, 1984, one week before Hedda's seventy-ninth birthday, I was sitting close to her bed, holding her hand, when she stopped breathing. I yelled, "Breathe, Hedda! Breathe!" She opened her eyes, looked at me for a moment, smiled, then closed her eyes again. After a second or two, she took her last breath. I knew she was gone but called for a nurse, who came running in, followed by a doctor. They confirmed that it was the end. I begged them to leave me alone. I phoned Eric, who said he would come as quickly as possible.

During the next half hour, I sat by my wife's side, holding her hand and thinking about our life together. I wept as I recalled the past. Eric arrived, and we phoned my daughter. Finally, a gurney arrived with two orderlies assigned to take Hedda's body away. As they wrapped her in a sheet, I leaned over to kiss her lips and say goodbye. Eric went downstairs with the body and left me in the room. I cried again, uncontrollably. We had been married for fifty-three years.

Hedda had always said she wanted to be cremated and preferred no funeral service. We respected her wishes. But on September 16 I invited a few close friends and neighbors to celebrate her birthday.

For the next several months I was alone and rarely went out of the house except to buy groceries or attend to business matters. Three or four times a day, I'd see something that would remind me of Hedda and break down and sob like a hurt child. At times I'd hear her voice calling me and I'd respond. Friends suggested that I move out of our house, but I refused. I wanted to be near the reminders. But time is a great healer, and after a while I was able to control my sudden spasms of grief.

There is no doubt in my mind that the luckiest decision I ever made was to marry Hedda. She was an extraordinary person: honest, forthright, sensitive, modest, and totally self-effacing, with an abundance of good sense; she was also a wise and loving mother. In addition, she had possessed a keen instinct for business. If I had taken her advice and invested in the real estate that she urged me to buy I could have become a rich man. As it was, the investments she did make over my protests have enabled me, with Social Security and my Directors Guild pension, to live comfortably.

I cannot conceive of any other woman tolerating my indiscretions, mistakes, and selfishness. Twice we were on the verge of separating, but not because of another woman—if Hedda was ever jealous, she never revealed it. Her anger arose because of my failure to appreciate her abilities, my criticism of the way she dressed, or my cruel lack of consideration for her feelings. At such times she'd stop speaking to me, become silently resentful for days, sometimes weeks, and not allow me to come close to her or touch her. In that sense we were complete opposites; I am slow to anger but quick to forget and forgive. But not Hedda. She was hypersensitive to criticism, took umbrage quickly, and held on to it. When she was treated with consideration and affection, she'd relent and permit a partial lowering of her guard, but she always kept it handy.

The truth is that Hedda was never openly free and easy or lavish with her affections; she always seemed hesitant, suspicious, and restricted. Although she never admitted it or dwelled on it, looking back I suspect that she was badly scarred when her mother, whom she and her sister adored, deserted them when they were very young and ran off with another man. She also suffered at age sixteen, when she discovered that her first lover had been unfaithful. She must have vowed never again to love anyone so deeply as to become vulnerable. Yet she never spoke critically of her mother; she described her as a sad, emotionally confused woman. She rarely mentioned her former lover.

She revealed one other traumatic experience. When the children were growing up, I suggested we get a puppy for them, and Hedda refused. I demanded to know why. She told me that after her dismal affair with her lover she came to her senses and began to study shorthand and typing, became an expert at both, and found a good job as a secretary. For companionship she acquired a small wire-haired terrier and became deeply attached to him. One weekend she went to visit a friend in the country and took the little dog. He was playing outside when a pit bull grabbed him and punctured his lungs. Hedda drove him back to New York as quickly as possible, and for six weeks she went every day before and after work to visit him at a veternarian's hospital. She spent half her salary to save the little dog, but he died. She made up her mind never to have another pet. I understood. We are the sum of our natures, ancestors, and experiences, so I could not fault Hedda. I have come to realize, as I never did before her death, her true worth.

During the next three years I gave up looking for jobs and traveled extensively, visiting friends and family. I attended my grandson David's graduation from Boston Medical College and took him and his sister Riva on a trip to the Orient. I went to Vienna, Georgia, my old hometown, when I was invited there to help celebrate the ninetieth birthday of Ruth Lewis, my former elocution teacher. During my visit, I spoke to the Kiwanis club. I also journeyed to the Soviet Union with a group under the auspices of the Directors Guild.

In 1987 I began to write, sporadically, this autobiography. In 1990 I was invited to attend the Jacksonville Film Festival in Florida by Todd Roobin, a relative of mine and a member of the staff; *Mr. Skeffington* was run, and I spoke to a crowded theater. In recent years the Los Angeles County Museum of Art has shown several of my films and asked me to speak. Occasionally I have been interviewed about film making during the forties and fifties, the so-called Golden Age of Hollywood. In 1994 I was invited by a film group called Cinephile to attend a showing of *The Hard Way*. Joan Leslie also appeared and the crowd was enthusiastic. We answered questions and signed autographs for over an hour.

Soon after, I was invited to lunch at the Four Seasons Hotel by Dena Drubinsky representing Ted Turner Classic Films. They were planning a Vincent Sherman Director of the Month short retrospective of my career for January 1995 and wanted to interview me on film. I was flattered. Dena arranged the interview and later sent me a copy. It was well done.

In February 1995 my part-time secretary and dear companion,

Donna Cameron, died of cancer. My loss of Donna, preceded by the deaths of Daniel Fuchs and Oscar Saul, two writers who were close friends, left me deeply depressed. The next few months were quiet; no one called for interviews and there were no showings of my films. I began to feel that the film world had forgotten me.

Postscript

Telluride is a small town beautifully located in the mountains of Colorado, and the film festival held there annually is organized by Bill and Stella Spence and Tom Luddy. In early July 1995, I received an invitation to attend the festival, where they planned to show *The Hard Way,* which I had directed in 1942. A chartered plane picked us up along with other guests at the Los Angeles airport on Thursday, August 27, and we landed at Montrose, where buses carried us up to the town.

I was curious to know why I had been invited. My son, who knows or is able to find out how many things occur nowadays in Hollywood, enlightened me. Eric learned that Philip Lopate, an essayist and film scholar from New York, who was the festival's guest curator that season, had been asked to suggest a "neglected" film. He chose *The Hard Way.* When someone suggested that they invite a director of the same period, Lopate recalled that I was still alive. That's how my trip came about. I took Eric and his son, Cosimo, along with me.

An attractive young woman, Chris Stanfield, was assigned to guide and assist us. After we were deposited in a comfortable condominium we learned that *The Hard Way* was scheduled to be shown Saturday morning at 9 A.M. I was not happy. Who would want to see an old film so early in the morning? I was sure no one would be in the theater. But I was wrong. It was filled. I was certain that, with the exception of Lopate, who introduced me and promised that I would answer questions after the showing, not six people in the audience had ever heard my name or knew anything about the film. It wasn't even on video. (Very few of my films are, which I still don't understand.) I didn't sense any anticipation or excitement in the air. They were simply polite movie buffs and merely curious to see a fifty-three-year-old movie.

The picture began, and the print was excellent, supplied, I think, by Ted Turner Classic Films. Slowly but surely I could feel surprise and interest from the crowd as they abandoned their slouched positions and straightened up in their seats. Laughs came in the right places, and couples glanced at each other and nodded approvingly as they discovered they were watching a film with pace and energy and dramatic problems that were modern, couched in terms that produced both conflict and drama. I relaxed and enjoyed the film as much as they did.

I was asked to go backstage five minutes before the film ended so that I could step out on stage at the finish. From there I heard a thunderous burst of applause at the end of the film. I came out, and the audience rose to its feet in a standing ovation. I was deeply touched, nearly moved to tears. I threw them kisses from my heart and explained why their reception meant so much to me: Irwin Shaw, who had written the screenplay had asked that his name be removed from the film because he did not like what I was doing with his script. Ida Lupino yelled at me at the end of the first week of shooting, "This picture is going to stink, and I'm going to stink in it!" Jack Warner had viewed the rough cut and said, "Boys, I think we've got a flop on our hands." If only they could have been present at this showing!

Enthusiasm, as we know, creates enthusiasm. By nightfall Todd McCarthy, film critic for *Daily Variety,* the Hollywood trade paper, told Eric that the buzz around Telluride was that *The Hard Way* was an undiscovered great film. That worried me for the audience who was to attend a second screening the following morning in a different theater. I was concerned lest they arrive determined to challenge the high praise. After all, how could a fifty-three-year-old film be that good? I spoke before the screening and begged them not to let their skepticism affect their enjoyment of the film. I said it was a good picture but not great.

I left the theater, had breakfast, and returned. When the picture was over, the applause was again most generous, and I discovered that Bertrand Tavernier, a well-known and excellent French director who had seen the film for the first time the day before, had volunteered to interrogate me. I was flattered and honored. His questions were acute and penetrating—only an experienced professional could have formulated such comments and inquiries. They concerned the photography, writing, editing, and the various performances. He liked them all but was particularly impressed by Dennis Morgan, whom he had seen in various films and thought was "dull and wooden." But in this part, "he came to life" and revealed a sense of humor and a depth of emotion that was never visible before. I accepted some of the credit but not all. Dennis deserved the major portion. It was the first role he had been given that allowed him to show his talent.

The audience understood why the New York film critics voted Ida Lupino the best actress, but they were equally impressed by the fact that Joan Leslie was only seventeen years old when she did the film. They also praised Jack Carson, a much underrated performer, and Gladys George, a standout in a small role. As I watched the film I felt a surge of pride for all of the performances, including the smaller roles. Reviewing the festival in *Variety,* McCarthy wrote, "The Hollywood discovery of the fest was Vincent Sherman's superb 1942 Warner Bros. meller *The Hard Way.*"

That day and the day before, I was stopped on the streets by dozens of people who wanted to know what other films I had directed and what it was like directing Bette Davis and Joan Crawford, Clark Gable, Errol Flynn, and Humphrey Bogart. I answered them as well as I could.

Early in the afternoon I was resting when Eric rushed in to tell me that Oliver Stone, director of *Platoon, Wall Street, JFK,* and *Born on the Fourth of July,* a great film about the Vietnam war, wanted to meet me. We were invited that evening to a barbecue at Stone's extraordinarily beautiful ranch outside Telluride. He had someone pick us up and drive us to his place. Oliver was a revelation to me. My impression of him, based on media reports, was that he was arrogant, aggressive, hostile, haughty, egotistical, contemptuous of old films, and altogether unpleasant. What I discovered was a warm-hearted, kind, generous, modest, intelligent, and obviously talented man. Several months before, when I read that Stone was going to do a film about George Washington, I wrote him a letter. For years I had been interested in Washington, had collected much material about him, and even tried to get Warner Bros. to let me make a film about him, one that would reveal that "as a God he was a disappointment but as a man a great fulfillment." The studio turned me down. I offered Stone my services and the use of my library without obligation simply because I thought it was time the American public learned about Washington the man. Janet Yang, the president of Stone's company, sent me a gracious reply; she said she was sending my letter to the writer of the screenplay and I would hear from him. But I never did. I had a chance to ask Oliver about the project, and he informed me that he had agreed to produce the film but that Robert Redford was in charge of developing the script. He would ask Redford to call me. I never heard from Redford, either, but I have since heard from Oliver that the project is on hold.

Oliver and I had a pleasant conversation about our films, and I was pleased to hear that he especially liked *Mr. Skeffington.* I imposed upon his friendliness and asked if he'd read a screenplay I had done years before and recently rewrote. He did, and within a few days he gave me his opinion, which was honest, acute, and enlightening. Later, he kindly agreed to read this autobiography and permitted me to quote his appraisal. Despite the furor Oliver's name on a film arouses, I consider him a tremendous talent and respect his desire to examine our mores, expand the technique of film making, and tackle difficult subjects.

The day following the barbecue I had lunch with Tavernier, who is not only an excellent film maker but also director of the Institut Lumière in Lyon, France. We were joined by his friend, Thierry Frémaux, manager of the Institut, and Pierre Rissient, who is associated with CIBY 2000. They brought with them a film history of the Institut and spoke at length about the Lumière brothers and their great contribution to films. The Institut hopes to acquire a sufficient number of prints of my films to invite me for a retrospective.

Since the festival and McCarthy's article, I have had requests for interviews and have been asked to speak to various film groups about the "old days" in the Hollywood studios. We all respond to praise, and the recent interest in my work has been like a shot in the arm for me. I'm happy to know that I have not been forgotten.

As I approach my ninetieth birthday I cannot resist looking back; although my films were not landmarks, they did win some recognition, and from the fan mail I have received over the years from all over the world I have reason to believe that they provided a few hours of entertainment. I hope they have also served to promote a greater understanding among people. I am frequently asked which film I think is my best and which I like the most. Out of the thirty productions, one of my favorites is *Saturday's Children.* The writers, the Epstein brothers, had recommended me and I was able to reveal a sweet and gentle John Garfield as opposed to the brash young men he had been portraying. The work also stands out for me because Claude Rains, who was a star in the New York theater when I was a bit player, approved of my directing. *Underground* is another favorite because it was one of the first serious anti-Nazi films that was successful, and it was made for a pittance. I also like *All Through the Night* because it treated the Nazi bundists in America with humor and contempt, led by Humphrey Bogart. It was, also commercially successful.

I am especially proud of *The Hard Way* because it allowed me to say much about the drive for success in our society, especially in the theater, and the ruthless behavior it often creates. I fondly remember *Old Acquaintance;* although it was considered lightweight women's magazine material, I was able through Bette Davis and Miriam Hopkins to give their relationships a sense of truth. *Mr. Skeffington* holds a special place in my heart because it was the best script I ever had. Even though Bette and Claude Rains were nominated by the Academy, I was only partially successful in achieving what I had hoped for; yet it said much that was worthwhile about beauty and love and race relations. About that time Jack Warner talked me into developing a minor story I had bought, *The Man Who Died Twice,* into a starring vehicle for Ann Sheridan. It was retitled *Nora Prentiss* and became a mild success as a film noir. This led to a second film with Sheridan, *The Unfaithful,* which followed the plot of Somerset Maugham's *The Letter* but delivered a different message: It pointed out that a marriage made in haste because of the war and an indiscretion under difficult circumstances should not be enough to break up a relationship that had developed (after the war) into love.

I must include in my list of favorites *The Adventures of Don Juan* starring Errol Flynn with Viveca Lindfors and Robert Douglas, mainly because it was my first color and action project and Errol had asked for me to direct him. The tongue-in-cheek approach, pageantry, and dueling scenes were, I felt, unusual and most enjoyable. *The Hasty Heart* is also a favorite because it deals with alienation and antisocial feelings and how, when they are overcome, the human spirit flourishes. I was especially proud of Richard Todd's performance (his first major role and an Academy nomination), as well as the work of Patricia Neal and Ronald Reagan. In London I received the National Film Award for 1950.

The Damned Don't Cry with Joan Crawford captured the drive of an ambitious woman to improve her life while she is still young enough to attract men, ignoring the cost and finally coming to grief. It also explored the gangster elements in our society and was the first film to touch on the Virginia Hill–Bugsy Siegel romance and tragedy. *Harriet Craig,* my second film with Joan, centered around a woman so obsessed with her home and material things and so determined to dominate her husband that she destroys her marriage. *Goodbye My Fancy,* also with Joan, was a story that I had high hopes for, but it failed because of improper casting. Still, I find the film worth viewing. I also consider worthwhile *The Young Philadelphians* with Paul Newman, Barbara Rush, Alexis Smith, and Robert Vaughn. It explores class conflicts and the importance of remaining true to oneself, and it received many excellent reviews along with audience approval. All of my other films were competently done, and I was never ashamed of any of the performances, but they were not stories that probed deeply into character or whose subject matter was important.

Regarding today's films, we have seen an enormous advance technically, with special effects and digital work accompanied by rapid-fire editing and imagery. But I am concerned, as many seem to be, with the excess of sex and violence and an overabundance of effects for their own sake. Of course, sex usually sells, and its excess is, I think, a rebellion, begun long ago, against years of Puritanism and repression. Violence, I believe, is caused by frustration, the breakdown of family life, and the ever-widening gulf between the haves and the have nots. Like sex, when used properly, violence does make for dramatic excitement and graphic action. Both, however, when overdone, leave audiences bored and the box office disappointing.

I have always preferred films that examine the human condition and depend on personal conflicts resolved by insight, truth, and understanding rather than gunplay. I am especially concerned about the lack of hope expressed in most films of today and how such an attitude affects the young. To live without hope can be devastatingly destructive. Unfortunately, most directors have to pay more attention to the marketplace and what will make a profit than with what will benefit mankind. I am not innocent of the charge; the lurking fear of poverty that left its mark on me during my early years in New York and the realization that a series of unsuccessful films can mean the end of a career often impelled me to accept assignments that I thought would be successful at the box office rather than wait and hope for one of great human values.

To become successful in films, whatever branch you choose, unless your family is wealthy, you must have not only talent, but you must be as sensitive as a filly in heat. You must also have the hide of a rhinoceros, for you will, at times, encounter insults and humiliation. It is a rough business, competition is furious, and some cannot take it; if you have talent and determination and can control your own ego you may make it.

As most of us who realize that the curtain must surely soon come down, I have accumulated many happy thoughts and some regrets. I regret that I did not do more in World War II to help in the fight against Hitler and his ally the Japanese; when America was drawn into the conflict, I registered for the draft, but because I was thirty-five years old, married, and raising a child, I was deferred. Several friends at Warner's enlisted, and when I offered to join them I was told that I would probably merely be transferred from a desk at Warner's to a desk at the Signal corps and assigned to make training films; I might as well remain at the studio and make films to help the war effort. I did so and used my salary to buy war bonds. At the time the only news that reached us about the anti-Semitism of the Nazis was that they were discriminating against the Jews. Later, we refused to believe the rumors of concentration camps and death squads. In fact, it was not until the war ended and liberation took place that the real truth became known. Some people even now refuse to believe what has been verified and written about. Ironically, Germany had been regarded as one of the most advanced and intelligent nations of the world. Its Jews were staunch patriots and some of its most prominent citizens: writers, artists, educators, scientists, musicians, statesmen, and businessmen. How such a nation could be led down the dark road of barbarism and brutality and set civilization so far back still haunts us. I wish I had done more to end the horror.

One of my deepest regrets is that my father never lived to enjoy what little success I had. I would have given anything if I could have sent a limousine for him and brought him to the studio where he could have seen at the stage entrance a sign reading "Sherman Co." and sat in a director's chair with my name on it. I also regret that I was not able to prevent my brother from becoming an alcoholic or to save my two sisters from cancer or my mother, who spent her last days with an ailing heart.

I am happy, however, that my father and mother had the courage to leave Russia and come to America. I am also grateful that I grew up in a small town in the South rather than in a confined ethnic section of a large city. It enabled me to feel comfortable with all kinds of people wherever I go.

I regret that I did not fight harder to get *The Treasure of Sierra Madre* and *Casablanca* and that I accepted many second-rate assignments, but I am also happy that since the beginning of my career in Hollywood, I have been able to earn a living, give my children a good education, help friends and relatives, and contribute to various charities. I have never coveted great wealth and power but wanted only enough to feel free and not beholden to any man.

Before the Telluride Festival I received a phone call from Mary Ann Anderson, who was Ida Lupino's conservator. She had kept me informed about Ida's health and activities during the past and now regretted to tell me that Ida had recently been diagnosed with colon cancer. Ida had asked to see me. I met Mary for lunch and we proceeded to Ida's apartment. She looked better than I had seen her in a long time. We spent a delightful afternoon together, laughing and joking about the past. Mary told me later that Ida said it was one of the best afternoons she had ever had. I was happy to hear it. A few weeks later, Ida was dead, and I attended a memorial service at the home of Mala Powers, an actress Ida had discovered. It was a fitting tribute to one of the great talents of our time.

I have seen much and gone through many changes of attitude toward life: from an idealistic and innocent boy to a disillusioned, cynical young man, to a more mature realization that the world is composed of good and evil; that in modern bourgeois society men generally act in their own interests, as do nations. They are driven by various factors: materialism, a quest for power, religious zeal, honor, sex, or ego satisfaction. Sometimes, however, human need and a drive for self-preservation propels them to work together to improve the human predicament. I hope we are on the verge of such a move.

I am reminded of a meeting of the Directors Guild years ago when D.W. Griffith was asked to speak. Seated down front, he rose and turned to us. He said very simply, "If you men would only realize, films speak a universal language, and you have in your hands the power to change the world." He was right. I can only hope that all of us who are in the field of entertainment and communication will use our talents to oppose hatred, violence, racism, greed, and corruption, to become more conscious of our environment, to support education, and to help those who are less fortunate than we are.

I am grateful to Providence for all its blessings, which have enabled me to enjoy an unexpected life, and I look forward to each day.

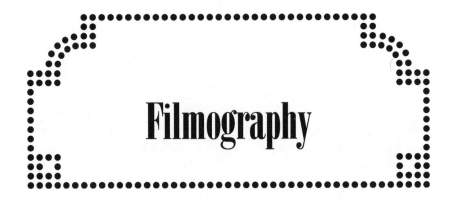

Filmography

Theatrical and Acting Work

Early 1930s: numerous Theater Guild productions, New York

1933: appeared in the film version of *Counsellor at Law* (Universal, directed by William Wyler)

1933: appeared in *Air Devils* and *Murder at Rexford Arms* (Columbia)

1934: appeared in *Highway Patrol* and *By Persons Unknown* (Columbia) and *Case of the Howling Dog* and *Midnight Alibi* (Warner)

1935-38: appeared in and/or directed the plays *Judgement Day, Volpone, Sailors of Catarro, Black Pit, Waiting for Lefty, Battle Hymn, Bitter Stream, It Can't Happen Here, Dead End,* and others

Script Writing

Crime School (Warner's, 86 minutes, released May 28, 1938)
> Cast: Humphrey Bogart, the Dead End Kids, Milburn Stone
> Director: Lewis Seiler
> Screenplay: Crane Wilbur, Vincent Sherman
> Dialogue Director: Vincent Sherman

My Bill (Warner's, 65 minutes, released July 9, 1938)
> Cast: Kay Francis, Dickie Moore, Bonita Granville, John Litel, Anita Louise
> Director: John Farrow
> Screenplay: Vincent Sherman, Robertson White
> Camera: Sid Hickox
> Editor: Frank Magee

Heart of the North (Warner's, 85 minutes, released December 10, 1938)
> Cast: Dickie Foran, Gloria Dickson, Patric Knowles
> Director: Lewis Seiler
> Screenplay: Lee Katz, Vincent Sherman
> Camera (Technicolor): Wilfred Cline

Camera: L.W. O'Connell
Editor: Louis Hesse

King of the Underworld (Warner's, 69 minutes, released January 14, 1939)
Cast: Humphrey Bogart, Kay Francis, James Stephenson
Director: Lewis Seiler
Screenplay: George Bricker, Vincent Sherman

Pride of the Bluegrass (Warner's, 65 minutes, released October 7, 1939)
Cast: Edith Fellows, James McCallion, Gantry the Great
Director: William McGann
Screenplay: Vincent Sherman
Camera: Ted McCord

Films Directed

The Return of Dr. X (Warner's, 62 minutes, released December 2, 1939)
Cast: Humphrey Bogart, Rosemary Lane, Dennis Morgan, Wayne
Morris, John Litel, Lya Lyss
Director: Vincent Sherman
Screenplay: Lee Katz
Camera: Sid Hickox
Editor: Thomas Pratt

Saturday's Children (Warner's, 101 minutes, released May 11, 1940)
Cast: John Garfield, Anne Shirley, Claude Rains, Lee Patrick, George
Tobias
Producers: Jack Warner, Hal Wallis
Associate Producer: Henry Blanke
Director: Vincent Sherman
Screenplay: Philip Epstein and Julius Epstein
Camera: James Wong Howe
Editor: Owen Marks

The Man Who Talked Too Much (Warner's, 75 minutes, released July 16,
1940)
Cast: George Brent, Virginia Bruce, Richard Barthelmess, William
Lundigan, George Tobias, John Litel, Marc Lawrence
Associate Producer: Edmund Grainger
Director: Vincent Sherman
Screenplay: Walter De Leon, Tom Reed
Camera: Sid Hickox
Editor: Thomas Pratt

Flight from Destiny (Warner's, 73 minutes, released February 8, 1941)
Cast: Geraldine Fitzgerald, Thomas Mitchell, Jeffrey Lynn, James
Stephenson, Mona Maris, Willie Best
Producer: Jack Warner

Associate Producer: Edmund Grainger
Director: Vincent Sherman
Screenplay: Barry Trivers
Camera: James Van Trees
Editor: Thomas Richards

Underground (Warner's, 95 minutes, released June 28, 1941)
Cast: Philip Dorn, Jeffrey Lynn, Kaaren Verne, Mona Maris, Martin
Kosleck
Producers: Bryan Foy, William Jacobs
Director: Vincent Sherman
Screenplay: Charles Grayson
Camera: Sid Hickox
Editor: Thomas Pratt

All through the Night (Warner's, 107 minutes, released January 10, 1942)
Cast: Humphrey Bogart, Conrad Veidt, Kaaren Verne, Jane Darwell,
Frank McHugh, Peter Lorre, Judith Anderson, William Demarest,
Phil Silvers, Jackie Gleason
Director: Vincent Sherman
Producer: Jerry Wald
Screenplay: Leonard Spigelgass, Edwin Gilbert
Camera: Sid Hickox
Editor: Rudi Fehr

The Hard Way (Warner's, 109 minutes, released September 21, 1942)
Cast: Ida Lupino, Dennis Morgan, Joan Leslie, Jack Carson, Gladys
George, Faye Emerson
Producer: Jerry Wald
Director: Vincent Sherman
Screenplay: Daniel Fuchs, Peter Viertel
Camera: James Wong Howe
Editor: Thomas Pratt

Old Acquaintance (Warner's, 110 minutes, released November 27, 1943)
Cast: Bette Davis, Miriam Hopkins, Gig Young, John Loder, Dolores
Moran, Anne Revere
Producer: Henry Blanke
Director: Vincent Sherman
Screenplay: John Van Druten, Leonore Coffee
Music: Franz Waxman
Camera: Sol Polito
Editor: Terry Morse

In Our Time (Warner's, 110 minutes, released February 19, 1944)
Cast: Ida Lupino, Paul Henreid, Nancy Coleman, Mary Boland, Victor
Francen, Alla Nazimova, Michael Chekhov

Producer: Jerry Wald
Director: Vincent Sherman
Screenplay: Ellis St. Joseph, Howard Koch
Music: Franz Waxman
Camera: Carl Guthrie
Editor: Rudi Fehr

Mr. Skeffington (Warner's, 146 minutes, released August 12, 1944)
Cast: Bette Davis, Claude Rains, Walter Abel, Richard Waring, George
Coulouris, Marjorie Riordan, Gigi Perreau
Producers: Philip Epstein and Julius Epstein
Director: Vincent Sherman
Screenplay: Philip Epstein and Julius Epstein
Music: Franz Waxman
Camera: Ernest Haller
Editor: Ralph Dawson

Pillow to Post (Warner's, 92 minutes, released June 9, 1945)
Cast: Ida Lupino, Sydney Greenstreet, William Prince, Stuart Erwin,
Willie Best, Louis Armstrong and his orchestra
Producer: Alex Gottlieb
Director: Vincent Sherman
Screenplay: Charles Hoffman
Camera: Wesley Anderson
Editor: Alan Crosland Jr.

Janie Gets Married (Warner's, 89 minutes, released June 22, 1946)
Cast: Joan Leslie, Robert Hutton, Edward Arnold, Ann Harding, Robert
Benchley, Dorothy Malone, Donald Meek, Mel Torme
Producer: Alex Gottlieb
Director: Vincent Sherman
Screenplay: Agnes Christine Johnston
Camera: Carl Guthrie
Editor: Christian Nyby

Nora Prentiss (Warner's, 111 minutes, released February 22, 1947)
Cast: Ann Sheridan, Kent Smith, Robert Alda, Bruce Bennett,
Rosemary De Camp, Wanda Henrix
Producer: William Jacobs
Director: Vincent Sherman
Screenplay: N. Richard Nash
Camera: James Wong Howe
Editor: Owen Marks

The Unfaithful (Warner's, 109 minutes, released June 5, 1947)
Cast: Ann Sheridan, Lew Ayres, Zachary Scott, Eve Arden
Producer: Jerry Wald

Director: Vincent Sherman
Screenplay: David Goodis, James Gunn
Music: Max Steiner
Camera: Ernest Haller
Editor: Alan Crosland Jr.

The (New) Adventures of Don Juan (Warner's, 110 minutes, released
December 24, 1948)
Cast: Errol Flynn, Viveca Lindfors, Robert Douglas, Alan Hale, Romney
   Brent, Ann Rutherford, Raymond Burr
Producer: Jerry Wald
Director: Vincent Sherman
Screenplay: George Oppenheimer, Harry Kurnitz
Art Director: Edward Carrere
Camera: Elwood Bredell
Editor: Alan Crosland Jr.

The Hasty Heart (Warner's, 99 minutes, released December 2, 1949)
Cast: Ronald Reagan, Patricia Neal, Richard Todd, Orlando Martens
Director: Vincent Sherman
Screenplay: Ranald MacDougall
Art Director: Terence Verity
Camera: Wilkie Cooper

Backfire (Warner's, 91 minutes, released February 11, 1950)
Cast: Virginia Mayo, Gordon MacRae, Edmund O'Brien, Dane Clark,
   Viveca Lindfors, Ed Begley, Monte Blue
Producer: Anthony Veiller
Director: Vincent Sherman
Screenplay: Larry Marcus
Camera: Carl Guthrie
Editor: Thomas Reilly

The Damned Don't Cry (Warner's, 103 minutes, released May 13, 1950)
Cast: Joan Crawford, David Brian, Steve Cochran, Kent Smith
Producer: Jerry Wald
Director: Vincent Sherman
Screenplay: Jerome Weidman, Harold Medford
Camera: Ted McCord
Editor: Rudi Fehr

Harriet Craig (Columbia, 94 minutes, released November 1950)
Cast: Joan Crawford, Wendell Corey, Lucille Watson, Allyn Joslyn
Producer: William Dozier
Director: Vincent Sherman
Screenplay: Ann Froelich, James Gunn
Camera: Joseph Walker
Editor: Viola Lawrence

Goodbye My Fancy (Warner's, 107 minutes, released May 19, 1951)
    Cast: Joan Crawford, Robert Young, Frank Lovejoy, Eve Arden, Janice
        Rule, Lurene Tuttle, John Qualen
    Producer: Henry Blanke
    Director: Vincent Sherman
    Screenplay: Ivan Goff, Ben Roberts
    Camera: Ted McCord
    Editor: Rudi Fehr

Lone Star (MGM, 94 minutes, released February 8, 1952)
    Cast: Clark Gable, Ava Gardner, Broderick Crawford, Lionel
        Barrymore, Beulah Bondi, Ed Begley
    Producer: Z. Wayne Griffin
    Director: Vincent Sherman
    Screenplay: Borden Chase
    Camera: Harold Rosson
    Editor: Ferris Webster

Affair in Trinidad (Columbia [Beckworth], 98 minutes, released September
1952)
    Cast: Rita Hayworth, Glenn Ford, Alexander Scourby, Valerie Bettis
    Producer: Vincent Sherman
    Director: Vincent Sherman
    Screenplay: Oscar Saul, James Gunn
    Camera: Joseph Walker
    Editor: Viola Lawrence

Defend My Love (Titanus, 88 minutes, made in 1955 in Italy, released in
United States October 1959)
    Cast: Martine Carol, Gabrielle Ferzetti, Vittorio Gassman
    Producer: Silvio Clementelli
    Director: Vincent Sherman, Giulio Macchi
    Screenplay: Giorgio Prosperi, Jacques Robert

Garment Jungle (Columbia, 88 minutes, released June 1957)
    Cast: Lee J. Cobb, Kerwin Matthews, Gia Scala, Richard Boone, Harold
        J. Stone, Adam Williams
    Producer: Harry Kleiner
    Director: Vincent Sherman, Robert Aldrich (uncredited)
    Screenplay: Harry Kleiner
    Camera: Joe Biroc
    Editor: William Lyon

The Naked Earth (Twentieth Century–Fox, 96 minutes, released June 1958)
    Cast: Juliette Greco, Richard Todd, Finlay Currie, Orlando Martens
    Producer: Adrian Worker
    Director: Vincent Sherman
    Screenplay: Milton Holmes

Art Director: Terence Verity
Camera: Erwin Hillier
Editor: E. Jarvis

The Young Philadelphians (Warner's, 136 minutes, released May 30, 1959)
Cast: Paul Newman, Barbara Rush, Alexis Smith, Brian Keith, Billie
Burke, Robert Vaughn, Otto Kruger, Robert Douglas
Director: Vincent Sherman
Screenplay: James Gunn
Camera: Harry Stradling
Editor: William Ziegler

Ice Palace (Warner's, 113 minutes, released July 2, 1960)
Cast: Richard Burton, Robert Ryan, Carolyn Jones, Martha Hyer, Jim
Backus, Ray Danton, Diane McBain, Karl Swenson, Shirley Knight,
George Takei
Producer: Henry Blanke
Director: Vincent Sherman
Music: Max Steiner
Camera: Joe Biroc
Editor: William Ziegler

A Fever in the Blood (Warner's, 117 minutes, released January 28, 1961)
Cast: Efrem Zimbalist Jr., Angie Dickinson, Jack Kelly, Don Ameche,
Ray Danton, Herbert Marshall, Carroll O'Connor
Producer: Roy Huggins
Director: Vincent Sherman
Screenplay: Roy Huggins, Harry Kleiner
Camera: J. Peverell Marley
Editor: William Ziegler

The Second Time Around (Twentieth Century–Fox, 99 minutes, released
December 1961)
Cast: Debbie Reynolds, Steve Forrest, Andy Griffith, Juliet Prowse,
Thelma Ritter
Producer: Jack Cummings
Director: Vincent Sherman
Screenplay: Oscar Saul, Cecil Dan Hansen
Camera: Ellis Carter
Editor: Betty Steinberg

Cervantes (The Young Rebel) (Landau/Unger, An Alexandre Salkind
Production, made in 1966-68, no official United States theatrical release,
distributed to television in the United States by American International
Pictures in 1972)
Cast: Horst Buchholz, Gina Lollobrigida, Jose Ferrer, Louis Jourdan,
Francisco Rabal, Fernando Rey

Executive Producer: Henry Weinstein
Producer: Alexandre Salkind
Director: Vincent Sherman
Screenplay: David Karp
Camera: Edmond Richard
Editor: Margarita Ochoa

Scenes Directed

Sea Hawk, 1940
Sergeant York, 1941 (one day)
Juke Girl, 1942 (four days)
Across the Pacific, 1942 (ten days)
Air Force, 1943
The Hanging Tree, 1959 (three days)

Television Movies Directed

The Last Hurrah, with Carroll O'Connor and Mariette Hartley
The Dream Merchants, with Mark Harmon and Morgan Fairchild
Women at West Point, with Linda Purl, Jameson Parker, and Andrew Stevens
Lady of the House, with Dyan Cannon and Armand Assante
Bogie: The Last Hero, produced by Charles Fries

Episodes of Television Series Directed

77 Sunset Strip
The Long Hot Summer
The Bold Ones
Medical Center
Alias Smith and Jones
The Waltons
Other pilots and episodes

Awards

1943 *The Hard Way,* New York Film Critics' Award for Ida Lupino
1944 *Mr. Skeffington,* Academy Award nominations for Bette Davis and
      Claude Rains
1949 *The (New) Adventures of Don Juan,* Academy Award nominations for
      Costume Design, Art, and Set Decoration
1949 *The Hasty Heart,* Academy Award nomination for Richard Todd;

London Daily Mail Film of the Year and National Film Award for Vincent Sherman

1950 *The Damned Don't Cry,* Photoplay Award for Joan Crawford

1959 *The Young Philadelphians,* Academy Award nomination for Robert Vaughn

Index

A Bell for Adano, 152
A Fever in the Blood, 273-74
A Man Called Peter, 192, 258
Abbott, George, 10
Abel, Walter, 136, 141, 147
Abeles, Arthur, 179, 250
Academy Award, 125, 133, 150, 192
Across the Pacific, 189-90
Act One, 24
Action in the North Atlantic, 117
Actor's Equity, 50
Actor's Lab, 152
Adams, Franklin P., 3
Adler, Buddy, 240
Adler, Luther, 48
Adonis, Joe, 147
Adventures of Don Juan, The (New),
     163-73, 279, 301
Affair in Trinidad, 236, 239
Affectionately Yours, 88, 90, 128
Agee, James, 136
Alarcon, Enrique, 280
Aldrich, Robert, 215, 252-54
Alger, Horatio, 6
Algonquin Hotel, 61
All in the Family, 291
All through the Night, 97-98, 101-3,
     105-6, 108, 223, 301
Allen, Woody, 292
Allied Artists, 251
Allyson, June, 205
Alvarado, Don, 158
Ameche, Don, 274
America Firsters, 94, 105
American International Pictures
     (AIP), 282, 287

American Mercury Magazine, 7
Amin, Idi, 258
Anderson, Judith, 99, 101, 103
Anderson, Mary Ann, 304
Anderson, Maxwell, 24, 85
Andrews, Dana 251
Angels with Dirty Faces, 81
Applebaum, Arthur, 42
Arden, Eve, 160, 212, 291
Arkoff, Sam, 282, 287
Arnold, Edward, 152
Arnold, Elliott, 252
Arno, Max, 65
Arrowsmith, 55
Arrowsmith, Martin, 60
As Time Goes By, 109
Assante, Armand, 290
Associated British Pictures Corp.
     (ABPC), 177-78, 256, 261
Astor, Mary, 189
Atkinson, Brooks, 54, 56
Atlanta Georgian, The, 5
Atlanta Journal, The, 5
Austin, Jerry, 167
Autumn Leaves, 215
Awake and Sing, 48
Ayres, Lew, 160

Babbitt, 54-55
Babbitt, George, 54, 60
Bacall, Lauren, 292
Backfire, 176-77
Backus, Jim, 272
Bacon, Lloyd, 90
Baer, Parley, 274
Baker, Diane, 289

Baker's Wife, The, 78
Ballard, Kaye, 291
Baltic Deputy, 78
Bandler, Lou, 24
bar mitzvah, 7
Barber, Phil, 52-54, 56
Bardette, Trevor, 223
Baretta, 152, 289
Barker, Betty, 216
Barry, Philip, Jr. 292
Barrymore, John, 35, 38-42, 164
Barrymore, Lionel, 219, 222
Barthelmess, Richard, 44, 87
Barton, James, 243
Bass, Alfie, 182
Battle Hymn, 51-52
Baum, Martin, 251, 274, 290, 292
Bautzer, Greg, 202
Beckworth Corp., 237
Beecher, Janet, 75
Begley, Ed, 223
Behrman, Sam, 61
Belasco, David, 20
Belasco Theater, 50
Bellamy, Ralph, 43
Benchley, Robert, 10, 152
Bennett, Constance, 69
Bennett, Joan, 69
Bennett, Richard, 69
Benny, Jack, 24, 95
Benson, Hugh, 291
Bergman, Ingrid, 80, 205, 231
Bernhardt, Curtis, 150
Bernhardt, Sarah, 117, 258
Bernie, Ben, 31
Best, Willie, 152
Best of Everything, The, 215
Bettis, Valerie, 232-34, 240
Bette and Joan: The Divine Feud,
    218
Bey, Hassan, 283
Bicycle Thief, 188-89
Bill of Divorcement, 41
Biltmore Hotel, 63
Biltmore Theater, 63
Biroc, Joe, 273
Bitter Stream, 48
Black Pit, 48
blacklist, 243-67
Blackwell, Earl, 215
Blake, Robert, 152
Blanke, Henry, 85-86, 89, 119-20,

122, 129, 212, 271
Blankfort, Michael, 51
Blinn, Holbrook, 10
Blon, Katherine T. Von, 42
Blondell, Joan, 67
Blue, Ben, 161-62
Bogart, Humphrey, 67, 71, 73, 75, 77,
    79, 97-98, 102-5, 107, 189, 291
Bohnen, Roman (Bud), 112
Boland, Mary, 134
Bond, Ward, 225, 246-47
Bondi, Beulah, 223
Boone, Richard, 253-54
Born on the Fourth of July, 300
Born Yesterday, 208
Borzage, Frank, 92
Boyd, Alex, 179, 187
Brecht, Bertolt, 101
Breitstein, 36
Brenner, Herb, 244
Brent, George, 67, 89
Brent, Romney, 167
Brewer, Roy, 225, 246-47
Brewster, Diane, 269
Bride Came C.O.D., The, 90
Brinkley, Don, 289
Briskin, Irving, 43, 237
Broadway, 10
Broccoli, Cubby, 240
Broder, Jane, 35-36, 45
Broidy, Steve, 251
Bromley, Sheila, 42, 63
Brophy, Ed, 99
Broun, Heywood, 9
Brown, Chamberlin, 11-12
Brown, Clarence, 222
Brown, John, 51, 251
Brown, Ned, 244
Browning Version, The, 184
Bruce, Virginia, 87
Buchholz, Horst, 265, 283-84
Buchman, Harold, 250, 263
Buck, Pearl, 32, 134
Bunker, Archie, 291
Burke, Billie, 269
Burke, James, 223
Burks, Robert, 157
Burns, George, 24
Burns, Lillian, 253
Burton, Richard, 258, 271
Bury the Dead, 107
Buttons, Red, 291

Cabinet of Dr. Caligari, The, 103
Caesar, Sid, 31
Cagney, James, 67, 71, 80-90, 112
Cain, James, 157
Caine Mutiny, The, 227
Camelot, 273
Cameron, Donna, 297
Camp Beekman, 23
Camp Copake, 23
Camp Tamiment, 24-25, 28
Cannon, Dyan, 290
Capek, Karel, 20
Capone, Al, 34
Capra, Frank, 209
Captain Blood, 81
Carlotta, 130
Carlson, Linda, 289
Carol, Martine, 250
Carr, Harry, 49
Carrere, Edward, 166
Carroll, Harrison, 211
Carroll, Madeleine, 210
Carson, Jack, 112, 115, 117, 164, 300
Casablanca, 80-81, 105, 109, 135, 304
Cassavetes, John, 292
Castle, William, 215
Cavens, Freddie, 167
Cervantes (The Young Rebel Cervantes),
    277-78, 280, 282
Chaliapin, 15
Chalk Dust, 51
Chaplin, Charlie, 291
Charge of the Light Brigade, The, 81
Charisse, Cyd, 289
Chase, Borden, 219, 224
Chekhov, Michael, 134-35
Chenkin, Victor, 19
Chimes at Midnight (Falstaff), 284
Cinephile, 112, 296
Ciro's, 171
City College of New York, 56
Clark, Dane, 177
Clark, Robert, 177, 179, 181, 187, 193,
    251-52, 264
Class Reunion, 20, 22-23
Cleopatra, 273, 276
Clurman, Harold, 20, 48
Cobb, Lee J., 44, 47-48, 63, 253-55
Coca, Imogene, 31
Cochran, Steve, 204
Cocoanut Grove, 195
Coffee, Leonore, 119

Cohn, Harry, 206-10, 227-32, 235-38,
    240-42, 267
Cohn, Joe, 226
Coleman, Nancy, 134-35
Collins, Joan, 258
Columbia Pictures, 206-11, 227-242,
    252-56, 267
communist party, 223, 250
Comoro, "Auntie" (Hedda's stepmother),
    27
Comoro, Claire (Hedda's sister), 27
Comoro, Hedda. *See* Hedda Sherman
Comoro, Leo (Hedda's stepbrother), 27
Confessions of a Nazi Spy, 92
Conley, Jim, 15
Connery, Sean, 262
Conrad, William, 223
Conroy, Frank, 269
Considine, Shaun, 218
Cooper, Gary, 112, 184, 205
Cooper, Wilkie, 185
Copland, Aaron, 15
Corby, Ellen, 289
Cornell, Katherine, 23
Corner Pocket, 75
Costello, Dolores, 39
Costello, Frank, 197
Costello, Maurice, 39
Coughlin, Father, 94
Counsellor at Law, 30, 35, 41-43, 46, 48,
    50, 65, 86
Courage, 75
Craig's Wife, 206-7
Crawford, Broderick, 219, 223, 227
Crawford, Cheryl, 14, 17, 24, 88
Crawford, Joan, 85, 192, 195-218, 302;
    Cathy (daughter), 197, 202; Christina
    (daughter), 197, 202, 213, 216-17;
    Christopher (son), 197, 202, 213, 216;
    Cindy (daughter), 197, 202
Crawford, Marion, 182
Crewe, Regina, 43
Crime and Punishment, 101
Crime School, 71-74, 96-97
Crisp, Donald, 67
Crosland, Alan, Sr., 44
Cross, Wilbur, 59
Cudahy, Michael, 195
Cukor, George, 180, 208
Culp, Robert, 291
Cummings, Jack, 274
Currie, Finlay, 261, 263

Curtis, Tony, 245
Curtiz, Michael, 81, 109, 127, 152, 164

Daly, James, 289
Damned Don't Cry, The, 207, 301-2
Dandridge, Dorothy, 249
Dantine, Helmut, 205
Danton, Ray, 272
Dark Victory, 119
Darwell, Jane, 98
Daves, Doctor, 6
Davidson, Reverend, 1
Davis, Bette, 88-90, 119-33, 135-50, 195,
    200-201, 203, 213, 215-16, 218, 271,
    276, 302; Ruthie (mother), 128
Davis, Donald, 32
Davis, Owen, 32
Deacon, Richard, 269
Dead End, 62-63, 66, 71-72
Dead End Kids (Gabriel Dell, Leo
    Gorcey, Huntz Hall, Billy Halop,
    Bobby Jordan, Bernard Punsley), 71
Dean, Vaughn, 179, 187
Death of a Salesman, 255
Dekker, Albert Van, 14
Delon, Alain, 280
del Rio, Dolores, 158
Deluxe Tour, 263
Demarest, William, 99-100, 102
Democratic Campaign to Elect
    Roosevelt, 31
De Mille, Cecil B., 4
De Sica, Vittorio, 188, 250
Deutsche, Armand, 258
Dickens, Charles, 179
Dickinson, Angie, 274
Dieterle, William, 240
Digges, Dudley, 16-17
Directors Guild of America, 256, 293,
    296, 305
Dirty Dozen, The, 256
Doctor Socrates, 76
Doctor's Hospital, 289
Dodge City, 81
Dodsworth (book, movie, play), 199
Dodsworth (character), 60
Don Quixote, 277, 283
Donati, William, 174
Donnelly, Ruth, 151
Dorn, Philip, 93
Dostoyevsky, 100
Douglas, Robert, 167, 170, 269, 289

Dozier, William (Bill), 192, 206-9
Draper, Ruth, 19
Dream Merchants, The, 291
Drink to Me Only, 274
Drubinsky, Dena, 296
Druten, John Van, 119
Duff, Howard, 291
Duff, Warren, 75
Durant, Will, 24
Duse, Eleanora, 15
Duvivier, Julian, 18
Dvorak, Ann, 76

Eastman, Max, 86
Eddington, Nora (Mrs. Errol Flynn),
    166, 171
Edison, Arthur, 190
Ehrlich, Leonard, 51
Eisler, Hans, 101
Eisley, Fred, 269
Elizabeth the Queen, 24-26
Ellenstein, Robert, 253
Elmer Gantry, 60
Elysia, 68
Emerson, Faye, 112
Emperor Jones, 18, 23-24
End of the Day, The, 135
Epstein, Julius (Julie), 85, 90, 109-10,
    135, 138, 143, 208, 301
Epstein, Philip. *See* Epstein, Julius
Erdman, Richard, 152
Erwin, Stuart, 151
Escape Me Never, 169
Essex, Lord, 25
Everett, Chad, 289
Everybody Comes to Rick's, 109-10
Excess Baggage, 125
Executive Suite, 289

Fahringer, Helen, 75
Fair Bride, The, 248
Fairbanks, Douglas, 196
Fairbanks, Douglas, Jr., 196
Fairchild, Morgan, 291
Fallon, Bill, 87
Fang, Mei Lan, 19
Farnesworth, Arthur (Farney), 127,
    131-32, 137-38, 144
Farnum, William, 223
Farrell, Glenda, 67
Farrow, John, 76
Federal Theater, 50, 52-53, 56

Fehr, Rudi, 101, 207
Fein, Irving, 24
Feldman, Charlie, 97, 235
Feldsers, The, 16
Female on the Beach, 215
Ferber, Edna, 270
Ferrer, Jose, 283, 291
Ferzetti, Gabrielle, 250
Feyder, Jacques, 78
Fier, Jack, 253
Finkle, Abem, 75, 85
Fishbein, Frieda, 10, 20, 22-23, 28
Fitzgerald, Geraldine, 91
Five Star Final, 249
Flanagan, Hallie, 50, 53-54
Fleming, Victor, 171, 205, 222
Flight from Destiny, 91, 93, 97
Florida Film Festival, 296
Flynn, Errol, 67, 80, 164-75, 279; Dierdre
   (daughter), 171
Fontanne, Lynn (Mrs. Alfred Lunt), 17,
   25-26, 29
For Us the Living, 60
Foran, Dick, 67
Ford, Glenn, 228, 231
Ford, John, 98, 250, 264, 291
Ford, Wally, 99
Forrest, Steve, 275
Fountainhead, The, 184
Four Daughters, 81, 86
Fowler, Gene, 41
Foxman, Aaron, 51
Foy, Bryan (Brynie), 63-80, 83, 87, 91-97
Francen, Victor, 134
Francis, Katy, 67, 75-77
Franco, General 78
Frank, Bruno, 277
Frank, Leo M., 15-16
Frasso, Countess di, 131
Frémaux, Thierry, 301
Friedman, Charles, 50
Fries, Charles, 292
Frings, Kurt, 248, 251
From Here to Eternity, 227
Front Page, The, 34
Fuchs, Daniel (Danny), 109-10, 114, 275,
   297
Fugitive, The, 273
Fulton County Tower, 5

Gabel, Martin, 62
Gable, Clark, 196, 219-20, 223-28

Gantry, Elmer, 55, 60
Gardenia, Vince, 291
Gardner, Ava, 219, 222, 236, 280-82
Garfield, John (Jules), 31, 85, 95, 152,
   301
Garment Jungle, 252, 256, 271
Garrett, Oliver, 92
Garson, Greer, 85
Gassman, Vittorio, 250
Gaudio, Tony, 119
Gay Sisters, The, 120
Geddes, Virgil, 50-51, 56
Geer, Will, 289
Gentle People, The, 91-92
George, Sen. Walter F., 16
George, Gladys, 112, 300
Georgi, Yvonne, 19
Geray, Steven, 236
Gerosi, Caesar, 248-49
Ghost of a Chance, 243-44
Gianninni, A.P., 97
Giant, 270
Gibbons, Cedric, 226
Gide, André, 15
Gielgud, John, 17, 103
Gilbert, John, 41
Gilda, 228-29, 232, 240-41
Gilpin, Charles, 23
Ginnis, Abe, 274
Girl Crazy, 110
Gleason, Jackie, 99-100
Glicksman, Frank, 277, 288-89
God's Angry Man, 51
God's in His Heaven, 47
Goff, Ivan, 176-77
Gogh, Vincent Van, 15
Gold, Michael, 51
Goldstein, Bob, 256, 265, 274
Goldwater, Barry, 193
Golub, Larry, 192
Good Earth, The, 32, 134
Goodbye My Fancy, 210, 212, 301-2
Goodnight Sweet Prince, 41
Gordon, Mike, 48
Gorse, Sol, 168
Gottlieb, Alex, 151
Goulding, Edmund, 119, 122
Gown of Glory, 274
Grady Hospital, 5
Grand Hotel, 41
Granet, Bert, 229
Grant, Cary (Archie Leach), 76, 155, 231

Granville, Bonita, 76
Grapes of Wrath, The, 98
Grasso, 15
Grayson, Charles, 92
Great Mouthpiece, The, 87
Greco, Juliette, 261, 263
Green, Jones &, 12-13
Greenstreet, Sydney, 20, 151, 189
Griffin, Z. Wayne, 220, 225
Griffith, Andy, 275
Griffith, D.W., 305
Group Theater, 47-48, 196
Guardino, Harry, 289
Gunn, James (Jimmy), 159-60, 209, 231, 268
Gump, Forrest, 6

Hagman, Larry, 289
Haines, Billy, 202
Hale, Alan, 67, 166-67, 172
Hall, Juanita, 236
Haller, Ernest, 141, 146
Hamlet, 39, 103
Haneghan, Steve, 154
Hansen, Harry, 9
Hard Way, The, 106-19, 134-35, 143, 296, 298
Harding, Ann, 152
Hardy, Thomas, 179
Harlequinade, 184
Harlow, Jean, 221
Harmon, Mark, 291
Harriet Craig, 192, 209-11, 231
Harris, Jed, 10, 42
Harris, Sam, 22
Harrison, Greg, 289
Harrow, Ben, 56-57
Hart, Bernie, 23
Hart, Moss, 22-24
Hartley, Mariette, 291
Hartman, Elizabeth, 289
Harvey, Paul, 112
Hasty Heart, The, 70, 176-93, 301
Havilland, Olivia De, 67, 85, 190, 205
Hawaiian Eye, 273
Hawk Island, 220
Hawks, Howard, 91, 106-7, 119-20
Hayes, Al, 242
Hayward, Leland, 91, 152
Hayworth, Rita (née Cansino), 228-39
Hearn, Lafcadio, 19
Hecht, Ben, 34

Hecht, Harold, 32
Hegger, Grace, 55, 199
Helburn, Terry, 29
Heller, George, 50
Hellinger, Mark, 70-71, 116-17
Hellman, Marcel, 251
Hemingway, Ernest, 261
Henderson, Peggy, 182
Henreid, Paul, 132, 134-35
Hepburn, Katharine, 59, 197
Hepburn, Dr. and Mrs., 59
Herbert, Hugh, 67
Herbert, F. Hugh, 247
Heston, Charlton, 246
Hickox, Sid, 79-80, 82, 100
High Sierra, 98
Hill, Virginia, 197
Hillier, Erwin, 261
Hitchcock, Alfred, 105, 109, 231
Hitler, Adolph, 78, 92, 94, 101
Hoffman, Charles, 151
Holder, Geoffrey, 235
Holliday, Judy, 230
Hollywood Reporter, The, 245
Holmes, Dr., 78
Holmes, Milton, 250
Holscher, Walter, 235
Hoover, Herbert, 21
House Unamerican Activities Committee (HUAC), 244-45
Hopkins, Arthur, 39
Hopkins, Harry, 53
Hopkins, Miriam, 13, 119-26
Hopper, Hedda, 129, 197
Horovitz, Dr. Morris, 36, 64; Dora (wife), 36; Leon (son), 37, 152
Horowitz, Vladimir, 19
Houston, Sam, 220
Howard, Leslie, 80
Howard, Sidney, 67, 86
Howe, James Wong (Jimmie), 111-13, 117-18
Howes, Reed, 4
Hud, 84
Huggins, Roy, 273-74, 276, 289
Hughes, Charles Evans, 33
Hughes, Howard, 91, 241
Humoresque, 200-201
Hush Hush, Sweet Charlotte, 215
Husing, Ted, 33
Hustler, The, 75
Huston, John, 86, 98, 130, 189-91, 205

Huston, Walter, 56
Hutton, Robert, 152
Hyer, Martha, 271-72

I Was a Male War Bride, 155
Ice Palace, 270-72
In Our Time, 132-37
In the Heat of the Night, 291
Inge, William, 268
Inspector General, The, 182
Institute for Rational Emotional
   Therapy, 293
Insull, Samuel, 34-35
Invisible Man, The, 33, 37
It Can't Happen Here, 52-53, 58, 86

Jackson, Andrew, 219
Jackson, Donald, 251
Jackson, Gordon, 180-81
Jacobs, William (Bill), 68, 94
Jacobs, Dr. Thornwell, 3, 7
Jaffe, Sam (actor), 50
Jaffee, Sam (agent), 2, 4, 6
Janie, 152
Janie Gets Married, 152
Jayhawker, 52
Jenkins, Allen, 67
Jenkins, Bill, 4
Jens, Salome, 289
Jews without Money, 51
Jezebel, 125
JFK, 300
Johnny Belinda, 164
Johnny Guitar, 215
Jolly, "Hash," 6
Jones, Carolyn, 271-72, 291
Jones, Robert Edmund, 26
Jonson, Ben, 16
Jordan, Bobby, 71
Joseph, Ellis St., 134
Josephson, Ben, 25, 30
Josephy, Bill, 248, 251
Jourdan, Louis, 283
Juarez, 130
Judgement Day, 45-47
Juke Girl, 70

Kael, Pauline, 118
Kahane, Ben, 237, 247
Kalmenson, Ben, 192
Kanin, Fay, 210
Kanin, Garson, 230

Kanter, Hal, 277
Kaplan, Hyman, 98
Karl, Harry, 276
Karns, Roscoe, 85
Karp, David, 278, 280-81
Katz, Lee, 79, 95, 190
Kaufman, George, 23-24
Kauser, Alice, 9-10
Kaye, Danny, 182
Keighley, William, 90, 135
Keith, Brian, 269
Kelly, Barry, 272
Kelly, Burt, 20
Kelly, Gene, 244
Kelly, George, 206
Kelly, Jack, 273
Kelly, Orry, 76, 138
Kenyon, Doris, 41
Kerensky, 34
Khan, Aga, 234
Khan, Ally, 228, 234
Kibbee, Guy, 67
Kid Galahad, 79, 81
King of the Underworld, 77, 97
Kingsley, Sidney, 62
Kissell, Bill, 100, 149
Kitzmiller, John, 261
Kleiner, Harry, 252-53, 271, 273
Knight, Shirley, 272
Kobal, John, 239
Koch, Howard (asst. dir.), 226
Kolodin, Irving, 29
Koppel, Ted, 193
Kosleck, Martin, 99
Krasna, Norman, 241
Kreutzberg, Harold, 19
Krims, Milton, 75
Kropotkin, 27
Kruger, Otto, 30-31, 269
Kurnitz, Harry, 165-66

La Bete Humaine, 78
La Grande Illusion, 78
La Kermesse Héroique, 78
La Maternelle, 278
Lachie, 178
Ladd, Alan, 205, 240
Lady of the House (film), 206, 208
Lady of the House (television movie), 290
Laemmle, Carl, 36, 42
Landau, Ely, 277, 281, 287
Landon, Michael, 2

Lane, Rosemary, 79
Lang, Fritz, 78, 101
Larimore, Earl, 33
Larwood, James (Jimmie), 1, 8-10, 19
Last Hurrah, The, 291
Latta, C.J., 179
Lawrence, Steve, 289
Lawrence, Viola (Vi), 210, 236
Lawson, John Howard, 117
Lazar, Irving "Swifty," 270
Lean, David, 111
Learned, Michael, 289
Leary, Brianne, 291
Le Blang, Joe, 10
Lee, Bob, 140
Lee, Lester, 233
Lenin in October, 51
Leonard, Bob, 179
Leporella, 167
Lerch, Freda (née Rosenblatt), 40, 204
LeRoy, Mervyn, 71
Leslie, Joan, 112, 114, 152, 296
Letter, The, 119, 159-60
Levathes, Pete, 276-77
Levee, Mike, 85, 91, 111
Leventhal, Jules, 62
Levin, Meyer, 46
Levy, Jean Benoit, 78
Lewis, Ruth, 16, 296
Lewis, Sinclair, 52-62, 86; Lou (secretary), 58, 61; Michael (son), 58, 60
Lewis and Clark, 246
Liebman, Max, 31
Light, James, 50-51
Light and Power, 34-35, 66
Lights of New York, 68
Lilies of the Field, 290
Lindbergh, Charles, 65, 95
Lincoln, Abraham, 51
Linden, Eric, 14
Lindfors, Viveca, 167, 177, 302
Litel, John, 67, 76, 79
Little Foxes, The, 119
Litvak, Anatole (Tola), 85, 92, 96
Lockwood, Gary, 277, 289
Loder, John, 120, 139
Loeb, Philip, 50
Loggia, Robert, 253
Lollobrigida, Gina, 282-84
Loman, Willy, 255
Lombardo, Geoffredo, 248-49
Lone Star, 219-20

Long Hot Summer, The, 277
Lopate, Philip, 298
Lorentz, Pare, 112-13
Lorre, Peter, 99-100
Los Angeles Times, 42, 215
Losey, Joseph, 52
Louise, Anita, 76
Lovejoy, Frank, 212-13
Lovsky, Celia, 100
Lubitsch, Ernst, 120-21
Luciano, Lucky, 241
Luddy, Tom, 298
Lundigan, William, 87
Lunt, Alfred, 14, 16-17, 25-26, 29
Lupino, Ida, 95, 112-19, 132-35, 141, 151-52, 169, 205, 299-300, 304-5
Lupino, Stanley, 113
Lynn, Jeffrey, 91-93
Lyss, Lya, 79

M, 101
MacArthur, Charles, 34
MacCauley, Dick, 75
MacDougall, Ranald, 215
MacKenzie, Aeneas, 75
Maclane, Barton, 67, 76
MacRae, Gordon, 177
Madame Tussaud's Gallery, 182
Maedchen in Uniform, 278
Mahler, 15
Mahoney, Jock, 167
Mailley, Bertha, 25, 30
Main Street, 55
Malone, Dorothy, 152
Maltese Falcon, The, 86, 105
Maltin, Leonard, 112
Maltz, Albert, 48
Mamoulian, Rouben, 14, 17, 20
Man Who Died Twice, The, 153, 302
Man Who Talked Too Much, The, 87, 97
Mann, Alonzo, 16
Mann, Anthony, 248-49
Mannix, Eddie, 224
Mantee, Duke, 80
Mantz, Paul, 263
Marco Millions, 14, 16-17, 19
Maricle, Leona, 112
Maris, Mona, 91-94
Marshall, Bruce, 248
Marshall, Herbert, 160, 274
Martin, Baby Face, 62, 73
Martins, Orlando, 182, 261

Massey, Raymond, 251
Mate, Rudy, 229
Matthews, Kerwin, 254
Mattison, Frank, 167
Mature, Victor, 248-49
Maugham, Somerset, 1
Maverick, 273
Maximilian, 130
Mayberry, Dick, 168, 172
Mayer, Edwin Justus, 92
Mayer, Louis B., 104, 154, 204
Mayerling, 92
Mayo, Virginia, 177
Mayor of Hell, The, 71
MCA, 121, 220, 243-46
McBain, Diane, 272
McCarey, Leo, 106-7
McCarthy, Todd, 299-301
McClellan, Ian, 83
McClintic, Guthrie, 23
McHugh, Frank, 67, 99-100
McQuade, Robert, 44
Medford, Harold, 198-99
Medical Center, 288
Meek, Donald, 152
Mein Kampf, 247
Meisner, Sanford (Sandy), 14, 17
Mencken, H.L., 7
Mercer, Johnny, 14
Meredith, Burgess, 291
Methot, Mayo, 100
MGM, 195-96, 243-45
Michael, Ralph, 182
Midnight Alibi, 44, 65, 87
Mierhold, 15
Mildred Pierce, 81, 195
Miles, Vera, 289
Miller, Arthur, 255
Miller, David, 215
Miller, Seton, 75
Miss Sadie Thompson, 1
Mitchell, Thomas, 91
Moeller, Philip, 16-17, 32
Moffitt, John C., 52-53
Molnar, 10
Monash, Paul, 277
Montand, Yves, 250
Montgomery, Ray, 112
Moore, Dinty, 85
Moran, Dolores, 120
Moreno, Rita, 289
Morgan, Chief, 6

Morgan, Dennis, 79-80, 83, 112-15,
    157, 299
Morris, Howard, 31
Morris, Wayne, 79-80, 83
Morrison, Tom, 181
Mortal Storm, The, 92
Mosca, 16
Moskowitz, Joe, 265
Motion Picture Alliance for the
    Preservation of American Ideals,
    225, 246
Mr. Moto, 101
Mr. Skeffington, 130, 132, 136, 138,
    150-51, 296, 301-2
Much Ado about Nothing, 26, 28-29
Mudlark, The, 189
Muhl, Ed, 244-46
Muni, Paul, 30, 35, 43, 67, 75-76, 85
Murray, Jan, 291
Murrow, Edward J., 180
Mussolini, 78
My Bill, 76, 96
My Days with Errol Flynn, 174

Naked Earth, The, 250-56
Nash, N. Richard, 156
Nathan, Paul, 90
Nation, 21, 31
Nazimova, Alla, 31, 134
Neal, Patricia, 180-84, 205, 302
Negulesco, Jean, 164, 189
Nelson, Ralph, 290-91
Nelson, Sam, 236
Nettleton, Lois, 289
New Masses Magazine, 247
New Republic, 21, 31
New York American, 43
New York Evening Journal, 11
New York Film Critics Award, 117
New York Herald Tribune, 191
New York Sun, 29
New Yorker, 118, 266
Newman, Paul, 268-70, 302
Nichols, Anthony, 182
Night Train, 135
Nora Prentiss, 156
Notorious, 231
Now, Voyager, 119, 135

O'Brien, Edmund, 176
O'Brien, Pat, 67, 71
O'Connor, Carroll, 274, 291

O'Connor, Donald, 244-45
O'Neill, Eugene, 14-18, 51
O'Neill, Peggy, 184
Ochoa, Margarita, 287
Odets, Clifford, 14, 48
Of Human Bondage, 127
Oglethorpe University, 1, 3, 5, 215
Old Acquaintance, 13, 119-20, 127-28, 136
Old Maid, The, 119-20, 122
Olsen, Moroni, 223
Once in a Lifetime, 22, 24
One Shot Fired, 54
Opatashu, David, 289
Oppenheimer, George, 164-65
Orovitz family: Harry (father), 2-7, 25, 28; Vinnie (mother), 2-7, 28; Abe (son, later Vincent Sherman), 2, 11; Nathan (son), 8, 20, 26, 48-49; Barbara (daughter), 49; Evelyn (daughter), 49; Minnie (daughter), 49; Tillie (daughter), 25, 49; Ben (uncle), 2, 36-37; Max (cousin), 49; Nat (cousin), 10, 25; Anna (Nat's wife), 10; Buddy (Nat's son), 10; Naomi (Nat's daughter), 10; Aunt Ida (Nat's stepmother), 10; Louis (Nat's stepbrother), 10; Bessie (Nat's stepsister), 10
Ottley, John, 5
Our Dancing Daughters, 195
Out of the Fog, 95
Outlaw, The, 91
Owen, Reginald, 10

Page, Don, 157
Pagnol, Marcel, 78
Paradise Lost, 48
Paramount Studios, 67
Park, Arthur, 214, 219-20, 244, 251, 269
Parker, Dorothy, 164-65, 270
Parker, Eleanor, 120, 169
Parker, Jameson, 291
Parrish, Bob, 274
Parsons, Louella, 129, 197, 232
Pasadena Playhouse, 42, 44, 63
Patrick, Lee, 85
Patton, General, 152
Pepper, Jack, 110
Pence, Bill and Stella, 298
Petchnikoff, Sergei, 226
Petrified Forest, The, 80

Pevney, Joseph, 18-19, 24, 32, 215
Peyton Place, 277
Phagan, Mary, 15
Philadelphians, The, 268. See *The Young Philadelphians*
Picasso, Pablo, 15
Picerni, Paul, 269
Pickfair, 196
Pickford, Mary, 196
Picnic, 268
Pillow to Post, 151-52
Platoon, 300
Play It Again, Sam, 292
Play's the Thing, The, 10, 24
Plymouth Adventure, 222
Poil de Carotte, 78
Polito, Sol, 119, 123
Porgy, 17
Portman, Eric, 184
Powell, Dick, 67
Powell, Michael, 262
Powers, Mala, 305
Pratt, Thomas (Tommy), 117
Pride of the Bluegrass, 77, 97
Prince, William (Bill), 151
Prinz, Leroy, 117
Punsley, Bernard, 71
Purl, Linda, 289, 291

Qualen, John, 36-37, 39, 41
Queen Bee, 215
Quine, Richard, 39
Quo Vadis, 189

Rabal, Francisco (Paco), 283
Racket, The, 24
Radio City Music Hall, 43
Raft, George, 98
Rain, 1
Raine, Norman Reilly, 75
Rains, Claude, 17, 32-33, 37, 67, 85-86, 136, 139, 147-48, 231, 301
Randolph, John, 289
Rapf, Harry, 195
Rapper, Irving, 120, 135, 215-16
Rattigan, Terence, 184
Ray, Nicholas (Nick), 215
Raye, Matha, 161-62
RCA, 61
Reagan, Ronald, 70, 180-84, 186-87, 193-94, 302
Rebecca, 99

Red Channels, 223
Red River, 219
Redellings, Lowell, 193
Redford, Robert, 300
Reed, Carol, 135
Reed, Robert, 289
Reiner, Carl, 31
Reinhardt, Max, 18
Renoir, Jean, 78
Return of Dr. X, The, 79, 84-85, 87
Rey, Fernando, 283
Reynolds, Debbie, 274-76
Reynolds, Joyce, 152
Rhodes, Leah, 167
Rice, Elmer, 30, 36, 41, 45, 50, 52
Richberg, Donald, 35
Risdon, Elizabeth, 85
Rissient, Pierre, 301
Ritter, Thelma, 275
RKO, 241
Road to Life, The, 78
Roaring Twenties, The, 71
Robbins, Harold, 291
Rober, Richard, 177
Roberts, Ben, 176-77, 210
Roberts, Pernell, 289
Robin Hood, 74, 81, 166, 173
Robinson, Casey, 75
Robinson, Edward G., 67, 79
Robinson, Seymour, 42
Robson, Mark, 252
Rogers, Ginger, 110-11
Rogers, Lela, 110
Roobin, Todd, 296
Rooney, Mickey, 171
Roosevelt, Franklin D., 31, 33-35, 50, 58, 79, 105, 224, 247; Eleanor (wife), 31, 34-35, 50, 105
Rossen, Robert, 71, 75, 91, 109
Rosson, Art, 227
Rosson, Harold (Hal), 221-22
Rosten, Leo, 98
Routh, Dr. James (Babe), 3
Rowlands, Gena, 292
Rubin, Stanley, 245
Rule, Janice, 212
Runyon, Damon, 70, 98
R.U.R., 20
Rush, Barbara, 269, 302
Russell, Rosalind, 206, 217
Rutherford, Ann, 167
Ryan, Mitchell, 289

Ryan, Robert, 271
Ryskind, Morrie, 225

Salkind, Alexandre (Alex), 278-87
Salkind, Michel (Miguel, Mischa), 278-87
Salome, 240
San Quentin, 71
Santa Fe Trail, 81
Sarnoff, David, 61
Saturday's Children, 85-89, 130
Saul, Oscar, 235, 267, 275, 297
Saunders, Russ, 44
Scala, Gia, 253
Scandal in Milan, 250
Schaeffer, Bill, 155
Schary, Dore, 23, 222, 227
Schwab's Drugstore, 79, 152
Schlesinger, Leon, 95
Schoenberg, 15
Schukin, Boris, 51
Schulberg, Budd, 98
Scott, Pippa, 289
Scott, Zachary, 160
Scourby, Alexander, 228, 232
Sea Hawk, 81
Second Time Around, 275
Secret Life of Walter Mitty, The, 182
Seiler, Lewis (Lew), 70-73, 77
Self, Bill, 276-77
Semperi, Julio, 280, 286
Serenade, 157-59
Sergeant York, 112
Sevaried, Eric, 95
Seventh Heaven, 4
Shakespeare, William, 26, 41
Shaw, Irwin, 91, 106-8, 111, 115, 117, 299
Show of Shows, 31
Sheridan, Ann, 67-71, 90, 154-62, 223, 236
Sherman, Eric (son), 163, 272, 278, 284
Sherman, Cosimo (grandson), 298
Sherman, Hedda Comoro, 22-23, 25-36, 42, 44-45, 47-49, 52, 55, 60, 63, 65-67, 75, 77-79, 87, 97, 101, 127, 129, 142, 146, 148, 155, 161, 163, 178, 184, 201, 205, 219, 240-41, 246, 250, 257, 268, 278, 280, 283, 287, 290, 293-96
Sherman, Hedwin (daughter), 127, 163, 235

Sherman, John, 182
Shipway, Maggie, 262
Shipway, Phil, 262
Shirer, William, 95
Shirley, Anne, 85-86
Shubert, J.J., 195
Sidney, Sylvia, 289
Siegel, Bugsy, 197, 204
Siegel, Don, 116-17
Signoret, Simone, 250
Silone, 48
Silver Chalice, The, 268
Silvers, Phil, 99-100
Simon, Michel, 135
Simon, Sylvan, 227
Simpson, Russell, 223
Sinatra, Frank, 223
Sinclair, Upton, 86
Skinner, Cornelia Otis, 19
Slaton, Governor, 16
Slater, James, 290
Small Agency, The, 41
Smith, Alexis, 269, 302
Smith, Kent, 152, 156
Smithers, William, 290
Somebody Up There Likes Me, 268
Sperling, Milton, 291
Spigelgass, Leonard, 98
Spring in New York, 70
Squall, The, 10, 12
Stage Door Canteen, 152
Stalin, 27
Stanfield, Chris, 298
Stanford, Sally, 290
Stanislavsky, 15
Steele, Alfred, 215
Steeple, The, 1
Stieglitz, 15
Stein, Gertrude, 15
Stendhal, 15
Stepanek, Karl, 236
Stephenson, James, 77, 160
Stern, Stewart, 269
Stevens, Andrew, 291
Stevenson, Philip, 47
Stewart, James (Jimmy), 85
Stiefel, Milton, 18-19
Stolen Life, 149-50
Stone, Oliver, 300-301
Story of Esther Costello, The, 215
Stradling, Harry, 269
Strange Interlude, 17

Strauss, Peter, 289
Stravinsky, 15
Street Scene, 36, 50
Sudden Fear, 215
Sullavan, Margaret, 207, 209
Sullivan, Barry, 289
Sullivan, Ed, 43
Sun Also Rises, The, 261
Suzuli, Sam, 23
Swenson, Karl, 272
Sweyd, Lester, 22, 76

Takei, George, 272
Taradash, Dan, 240, 291
Tau Epsilon Phi, 3
Tavernier, Bertrand, 299
Taylor, Elizabeth, 248
Taylor, Robert, 42
Telluride Film Festival, 299, 304
Temple, Shirley, 277
Ten Commandments, The, 4
Terrible Turk, The, 42
Terry, Phillip, 197
Thatcher, Torin, 228
Theater Guild, 14, 16, 20, 24-26, 28-29, 32, 48, 69, 86, 134
They Drive by Night, 112
Thief of Bagdad, The, 103
Third Man, The, 193
This Is the Army, 81
Thomas, Richard, 290
Thompson, Big Bill, 34
Thompson, Dorothy, 52-55, 60-62, 87
Thompson, Ernest, 290
Tobias, George, 85
Todd, Richard, 181, 192, 258, 301-2
Tone, Franchot, 196
Topaze, 41
Torch Song, 215
Torme, Mel, 152
Tracy, Spencer, 222, 227, 291
Trapper John, 289
Treasure of the Sierra Madre, The, 86, 304
Trial, The, 278
Trial and Error, 91
Trilling, Steve, 115, 158-59, 161, 167, 176, 207, 210, 212-13, 242, 244, 267-68, 270-71, 273
Turner, Don, 168
Turner Classic Films, 296
Twentieth Century-Fox, 192

Un carnet de bal, 78
Underground, 92, 94-98
Unfaithful, The, 158-59, 161, 163, 209, 231, 301-2
Unger, Oliver, 277-79, 281
Universal Pictures, 35, 38, 42, 244-45
Untermeyer, Louis, 61
Upp, Virginia Van, 229-31
Upton, Gabby, 274

Vachtangov, 15
Vanel, Charles, 250
Variety, 115, 299-300
Vaughn, Robert, 269, 302
Veidt, Conrad, 99, 103; Mrs., 104
Veiller, Anthony (Tony), 176
Verga, 248
Verity, Terence, 179, 261
Verne, Kaaren, 93-100
Vickers, Ann, 60
Victim, The, 195, 197-98, 207. See also *The Damned Don't Cry*
Vidor, Charles, 229
Viertel, Peter, 117
Villard, Oswald Garrison, 51
Volpone (play), 16-17, 19
Volpone (character), 16-17, 19
Voltore, 17
Voscovec, George, 236

Waiting for Lefty, 48
Wald, Jerry, 75, 97-99, 105-8, 112, 115, 117, 132, 134, 156-60, 164-65, 167, 173, 195-99, 240-42, 244
Walk with the Devil, 252, 267
Walker, Joe, 209, 236
Wall Street, 300
Wallach, Ira, 274
Wallis, Hal, 67, 70-71, 85-90, 97, 102, 106-10, 115, 120, 130-35, 156-60
Walsh, Raoul, 98, 164, 166, 173
Walter, Jessica, 289
Walters, Chuck, 215
Waltons, The, 289
Wanamaker, Sam, 210
Ward, Al, 289
Waring, Richard, 136
Warner, Jack, 64-66, 70-71, 74-75, 79-82, 84, 86-88, 91-93, 95-97, 99, 111, 114-117, 126, 128, 130, 132, 139, 142-43, 149, 151-154, 156-61, 164-65, 167-74, 176, 178, 190-91,
204, 210, 212-13, 215, 244, 247, 264-65, 267-68, 270-72, 274, 299; Jackie Jr. (son), 177-79; 187-89; Barbara (wife), 187
Warner Bros. Studios, 44, 63-64, 67-195, 267-74
Warwick, Robert, 44, 167
Washington, George, 300
Washington, Ned, 233
Wasserman, Lew, 121, 246
Waters, Johnny, 227
Watson, Tom, 16
Wayne, John, 225, 250
Webster, Paul, 153, 246
Weidman, Jerome (Jerry), 198-99
Weinstein, Henry, 277-78, 280-81
Weiss, Morris, 49
Welles, Orson, 234, 278
Wells, H.G., 33
Werfel, Franz, 20
West, Adam, 269
Westmore, Perc, 138, 142, 172
Westside Medical, 289
What Makes Sammy Run? 98
What Price Glory? 7
What Ever Happened to Baby Jane? 215-16
Wheeler, William (investigator), 252
Where's the Rest of Me? 193
White, Jesse, 274
White Cargo, 24
White Christmas, 81
White House, the, 33
Wigman, Mary, 19
Wilbur, Crane, 71, 75
Wiles, Buster, 174
William, Warren, 87
Williams, John, 269
Williams, Tennessee, 188
Winsten, Archer, 87
Wise, Robert, 268
With a Feather on My Nose, 270
Wolfson, Marty, 35
Wolfson, Victor, 48
Women at West Point, 291
Woollcott, Alexander 9
Woolfenden, Bill, 36, 44
Wright, Tenney, 74, 79, 157
Wyler, William (Willy), 36, 38, 40-43, 71-73, 106-7, 127, 204
Wyman, Jane, 67, 164, 181
Wymore, Patrice, 205

Wynter, Dana, 289

Yang, Janet, 300
Yankee Doodle Dandy, 81, 112
Youma, 19-20
Young, Gig, 120
Young, Ned, 244-45
Young, Robert, 212
Young Philadelphians, The, 270-71, 288, 301

Young Rebel (Cervantes), The, 280
Yurka, Blanche, 10

Zanuck, Darryl F., 87, 261-65, 277, 287
Zanuck, Richard (Dick), 264, 277
Ziegler, William (Bill), 270
Zimbalist, Efrem, Jr., 273
Zinnemann, Fred, 240
Zweig, Stefan, 16, 95